250
Poems
A Portable Anthology

Edited by

PETER SCHAKEL

Hope College

JACK RIDL

Hope College

Bedford/St. Martin's   BOSTON ◆ NEW YORK

For Bedford/St. Martin's

Developmental Editors: Emily Goodall and Stephen A. Scipione
Production Editors: Thomas P. Crehan and Kerri Cardone
Production Supervisor: Jennifer Wetzel
Marketing Manager: Jenna Bookin Barry
Copyeditor: Jane Zanichkowsky
Text Design: Sandra Rigney
Cover Design: Donna Lee Dennison
Cover Art: St. Clair Whitman House © 1991 Christian Harkness.
Composition: Stratford Publishing Services, Inc.
Printing and Binding: Haddon Craftsmen, Inc., an R.R. Donnelley & Sons Company

President: Joan E. Feinberg
Editor in Chief: Karen S. Henry
Director of Marketing: Karen Melton
Director of Editing, Design, and Production: Marcia Cohen
Managing Editor: Elizabeth M. Schaaf

Library of Congress Control Number: 2002108134

Manufactured in the United States of America

8 7 6 5 4 3
f e d c b a

For information, write: Bedford/St. Martin's, 75 Arlington Street, Boston, MA 02116 (617-399-4000)

ISBN: 0-312-40238-4

Acknowledgments and copyrights are listed at the back of the book on pages 396–401, which constitute an extension of the copyright page. It is a violation of the law to reproduce these selections by any means whatsoever without the written permission of the copyright holder.

Ai. "Why Can't I Leave You?" from *Vice: New and Selected Poems* by Ai. Copyright © 1973 by Ai. Reprinted by permission of W.W. Norton & Company, Inc.

Sherman Alexie. "Postcards to Columbus" from *Old Shirts and New Skins* (Los Angeles, CA: American Indian Studies Center, 1993). Copyright © 1993 by Sherman Alexie. Reprinted by permission.

Agha Shahid Ali. "I Dream It Is Afternoon When I Return to Delhi" from *The Half-Inch Himalayas*. Copyright © 1987 by Agha Shahid Ali. Wesleyan University Press.

Tom Andrews. "The Hemophiliac's Motorcycle" from *The Hemophiliac's Motorcycle*. Copyright © 1994 by Tom Andrews. Reprinted by permission of the University of Iowa Press.

Preface for Instructors

250 Poems: A Portable Anthology is a compact collection of poems, classic and contemporary, that is rewarding to teach and enjoyable to read. In preparing this volume, we sought to include many canonical poets along with poets writing since 1950 who have received considerable critical attention. We also included some poets who are deserving of such attention but who have been by and large undervalued, as well as recent poets we think will receive critical recognition in the future. We recognize, of course, that prognostication in any art is hazardous and realize that we have, reluctantly but necessarily, left out many poets worthy of inclusion. We tried to represent a wide variety of poetic strategies and forms in order to illustrate the diversity of approaches to the art. And we chose a range of poems that reveals the impact of ethnic diversity on poetry written in English.

The poems are arranged chronologically by birth date of the authors, to guide readers toward a sense of the historical development of poetry in English and the influence of earlier poets and poems on later ones. The dates given below the poems indicate earliest publication in a book, preceded in some cases by the probable date of composition, in *italics*, where that information seems useful. We have kept the apparatus in the book to a minimum. Glosses are provided for vocabulary that cannot be found readily in a current dictionary. Annotation is added to clarify lines that draw on ideas requiring specialized knowledge or practices not readily familiar in our time or outside a specific culture. The appendices include biographical sketches for every poet in the book, to indicate their historical, cultural, and personal contexts, and a glossary.

The *250 Poems* companion Web site at bedfordstmartins.com/250poems provides additional resources. LitLinks presents concise annotations and links to hundreds of Web sites that contain useful biographical information about the poets included in this anthology. Links to the Academy of American Poets and Modern American Poetry Web sites provide further biographical information. VirtuaLit, an interactive poetry tutorial, offers exercises designed to promote close readings of poems. A brief introduction, "How to Read a Poem—and Why," is also available on the Web site, along with groupings of poems by form as well as by subject matter and theme.

ACKNOWLEDGMENTS

For assistance in selecting and annotating particular poets presented in this anthology, we are indebted to several Hope College colleagues: Susan Atefat Peckham, Marla Lunderberg, Jesse Montaño, and William Pannapacker. We are grateful to Charles Huttar, who provided valuable assistance with the biographical sketches, glossary, glosses, and annotations. Myra Kohsel, office manager for the Department of English at Hope College, helped us in a variety of ways with her usual graciousness, patience, and competence.

We want also to express our appreciation to those at Bedford/ St. Martin's who helped make this book possible: to Charles Christensen and Joan Feinberg for supporting the project; to Steve Scipione for believing in it and in us and for his wise counsel all along the way; to Elizabeth Schaaf, Tom Crehan, and Kerri Cardone, for seeing the book through production; to Jane Zanichkowsky for her careful copyediting; to Arthur Johnson for arranging permissions; and to Emily Goodall for her perceptive questions, creative ideas, and alert, attentive work as the book's editor.

Contents

ANONYMOUS

Lord Randal

1

"O where ha' you been, Lord Randal, my son?
And where ha' you been, my handsome young man?"
"I ha' been at the greenwood; mother, mak my bed soon,
For I'm wearied wi' huntin', and fain wad° lie down."   *gladly would*

2

"And wha° met ye there, Lord Randal, my son?   *who*   5
And wha met you there, my handsome young man?"
"O I met wi' my true-love; mother, mak my bed soon,
For I'm wearied wi' huntin', and fain wad lie down."

3

"And what did she give you, Lord Randal, my son?
And what did she give you, my handsome young man?"   10
"Eels fried in a pan; mother, mak my bed soon,
For I'm wearied wi' huntin', and fain wad lie down."

4

"And wha gat your leavin's, Lord Randal, my son?
And wha gat your leavin's, my handsome young man?"
"My hawks and my hounds; mother, mak my bed soon,   15
For I'm wearied wi' huntin', and fain wad lie down."

5

"And what becam of them, Lord Randal, my son?
And what becam of them, my handsome young man?"
"They stretched their legs out and died; mother, mak my bed soon,
For I'm wearied wi' huntin', and fain wad lie down."   20

6

"O I fear you are poisoned, Lord Randal, my son!
I fear you are poisoned, my handsome young man!"
"O yes, I am poisoned; mother, mak my bed soon,
For I'm sick at the heart, and I fain wad lie down."

7

"What d' ye leave to your mother, Lord Randal, my son?   25
What d' ye leave to your mother, my handsome young man?"

1

"Four and twenty milk kye;° mother, mak my bed soon,   *cows*
For I'm sick at the heart, and I fain wad lie down."

8

"What d' ye leave to your sister, Lord Randal, my son?
What d' ye leave to your sister, my handsome young man?"   30
"My gold and my silver; mother, mak my bed soon,
For I'm sick at the heart, and I fain wad lie down."

9

"What d' ye leave to your brother, Lord Randal, my son?
What d' ye leave to your brother, my handsome young man?"
"My houses and my lands; mother, mak my bed soon,   35
For I'm sick at the heart, and I fain wad lie down."

10

"What d' ye leave to your true-love, Lord Randal, my son?
What d' ye leave to your true-love, my handsome young man?"
"I leave her hell and fire; mother, mak my bed soon,
For I'm sick at the heart, and I fain wad lie down."   40

[1803]

ANONYMOUS

Sir Patrick Spens

The king sits in Dumferling town,
   Drinking the blude-reid° wine;   *blood-red*
"O whar will I get guid sailor,
   To sail this ship of mine?"

Up and spak an eldern° knicht,°   *elderly/knight*   5
   Sat at the king's richt° knee: *right*
"Sir Patrick Spens is the best sailor
   That sails upon the sea."

The king has written a braid° letter   *broad (clear)*
   And signed it wi' his hand,   10
And sent it to Sir Patrick Spens,
   Was walking on the sand.

The first line that Sir Patrick read,
   A loud lauch° lauched he;   *laugh*

The next line that Sir Patrick read,   15
   The tear blinded his ee.°   *eye*

"O wha° is this has done this deed,   *who*
   This ill deed done to me,
To send me out this time o' the year,
   To sail upon the sea?   20

"Mak haste, mak haste, my mirry men all,
   Our guid ship sails the morn."
"O say na° sae,° my master dear,   *not/so*
   For I fear a deadly storm.

"Late, late yestre'en I saw the new moon   25
   Wi' the auld moon in hir arm,
And I fear, I fear, my dear master,
   That we will come to harm."

O our Scots nobles were richt laith°   *loath*
   To weet° their cork-heeled shoon,°   *wet/shoes* 30
But lang or° a' the play were played   *before*
   Their hats they swam aboon.°   *above*

O lang, lang may their ladies sit,
   Wi' their fans into their hand,
Or ere they see Sir Patrick Spens   35
   Come sailing to the land.

O lang, lang may the ladies stand
   Wi' their gold kems° in their hair,   *combs*
Waiting for their ain° dear lords,   *own*
   For they'll see them na mair.°   *more*   40

Half o'er, half o'er to Aberdour
   It's fifty fadom° deep,   *fathoms*
And there lies guid Sir Patrick Spens
   Wi' the Scots lords at his feet.

[1765]

SIR THOMAS WYATT   [1503–1542]

They flee from me

They flee from me, that sometime did me seek,
With naked foot stalking in my chamber.
I have seen them, gentle, tame, and meek,

That now are wild, and do not remember
That sometime they put themselves in danger   5
To take bread at my hand; and now they range,
Busily seeking with a continual change.

Thankèd be fortune it hath been otherwise,
Twenty times better; but once in special,
In thin array, after a pleasant guise,°   *manner of dress* 10
When her loose gown from her shoulders did fall,
And she me caught in her arms long and small,°   *slender*
Therewithall sweetly did me kiss
And softly said, "Dear heart,° how like you this?"

It was no dream, I lay broad waking.   15
But all is turned, thorough° my gentleness,   *through*
Into a strange fashion of forsaking;
And I have leave to go, of° her goodness,   *out of (motivated by)*
And she also to use newfangleness.
But since that I so kindly° am served,   20
I fain would know what she hath deserved.

[from an undated manuscript]

14. **Dear heart** (pun): Heart, and hart (deer).
20. **kindly** (pun): Graciously (ironic), and "in kind"; i.e., in a way typical of female
nature.

QUEEN ELIZABETH I   [1533–1603]

When I was fair and young

When I was fair and young, and favor graced me,
Of many was I sought, their mistress for to be;
But I did scorn them all, and answered them therefore,
        "Go, go, go seek some otherwhere,
                Importune me no more!"   5

How many weeping eyes I made to pine with woe,
How many sighing hearts, I have no skill to show;
Yet I the prouder grew, and answered them therefore,
        "Go, go, go seek some otherwhere,
                Importune me no more!"   10

Then spake fair Venus' son,° that proud victorious boy,   *Cupid*
And said: "Fine dame, since that you be so coy,

I will so pluck your plumes that you shall say no more,
   'Go, go, go seek some otherwhere,
      Importune me no more!'"   15

When he had spake these words, such change grew in my breast
That neither night nor day since that, I could take any rest.
Then lo! I did repent that I had said before,
   "Go, go, go seek some otherwhere,
      Importune me no more!"   20

                    [*c. 1580s*]

EDMUND SPENSER   [1552–1599]

One day I wrote her name
upon the strand

One day I wrote her name upon the strand,
But came the waves and washèd it away:
Again I wrote it with a second hand,
But came the tide, and made my pains his prey.
"Vain man," said she, "that dost in vain assay,   5
A mortal thing so to immortalize,
For I myself shall like to this decay,
And eek° my name be wipèd out likewise."   *also*
"Not so," quod° I, "let baser things devise,   *quoth (said)*
To die in dust, but you shall live by fame: 10
My verse your virtues rare shall eternize,
And in the heavens write your glorious name.
Where whenas death shall all the world subdue,
Our love shall live, and later life renew."

                    [1595]

SIR PHILIP SIDNEY   [1554–1586]

Loving in truth, and fain in verse
my love to show

Loving in truth, and fain in verse my love to show,
That the dear she might take some pleasure of my pain,
Pleasure might cause her read, reading might make her know,

Knowledge might pity win, and pity grace obtain,
   I sought fit words to paint the blackest face of woe: 5
Studying inventions fine, her wits to entertain,
Oft turning others' leaves, to see if thence would flow
Some fresh and fruitful showers upon my sunburned brain.
   But words came halting forth, wanting° Invention's stay;°
Invention, Nature's child, fled step-dame Study's blows,
And others' feet still seemed but strangers in my way.   10
Thus great with child to speak, and helpless in my throes,
   Biting my truant pen, beating myself for spite,
   "Fool," said my Muse to me, "look in thy heart and write."

                         [1582]

9. **wanting:** Lacking; **stay:** Support.

MARY (SIDNEY) HERBERT,
COUNTESS OF PEMBROKE   [1561–1621]

Psalm 100 *Jubilate Deo*

O all you lands, the treasures of your joy
   In merry shout upon the Lord bestow:
Your service cheerfully on him employ,
   With triumph song into his presence go.
Know first that he is God; and after know
   This God did us, not we ourselves create: 5
We are his flock, for us his feedings grow:
   We are his folk, and he upholds our state.
With thankfulness O enter then his gate:
   Make through each porch of his your praises ring,
All good, all grace, of his high name relate,   10
   He of all grace and goodness is the spring.
Time in no terms his mercy comprehends,
From age to age his truth itself extends.

                     [*c. 1595;* 1823]

MICHAEL DRAYTON   [1563–1631]

Since there's no help, come let us kiss and part

Since there's no help, come let us kiss and part;
Nay, I have done, you get no more of me,
And I am glad, yea glad with all my heart
That thus so cleanly I myself can free;
Shake hands forever, cancel all our vows,   5
And when we meet at any time again,
Be it not seen in either of our brows
That we one jot of former love retain.
Now at the last gasp of love's latest breath,
When, his pulse failing, passion speechless lies,   10
When faith is kneeling by his bed of death,
And innocence is closing up his eyes,
   Now if thou wouldst, when all have given him over,
   From death to life thou mightst him yet recover.

[1619]

CHRISTOPHER MARLOWE   [1564–1593]

The Passionate Shepherd to His Love

Come live with me and be my love,
And we will all the pleasures prove
That valleys, groves, hills, and fields,
Woods, or steepy mountain yields.

And we will sit upon the rocks,   5
Seeing the shepherds feed their flocks,
By shallow rivers, to whose falls
Melodious birds sing madrigals.

And I will make thee beds of roses
And a thousand fragrant posies,   10
A cap of flowers, and a kirtle
Embroidered all with leaves of myrtle.

A gown made of the finest wool
Which from our pretty lambs we pull,

Fair lined slippers for the cold,   15
With buckles of the purest gold.

A belt of straw and ivy buds,
With coral clasps and amber studs,
And if these pleasures may thee move,
Come live with me, and be my love.   20

The shepherd swains shall dance and sing
For thy delight each May morning.
If these delights thy mind may move,
Then live with me and be my love.

[1599]

WILLIAM SHAKESPEARE   [1564–1616]

Sonnet 18

Shall I compare thee to a summer's day?
Thou art more lovely and more temperate:
Rough winds do shake the darling buds of May,
And summer's lease° hath all too short a date;°   *allotted time/duration*
Sometimes too hot the eye of heaven shines,   5
And often is his gold complexion dimmed;
And every fair° from fair° sometimes declines,   *beautiful thing/beauty*
By chance or nature's changing course untrimmed;°   *stripped of its beauty*
But thy eternal summer shall not fade,
Nor lose possession of that fair thou ow'st;°   *beauty you own* 10
Nor shall death brag thou wand'rest in his shade,
When in eternal lines° to time thou grow'st:°
     So long as men can breathe, or eyes can see,
     So long lives this,° and this gives life to thee.   *this sonnet*

[1609]

12. **lines:** (Of poetry); **grow'st:** You are grafted to time.

WILLIAM SHAKESPEARE   [1564–1616]

Sonnet 73

That time of year thou mayst in me behold
When yellow leaves, or none, or few, do hang
Upon those boughs which shake against the cold,
Bare ruined choirs,° where late° the sweet birds sang.   *choirstalls/lately*
In me thou seest the twilight of such day   5
As after sunset fadeth in the west,
Which by and by black night doth take away,
Death's second self, that seals up all in rest.
In me thou seest the glowing of such fire
That on the ashes of his youth doth lie,   10
As the deathbed whereon it must expire,
Consumed with that which it was nourished by.
   This thou perceiv'st, which makes thy love more strong,
   To love that well which thou must leave ere long.

[1609]

WILLIAM SHAKESPEARE   [1564–1616]

Sonnet 116

Let me not to the marriage of true minds
Admit impediments. Love is not love
Which alters when it alteration finds,
Or bends with the remover to remove.
O, no, it is an ever-fixèd mark   5
That looks on tempests and is never shaken;
It is the star to every wandering bark,
Whose worth's unknown, although his height be taken.°   *is measured*
Love's not time's fool, though rosy lips and cheeks
Within his bending sickle's compass come;   10
Love alters not with his brief hours and weeks,
But bears it out even to the edge of doom.°   *Judgment Day*
   If this be error and upon me proved,
   I never writ, nor no man ever loved.

[1609]

WILLIAM SHAKESPEARE   [1564–1616]

Sonnet 130

My mistress' eyes are nothing like the sun;
Coral is far more red than her lips' red;
If snow be white, why then her breasts are dun;°   *dull grayish brown*
If hairs be wires, black wires grow on her head.
I have seen roses damasked,° red and white,   *variegated*   5
But no such roses see I in her cheeks;
And in some perfumes is there more delight
Than in the breath that from my mistress reeks.
I love to hear her speak, yet well I know
That music hath a far more pleasing sound.   10
I grant I never saw a goddess go;°   *walk*
My mistress, when she walks, treads on the ground.
   And yet, by heaven, I think my love as rare
   As any she° belied° with false compare.   *woman/misrepresented*

[1609]

THOMAS CAMPION   [1567–1620]

When thou must home

When thou must home to shades of underground,
And there arrived, a new admirèd guest,
The beauteous spirits do engirt° thee round,   *encircle*
White Iope, blithe Helen,° and the rest,
To hear the stories of thy finished love
From that smooth tongue whose music hell can move,   5

Then wilt thou speak of banqueting delights,
Of masques and revels which sweet youth did make,
Of tourneys and great challenges of knights,
And all these triumphs for thy beauty's sake;
When thou hast told these honors done to thee,   10
Then tell, Oh tell, how thou didst murther° me.   *murder*

[1601]

---

4. Iope, Helen: In Greek mythology, Iope, or Cassiopeia, was known for her beauty and vanity; Helen was known for loveliness, liveliness, and inconstancy.

JOHN DONNE   [1572–1631]

A Valediction: Forbidding Mourning

As virtuous men pass mildly away,
  And whisper to their souls to go,
Whilst some of their sad friends do say
  The breath goes now, and some say, No;

So let us melt, and make no noise,   5
  No tear-floods, nor sigh-tempests move;
'Twere profanation of our joys
  To tell the laity our love.

Moving of th' earth brings harms and fears,
  Men reckon what it did and meant;   10
But trepidation of the spheres,
  Though greater far, is innocent.

Dull sublunary° lovers' love   *under the moon; hence, inconstant*
  (Whose soul is sense) cannot admit
Absence, because it doth remove   15
  Those things which elemented° it.   *composed*

But we, by a love so much refined
  That our selves know not what it is,
Inter-assurèd of the mind,
  Care less, eyes, lips, and hands to miss.   20

Our two souls therefore, which are one,
  Though I must go, endure not yet
A breach, but an expansion,
  Like gold to airy thinness beat.

If they be two, they are two so   25
  As stiff twin compasses° are two;   *drawing compasses*
Thy soul, the fixed foot, makes no show
  To move, but doth, if th' other do.

And though it in the center sit,
  Yet when the other far doth roam,   30
It leans and hearkens after it,
  And grows erect, as that comes home.

Such wilt thou be to me, who must,
  Like th' other foot, obliquely run;
Thy firmness makes my circle just,   35
  And makes me end where I begun.

[1633]

JOHN DONNE   [1572–1631]

The Flea

Mark but this flea, and mark in this,
How little that which thou deny'st me is;
Me it sucked first, and now sucks thee,
And in this flea, our two bloods mingled be;°
Confess it, this cannot be said°   *called* 5
A sin, or shame, or loss of maidenhead,°   *virginity*
 Yet this enjoys before it woo,
 And pampered swells with one blood made of two,
 And this, alas, is more than we would do.

Oh stay,° three lives in one flea spare,   10
Where we almost, nay more than married are.
This flea is you and I, and this
Our marriage bed, and marriage temple is;
Though parents grudge, and you, we are met,
And cloistered in these living walls of jet.   15
 Though use° make you apt to kill me,   *habit*
 Let not to this, self murder added be,
 And sacrilege, three sins in killing three.°

Cruel and sudden, hast thou since
Purpled thy nail, in blood of innocence?   20
In what could this flea guilty be,
Except in that drop which it sucked from thee?
Yet thou triumph'st, and say'st that thou
Find'st not thyself, nor me the weaker now;
 'Tis true, then learn how false, fears be;   25
 Just so much honour, when thou yield'st to me,
 Will waste, as this flea's death took life from thee.

[1633]

4. our two bloods mingled be: Renaissance medical theory held that blood was mingled during sexual intercourse, the "little" act the lady is denying the speaker (l. 2); such mingling leads to conception and pregnancy (l. 8).
10. stay: Stop; refrain from killing the flea. "Die" and "kill" were Renaissance slang terms for orgasm (the sexual act, with its loss of blood, was believed to reduce the length of a man's life).
18. three sins: Murder, suicide, and sacrilege (destroying a "marriage temple").

JOHN DONNE   [1572–1631]

Batter my heart, three-personed God

Batter my heart, three-personed God, for you
As yet but knock, breathe, shine, and seek to mend;
That I may rise and stand, o'erthrow me, and bend
Your force to break, blow, burn, and make me new.
I, like an usurped town, to another due,   5
Labor to admit you, but oh, to no end;
Reason, your viceroy in me, me should defend,
But is captived, and proves weak or untrue.
Yet dearly I love you, and would be lovèd fain,
But am betrothed unto your enemy;   10
Divorce me, untie or break that knot again,
Take me to you, imprison me, for I,
Except you enthrall me, never shall be free,
Nor ever chaste, except you ravish me.

[1633]

BEN JONSON   [1572–1637]

On My First Son

Farewell, thou child of my right hand,° and joy;
My sin was too much hope of thee, loved boy:
Seven years thou'wert lent to me, and I thee pay,
Exacted by thy fate, on the just day.
O could I lose all father now! for why   5
Will man lament the state he should envy,
To have so soon 'scaped world's and flesh's rage,
And, if no other misery, yet age?
Rest in soft peace, and asked, say, "Here doth lie
Ben Jonson his best piece of poetry."   10
For whose sake henceforth all his° vows be such   *(the father's)*
As what he loves may never like° too much.

[1616]

1. **child . . . hand:** A literal translation of the Hebrew name "Benjamin." The boy, named for his father, was born in 1596 and died on his birthday ("the just day") in 1603.
12. **like:** Archaic meaning "please."

LADY MARY WROTH   [c. 1587–c. 1651]

Am I thus conquered?

Am I thus conquered? Have I lost the powers
   That° to withstand, which joys° to ruin me?   *(love)/delights*
Must I be still while it my strength devours,
   And captive leads me prisoner, bound, unfree?
Love first shall leave men's fant'sies to them free,   5
   Desire shall quench love's flames, spring hate sweet showers,
Love shall loose all his darts, have sight, and see
   His shame, and wishings hinder happy hours.
Why should we not love's purblind° charms resist?   *completely blind*
   Must we be servile, doing what he list?°   *pleases* 10
No, seek some host to harbor thee: I fly
Thy babish° tricks, and freedom do profess.   *childish*
   But O my hurt makes my lost heart confess
   I love, and must: So farewell liberty.

            [1621]

ROBERT HERRICK   [1591–1674]

To the Virgins, to Make Much of Time

Gather ye rosebuds while ye may,
   Old time is still a-flying;
And this same flower that smiles today
   Tomorrow will be dying.

The glorious lamp of heaven, the sun,   5
   The higher he's a-getting,
The sooner will his race be run,
   And nearer he's to setting.

That age is best which is the first,
   When youth and blood are warmer;   10
But being spent, the worse, and worst
   Times still succeed the former.

Then be not coy, but use your time,
   And while ye may, go marry;
For having lost but once your prime,   15
   You may forever tarry.

            [1648]

GEORGE HERBERT   [1593–1633]

Easter-wings°

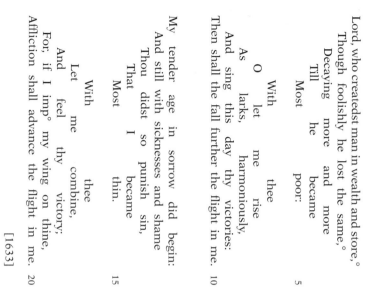

Lord, who createdst man in wealth and store,°
Though foolishly he lost the same,°
Decaying more and more
Till he became
Most poor: 5
          With thee
          O let me rise
          As larks, harmoniously,
And sing this day thy victories:
Then shall the fall further the flight in me.   10

My tender age in sorrow did begin:
And still with sicknesses and shame
Thou didst so punish sin,
That I became
Most thin.   15
          With thee
          Let me combine,
          And feel this day thy victory;
For, if I imp° my wing on thine,
Affliction shall advance the flight in me.   20

[1633]

Easter-wings: Originally the stanzas were printed on facing pages, lines 1–10 on the left page, to be read first, then lines 11–20 on the right page. **Store (l. 1):** abundance. **"Lost the same" (l. 2):** through the Fall in the Garden of Eden. Early editions include the words "this day" in line 18 (perhaps repeated by mistake from line 9); they do not appear in the only surviving manuscript and are not required for the meter. **Imp (l. 19):** a term from falconry—to graft additional feathers onto the wings of a hawk to improve its flight.

GEORGE HERBERT   [1593–1633]

The Pulley

When God at first made man,
Having a glass of blessings standing by,
"Let us," said he, "pour on him all we can.
Let the world's riches, which dispersèd lie,
    Contract into a span."   5

So strength first made a way;
Then beauty flowed, then wisdom, honor, pleasure.
When almost all was out, God made a stay,

Perceiving that, alone of all his treasure,
   Rest in the bottom lay.   10

   "For if I should," said he,
"Bestow this jewel also on my creature,
He would adore my gifts instead of me,
And rest in Nature, not the God of Nature;
   So both should losers be.   15

   "Yet let him keep the rest,
But keep them with repining restlessness.
Let him be rich and weary, that at least,
If goodness lead him not, yet weariness
   May toss him to my breast."   20

[1633]

EDMUND WALLER   [1606–1687]

Song

   Go, lovely rose!
Tell her that wastes her time and me
   That now she knows,
When I resemble her to thee,
How sweet and fair she seems to be.   5

   Tell her that's young,
And shuns to have her graces spied,
   That hadst thou sprung
In deserts, where no men abide,
Thou must have uncommended died.   10

   Small is the worth
Of beauty from the light retired;
   Bid her come forth,
Suffer herself to be desired,
And not blush so to be admired.   15

   Then die! that she
The common fate of all things rare
   May read in thee;
How small a part of time they share
That are so wondrous sweet and fair!   20

[1645]

JOHN MILTON   [1608–1674]

When I consider how my light is spent

When I consider how my light is spent°
  Ere half my days, in this dark world and wide,
  And that one talent which is death to hide
  Lodged with me useless, though my soul more bent
To serve therewith my Maker, and present   5
  My true account, lest he returning chide.
  "Doth God exact day-labor, light denied?"
  I fondly ask; but patience to prevent
That murmur, soon replies, "God doth not need
  Either man's work or his own gifts; who best   10
  Bear his mild yoke, they serve him best. His state
Is kingly. Thousands at his bidding speed
  And post o'er land and ocean without rest:
  They also serve who only stand and wait."

[*c. 1652;* 1673]

1. **when . . . spent:** Milton went blind in 1652. Lines 1–2 allude to Matthew 25:1–13; line 3, to Matthew 25:14–30; and line 11, to Matthew 11:30.

JOHN MILTON   [1608–1674]

Lycidas

In this monody° the author bewails a learned friend, unfortunately drowned in his passage from Chester on the Irish Seas, 1637. And by occasion foretells the ruin of our corrupted clergy, then in their height.

Yet once more, O ye laurels,° and once more,
Ye myrtles brown,° with ivy never sere,   *dark*
I come to pluck your berries harsh and crude,°   *unripe*

monody: A monody is an elegy or dirge sung by a single voice. The poem draws on the traditions of the pastoral elegy. It appeared in a collection of poems published as a tribute to Edward King, Milton's "learned friend" and fellow student at Cambridge.
1. **ye laurels:** Laurel, sacred to Apollo, was the emblem of poetic achievement. Myrtle is the crown of Venus and ivy of Bacchus. All three are evergreen, thus "never sere" (dry, withered).

And with forced fingers rude
Shatter your leaves before the mellowing year.   5
Bitter constraint, and sad occasion dear,
Compels me to disturb your season due:
For Lycidas is dead, dead ere his prime,
Young Lycidas, and hath not left his peer.
Who would not sing for Lycidas? He knew   10
Himself to sing, and build the lofty rhyme.
He must not float upon his watery bier
Unwept, and welter° to the parching wind,   *roll about*
Without the meed° of some melodious tear.   *reward*
   Begin then, sisters of the sacred well°   15
That from beneath the seat of Jove doth spring,
Begin, and somewhat loudly sweep the string.
Hence with denial vain, and coy° excuse,   *reticent*
So may some gentle Muse
With lucky words favor my destined urn,   20
And as he passes turn,
And bid fair peace be to my sable° shroud.   *black*
For we were nursed upon the self-same hill,
Fed the same flock, by fountain, shade, and rill.
   Together both, ere the high lawns° appeared   *pastures* 25
Under the opening eyelids of the morn,
We drove afield, and both together heard
What time the grey-fly winds° her sultry horn,   *blows*
Battening° our flocks with the fresh dews of night,   *fattening*
Oft till the star that rose, at evening, bright   30
Toward heaven's descent had sloped his westering wheel.
Meanwhile the rural ditties were not mute,
Tempered to the oaten flute;°
Rough satyrs danced, and fauns with cloven heel
From the glad sound would not be absent long,   35
And old Damaetas° loved to hear our song.
   But O the heavy change, now thou art gone,
Now thou art gone, and never must return!
Thee, shepherd, thee the woods and desert caves,
With wild thyme and the gadding° vine o'ergrown,   *wandering* 40
And all their echoes mourn.
The willows and the hazel copses° green   *thickets*

15. sisters . . . well: The muses; the well sacred to them was Aganippe near
Mount Helicon.
33. oaten flute: Instrument symbolic of pastoral poetry.
36. Damaetas: A pastoral name, referring probably to a Cambridge tutor.

Shall now no more be seen
Fanning their joyous leaves to thy soft lays.
As killing as the canker° to the rose,   *cankerworm* 45
Or taint-worm to the weanling herds that graze,
Or frost to flowers, that their gay wardrobe wear,
When first the white-thorn blows;°   *hawthorn blossoms*
Such, Lycidas, thy loss to shepherd's ear.
   Where were ye, nymphs, when the remorseless deep   50
Closed o'er the head of your loved Lycidas?
For neither were ye playing on the steep
Where your old bards, the famous Druids, lie,
Nor on the shaggy top of Mona high,
Nor yet where Deva spreads her wizard stream.°   55
Ay me, I fondly° dream,   *foolishly*
Had ye been there!—for what could that have done?
What could the Muse herself that Orpheus bore,
The Muse herself,° for her enchanting son
Whom universal nature did lament,   60
When by the rout that made the hideous roar
His gory visage down the stream was sent,
Down the swift Hebrus to the Lesbian shore?
   Alas! what boots° it with uncessant care   *profits*
To tend the homely slighted shepherd's trade,   65
And strictly meditate the thankless Muse?
Were it not better done as others use,
To sport with Amaryllis in the shade,
Or with the tangles of Neaera's hair?°
Fame is the spur that the clear spirit doth raise   70
(That last infirmity of noble mind)
To scorn delights, and live laborious days;
But the fair guerdon° when we hope to find,   *reward*
And think to burst out into sudden blaze,
Comes the blind Fury with the abhorrèd shears,°   75

55. Deva . . . stream: The River Dee in Cheshire, "wizard" because it was said to be able to change the size and position of its channel. "Mona" is the island of Anglesey, in northwest Wales. Both are in the west country near where King died.
59. The Muse herself: Calliope. Her son Orpheus was torn apart by a mob ("rout") of screaming Thracian women (Bacchantes). His bloody head floated down the river Hebrus, across the Aegean to the island of Lesbos.
68–69. Amaryllis, Neaera: Conventional names for shepherdesses.
75. Fury: Atropos, one of the three Fates in Greek mythology, used her scissors to cut the thread of human life, after it had been spun and measured by her sisters. For the Greeks and Romans the Furies had a different role, but even in classical literature "Fury" and "Fate" were often used interchangeably.

And slits the thin-spun life. "But not the praise,"
Phoebus replied, and touched my trembling ears:
"Fame is no plant that grows on mortal soil,
Nor in the glistering foil°
Set off to the world, nor in broad rumor lies,   80
But lives and spreads aloft by those pure eyes
And perfect witness of all-judging Jove;
As he pronounces lastly on each deed,
Of so much fame in heaven expect thy meed.'
   O fountain Arethuse,° and thou honored flood,   85
Smooth-sliding Mincius,° crowned with vocal reeds,
That strain I heard was of a higher mood.
But now my oat proceeds,
And listens to the herald of the sea°
That came in Neptune's plea.   90
He asked the waves, and asked the felon winds,
What hard mishap hath doomed this gentle swain?
And questioned every gust of rugged wings
That blows from off each beakèd promontory—
They knew not of his story,   95
And sage Hippotades° their answer brings,
That not a blast was from his dungeon strayed;
The air was calm, and on the level brine
Sleek Panope° with her all sisters played.
It was that fatal and perfidious bark,   100
Built in the eclipse, and rigged with curses dark,
That sunk so low that sacred head of thine.
   Next Camus,° reverend sire, went footing slow,
His mantle hairy, and his bonnet sedge,°   *plants growing near water*
Inwrought with figures dim, and on the edge   105
Like to that sanguine flower° inscribed with woe.

---

79. **glistering foil:** Gold or silver leaf set under jewels to increase their brilliance.
85. **Arethuse:** A fountain in Sicily associated with the pastoral poetry of Theocritus.
86. **Mincius:** A river in Lombardy associated with the *Eclogues* of Virgil.
89. **herald of the sea:** The merman Triton, who pleads Neptune's innocence in Lycidas's death.
96. **Hippotades:** Aeolus, the wind god, son of Hippotas.
99. **Panope:** The greatest of the Nereids (sea nymphs).
103. **Camus:** God of the river Cam, representing the ancient University of Cambridge.
106. **sanguine flower:** The blood-colored hyacinth; marks on its leaves supposedly are the Greek letters AIAI, expressing woe.

"Ah, who hath reft," quoth he, "my dearest pledge?"°   *child (hopefulness)*
Last came, and last did go,
The Pilot° of the Galilean lake;
Two massy keys he bore of metals twain   110
(The golden opes, the iron shuts amain).°   *with force*
He shook his mitred locks, and stern bespake:
"How well could I have spared for thee, young swain,
Enow° of such as for their bellies' sake   *enough*
Creep and intrude and climb into the fold!°   115
Of other care they little reckoning make
Than how to scramble at the shearers' feast,
And shove away the worthy bidden guest.
Blind mouths!° that scarce themselves know how to hold
A sheep-hook, or have learned aught else the least   120
That to the faithful herdman's art belongs!
What recks° it them? What need they? They are sped;°
And when they list,° their lean and flashy songs   *want*
Grate on their scrannel° pipes of wretched straw   *thin, feeble*
The hungry sheep look up, and are not fed,   125
But swoln with wind, and the rank mist they draw,
Rot inwardly, and foul contagion spread,
Besides what the grim wolf° with privy paw
Daily devours apace, and nothing said;
But that two-handed engine° at the door   130
Stands ready to smite once, and smite no more,"
    Return, Alpheus,° the dread voice is past
That shrunk thy streams; return, Sicilian Muse,
And call the vales, and bid them hither cast
Their bells and flowerets of a thousand hues.   135

109. The Pilot: Saint Peter, Galilean fisherman, first bishop of the church (thus his "mitred" locks—entitled to wear a bishop's mitre); to him Christ promised "the keys of the kingdom" (Matthew 16:19) to open and close the gates of heaven.
115. Creep . . . fold: Alluding to John 10:1—"Anyone who does not enter the sheepfold by the gate but climbs in by another way is a thief and a bandit."
119. Blind mouths!: A reference to the greed of the bishops: a bishop *(episcopus)* is one who oversees, and a pastor is one who feeds his flock.
122. recks: Matters to them; **are sped:** Have more than enough.
128. grim wolf: The Roman Catholic Church, secretly ("privy") opposing Protestantism.
130. two-handed engine: An apocalyptic instrument of revenge against clergy who neglect their responsibilities.
132. Alpheus: The reference to this river god who fell in love with the nymph Arethusa brings the poem back to the pastoral mode.

Ye valleys low where the mild whispers use°   *frequent (verb)*
Of shades and wanton winds and gushing brooks,
On whose fresh lap the swart star° sparely looks,   *Sirius*
Throw hither all your quaint enamelled eyes,
That on the green turf suck the honied showers,   140
And purple all the ground with vernal flowers.
Bring the rathe° primrose that forsaken dies,   *early*
The tufted crowtoe, and pale jessamine,
The white pink, and the pansy freaked° with jet,   *flecked*
The glowing violet,   145
The musk-rose, and the well-attired woodbine,
With cowslips wan that hang the pensive head,
And every flower that sad embroidery wears.
Bid amaranthus all his beauty shed,
And daffadillies fill their cups with tears,   150
To strew the laureate hearse where Lycid lies.
For so to interpose a little ease,
Let our frail thoughts dally with false surmise;
Ay me! whilst thee the shores and sounding seas
Wash far away, where'er thy bones are hurled,   155
Whether beyond the stormy Hebrides,
Where thou perhaps under the whelming° tide   *engulfing*
Visit'st the bottom of the monstrous world;
Or whether thou, to our moist vows° denied,   *tearful prayers*
Sleep'st by the fable of Bellerus° old,   160
Where the great vision of the guarded mount°
Looks toward Namancos and Bayona's hold:°
Look homeward, Angel,° now, and melt with ruth;°
And, O ye dolphins,° waft the hapless youth.
   Weep no more, woeful shepherds, weep no more,   165
For Lycidas your sorrow is not dead,
Sunk though he be beneath the watery floor;
So sinks the day-star° in the ocean bed,   *the sun*

---

160. Bellerus: A fabulous giant for whom Land's End (the southwestern tip of Cornwall) was called Bellerium in Roman times.
161. the guarded mount: Saint Michael's Mount, in Cornwall.
162. Namancos and Bayona: A mountain range and a fortress on the coast of northern Spain.
163. Angel: The archangel Michael, patron of mariners, imagined as standing on Saint Michael's Mount, looking southward; **ruth:** Pity.
164. ye dolphins: Dolphins brought the Greek poet Arion safely to shore and carried Melicertes to land, where he was transformed to a sea god, Palaemon.

And yet anon repairs° his drooping head,   *returns (raises)*
And tricks° his beams, and with new-spangled ore   *plays tricks with* 170
Flames in the forehead of the morning sky:
So Lycidas sunk low, but mounted high,
Through the dear might of him that walked the waves,°   *(Christ)*
Where, other groves and other streams along,
With nectar pure his oozy locks he laves,°   *bathes* 175
And hears the unexpressive° nuptial song   *inexpressible*
In the blest kingdoms meek of joy and love.
There entertain him all the saints above,
In solemn troops and sweet societies
That sing, and singing in their glory move,   180
And wipe the tears for ever from his eyes.
Now, Lycidas, the shepherds weep no more;
Henceforth thou art the Genius of the Shore,
In thy large recompense, and shalt be good
To all that wander in that perilous flood.   185
   Thus sang the uncouth° swain to the oaks and rills,   *uneducated*
While the still morn went out with sandals grey;
He touched the tender stops of various quills,
With eager thought warbling his Doric lay.°   *pastoral song*
And now the sun had stretched out all the hills,   190
And now was dropped into the western bay;
At last he rose, and twitched his mantle blue:
Tomorrow to fresh woods, and pastures new.

[1638]

ANNE BRADSTREET   [c. 1612–1672]

To My Dear and Loving Husband

If ever two were one, then surely we.
If ever man were loved by wife, then thee;
If ever wife was happy in a man,
Compare with me ye women if you can.
I prize thy love more than whole mines of gold,   5
Or all the riches that the East doth hold.
My love is such that rivers cannot quench,
Nor ought but love from thee give recompense.
Thy love is such I can no way repay;

The heavens reward thee manifold, I pray.   10
Then while we live, in love let's so persever,
That when we live no more we may live ever.

[1678]

RICHARD LOVELACE   [1618–1657]

To Lucasta, Going to the Wars

Tell me not, Sweet, I am unkind,
   That from the nunnery
Of thy chaste breast and quiet mind
   To war and arms I fly.

True, a new mistress now I chase,   5
   The first foe in the field;
And with a stronger faith embrace
   A sword, a horse, a shield.

Yet this inconstancy is such
   As you too shall adore;   10
I could not love thee, dear, so much,
   Loved I not honor more.

[1649]

ANDREW MARVELL   [1621–1678]

To His Coy Mistress°

   Had we but world enough, and time,
This coyness, lady, were no crime.
We would sit down, and think which way
To walk, and pass our long love's day.
Thou by the Indian Ganges' side   5
Shouldst rubies find; I by the tide

Coy: In the seventeenth century, "coy" could carry its older meaning, "shy," or the
modern sense of "coquettish."

Of Humber would complain.° I would
Love you ten years before the Flood,
And you should, if you please, refuse
Till the conversion of the Jews.°   10
My vegetable° love should grow   *living and growing*
Vaster than empires, and more slow;
An hundred years should go to praise
Thine eyes, and on thy forehead gaze;
Two hundred to adore each breast,   15
But thirty thousand to the rest;
An age at least to every part,
And the last age should show your heart.
For, lady, you deserve this state,°   *dignity*
Nor would I love at lower rate.   20
    But at my back I always hear
Time's wingèd chariot hurrying near;
And yonder all before us lie
Deserts of vast eternity.
Thy beauty shall no more be found,   25
Nor, in thy marble vault, shall sound
My echoing song; then worms shall try
That long-preserved virginity,
And your quaint honor turn to dust,
And into ashes all my lust: 30
The grave's a fine and private place,
But none, I think, do there embrace.
    Now therefore, while the youthful hue
Sits on thy skin like morning dew,
And while thy willing soul transpires°   *breathes forth* 35
At every pore with instant fires,°   *urgent passion*
Now let us sport us while we may,
And now, like amorous birds of prey,
Rather at once our time devour
Than languish in his slow-chapped° power.   40
Let us roll all our strength and all

5–7. **Indian Ganges', Humber:** The Ganges River in India, with its distant, romantic associations, contrasts with the Humber River, running through Hull in northeast England, Marvell's home town.
10. **conversion . . . Jews:** An occurrence foretold, in some traditions, as one of the concluding events of human history.
40. **slow-chapped:** Slow-jawed, devouring slowly.

Our sweetness up into one ball,
And tear our pleasures with rough strife
Thorough° the iron gates of life;   *through*
Thus, though we cannot make our sun   45
Stand still,° yet we will make him run.

[*c. 1650;* 1681]

45–46. make our sun stand still: An allusion to Joshua 10:12. In answer to
Joshua's prayer, God made the sun stand still, to prolong the day and give the
Israelites more time to defeat the Amorites.

APHRA BEHN   [1640–1689]

On Her Loving Two Equally

I

How strong does my passion flow,
Divided equally twixt two?
Damon had ne'er subdued my heart
Had not Alexis° took his part;
Nor could Alexis powerful prove,   5
Without my Damon's aid, to gain my love.

II

When my Alexis present is,
Then I for Damon sigh and mourn;
But when Alexis I do miss,
Damon gains nothing but my scorn.   10
But if it chance they both are by,
For both alike I languish, sigh, and die.

III

Cure then, thou mighty wingèd god,
This restless fever in my blood;
One golden-pointed dart take back: 15
But which, O Cupid, wilt thou take?
If Damon's, all my hopes are crossed;
Or that of my Alexis, I am lost.

[1684]

3–4. Damon, Alexis: Traditional names in poetry.

EDWARD TAYLOR   [c.1642–1729]

Housewifery

Make me, O Lord, thy spinning wheel complete.°
  Thy holy word my distaff make for me.
Make mine affections thy swift flyers neat,
  And make my soul thy holy spool to be.
  My conversation make to be thy reel,   5
  And reel the yarn thereon spun on thy wheel.

Make me thy loom then, knit therein this twine;
  And make thy holy spirit, Lord, wind quills.°
Then weave the web thyself. The yarn is fine.
  Thine ordinances make my fulling mills.   10
  Then dye the same in heavenly colors choice,
  All pinked° with varnished° flowers of paradise.   *ornamented/lustrous*

Then clothe therewith mine understanding, will,
  Affections, judgment, conscience, memory,
My words, and actions, that their shine may fill   15
  My ways with glory and thee glorify.
  Then mine apparel shall display before ye
  That I am clothed in holy robes for glory.

[*1682–1683;* 1939]

1. **spinning wheel complete:** In a spinning wheel, the distaff holds the raw wool or flax to be spun; the flyers twist and guide the thread; the thread is wound onto the spool as it is spun; and the reel receives the finished thread.
8. **quills:** The spools of a loom.

ANNE FINCH, COUNTESS OF
WINCHILSEA   [1661–1720]

The Introduction

Did I my lines intend for public view,
How many censures° would their faults pursue,   *criticisms*
Some would, because such words they do affect,
Cry they're insipid, empty, uncorrect.
And many have attained, dull and untaught,   5
The name of wit,° only by finding fault.   *perceptive person*

True judges might condemn their want° of wit,°   *lack/cleverness*
And all might say, they're by a woman writ.
Alas! a woman that attempts the pen,
Such an intruder on the rights of men,   10
Such a presumptuous creature, is esteemed,
The° fault can by no virtue be redeemed.   *That the*
They tell us we mistake our sex and way;
Good breeding, fashion, dancing, dressing, play
Are the accomplishments we should desire;   15
To write, or read, or think, or to inquire
Would cloud our beauty, and exhaust our time,
And interrupt the conquests° of our prime;°   *(amorous)/best years*
Whilst the dull manage of a servile house°   *household with servants*
Is held by some our utmost art, and use.   20
    Sure 'twas not ever thus, nor are we told
Fables° of women that excelled of old;   *stories conveying lessons*
To whom, by the diffusive° hand of Heaven   *scattering*
Some share of wit and poetry was given.

                        • • •

How are we fallen, fallen by mistaken rules?
And education's, more than nature's, fools,
Debarred from all improvements of the mind,
And to be dull, expected and designed;°   *shaped, formed*
And if someone would soar above the rest,   55
With warmer fancy° and ambition pressed,   *inventiveness*
So strong th' opposing faction still appears,
The hopes to thrive can ne'er outweigh the fears.
Be cautioned then my Muse, and still retired;
Nor be despised, aiming to be admired;   60
Conscious of wants, still with contracted wing,
To some few friends and to thy sorrows sing;
For groves of laurel° thou wert never meant;
Be dark enough thy shades, and be thou
    there content.

                                                            [1689]

63. **groves of laurel:** Leaves worn as a mark of distinction.

JONATHAN SWIFT   [1667–1745]

A Description of the Morning

Now hardly here and there a hackney-coach
Appearing, showed the ruddy morn's approach.
Now Betty from her master's bed had flown,
And softly stole to discompose her own;
The slip-shod 'prentice from his master's door   5
Had pared the dirt and sprinkled round the floor.
Now Moll had whirled her mop with dext'rous airs,
Prepared to scrub the entry and the stairs.
The youth with broomy stumps° began to trace   *worn broom*
The kennel-edge,° where wheels had worn the place.   *gutter*   10
The small-coal man° was heard with cadence deep,   *coal vendor*
Till drowned in shriller notes of chimney-sweep:
Duns° at his lordship's gate began to meet;   *debt collectors*
And brickdust Moll° had screamed through half the street
The turnkey now his flock returning sees,   15
Duly let out a-nights to steal for fees:
The watchful bailiffs take their silent stands,
And schoolboys lag with satchels in their hands.

[1709]

14. **brickdust Moll:** Woman selling powdered brick.

ALEXANDER POPE   [1688–1744]

The Rape of the Lock°

CANTO I

What dire offence from amorous causes springs,
What mighty quarrels rise from trivial things,

The Rape of the Lock: The poem is based on an actual incident: Lord Petre had
cut a lock of hair from the head of Arabella Fermor, which led to an estrangement
between the two prominent families. Pope's friend John Caryll, to whom the poem
is addressed (I.3), suggested that Pope write a humorous poem about the incident
that might lead to a reconciliation. The poem printed here is the original version
in two cantos, which Pope said was written in less than two weeks. It was widely
admired and praised when it appeared in 1712. Two years later Pope published an
expanded version in five cantos.

I sing—This verse to Caryll, Muse, is due:
This, even Belinda may vouchsafe to view:
Slight is the subject, but not so the praise,   5
If she inspire, and he approve my lays.
   Say what strange motive, Goddess, could compel
A well-bred lord to assault a gentle belle?
Oh, say what stranger cause, yet unexplored,
Could make a gentle belle reject a lord?   10
And dwells such rage in softest bosoms then?
And lodge such daring souls in little men?
   Sol° through white curtains did his beams display,   *the sun*
And oped those eyes which brighter shine than they.
Shock° just had given himself the rowzing shake,   15
And nymphs° prepared their chocolate to take.   *beautiful young women*
Thrice the wrought slipper knocked against the ground,°
And striking watches the tenth hour resound.
Belinda rose, and 'midst attending dames,
Launched on the bosom of the silver Thames.   20
A train of well-dressed youths around her shone,
And every eye was fixed on her alone;
On her white breast a sparkling cross she wore,
Which Jews might kiss, and infidels adore.
Her lively looks a sprightly mind disclose,   25
Quick as her eyes, and as unfixed as those:
Favors to none, to all she smiles extends;
Oft she rejects, but never once offends.
Bright as the sun, her eyes the gazers strike,
And, like the sun, they shine on all alike.   30
Yet graceful ease, and sweetness void of pride,
Might hide her faults, if belles had faults to hide:
If to her share some female errors fall,
Look on her face, and you'll forgive 'em all.
   This nymph, to the destruction of mankind,   35
Nourished two locks which graceful hung behind
In equal curls, and well conspired to deck
With shining ringlets her smooth ivory neck.
Love in these labyrinths his slaves detains,
And mighty hearts are held in slender chains.   40
With hairy springes° we the birds betray,   *snares*
Slight lines of hair surprize the finny prey,°   *fish*

I.15. **Shock:** The conventional name for a lapdog with very long hair.
I.17. **slipper . . . ground:** To summon a servant; bells were not introduced until
the late 1700s.

Fair tresses man's imperial race ensnare,
And beauty draws us with a single hair.
   The adventrous baron the bright locks admired,   45
He saw, he wished, and to the prize aspired.
Resolved to win, he meditates the way,
By force to ravish, or by fraud betray;
For when success a lover's toil attends,
Few ask if fraud or force attained his ends.   50
   For this, ere Phoebus° rose, he had implored   *the sun*
Propitious heaven, and every power adored,
But chiefly love—to love an altar built,
Of twelve vast French romances, neatly gilt.
There lay the sword-knot° Sylvia's hands had sewn,   55
With Flavia's busk° that oft had wrapped his own:
A fan, a garter, half a pair of gloves,
And all the trophies of his former loves.
With tender billet-doux° he lights the pyre,   *love letters*
And breaths three amorous sighs to raise the fire.   60
Then prostrate falls, and begs with ardent eyes
Soon to obtain, and long possess the prize:
The powers gave ear, and granted half his prayer,
The rest, the winds dispersed in empty air.
   Close by those meads° forever crowned with flowers,   *meadows* 65
Where Thames with pride surveys his rising towers,
There stands a structure of majestic frame,
Which from the neighboring Hampton° takes its name.
Here Britain's statesmen oft the fall foredoom
Of foreign tyrants, and of nymphs at home;   70
Here thou, great Anna,° whom three realms obey,
Dost sometimes counsel take—and sometimes tea.°
   Hither our nymphs and heroes did resort,
To taste awhile the pleasures of a court;

I.55. sword-knot: A ribbon or tassel tied to the hilt of a sword, sometimes the work of the sword owner's lady.
I.56. busk: Usually a strip of wood, whalebone, steel, or other rigid material used to stiffen the front of a corset. It probably refers here to the whole corset, which the baron often has wrapped around his hand (or waist).
I.68. Hampton: Hampton Court Palace, about fifteen miles up the Thames from central London.
I.71. Anna: Queen Anne (1665–1714) was ruler of Great Britain and Ireland (1702–1714), and the English Crown continued its old claim to rule France as well.
I.72. tea: In seventeenth-century pronunciation, "tea" and "obey" were perfect rhymes, as were "found" and "wound" (II. 102–03) and "hair" and "sphere" (II. 183–84).

In various talk the cheerful hours they passed,   75
Of, who was bit,° or who capotted last:°
This speaks the glory of the British Queen,
And that describes a charming Indian screen;
A third interprets motions, looks, and eyes;
At every word a reputation dies.   80
Snuff, or the fan, supply each pause of chat,
With singing, laughing, ogling, and all that.
   Now, when declining from the noon of day,
The sun obliquely shoots his burning ray;
When hungry judges soon the sentence sign,   85
And wretches hang that jurymen may dine;
When merchants from the Exchange return in peace,
And the long labors of the toilet° cease—   *dressing-table*
The board's with cups and spoons, alternate, crowned;
The berries crackle, and the mill turns round;°   90
On shining altars of Japan° they raise
The silver lamp, and fiery spirits blaze:
From silver spouts the grateful liquors glide,
And China's earth receives the smoking tide.
At once they gratify their smell and taste,   95
While frequent cups prolong the rich repast.
Coffee (which makes the politician wise,
And see through all things with his half-shut eyes)
Sent up in vapors to the Baron's brain
New stratagems, the radiant lock to gain.   100
Ah, cease, rash youth! desist ere 'tis too late,
Fear the just Gods, and think of Scylla's fate!°
Changed to a bird, and sent to flit in air,
She dearly pays for Nisus' injured hair!
   But when to mischief mortals bend their mind,   105
How soon fit instruments of ill they find.
Just then, Clarissa drew with tempting grace
A two-edged weapon° from her shining case: *scissors*

I.76. **was bit:** Taken in, made the butt of a joke, or cheated in a card game; **capotted:** Lost all the tricks in the card game Piquet.
I.90. **berries . . . round:** Denotes the roasting and grinding of coffee beans.
I.91. **altars of Japan:** A table work decorated and finished in the Japanese style,
with a varnish of exceptional hardness.
I.102. **Scylla's fate!:** This Scylla, daughter of Ninus, cut from his head a lock of
hair that protected him to give it to her lover, Minos of Crete, who was laying siege
to her father's city of Megara. Minos was shocked and refused to accept it, and
Scylla was turned into a seabird (Ovid, *Metamorphoses*, VIII).

So ladies in romance assist their knight,
Present the spear, and arm him for the fight.   110
He takes the gift with reverence, and extends
The little engine on his fingers' ends;
This just behind Belinda's neck he spread,
As o'er the fragrant steams she bends her head.
He first expands the glittering forfex° wide   115
To enclose the lock; then joins it, to divide;
One fatal stroke the sacred hair does sever
From the fair head, forever and forever!
   The living fires come flashing from her eyes,
And screams of horror rend the affrighted skies.   120
Not louder shrieks by dames to heaven are cast,
When husbands die, or lapdogs breathe their last,
Or when rich china vessels fallen from high,
In glittering dust and painted fragments lie.
   "Let wreaths of triumph now my temples twine,"   125
The victor cried, "The glorious prize is mine!
While fish in streams, or birds delight in air,
Or in a coach and six the British fair,
As long as *Atalantis*° shall be read,
Or the small pillow grace a lady's bed,   130
While visits shall be paid on solemn days,
When numerous wax-lights in bright order blaze,
While nymphs take treats, or assignations give,
So long my honor, name, and praise shall live!
   "What time would spare, from steel receives its date,   135
And monuments, like men, submit to fate!
Steel did the labor of the Gods destroy,
And strike to dust the aspiring towers of Troy;
Steel could the works of mortal pride confound,
And hew triumphal arches to the ground.   140
What wonders then, fair nymph, thy hairs should feel
The conquering force of unresisted steel?"

CANTO II

But anxious cares the pensive nymph oppressed,
And secret passions labored in her breast.
Not youthful kings in battle seized alive,

I.115. forfex: Latin for scissors.
I.129. *Atalantis*: *New Atlantis* (1709) by Delarivière Manley was popular at the time because of its accounts of court scandal.

Not scornful virgins who their charms survive,
Not ardent lover robbed of all his bliss,   5
Not ancient lady when refused a kiss,
Not tyrants fierce that unrepenting die,
Not Cynthia° when her manteau's pinned awry,   *conventional name*
E'er felt such rage, resentment, and despair,
As thou, sad virgin, for thy ravished hair.   10
    While her racked soul repose and peace requires,
The fierce Thalestris° fans the rising fires.
"O wretched maid!" she spreads her hands, and cried,
And Hampton's echoes, "Wretched maid!" replied,
"Was it for this you took such constant care,   15
Combs, bodkins, leads, pomatums to prepare?°
For this your locks in paper durance bound,
For this with torturing irons wreathed around?
Oh, had the youth but been content to seize
Hairs less in sight — or any hairs but these!   20
Gods! shall the ravisher display this hair,
While the fops envy, and the ladies stare?
Honor forbid! at whose unrivaled shrine
Ease, pleasure, virtue, all, our sex resign.
Methinks already I your tears survey,   25
Already hear the horrid things they say,
Already see you a degraded toast,°
And all your honor in a whisper lost!
How shall I, then, your helpless fame defend?
'Twill then be infamy to seem your friend!   30
And shall this prize, the inestimable prize,
Exposed through crystal to the gazing eyes,
And heightened by the diamond's circling rays,
On that rapacious hand forever blaze?°
Sooner shall grass in Hyde Park Circus° grow,   35

II.12. Thalestris: A character named for a queen of the Amazons, thus a fierce and militant warrior.
II.16. bodkin: A long pin or pin-shaped ornament used by women to fasten up their hair; **leads:** Black lead combs were used to darken hair.
II.27. toast: "A celebrated woman whose health is often drunk" (from Samuel Johnson's *Dictionary of the English Language* [1755]).
II.33–34. diamond's . . . blaze: The baron intends to encase the lock in crystal and mount it on a ring.
II.35. Hyde Park Circus: A circular drive in Hyde Park, a popular gathering place for the upper classes.

And wits take lodgings in the sound of Bow;°
Sooner let earth, air, sea, to chaos fall,
Men, monkeys, lapdogs, parrots, perish all!"
　She said; then raging to Sir Plume repairs,
And bids her beau demand the precious hairs   40
(Sir Plume, of amber snuffbox justly vain,
And the nice conduct of a clouded cane).°
With earnest eyes, and round unthinking face,
He first the snuffbox opened, then the case,
And thus broke out—"My Lord, why, what the devil?   45
Zounds!° damn the lock! 'fore Gad, you must be civil!
Plague on 't! 'tis past a jest—nay prithee, pox!
Give her the hair"—he spoke, and rapped his box.
　"It grieves me much," replied the Peer again,
"Who speaks so well should ever speak in vain.   50
But by this lock, this sacred lock, I swear
(Which never more shall join its parted hair,
Which never more its honors shall renew,
Clipped from the lovely head where once it grew),
That while my nostrils draw the vital air,   55
This hand, which won it, shall forever wear."
He spoke, and speaking, in proud triumph spread
The long-contended honors of her head.
　But see! the nymph in sorrow's pomp appears,
Her eyes half languishing, half drowned in tears;   60
Now livid pale her cheeks, now glowing red;
On her heaved bosom hung her drooping head,
Which, with a sigh, she raised; and thus she said:
　"Forever cursed be this detested day,
Which snatched my best, my favorite curl away!   65
Happy! ah, ten times happy had I been,
If Hampton Court these eyes had never seen!
Yet am not I the first mistaken maid,
By love of courts to numerous ills betrayed.
Oh, had I rather unadmired remained   70
In some lone isle, or distant northern land;

II.36. Bow: Lodgings within hearing distance of the bells of Saint Mary-le-Bow Church would be in an unfashionable part of London.
II.42. clouded cane: Canes with heads of mottled or veined stones were considered stylish.
II.46. Zounds!: A euphemistic abbreviation of "by God's wounds" used in oaths and asseverations.

Where the gilt chariot never marked the way,
Where none learn ombre, none e'er taste bohea!°
There kept my charms concealed from mortal eye,
Like roses that in deserts bloom and die.   75
What moved my mind with youthful lords to roam?
Oh, had I stayed, and said my prayers at home!
'Twas this the morning omens did foretell;
Thrice from my trembling hand the patch box° fell;
The tottering china shook without a wind,   80
Nay, Poll sat mute, and shock was most unkind.
See the poor remnants of this slighted hair:
My hands shall rend what ev'n thy own did spare.
This, in two sable ringlets taught to break,
Once gave new beauties to the snowy neck.   85
The sister lock now sits uncouth, alone,
And in its fellow's fate foresees its own;
Uncurled it hangs! the fatal shears demands,
And tempts once more thy sacrilegious hands."
    She said: the pitying audience melt in tears,   90
But fate and Jove had stopped the baron's ears.
In vain Thalestris with reproach assails,
For who can move when fair Belinda fails?
Not half so fixed the Trojan° could remain,
While Anna begged and Dido raged in vain.   95
"To arms, to arms!" the bold Thalestris cries,
And swift as lightning to the combat flies.
All side in parties, and begin the attack;
Fans clap, silks rustle, and tough whalebones crack;
Heroes' and heroines' shouts confusedly rise,   100
And bass and treble voices strike the skies.
No common weapons in their hands are found,
Like Gods they fight, nor dread a mortal wound.
    So when bold Homer makes the Gods engage,
And heavenly breasts with human passions rage;   105

II.73. ombre: A popular card game played by three persons; bohea: In the early
1700s, referred to the finest kinds of black tea.
II.79. patch box: A box for holding patches, the small pieces of black silk or
court-plaster worn on the face by men and especially women of fashion in the
1600s and 1700s, either to hide a blemish or to show off the complexion by contrast.
II.94–95. the Trojan: Aeneas, who abandoned Dido at the bidding of the gods,
despite Dido's reproaches (*Aeneid* 4.305–92) and the pleadings of her sister Anna
that he stay (4.416–49).

'Gainst Pallas, Mars; Latona, Hermes arms;°
And all Olympus rings with loud alarms.
Jove's thunder roars, heaven trembles all around;
Blue Neptune storms, the bellowing deeps resound;
Earth shakes her nodding towers, the ground gives way,   110
And the pale ghosts start at the flash of day.
   While through the press enraged Thalestris flies,
And scatters deaths around from both her eyes,°
A beau and witling perished in the throng,
One died in metaphor, and one in song.   115
"O cruel nymph! a living death I bear,"
Cried Dapperwit, and sunk beside his chair.
A mournful glance Sir Fopling° upwards cast,
"Those eyes are made so killing"—was his last.
Thus on Meander's flowery margin lies   120
The expiring swan, and as he sings he dies.°
   As bold Sir Plume had drawn Clarissa down,
Chloe stepped in, and killed him with a frown;
She smiled to see the doughty hero slain,
But at her smile, the beau revived again.   125
   Now Jove suspends his golden scales in air,°
Weighs the men's wits against the lady's hair;
The doubtful beam long nods from side to side;
At length the wits mount up, the hairs subside.
   See, fierce Belinda on the baron flies,   130
With more than usual lightning in her eyes;
Nor feared the chief the unequal fight to try,
Who sought no more than on his foe to die.
But this bold lord, with manly strength indued,
She with one finger and a thumb subdued: 135

II.106. **Pallas . . . Hermes:** In the *Illiad* 20.91ff, Pallas (Athena) and Hermes sided with the Greeks, Mars and Latona (Leto, mother of Apollo and Diana), with the Trojans.
II.113. Lines 113–47 include sexual innuendos, particularly the double entendre in which "die" or "kill" can mean orgasm as well as physical death.
II.117–18. **Dapperwit, Fopling:** Names of characters borrowed from recent satiric comedies.
II.120–21. **expiring swan:** Legends hold that the mute swan, a royal bird in England since 1462, uses its voice only as it dies. **Meander's flowery margin:** "Thus, at the summons of fate, casting himself down amid the watery grasses by the shallows of Meander, sings the white swan" (Ovid, *Heroides* 7:1–2).
II.126. **Jove . . . air:** In the *Iliad* (16.783ff, 22.271ff), the *Aeneid* (12.725ff), and *Paradise Lost* (4.996ff), scales are used by the gods to determine the course of future events.

Just where the breath of life his nostrils drew,
A charge of snuff the wily virgin threw;
Sudden, with starting tears each eye o'erflows,
And the high dome re-echoes to his nose.
    "Now meet thy fate," the incensed Virago° cried,   *female warrior*   140
And drew a deadly bodkin° from her side.
"Boast not my fall," he said, "insulting foe!
Thou by some other shalt be laid as low.
Nor think, to die dejects my lofty mind;
All that I dread, is leaving you behind!   145
Rather than so, ah, let me still survive,
And still burn on, in Cupid's flames, alive."
    "Restore the lock!" she cries; and all around
"Restore the lock!" the vaulted roofs rebound.
Not fierce Othello in so loud a strain   150
Roared for the handkerchief that caused his pain.°
But see how oft ambitious aims are crossed,
And chiefs contend till all the prize is lost.
The lock, obtained with guilt, and kept with pain,
In every place is sought, but sought in vain: 155
With such a prize no mortal must be blessed,
So heaven decrees! with heaven who can contest?
    Some thought it mounted to the lunar sphere,
Since all that man e'er lost is treasured there.
There heroes' wits are kept in ponderous vases,   160
And beaux' in snuffboxes and tweezer cases.
There broken vows and deathbed alms are found,
And lovers' hearts with ends of riband bound;
The courtiers' promises, and sick man's prayers,
The smiles of harlots, and the tears of heirs;   165
Cages for gnats, and chains to yoke a flea,
Dried butterflies, and tomes of casuistry.
    But trust the Muse—she saw it upward rise,
Though marked by none but quick, poetic eyes
(Thus Rome's great founder to the heavens withdrew,   170
To Proculus alone confessed in view).°
A sudden star, it shot through liquid air,
And drew behind a radiant trail of hair.

II.141. bodkin: A short pointed weapon, or dagger, or (as in II.16 above) a long
pin or pin-shaped ornament used to fasten up the hair.
II.150–51. Othello . . . pain: *Othello* 3.4.55–98.
II.170–71. (Thus . . . view): Romulus' removal to heaven in a storm cloud was
observed only by the senator Proculus.

Not Berenice's locks first rose so bright,°
The skies bespangling with disheveled light.   175
This, the beau monde shall from the Mall survey, ⎫
As through the moonlight shade they nightly stray, ⎬
And hail with music its propitious ray.   ⎭
This Partridge soon shall view in cloudless skies,
When next he looks through Galileo's eyes;°   *telescope*   180
And hence the egregious wizard shall foredoom
The fate of Louis,° and the fall of Rome.
    Then cease, bright nymph, to mourn the ravished hair,
Which adds new glory to the shining sphere.
Not all the tresses that fair head can boast   185
Shall draw such envy as the lock you lost.
For, after all the murders of your eye,
When, after millions slain, yourself shall die;
When those fair suns shall set, as set they must,
And all those tresses shall be laid in dust;   190
This lock the Muse shall consecrate to fame,
And 'midst the stars inscribe Belinda's name.

[1712]

II.174. **Berenice:** Wife of Ptolemy III who offered a lock of her hair to Aphrodite
to ensure her husband's safe return from war; the hair disappeared from
Aphrodite's temple and was turned into a constellation.
II.179–82. "John Partridge was a ridiculous Star-gazer, who in his Almanacks
every year, never fail'd to predict the downfall of the Pope, and the King of France,
then at war with the English" (Pope's note).

THOMAS GRAY   [1716–1771]

Elegy Written in a Country Churchyard

The curfew° tolls the knell of parting day,   *evening bell*
    The lowing herd wind slowly o'er the lea,
The plowman homeward plods his weary way,
    And leaves the world to darkness and to me.

Now fades the glimmering landscape on the sight,   5
    And all the air a solemn stillness holds,
Save where the beetle wheels his droning flight,
    And drowsy tinklings lull the distant folds;

Save that from yonder ivy-mantled tower
    The moping owl does to the moon complain   10

Of such, as wandering near her secret bower,
    Molest her ancient solitary reign.

Beneath those rugged elms, that yew tree's shade,
    Where heaves the turf in many a moldering heap,
Each in his narrow cell forever laid,   15
    The rude forefathers° of the hamlet sleep.   *humble ancestors*

The breezy call of incense-breathing morn,
    The swallow twittering from the straw-built shed,
The cock's shrill clarion, or the echoing horn,°   *(of a hunter)*
    No more shall rouse them from their lowly bed.   20

For them no more the blazing hearth shall burn,
    Or busy housewife ply her evening care;
No children run to lisp their sire's return,
    Or climb his knees the envied kiss to share.

Oft did the harvest to their sickle yield,   25
    Their furrow oft the stubborn glebe° has broke;   *soil*
How jocund did they drive their team afield!
    How bowed the woods beneath their sturdy stroke!

Let not Ambition mock their useful toil,
    Their homely joys, and destiny obscure;   30
Nor Grandeur hear with a disdainful smile
    The short and simple annals of the poor.

The boast of heraldry,° the pomp of power,   *noble ancestry*
    And all that beauty, all that wealth e'er gave,
Awaits alike the inevitable hour.   35
    The paths of glory lead but to the grave.

Nor you, ye proud, impute to these the fault,
    If memory o'er their tomb no trophies° raise,   *memorials*
Where through the long-drawn aisle and fretted° vault   *ornamented*
    The pealing anthem swells the note of praise.   40

Can storied° urn or animated° bust   *decorated/lifelike*
    Back to its mansion call the fleeting breath?
Can Honor's voice provoke° the silent dust,   *call forth*
    Or Flattery soothe the dull cold ear of Death?

Perhaps in this neglected spot is laid   45
    Some heart once pregnant with celestial fire;
Hands that the rod of empire might have swayed,
    Or waked to ecstasy the living lyre.

But Knowledge to their eyes her ample page
  Rich with the spoils of time did ne'er unroll;   50
Chill Penury repressed their noble rage,
  And froze the genial current of the soul.

Full many a gem of purest ray serene,
  The dark unfathomed caves of ocean bear:
Full many a flower is born to blush unseen,   55
  And waste its sweetness on the desert air.

Some village Hampden,° that with dauntless breast
  The little tyrant of his fields withstood;
Some mute inglorious Milton here may rest,
  Some Cromwell guiltless of his country's blood.   60

The applause of listening senates to command,
  The threats of pain and ruin to despise,
To scatter plenty o'er a smiling land,
  And read their history in a nation's eyes,

Their lot forbade: nor° circumscribed alone   *not* 65
  Their growing virtues, but their crimes confined;
Forbade to wade through slaughter to a throne,
  And shut the gates of mercy on mankind,

The struggling pangs of conscious truth to hide,
  To quench the blushes of ingenuous shame,   70
Or heap the shrine of Luxury and Pride
  With incense kindled at the Muse's flame.

Far from the madding crowd's ignoble strife,
  Their sober wishes never learned to stray;
Along the cool sequestered vale of life   75
  They kept the noiseless tenor of their way.

Yet even these bones from insult to protect
  Some frail memorial° still erected nigh,   *(simple tombstone)*
With uncouth rhymes and shapeless sculpture decked,
  Implores the passing tribute of a sigh.   80

Their name, their years, spelt by the unlettered Muse,
  The place of fame and elegy supply:
And many a holy text around she strews,
  That teach the rustic moralist to die.

57–60. Hampden, Cromwell: John Hampden (1594–1643) refused to pay a special tax imposed in 1636 and led a defense of the people's rights in Parliament. Oliver Cromwell (1599–1658) was a rebel leader in the English Civil War.

For who to dumb Forgetfulness a prey,   85
    This pleasing anxious being e'er resigned,
Left the warm precincts of the cheerful day,
    Nor cast one longing lingering look behind?

On some fond breast the parting soul relies,
    Some pious drops° the closing eye requires;   *tears* 90
Even from the tomb the voice of Nature cries,
    Even in our ashes live their wonted fires.

For thee,° who mindful of the unhonored dead   *(the poet himself)*
    Dost in these lines their artless tale relate;
If chance, by lonely contemplation led,   95
    Some kindred spirit shall inquire thy fate,

Haply° some hoary-headed swain° may say,   *perhaps, elderly shepherd*
    "Oft have we seen him° at the peep of dawn   *the poet*
Brushing with hasty steps the dews away
    To meet the sun upon the upland lawn.   100

"There at the foot of yonder nodding beech
    That wreathes its old fantastic roots so high,
His listless length at noontide would he stretch,
    And pore upon the brook that babbles by.

"Hard by yon wood, now smiling as in scorn,   105
    Muttering his wayward fancies he would rove,
Now drooping, woeful wan, like one forlorn,
    Or crazed with care, or crossed in hopeless love.

"One morn I missed him on the customed hill,
    Along the heath and near his favorite tree;   110
Another° came; nor yet beside the rill,   *(another day)*
    Nor up the lawn, nor at the wood was he;

"The next with dirges due in sad array
    Slow through the churchway path we saw him borne.
Approach and read (for thou canst read) the lay,   115
    Graved on the stone beneath yon aged thorn."

THE EPITAPH

Here rests his head upon the lap of Earth
    A youth to fortune and to Fame unknown.
Fair Science° frowned not on his humble birth,   *learning*
    And Melancholy marked him for her own.   120

Large was his bounty, and his soul sincere,
    Heaven did a recompense as largely send:

He gave to Misery all he had, a tear,
  He gained from Heaven ('twas all he wished) a friend.

No farther seek his merits to disclose,   125
  Or draw his frailties from their dread abode
(There they alike in trembling hope repose),
  The bosom of his Father and his God.

[1751]

CHRISTOPHER SMART   [1722–1771]

From Jubilate Agno°

For I will consider my Cat Jeoffry.
For he is the servant of the Living God, duly and daily serving him.
For at the first glance of the glory of God in the East he worships
  in his way.
For is this done by wreathing his body seven times round with elegant
  quickness.
For then he leaps up to catch the musk, which is the blessing of God
  upon his prayer.   5
For he rolls upon prank° to work it in.   *prankishly*
For having done duty and received blessing he begins to consider
  himself.
For this he performs in ten degrees.
For first he looks upon his forepaws to see if they are clean.
For secondly he kicks up behind to clear away there.   10
For thirdly he works it upon stretch with the forepaws extended.
For fourthly he sharpens his paws by wood.
For fifthly he washes himself.
For sixthly he rolls upon wash.
For seventhly he fleas himself, that he may not be interrupted
  upon the beat.°   15
For eighthly he rubs himself against a post.
For ninthly he looks up for his instructions.
For tenthly he goes in quest of food.

Jubilate Agno: "Rejoice in the Lamb" (Latin); i.e., in Jesus, the Lamb of God. The
poem was written while Smart was confined for madness from 1759 to 1763. It is
influenced by the form of Hebrew poetry, particularly the biblical psalms. The
best-known section is that concerning his cat Jeoffry, his companion during his
confinement.
15. that . . . beat: Not need to stop to scratch while on his daily rounds of hunting.

For having considered God and himself he will consider his neighbor.
For if he meets another cat he will kiss her in kindness.   20
For when he takes his prey he plays with it to give it a chance.
For one mouse in seven escapes by his dallying.
For when his day's work is done his business more properly begins.
For he keeps the Lord's watch in the night against the adversary.
For he counteracts the powers of darkness by his electrical skin and
   glaring eyes.   25
For he counteracts the Devil, who is death, by brisking about the life.
For in his morning orisons he loves the sun and the sun loves him.
For he is of the tribe of Tiger.
For the Cherub Cat is a term of the Angel Tiger.°
For he has the subtlety and hissing of a serpent, which in goodness
   he suppresses.   30
For he will not do destruction if he is well-fed, neither will he spit
   without provocation.
For he purrs in thankfulness when God tells him he's a good Cat.
For he is an instrument for the children to learn benevolence upon.
For every house is incomplete without him, and a blessing is lacking
   in the spirit.
For the Lord commanded Moses concerning the cats at the departure
   of the Children of Israel from Egypt.   35
For every family had one cat at least in the bag.°
For the English Cats are the best in Europe.
For he is the cleanest in the use of his forepaws of any quadruped.
For the dexterity of his defense is an instance of the love of God to him
   exceedingly.
For he is the quickest to his mark of any creature.   40
For he is tenacious of his point.
For he is a mixture of gravity and waggery.
For he knows that God is his Savior.
For there is nothing sweeter than his peace when at rest.
For there is nothing brisker than his life when in motion.   45
For he is of the Lord's poor, and so indeed is he called by benevolence
   perpetually—Poor Jeoffry! poor Jeoffry! the rat has bit thy throat.
For I bless the name of the Lord Jesus that Jeoffry is better.
For the divine spirit comes about his body to sustain it in complete cat.
For his tongue is exceeding pure so that it has in purity what
   it wants° in music.   *lacks*

29. Cherub . . . Tiger: As a cherub is a small angel, so a cat is like a small tiger.
36. cat . . . bag: No cats are mentioned in the biblical account of the Exodus, but
Smart may have been aware that images of cats were among the Egyptian gods
and may be speculating that cats were among the jewelry of silver and gold the
Egyptians gave the Israelites as they left (Exodus 12:35–36).

For he is docile and can learn certain things.   50
For he can sit up with gravity, which is patience upon approbation.
For he can fetch and carry, which is patience in employment.
For he can jump over a stick, which is patience upon proof positive.
For he can spraggle upon waggle° at the word of command.
For he can jump from an eminence into his master's bosom.   55
For he can catch the cork and toss it again.
For he is hated by the hypocrite and miser.
For the former is afraid of detection.
For the latter refuses the charge.
For he camels his back to bear the first notion of business.   60
For he is good to think on, if a man would express himself neatly.
For he made a great figure in Egypt for his signal services.
For he killed the Ichneumon rat, very pernicious by land.°
For his ears are so acute that they sting again.
For from this proceeds the passing quickness of his attention.   65
For by stroking of him I have found out electricity.
For I perceived God's light about him both wax and fire.
For the electrical fire is the spiritual substance which God sends from
    heaven to sustain the bodies both of man and beast.
For God has blessed him in the variety of his movements.
For, though he cannot fly, he is an excellent clamberer.   70
For his motions upon the face of the earth are more than any other
    quadruped.
For he can tread to all the measures upon the music.
For he can swim for life.
For he can creep.

[*c. 1760;* 1939]

54. **spraggle upon waggle:** Sprawl when his master waggles a finger.
63. **Ichneumon:** Egyptian species of mongoose that somewhat resembles a large
rat. It is, however, regarded as beneficial and was domesticated by the ancient
Egyptians.

PHILIP FRENEAU   [1752–1832]

The Indian Burying Ground

In spite of all the learned have said,
    I still my opinion keep;
The posture, that we give the dead,
    Points out the soul's eternal sleep.

Not so the ancients of these lands°—   5
   The Indian, when from life released,
Again is seated with his friends,°
   And shares again the joyous feast.

His imaged birds, and painted bowl,
   And venison, for a journey dressed,°   10
Bespeak the nature of the soul,
   Activity, that knows no rest.

His bow, for action ready bent,
   And arrows, with a head of stone,
Can only mean that life is spent,   15
   And not the old ideas gone.

Thou, stranger, that shalt come this way,
   No fraud upon the dead commit—
Observe the swelling turf, and say
   They do not lie, but here they sit.   20

Here still a lofty rock remains,
   On which the curious eye may trace
(Now wasted, half, by wearing rains)
   The fancies of a ruder° race.   *more primitive*

Here still an aged elm aspires,   25
   Beneath whose far-projecting shade
(And which the shepherd still admires)
   The children of the forest played!

There oft a restless Indian queen
   (Pale Shebah,° with her braided hair)   30
And many a barbarous form is seen
   To chide the man that lingers there.

By midnight moons, o'er moistening dews;
   In habit for the chase arrayed,
The hunter still the deer pursues,   35
   The hunter and the deer, a shade!

---

5. these lands: America or the Americas.
7. seated . . . friends: Refers to the Native American custom of burying the dead
in a sitting position.
10. for a journey dressed (pun): To prepare for cooking as well as to clothe.
30. Pale Shebah: The Queen of Sheba (here thought of as in Africa) visited
Solomon (1 Kings 10:1–13). The queen of line 29 is pale by contrast with her
African counterpart.

And long shall timorous fancy see
  The painted chief, and pointed spear,
And Reason's self shall bow the knee
  To shadows and delusions here.   40

                                             [1788]

WILLIAM BLAKE   [1757–1827]

The Lamb

  Little Lamb, who made thee?
  Dost thou know who made thee?
Gave thee life & bid thee feed,
By the stream & o'er the mead;
Gave thee clothing of delight,   5
Softest clothing wooly bright;
Gave thee such a tender voice,
Making all the vales rejoice!
  Little Lamb who made thee?
  Dost thou know who made thee?   10

  Little Lamb I'll tell thee,
  Little Lamb I'll tell thee!
He is callèd by thy name,
For he calls himself a Lamb:
He is meek & he is mild,   15
He became a little child:
I a child & thou a lamb,
We are callèd by his name.
  Little Lamb God bless thee.
  Little Lamb God bless thee.   20

                                             [1789]

WILLIAM BLAKE   [1757–1827]

The Tyger

Tyger, Tyger, burning bright
In the forests of the night,
What immortal hand or eye
Could frame thy fearful symmetry?

In what distant deeps or skies   5
Burnt the fire of thine eyes?
On what wings dare he aspire?
What the hand, dare seize the fire?

And what shoulder, & what art,
Could twist the sinews of thy heart?   10
And when thy heart began to beat,
What dread hand? & what dread feet?

What the hammer? what the chain?
In what furnace was thy brain?
What the anvil? what dread grasp   15
Dare its deadly terrors clasp?

When the stars threw down their spears
And water'd heaven with their tears,
Did he smile his work to see?
Did he who made the Lamb make thee?   20

Tyger, Tyger, burning bright
In the forests of the night,
What immortal hand or eye
Dare frame thy fearful symmetry?

[1794]

WILLIAM BLAKE   [1757–1827]

London

I wander through each chartered street,
Near where the chartered Thames does flow,
And mark in every face I meet
Marks of weakness, marks of woe.

In every cry of every man,   5
In every infant's cry of fear,
In every voice, in every ban,
The mind-forged manacles I hear.

How the chimney-sweeper's cry
Every black'ning church appalls;   10
And the hapless soldier's sigh
Runs in blood down palace walls.

But most through midnight streets I hear
How the youthful harlot's curse
Blasts the new-born infant's tear,   15
And blights with plagues the marriage hearse.

[1794]

ROBERT BURNS   [1759–1796]

A Red, Red Rose

O my luve's like a red, red rose,
    That's newly sprung in June;
O my luve's like the melodie
    That's sweetly played in tune.

As fair art thou, my bonnie lass,   5
    So deep in luve am I;
And I will luve thee still, my dear,
    Till a' the seas gang dry.

Till a' the seas gang dry, my dear,
    And the rocks melt wi' the sun: 10
O I will love thee still, my dear,
    While the sands o' life shall run.

And fare thee weel, my only luve,
    And fare thee weel awhile!
And I will come again, my luve,   15
    Though it were ten thousand mile.

[1796]

WILLIAM WORDSWORTH   [1770–1850]

I wandered lonely as a cloud

I wandered lonely as a cloud
That floats on high o'er vales and hills,
When all at once I saw a crowd,
A host, of golden daffodils;

Beside the lake, beneath the trees,   5
Fluttering and dancing in the breeze.

Continuous as the stars that shine
And twinkle on the milky way,
They stretched in never-ending line
Along the margin of a bay: 10
Ten thousand saw I at a glance,
Tossing their heads in sprightly dance.

The waves beside them danced; but they
Outdid the sparkling waves in glee:
A poet could not but be gay,   15
In such a jocund company:
I gazed—and gazed—but little thought
What wealth the show to me had brought:

For oft, when on my couch I lie
In vacant or in pensive mood,   20
They flash upon that inward eye
Which is the bliss of solitude;
And then my heart with pleasure fills,
And dances with the daffodils.

[1807]

WILLIAM WORDSWORTH   [1770–1850]

Lines

*Composed a Few Miles above Tintern Abbey°
on Revisiting the Banks of the Wye
During a Tour. July 13, 1798*

    Five years have passed; five summers, with the length
Of five long winters! and again I hear
These waters, rolling from their mountain-springs
With a soft inland murmur. Once again

Tintern Abbey: The ruins of a medieval abbey that Wordsworth had visited in
August 1793. Wordsworth says that he composed the poem in his head in four or
five hours as he walked from Tintern to Bristol in 1798, and then wrote it down
without revisions.

Do I behold these steep and lofty cliffs,   5
That on a wild secluded scene impress
Thoughts of more deep seclusion; and connect
The landscape with the quiet of the sky.
The day is come when I again repose
Here, under this dark sycamore, and view   10
These plots of cottage ground, these orchard tufts,
Which at this season, with their unripe fruits,
Are clad in one green hue, and lose themselves
'Mid groves and copses. Once again I see
These hedgerows, hardly hedgerows, little lines   15
Of sportive wood run wild; these pastoral farms,
Green to the very door; and wreaths of smoke
Sent up, in silence, from among the trees!
With some uncertain notice, as might seem
Of vagrant dwellers in the houseless woods,   20
Or of some Hermit's cave, where by his fire
The Hermit sits alone.

                These beauteous forms,
Through a long absence, have not been to me
As is a landscape to a blind man's eye;
But oft, in lonely rooms, and 'mid the din   25
Of towns and cities, I have owed to them,
In hours of weariness, sensations sweet,
Felt in the blood, and felt along the heart;
And passing even into my purer mind,
With tranquil restoration—feelings too   30
Of unremembered pleasure; such, perhaps,
As have no slight or trivial influence
On that best portion of a good man's life,
His little, nameless, unremembered, acts
Of kindness and of love. Nor less, I trust,   35
To them I may have owed another gift,
Of aspect more sublime; that blessed mood,
In which the burthen of the mystery,
In which the heavy and the weary weight
Of all this unintelligible world,   40
Is lightened—that serene and blessed mood,
In which the affections gently lead us on—
Until, the breath of this corporeal frame
And even the motion of our human blood
Almost suspended, we are laid asleep   45
In body, and become a living soul;

While with an eye made quiet by the power
Of harmony, and the deep power of joy,
We see into the life of things.

                         If this
Be but a vain belief, yet, oh! how oft—   50
In darkness and amid the many shapes
Of joyless daylight; when the fretful stir
Unprofitable, and the fever of the world,
Have hung upon the beatings of my heart—
How oft, in spirit, have I turned to thee,   55
O sylvan° Wye! thou wanderer through the woods,   *wooded*
How often has my spirit turned to thee!

   An now, with gleams of half-extinguished thought,
With many recognitions dim and faint,
And somewhat of a sad perplexity,   60
The picture of the mind revives again;
While here I stand, not only with the sense
Of present pleasure, but with pleasing thoughts
That in this moment there is life and food
For future years. And so I dare to hope,   65
Though changed, no doubt, from what I was when first
I came among these hills; when like a roe
I bounded o'er the mountains, by the sides
Of the deep rivers, and the lonely streams,
Wherever nature led—more like a man   70
Flying from something that he dreads than one
Who sought the thing he loved. For nature then
(The coarser pleasures of my boyish days,
And their glad animal movements all gone by)
To me was all in all.—I cannot paint   75
What then I was. The sounding cataract
Haunted me like a passion; the tall rock,
The mountain, and the deep and gloomy wood,
Their colors and their forms, were then to me
An appetite; a feeling and a love,   80
That had no need of a remoter charm,
By thought supplied, nor any interest
Unborrowed from the eye.—That time is past,
And all its aching joys are now no more,
And all its dizzy raptures. Not for this   85
Faint° I, nor mourn nor murmur; other gifts   *become discouraged*
Have followed; for such loss, I would believe,

Abundant recompense. For I have learned
To look on nature, not as in the hour
Of thoughtless youth; but hearing oftentimes   90
The still, sad music of humanity,
Nor harsh nor grating, though of ample power
To chasten and subdue. And I have felt
A presence that disturbs me with the joy
Of elevated thoughts; a sense sublime   95
Of something far more deeply interfused,
Whose dwelling is the light of setting suns,
And the round ocean and the living air,
And the blue sky, and in the mind of man:
A motion and a spirit, that impels   100
All thinking things, all objects of all thought,
And rolls through all things. Therefore am I still
A lover of the meadows and the woods,
And mountains; and of all that we behold
From this green earth; of all the mighty world   105
Of eye, and ear—both what they half create,
And what perceive; well pleased to recognize
In nature and the language of the sense
The anchor of my purest thoughts, the nurse,
The guide, the guardian of my heart, and soul   110
Of all my moral being.

                Nor perchance,
If I were not thus taught, should I the more
Suffer my genial spirits° to decay: *creative powers*
For thou art with me here upon the banks
Of this fair river; thou my dearest Friend,°   115
My dear, dear Friend; and in thy voice I catch
The language of my former heart, and read
My former pleasures in the shooting lights
Of thy wild eyes. Oh! yet a little while
May I behold in thee what I was once,   120
My dear, dear Sister! and this prayer I make,
Knowing that Nature never did betray
The heart that loved her; 'tis her privilege,
Through all the years of this our life, to lead
From joy to joy: for she can so inform   125
The mind that is within us, so impress

115. Friend: Wordsworth's sister Dorothy, who is made to sound younger by more than the year and a half that separated them.

With quietness and beauty, and so feed
With lofty thoughts, that neither evil tongues,
Rash judgments, nor the sneers of selfish men,
Nor greetings where no kindness is, nor all   130
The dreary intercourse of daily life,
Shall e'er prevail against us, or disturb
Our cheerful faith, that all which we behold
Is full of blessings. Therefore let the moon
Shine on thee in thy solitary walk;   135
And let the misty mountain winds be free
To blow against thee: and, in after years,
When these wild ecstasies shall be matured
Into a sober pleasure; when thy mind
Shall be a mansion for all lovely forms,   140
Thy memory be as a dwelling place
For all sweet sounds and harmonies; oh! then,
If solitude, or fear, or pain, or grief
Should be thy portion, with what healing thoughts
Of tender joy wilt thou remember me,   145
And these my exhortations! Nor, perchance—
If I should be where I no more can hear
Thy voice, nor catch from thy wild eyes these gleams
Of past existence—wilt thou then forget
That on the banks of this delightful stream   150
We stood together; and that I, so long
A worshiper of Nature, hither came
Unwearied in that service; rather say
With warmer love—oh! with far deeper zeal
Of holier love. Nor wilt thou then forget,   155
That after many wanderings, many years
Of absence, these steep woods and lofty cliffs,
And this green pastoral landscape, were to me
More dear, both for themselves and for thy sake!

                                                        [1798]

WILLIAM WORDSWORTH   [1770–1850]

Ode

Intimations of Immortality from Recollections
of Early Childhood

The Child is father of the Man;
And I could wish my days to be
Bound each to each by natural piety.°

1

There was a time when meadow, grove, and stream,
The earth, and every common sight,
  To me did seem
  Appareled in celestial light,
The glory and the freshness of a dream.   5
It is not now as it hath been of yore—
  Turn whereso'er I may,
   By night or day,
The things which I have seen I now can see no more.

2

  The Rainbow comes and goes,   10
  And lovely is the Rose,
  The Moon doth with delight
Look round her when the heavens are bare,
  Waters on a starry night
  Are beautiful and fair;   15
 The sunshine is a glorious birth;
 But yet I know, where'er I go,
That there hath passed away a glory from the earth.

3

Now, while the birds thus sing a joyous song,
  And while the young lambs bound   20
   As to the tabor's° sound,
To me alone there came a thought of grief:
A timely utterance gave that thought relief,

Epigraph: The final lines of Wordsworth's "My Heart Leaps Up."
21. tabor: A small drum, used chiefly as an accompaniment to the pipe or trumpet.

And I again am strong:
The cataracts blow their trumpets from the steep;   25
No more shall grief of mine the season wrong;
I hear the Echoes through the mountains throng,
The Winds come to me from the fields of sleep,
    And all the earth is gay;
       Land and sea   30
    Give themselves up to jollity,
     And with the heart of May
    Doth every Beast keep holiday—
      Thou Child of Joy,
Shout round me, let me hear thy shouts, thou happy Shepherd-boy!   35

4

Ye blessèd Creatures, I have heard the call
  Ye to each other make; I see
The heavens laugh with you in your jubilee;
  My heart is at your festival,
   My head hath its coronal,°   40
The fullness of your bliss, I feel—I feel it all.
    Oh, evil day! if I were sullen
    While Earth herself is adorning,
     This sweet May morning,
    And the Children are culling   45
     On every side,
    In a thousand valleys far and wide,
    Fresh flowers; while the sun shines warm,
And the Babe leaps up on his Mother's arm—
    I hear, I hear, with joy I hear!   50
    —But there's a Tree, of many, one,
A single Field which I have looked upon,
Both of them speak of something that is gone:
    The Pansy at my feet
    Doth the same tale repeat: 55
Whither is fled the visionary gleam?
Where is it now, the glory and the dream?

5

Our birth is but a sleep and a forgetting:
The Soul that rises with us, our life's Star,
    Hath had elsewhere its setting,   60

40. **coronal:** A wreath of flowers or leaves for the head; a garland.

And cometh from afar:
Not in entire forgetfulness,
And not in utter nakedness,
But trailing clouds of glory do we come
    From God, who is our home: 65
Heaven lies about us in our infancy!
Shades of the prison-house begin to close
    Upon the growing Boy
        But he
Beholds the light, and whence it flows,   70
    He sees it in his joy;
The Youth, who daily farther from the east
    Must travel, still is Nature's Priest,
    And by the vision splendid
    Is on his way attended;   75
At length the Man perceives it die away,
And fade into the light of common day.°

6

Earth fills her lap with pleasures of her own;
Yearnings she hath in her own natural kind,
And, even with something of a Mother's mind,   80
    And no unworthy aim,
    The homely° Nurse doth all she can   *simple, kindly*
To make her foster child, her Inmate Man,
    Forget the glories he hath known,
And that imperial palace whence he came.   85

7

Behold the Child among his newborn blisses,
A six-years' Darling of a pygmy size!
See, where 'mid work of his own hand he lies,
Fretted° by sallies of his mother's kisses,   *annoyed*
With light upon him from his father's eyes!   90
See, at his feet, some little plan or chart,

---

77. Lines 58–77 reflect Plato's belief that human souls inhabit "a pre-existent state" (in Wordsworth's terms) before being born into this world. Though imprisoned in a physical body and the material world, the soul of the infant has recollections of and longs to return to the perfect world of ideas. As the child grows older, those memories begin to fade, though reminders of that primal glory recur (usually from experiences with things in nature). By adulthood, such glimpses become rare and the adult becomes reconciled to the material world and its values.

Some fragrant from his dream of human life,
Shaped by himself with newly-learnèd art;
  A wedding or a festival,
  A mourning or a funeral;   95
   And this hath now his heart,
   And unto this he frames his song;
    Then will he fit his tongue
To dialogues of business, love, or strife;
   But it will not be long   100
   Ere this be thrown aside,
  And with new joy and pride
The little Actor cons° another part;   *learns*
Filling from time to time his "humorous stage"°
With all the Persons,° down to palsied Age, *dramatis personae* 105
That Life brings with her in her equipage;°
   As if his whole vocation
   Were endless imitation.

8

Thou, whose exterior semblance doth belie
   Thy Soul's immensity;   110
Thou best Philosopher, who yet dost keep
Thy heritage, thou Eye among the blind,
That, deaf and silent, read'st the eternal deep,
Haunted forever by the eternal mind—
   Mighty Prophet! Seer blest!   115
   On whom those truths do rest,
Which we are toiling all our lives to find,
In darkness lost, the darkness of the grave;
Thou, over whom thy Immortality
Broods like the Day, a Master o'er a Slave,   120
A Presence which is not to be put by;
Thou little Child, yet glorious in the might
Of heaven-born freedom on thy being's height,
Why with such earnest pains dost thou provoke
The years to bring the inevitable yoke,   125
Thus blindly with thy blessedness at strife?

---

104. "humorous . . . stage: Quoted from a sonnet by the Elizabethan poet Samuel Daniel: the varied temperaments (humors) of characters represented on the stage. Lines 103–05 echo Jaques's "All the world's a stage" speech in Shakespeare's *As You Like It* (2.7.138–65), with its description of the "seven ages" in the life of a person. **105–06. all . . . equipage:** All that is needed for a military operation, a journey, or a domestic establishment.

Full soon thy Soul shall have her earthly freight,
And custom lie upon thee with a weight,
Heavy as frost, and deep almost as life!

9

O joy! that in our embers   130
Is something that doth live,
That nature yet remembers
What was so fugitive!
The thought of our past years in me doth breed
Perpetual benediction: not indeed   135
For that which is most worthy to be blest;
Delight and liberty, the simple creed
Of Childhood, whether busy or at rest,
With new-fledged hope still fluttering in his breast —
Not for these I raise   140
The song of thanks and praise;
But for those obstinate questionings
Of sense and outward things,
Fallings from us, vanishings;
Blank misgivings of a Creature   145
Moving about in worlds not realized,°   *not seeming real*
High instincts before which our mortal Nature
Did tremble like a guilty Thing surprised;
But for those first affections,
Those shadowy recollections,   150
Which, be they what they may,
Are yet the fountain light of all our day,
Are yet a master light of all our seeing;
Uphold us, cherish, and have power to make
Our noisy years seem moments in the being   155
Of the eternal Silence: truths that wake,
To perish never;
Which neither listlessness, nor mad endeavor,
Nor Man nor Boy,
Nor all that is at enmity with joy,   160
Can utterly abolish or destroy!
Hence in a season of calm weather
Though inland far we be,
Our Souls have sight of that immortal sea
Which brought us hither,   165
Can in a moment travel thither,
And see the Children sport upon the shore,
And hear the mighty waters rolling evermore.

10

Then sing, ye Birds, sing, sing a joyous song!
    And let the young Lambs bound   170
    As to the tabor's sound!
We in thought will join your throng,
    Ye that pipe and ye that play,
    Ye that through your hearts today
    Feel the gladness of the May!   175
What though the radiance which was once so bright
Be now forever taken from my sight,
    Though nothing can bring back the hour
Of splendor in the grass, of glory in the flower;
    We will grieve not, rather find   180
    Strength in what remains behind;
    In the primal sympathy
    Which having been must ever be;
    In the soothing thoughts that spring
    Out of human suffering;   185
    In the faith that looks through death,
In years that bring the philosophic mind.

11

And O, ye Fountains, Meadows, Hills, and Groves,
Forebode not any severing of our loves!
Yet in my heart of hearts I feel your might;   190
I only have relinquished one delight
To live beneath your more habitual sway.
I love the Brooks which down their channels fret,°   *move in agitated waves*
Even more than when I tripped lightly as they;
The innocent brightness of a newborn Day   195
    Is lovely yet;
The clouds that gather round the setting sun
Do take a sober coloring from an eye
That hath kept watch o'er man's mortality;
Another race hath been, and other palms° are won.   *symbols of victory* 200
Thanks to the human heart by which we live,
Thanks to its tenderness, its joys, and fears,
To me the meanest° flower that blows° can give   *most ordinary/blooms*
Thoughts that do often lie too deep for tears.

[1807]

WILLIAM WORDSWORTH   [1770–1850]

The world is too much with us

The world is too much with us; late and soon,
Getting and spending, we lay waste our powers;
Little we see in Nature that is ours;
We have given our hearts away, a sordid boon!°   *gift*
This Sea that bares her bosom to the moon,   5
The winds that will be howling at all hours,
And are up-gathered now like sleeping flowers,
For this, for everything, we are out of tune;
It moves us not.—Great God! I'd rather be
A Pagan suckled in a creed outworn;   10
So might I, standing on this pleasant lea,°   *open meadow*
Have glimpses that would make me less forlorn;
Have sight of Proteus° rising from the sea;
Or hear old Triton° blow his wreathèd° horn.

[1807]

13. **Proteus:** In Greek mythology, a sea god who could change his own form or
appearance at will.
14. **Triton:** A Greek sea god with the head and upper body of a man and the tail of
a fish, usually pictured as playing on a conch-shell trumpet; **wreathèd:** Curved.

SAMUEL TAYLOR COLERIDGE   [1772–1834]

Kubla Khan

Or, a Vision in a Dream. A Fragment°

In Xanadu did Kubla Khan
A stately pleasure dome decree:°

Or, a Vision . . . A Fragment: Coleridge stated in a preface that this poem composed itself in his mind during "a profound sleep" (actually an opium-induced
reverie); that he began writing it down immediately upon waking but was interrupted by a caller; and that when he returned to his room an hour later he could
not complete it.
1–2. In . . . decree: "In Xamdu did Cublai Can build a stately Palace, encompass-
ing sixteene miles of plaine ground with a wall" (Samuel Purchas, *Purchas his
Pilgrimage* [1613]). The historical Kublai Khan (1215–1294) was the founder of
the Yüan dynasty of China and overlord of the Mongol Empire.

Where Alph,° the sacred river, ran
Through caverns measureless to man
   Down to a sunless sea.   5
So twice five miles of fertile ground
With walls and towers were girdled round:
And there were gardens bright with sinuous rills,
Where blossomed many an incense-bearing tree;
And here were forests ancient as the hills,   10
Enfolding sunny spots of greenery.

But oh! that deep romantic chasm which slanted
Down the green hill athwart a cedarn cover!
A savage place! as holy and enchanted
As e'er beneath a waning moon was haunted   15
By woman wailing for her demon lover!
And from this chasm, with ceaseless turmoil seething,
As if this earth in fast thick pants were breathing,
A mighty fountain momently was forced:
Amid whose swift half-intermitted burst   20
Huge fragments vaulted like rebounding hail,
Or chaffy grain beneath the thresher's flail:
And 'mid these dancing rocks at once and ever
It flung up momently the sacred river.
Five miles meandering with a mazy motion   25
Through wood and dale the sacred river ran,
Then reached the caverns measureless to man,
And sank in tumult to a lifeless ocean:
And 'mid this tumult Kubla heard from far
Ancestral voices prophesying war!   30
   The shadow of the dome of pleasure
   Floated midway on the waves;
   Where was heard the mingled measure
   From the fountain and the caves.
It was a miracle of rare device,   35
A sunny pleasure dome with caves of ice!

   A damsel with a dulcimer
   In a vision once I saw:
   It was an Abyssinian maid,

---

3. **Alph:** Probably derived from the name of the River Alpheus in southern
Greece, which according to mythology ran under the sea and emerged at Syracuse
(Italy) in the fountain of Arethusa.

And on her dulcimer she played,   40
Singing of Mount Abora.°
Could I revive within me
Her symphony and song,
To such a deep delight 'twould win me,
That with music loud and long,   45
I would build that dome in air,
That sunny dome! those caves of ice!
And all who heard should see them there,
And all should cry, Beware! Beware!
His flashing eyes, his floating hair!   50
Weave a circle round him thrice,
And close your eyes with holy dread,
For he on honey-dew hath fed,
And drunk the milk of Paradise.

[c. 1797–1798; 1813]

39–41. Abyssinian . . . Abora: See *Paradise Lost* 4.280–82: "where Abassin Kings
their issue Guard, / Mount Amara, though this by some supposed / True Paradise
under the Ethiop Line."

GEORGE GORDON, LORD BYRON   [1788–1824]

She walks in beauty

1

She walks in beauty, like the night
    Of cloudless climes and starry skies;
And all that's best of dark and bright
    Meet in her aspect and her eyes:
Thus mellowed to that tender light   5
    Which heaven to gaudy day denies.

2

One shade the more, one ray the less,
    Had half impaired the nameless grace
Which waves in every raven tress,
    Or softly lightens o'er her face;   10
Where thoughts serenely sweet express
    How pure, how dear their dwelling place.

3

And on that cheek, and o'er that brow,
  So soft, so calm, yet eloquent,
The smiles that win, the tints that glow,   15
  But tell of days in goodness spent,
A mind at peace with all below,
  A heart whose love is innocent!

[1815]

PERCY BYSSHE SHELLEY   [1792–1822]

Ozymandias°

I met a traveler from an antique land
Who said: Two vast and trunkless legs of stone
Stand in the desert. Near them, on the sand,
Half sunk, a shattered visage lies, whose frown,
And wrinkled lip, and sneer of cold command,   5
Tell that its sculptor well those passions read
Which yet survive, stamped on these lifeless things,
The hand that mocked them, and the heart that fed:
And on the pedestal these words appear:
"My name is Ozymandias, king of kings: 10
Look on my works, ye Mighty, and despair!"
Nothing beside remains. Round the decay
Of that colossal wreck, boundless and bare
The lone and level sands stretch far away.

[1818]

Ozymandias: The Greek name for Ramses II of Egypt (thirteenth century B.C.E.),
who erected the largest statue in Egypt as a memorial to himself.

PERCY BYSSHE SHELLEY   [1792–1822]

Ode to the West Wind

1

O wild West Wind, thou breath° of Autumn's being,
Thou, from whose unseen presence the leaves dead
Are driven, like ghosts from an enchanter fleeing,

Yellow, and black, and pale, and hectic red,
Pestilence-stricken multitudes: O thou,   5
Who chariotest to their dark wintry bed

The wingèd seeds, where they lie cold and low,
Each like a corpse within its grave, until
Thine azure sister of the Spring shall blow

Her clarion o'er the dreaming earth, and fill   10
(Driving sweet buds like flocks to feed in air)
With living hues and odors plain and hill:

Wild Spirit, which art moving everywhere;
Destroyer and preserver; hear, oh, hear!

2

Thou on whose stream, mid the steep sky's commotion,   15
Loose clouds like earth's decaying leaves are shed,
Shook from the tangled boughs of Heaven and Ocean,

Angels of rain and lightning: there are spread
On the blue surface of thine airy surge,
Like the bright hair uplifted from the head   20

Of some fierce Maenad,° even from the dim verge
Of the horizon to the zenith's height,
The locks of the approaching storm. Thou dirge

Of the dying year, to which this closing night
Will be the dome of a vast sepulcher,   25
Vaulted with all thy congregated might

---

1. **breath:** In many ancient languages, the words for *breath, wind, soul,* and *inspiration* are the same or closely related: in Latin, *spiritus.* Shelley uses this to interconnect nature and artistic inspiration (poetry) in his poem.
21. **Maenad:** A female votary of Dionysus, Greek god of wine and vegetation, who took part in the wild, orgiastic rites that characterize his worship.

Of vapors, from whose solid atmosphere
Black rain, and fire, and hail will burst: oh, hear!

3

Thou who didst waken from his summer dreams
The blue Mediterranean, where he lay,   30
Lulled by the coil of his crystàlline streams,

Beside a pumice isle in Baiae's bay,°
And saw in sleep old palaces° and towers
Quivering within the wave's intenser day,

All overgrown with azure moss and flowers   35
So sweet, the sense faints picturing them! Thou
For whose path the Atlantic's level powers

Cleave themselves into chasms, while far below
The sea-blooms and the oozy woods which wear
The sapless foliage of the ocean, know   40

Thy voice, and suddenly grow gray with fear,
And tremble and despoil themselves: oh, hear!

4

If I were a dead leaf thou mightest bear;
If I were a swift cloud to fly with thee;
A wave to pant beneath thy power, and share   45

The impulse of thy strength, only less free
Than thou, O uncontrollable! If even
I were as in my boyhood, and could be

The comrade of thy wanderings over Heaven,
As then, when to outstrip thy skyey speed   50
Scarce seemed a vision; I would ne'er have striven

As thus with thee in prayer in my sore need.
Oh, lift me as a wave, a leaf, a cloud!
I fall upon the thorns of life! I bleed!

A heavy weight of hours has chained and bowed   55
One too like thee: tameless, and swift, and proud.

---

32. pumice: Porous volcanic stone; **Baiae's bay:** West of Naples, Italy.
33. old palaces: Villas built by the Roman emperors.

5

Make me thy lyre,° even as the forest is:
What if my leaves are falling like its own!
The tumult of thy mighty harmonies

Will take from both a deep, autumnal tone,   60
Sweet though in sadness. Be thou, Spirit fierce,
My spirit! Be thou me, impetuous one!

Drive my dead thoughts over the universe
Like withered leaves to quicken a new birth!
And, by the incantation of this verse,   65

Scatter, as from an unextinguished hearth
Ashes and sparks, my words among mankind!
Be through my lips to unawakened earth

The trumpet of a prophecy! O Wind,
If Winter comes, can Spring be far behind?   70

[1820]

57. lyre: An Aeolian harp, whose strings produce a sequence of rising and falling harmonies as air blows over them.

JOHN KEATS   [1795–1821]

When I have fears
that I may cease to be

When I have fears that I may cease to be
    Before my pen has gleaned my teeming brain,
Before high piled books, in charactry,°   *writing*
    Hold like rich garners the full ripened grain;
When I behold, upon the night's starred face,   5
    Huge cloudy symbols of a high romance,
And think that I may never live to trace
    Their shadows, with the magic hand of chance;
And when I feel, fair creature of an hour,
    That I shall never look upon thee more,   10
Never have relish in the fairy power
    Of unreflecting love;—then on the shore

Of the wide world I stand alone, and think
Till love and fame to nothingness do sink.

[*1818;* 1848]

JOHN KEATS   [1795–1821]

The Eve of St. Agnes°

1

St. Agnes' Eve—Ah, bitter chill it was!
The owl, for all his feathers, was a-cold;
The hare limped trembling through the frozen grass,
And silent was the flock in woolly fold:
Numb were the Beadsman's° fingers, while he told   5
His rosary, and while his frosted breath,
Like pious incense from a censer old,
Seemed taking flight for heaven, without a death,
Past the sweet Virgin's picture, while his prayer he saith.

2

His prayer he saith, this patient, holy man;   10
Then takes his lamp, and riseth from his knees,
And back returneth, meagre, barefoot, wan,
Along the chapel aisle by slow degrees:
The sculptured dead, on each side, seem to freeze,
Emprisoned in black, purgatorial rails: 15
Knights, ladies, praying in dumb orat'ries,°   *silent chapels*
He passeth by; and his weak spirit fails
To think how they may ache in icy hoods and mails.

3

Northward he turneth through a little door,
And scarce three steps, ere Music's golden tongue   20

St. Agnes: According to legend, a young woman who performs the proper ritual will
dream of her future husband on Saint Agnes's Eve (January 20). Keats unites this
legend with the Romeo and Juliet theme of young love hindered by feuding families.
(Saint Agnes, martyred c. 303 at the age of thirteen, is the patron saint of virgins.)
5. Beadsman: Someone paid to pray for a benefactor, counting ("telling") the
beads of the rosary.

Flattered° to tears this aged man and poor;   *beguiled*
But no—already had his deathbell rung;
The joys of all his life were said and sung:
His was harsh penance on St. Agnes' Eve:
Another way he went, and soon among   25
Rough ashes sat he for his soul's reprieve,
And all night kept awake, for sinners' sake to grieve.

4

That ancient Beadsman heard the prelude soft;
And so it chanced, for many a door was wide,
From hurry to and fro. Soon, up aloft,   30
The silver, snarling trumpets 'gan to chide:
The level chambers, ready with their pride,
Were glowing to receive a thousand guests:
The carved angels, ever eager-eyed,
Star'd, where upon their heads the cornice rests,   35
With hair blown back, and wings put cross-wise on their breasts.

5

At length burst in the argent revelry,°   *revelers adorned with silver*
With plume, tiara, and all rich array,
Numerous as shadows haunting fairily°   *in a fairy-like manner*
The brain, new stuffed, in youth, with triumphs gay
Of old romance. These let us wish away,   40
And turn, sole-thoughted, to one Lady there,
Whose heart had brooded, all that wintry day,
On love, and winged St. Agnes' saintly care,
As she had heard old dames full many times declare.   45

6

They told her how, upon St. Agnes' Eve,
Young virgins might have visions of delight,
And soft adorings from their loves receive
Upon the honeyed middle of the night,
If ceremonies due they did aright;
As, supperless to bed they must retire,   50
And couch supine their beauties,° lily white;
Nor look behind, nor sideways, but require
Of heaven with upward eyes for all that they desire.

---

52. couch supine their beauties: To lay themselves (their beauties) face-up.

7

Full of this whim was thoughtful Madeline: 55
The music, yearning like a god in pain,
She scarcely heard: her maiden eyes divine,
Fix'd on the floor, saw many a sweeping train
Pass by—she heeded not at all: in vain
Came many a tiptoe,° amorous cavalier,   *ambitious (straining upwards)* 60
And back retired, not cooled by high disdain;
But she saw not: her heart was otherwhere:
She sighed for Agnes' dreams, the sweetest of the year.

8

She danced along with vague, regardless eyes,
Anxious her lips, her breathing quick and short: 65
The hallowed hour was near at hand: she sighs
Amid the timbrels,° and the thronged resort
Of whisperers in anger, or in sport;
'Mid looks of love, defiance, hate, and scorn,
Hoodwinked with faery° fancy; all amort,°   *visionary, unreal/as if dead* 70
Save to St. Agnes and her lambs unshorn,°
And all the bliss to be before to-morrow morn.

9

So, purposing each moment to retire,
She lingered still. Meantime, across the moors,
Had come young Porphyro, with heart on fire   75
For Madeline. Beside the portal doors,
Buttressed° from moonlight, stands he, and implores
All saints to give him sight of Madeline,
But for one moment in the tedious hours,
That he might gaze and worship all unseen;   80
Perchance speak, kneel, touch, kiss—in sooth such things have been.

10

He ventures in: let no buzzed whisper tell:
All eyes be muffled, or a hundred swords
Will storm his heart, Love's feverous citadel:
For him, those chambers held barbarian hordes,   85

67. **timbrel:** A hand-held percussion instrument, similar to a tambourine.
71. **Save . . . unshorn:** On Saint Agnes's Day, the wool of two lambs was offered at the altar during Mass and later spun and woven into cloth by nuns.
77. **Buttressed:** Sheltered by buttresses.

Hyena foemen, and hot-blooded lords,
Whose very dogs would execrations howl
Against his lineage: not one breast affords
Him any mercy, in that mansion foul,
Save one old beldame,° weak in body and in soul.   *old woman, hag*   90

11

Ah, happy chance! the aged creature came,
Shuffling along with ivory-headed wand,°   *staff*
To where he stood, hid from the torch's flame,
Behind a broad hall-pillar, far beyond
The sound of merriment and chorus bland:°   *soft*   95
He startled her; but soon she knew his face,
And grasped his fingers in her palsied hand,
Saying, "Mercy, Porphyro! hie thee from this place;
They are all here to-night, the whole blood-thirsty race!

12

"Get hence! get hence! there's dwarfish Hildebrand;   100
He had a fever late, and in the fit
He cursed thee and thine, both house and land:
Then there's that old Lord Maurice, not a whit
More tame for his gray hairs—Alas me! flit!
Flit like a ghost away."—"Ah, Gossip° dear,   *friend*   105
We're safe enough; here in this arm-chair sit,
And tell me how"—"Good Saints! not here, not here;
Follow me, child, or else these stones will be thy bier."

13

He followed through a lowly arched way,
Brushing the cobwebs with his lofty plume,   110
And as she muttered "Well-a—well-a-day!"
He found him in a little moonlight room,
Pale, latticed, chill, and silent as a tomb.
"Now tell me where is Madeline," said he,
"O tell me, Angela, by the holy loom   115
Which none but secret sisterhood may see,
When they St. Agnes' wool are weaving piously."

14

"St. Agnes! Ah! it is St. Agnes' Eve—
Yet men will murder upon holy days:

Thou must hold water in a witch's sieve,°   120
And be liege-lord of all the Elves and Fays,
To venture so: it fills me with amaze
To see thee, Porphyro! — St. Agnes' Eve!
God's help! my lady fair the conjuror plays
This very night: good angels her deceive!   125
But let me laugh awhile, I've mickle° time to grieve."   *much*

15

Feebly she laugheth in the languid moon,
While Porphyro upon her face doth look,
Like puzzled urchin on an aged crone
Who keepeth closed a wonderous riddle-book,   130
As spectacled she sits in chimney nook.
But soon his eyes grew brilliant, when she told
His lady's purpose; and he scarce could brook°
Tears, at the thought of those enchantments cold,
And Madeline asleep in lap of legends old.   135

16

Sudden a thought came like a full-blown rose,
Flushing his brow, and in his pained heart
Made purple riot: then doth he propose
A stratagem, that makes the beldame start:
"A cruel man and impious thou art: 140
Sweet lady, let her pray, and sleep, and dream
Alone with her good angels, far apart
From wicked men like thee. Go, go! — I deem
Thou canst not surely be the same that thou didst seem."

17

"I will not harm her, by all saints I swear,"   145
Quoth Porphyro: "O may I ne'er find grace
When my weak voice shall whisper its last prayer,
If one of her soft ringlets I displace,
Or look with ruffian passion in her face:
Good Angela, believe me by these tears;   150
Or I will, even in a moment's space,
Awake, with horrid shout, my foemen's ears,
And beard them, though they be more fanged than wolves and bears."

120. **witch's sieve:** A sieve bewitched so that it can hold water.
133. **brook:** Usually "endure," but here "hold back."

18

"Ah! why wilt thou affright a feeble soul?
A poor, weak, palsy-stricken, churchyard thing,   155
Whose passing-bell may ere the midnight toll;
Whose prayers for thee, each morn and evening,
Were never miss'd."—Thus plaining, doth she bring
A gentler speech from burning Porphyro;
So woeful, and of such deep sorrowing,   160
That Angela gives promise she will do
Whatever he shall wish, betide her weal or woe.

19

Which was, to lead him, in close secrecy,
Even to Madeline's chamber, and there hide
Him in a closet, of such privacy   165
That he might see her beauty unespied,
And win perhaps that night a peerless bride,
While legioned fairies paced the coverlet,
And pale enchantment held her sleepy-eyed.
Never on such a night have lovers met,   170
Since Merlin paid his Demon° all the monstrous debt.

20

"It shall be as thou wishest," said the Dame:
"All cates° and dainties shall be stored there   *delicacies*
Quickly on this feast-night: by the tambour frame°
Her own lute thou wilt see: no time to spare,   175
For I am slow and feeble, and scarce dare
On such a catering trust my dizzy head.
Wait here, my child, with patience; kneel in prayer
The while: Ah! thou must needs the lady wed,
Or may I never leave my grave among the dead."   180

21

So saying, she hobbled off with busy fear.
The lover's endless minutes slowly passed;
The dame returned, and whispered in his ear
To follow her; with aged eyes aghast
From fright of dim espial. Safe at last,   185

171. his Demon: Presumably the temptress Vivian, in the Arthurian legends, who turned one of Merlin's own spells against him.
174. tambour frame: A drum-shaped embroidery frame.

Through many a dusky gallery, they gain
The maiden's chamber, silken, hushed, and chaste;
Where Porphyro took covert,° pleased amain.°   *a hiding place/greatly*
His poor guide hurried back with agues° in her brain.   *feverish disturbance*

22

Her faltering hand upon the balustrade,   190
Old Angela was feeling for the stair,
When Madeline, St. Agnes' charmed maid,
Rose, like a missioned spirit,° unaware:
With silver taper's light, and pious care,
She turned, and down the aged gossip led   195
To a safe level matting. Now prepare,
Young Porphyro, for gazing on that bed;
She comes, she comes again, like ring-dove frayed° and fled.   *frightened*

23

Out went the taper as she hurried in;
Its little smoke, in pallid moonshine, died: 200
She closed the door, she panted, all akin
To spirits of the air, and visions wide:
No uttered syllable, or, woe betide!
But to her heart, her heart was voluble,
Paining with eloquence her balmy side;   205
As though a tongueless nightingale should swell
Her throat in vain, and die, heart-stifled, in her dell.

24

A casement° high and triple-arched there was,   *a type of window*
All garlanded with carven imag'ries
Of fruits, and flowers, and bunches of knot-grass,   210
And diamonded with panes of quaint device,
Innumerable of stains and splendid dyes,
As are the tiger-moth's deep-damasked° wings;   *variegated*
And in the midst, 'mong thousand heraldries,
And twilight saints, and dim emblazonings,   215
A shielded scutcheon blushed with blood of queens and kings.°

193. **missioned spirit:** An angel on a mission.
216. **scutcheon:** The escutcheon (shield emblazoned with a coat of arms) reveals the royal lineage of the family. **Blushed:** Points to "gules" (red) in line 218 as the moon reflecting off the shield reddening her breast.

25

Full on this casement shone the wintry moon,
And threw warm gules° on Madeline's fair breast,
As down she knelt for heaven's grace and boon;°   *gift, blessing*
Rose-bloom fell on her hands, together prest,   220
And on her silver cross soft amethyst,
And on her hair a glory, like a saint:
She seemed a splendid angel, newly drest,
Save wings, for heaven:— Porphyro grew faint:
She knelt, so pure a thing, so free from mortal taint.   225

26

Anon his heart revives: her vespers° done,   *evening prayers*
Of all its wreathed pearls her hair she frees;
Unclasps her warmed jewels one by one;
Loosens her fragrant bodice; by degrees
Her rich attire creeps rustling to her knees: 230
Half-hidden, like a mermaid in sea-weed,
Pensive awhile she dreams awake, and sees,
In fancy, fair St. Agnes in her bed,
But dares not look behind, or all the charm is fled.

27

Soon, trembling in her soft and chilly nest,   235
In sort of wakeful swoon, perplexed she lay,
Until the poppied warmth of sleep oppressed
Her soothed limbs, and soul fatigued away;
Flown, like a thought, until the morrow-day;
Blissfully havened both from joy and pain;   240
Clasped like a missal where swart Paynims pray;°
Blinded alike from sunshine and from rain,
As though a rose should shut, and be a bud again.

28

Stol'n to this paradise, and so entranced,
Porphyro gazed upon her empty dress,   245
And listened to her breathing, if it chanced
To wake into a slumberous tenderness;
Which when he heard, that minute did he bless,

218. **gules:** The heraldic name for red.
241. **Clasped . . . pray:** Kept shut as a Christian prayer book would be where
dark-skinned pagans (presumably Muslims) pray.

And breathed himself: then from the closet crept,
Noiseless as fear° in a wide wilderness,   *a fearful person* 250
And over the hushed carpet, silent, stepped,
And 'tween the curtains peeped, where, lo!—how fast she slept.

29

Then by the bed-side, where the faded moon
Made a dim, silver twilight, soft he set
A table, and, half anguished, threw thereon   255
A cloth of woven crimson, gold, and jet:—
O for some drowsy Morphean amulet!°   *sleep inducing charm*
The boisterous, midnight, festive clarion,°   *a shrill-sounding trumpet*
The kettle-drum, and far-heard clarionet,°   *clarinet*
Affray° his ears, though but in dying tone:—   *assault* 260
The hall door shuts again, and all the noise is gone.

30

And still she slept an azure-lidded sleep,
In blanchèd linen, smooth, and lavendered,
While he from forth the closet brought a heap
Of candied apple, quince, and plum, and gourd;   265
With jellies soother° than the creamy curd,   *smoother*
And lucent syrups, tinct° with cinnamon;   *tinctured*
Manna and dates, in argosy transferred
From Fez,° and spiced dainties, every one,
From silken Samarcand° to cedared Lebanon.   270

31

These delicates he heaped with glowing hand
On golden dishes and in baskets bright
Of wreathed silver: sumptuous they stand
In the retired quiet of the night,
Filling the chilly room with perfume light.—   275
"And now, my love, my seraph fair, awake!
Thou art my heaven, and I thine eremite:°   *hermit*
Open thine eyes, for meek St. Agnes' sake,
Or I shall drowse beside thee, so my soul doth ache."

32

Thus whispering, his warm, unnervèd arm   280
Sank in her pillow. Shaded was her dream

269. **Fez:** A commercial city in northern Morocco.
270. **Samarcand:** A city now in southern Russia, still noted for its silks.

By the dusk curtains:—'twas a midnight charm
Impossible to melt as iced stream:
The lustrous salvers in the moonlight gleam;
Broad golden fringe upon the carpet lies: 285
It seemed he never, never could redeem
From such a stedfast spell his lady's eyes;
So mused awhile, entoiled in woofèd° phantasies.   *woven*

33

Awakening up, he took her hollow lute,—
Tumultuous,—and, in chords that tenderest be,   290
He played an ancient ditty, long since mute,
In Provence called, "La belle dame sans mercy":°
Close to her ear touching the melody;—
Wherewith disturbed, she uttered a soft moan:
He ceased—she panted quick—and suddenly   295
Her blue affrayed eyes wide open shone:
Upon his knees he sank, pale as smooth-sculptured stone.

34

Her eyes were open, but she still beheld,
Now wide awake, the vision of her sleep:
There was a painful change, that nigh expelled   300
The blisses of her dream so pure and deep:
At which fair Madeline began to weep,
And moan forth witless words with many a sigh;
While still her gaze on Porphyro would keep;
Who knelt, with joinèd hands and piteous eye,   305
Fearing to move or speak, she look'd so dreamingly.

35

"Ah, Porphyro!" said she, "but even now
Thy voice was at sweet tremble in mine ear,
Made tuneable with every sweetest vow;
And those sad eyes were spiritual and clear: 310
How changed thou art! how pallid, chill, and drear!
Give me that voice again, my Porphyro,
Those looks immortal, those complainings dear!
Oh leave me not in this eternal woe,
For if thou diest, my love, I know not where to go."   315

---

292. "La . . . mercy": "The Beautiful Lady without Pity": title of a poem by the
medieval French poet Alain Chartier and later of a poem by Keats.

36

Beyond a mortal man impassioned far
At these voluptuous accents, he arose,
Ethereal, flushed, and like a throbbing star
Seen mid the sapphire heaven's deep repose;
Into her dream he melted, as the rose   320
Blendeth its odor with the violet, —
Solution sweet: meantime the frost-wind blows
Like Love's alarum pattering the sharp sleet
Against the window-panes; St. Agnes' moon hath set.

37

'Tis dark: quick pattereth the flaw-blown° sleet: *gust-blown* 325
"This is no dream, my bride, my Madeline!"
'Tis dark: the icèd gusts still rave and beat:
"No dream, alas! alas! and woe is mine!
Porphyro will leave me here to fade and pine. —
Cruel! what traitor could thee hither bring?   330
I curse not, for my heart is lost in thine,
Though thou forsakest a deceived thing; —
A dove forlorn and lost with sick unprunèd wing."

38

"My Madeline! sweet dreamer! lovely bride!
Say, may I be for aye thy vassal blest?   335
Thy beauty's shield, heart-shaped and vermeil° dyed?   *vermilion*
Ah, silver shrine, here will I take my rest
After so many hours of toil and quest,
A famished pilgrim, — saved by miracle.
Though I have found, I will not rob thy nest   340
Saving of thy sweet self; if thou thinkest well
To trust, fair Madeline, to no rude infidel.

39

"Hark! 'tis an elfin-storm from faery land,
Of haggard° seeming, but a boon indeed!   *wild*
Arise — arise! the morning is at hand; —   345
The bloated wassaillers° will never heed: —   *drunken revelers*
Let us away, my love, with happy speed;
There are no ears to hear, or eyes to see, —
Drowned all in Rhenish° and the sleepy mead:°

349. **Rhenish:** Rhine wine; **mead:** A heavy fermented liquor made of malt and
honey.

Awake! arise! my love, and fearless be,   350
For o'er the southern moors I have a home for thee."

40

She hurried at his words, beset with fears,
For there were sleeping dragons° all around,
At glaring watch, perhaps, with ready spears—
Down the wide stairs a darkling way they found.—   355
In all the house was heard no human sound.
A chain-drooped lamp was flickering by each door;
The arras,° rich with horseman, hawk, and hound,   *tapestry*
Fluttered in the besieging wind's uproar;
And the long carpets rose along the gusty floor.   360

41

They glide, like phantoms, into the wide hall;
Like phantoms, to the iron porch, they glide;
Where lay the Porter, in uneasy sprawl,
With a huge empty flaggon by his side:
The wakeful bloodhound rose, and shook his hide,   365
But his sagacious eye an inmate owns:°
By one, and one, the bolts full easy slide:—
The chains lie silent on the footworn stones;—
The key turns, and the door upon its hinges groans.

42

And they are gone: aye, ages long ago   370
These lovers fled away into the storm.
That night the Baron dreamt of many a woe,
And all his warrior-guests, with shade and form
Of witch, and demon, and large coffin-worm,
Were long be-nightmared. Angela the old   375
Died palsy-twitched, with meagre face deform;
The Beadsman, after thousand aves° told,
For aye unsought for slept among his ashes cold.

[1820]

---

353. sleeping dragons: Sentries; i.e., commissioned to watch like dragons over a treasure.
366. sagacious . . . owns: Recognizes a member of his household.
377. aves: Prayers beginning *Ave Maria* ("Hail Mary").

JOHN KEATS   [1795–1821]

Ode on a Grecian Urn

1

Thou still unravished bride of quietness,
  Thou foster child of silence and slow time,
Sylvan historian, who canst thus express
  A flowery tale more sweetly than our rhyme:
What leaf-fringed legend haunts about thy shape   5
  Of deities or mortals, or of both,
    In Tempe or the dales of Arcady?°
  What men or gods are these? What maidens loath?
What mad pursuit? What struggle to escape?
    What pipes and timbrels? What wild ecstasy?   10

2

Heard melodies are sweet, but those unheard
  Are sweeter; therefore, ye soft pipes, play on;
Not to the sensual ear,° but, more endeared,
  Pipe to the spirit ditties of no tone:
Fair youth, beneath the trees, thou canst not leave   15
  Thy song, nor ever can those trees be bare;
    Bold lover, never, never canst thou kiss,
Though winning near the goal—yet, do not grieve;
    She cannot fade, though thou hast not thy bliss,
  Forever wilt thou love, and she be fair!   20

3

Ah, happy, happy boughs! that cannot shed
  Your leaves, nor ever bid the spring adieu;
And, happy melodist, unwearièd,
  Forever piping songs forever new;
More happy love! more happy, happy love!   25
  Forever warm and still to be enjoyed,
    Forever panting, and forever young;
All breathing human passion far above,
    That leaves a heart high-sorrowful and cloyed,
  A burning forehead, and a parching tongue.   30

---

7. Tempe, Arcady: Tempe, a valley in Greece, and Arcadia ("Arcady"), a region of
ancient Greece, represent ideal pastoral landscapes.
13. not . . . ear: Not to the ear of the senses, but to the imagination.

4

Who are these coming to the sacrifice?
  To what green altar, O mysterious priest,
Lead'st thou that heifer lowing at the skies,
  And all her silken flanks with garlands dressed?
What little town by river or sea shore,   35
  Or mountain-built with peaceful citadel,
    Is emptied of this folk, this pious morn?
And, little town, thy streets forevermore
  Will silent be; and not a soul to tell
    Why thou art desolate, can e'er return.   40

5

O Attic° shape! Fair attitude! with brede°
  Of marble men and maidens overwrought,
With forest branches and the trodden weed;
  Thou, silent form, dost tease us out of thought
As doth eternity: Cold Pastoral!   45
  When old age shall this generation waste,
    Thou shalt remain, in midst of other woe
Than ours, a friend to man, to whom thou say'st,
"Beauty is truth, truth beauty,"° — that is all
  Ye know on earth, and all ye need to know.   50

[1820]

41. **Attic:** Greek, specifically Athenian; **brede:** Interwoven pattern.
49. **Beauty . . . beauty:** The quotation marks around this phrase were found in its
earliest printing, in an 1820 volume of poetry by Keats, but not in a printing later
that year or in written transcripts. This discrepancy has led to considerable critical controversy concerning the last two lines. Critics disagree whether "Beauty is
truth, truth beauty" is spoken by the urn (and thus perhaps expressing a limited
perspective not to be taken at face value) or by the speaker in the poem, or
whether the last two lines in their entirety are said by the urn (some recent editors
enclose both lines in parentheses to make this explicit) or by the speaker.

JOHN KEATS   [1795–1821]

To Autumn

I

Season of mists and mellow fruitfulness,
  Close bosom-friend of the maturing sun;
Conspiring with him how to load and bless
  With fruit the vines that round the thatch-eves run;
To bend with apples the mossed cottage-trees,   5
  And fill all fruit with ripeness to the core;
    To swell the gourd, and plump the hazel shells
With a sweet kernel; to set budding more,
  And still more, later flowers for the bees,
  Until they think warm days will never cease,   10
    For Summer has o'er-brimmed their clammy cells.

II

Who hath not seen thee oft amid thy store?
  Sometimes whoever seeks abroad may find
Thee sitting careless on a granary floor,
  Thy hair soft-lifted by the winnowing wind;   15
Or on a half-reaped furrow sound asleep,
  Drowsed with the fume of poppies, while thy hook°   *scythe*
    Spares the next swath and all its twinèd flowers:
And sometimes like a gleaner thou dost keep
  Steady thy laden head across a brook;   20
  Or by a cider-press, with patient look,
    Thou watchest the last oozings hours by hours.

III

Where are the songs of Spring? Aye, where are they?
  Think not of them, thou hast thy music too,—
While barrèd clouds bloom the soft-dying day,   25
  And touch the stubble-plains with rosy hue;
Then in a wailful choir the small gnats mourn
  Among the river sallows,° borne aloft   *willows*
    Or sinking as the light wind lives or dies;
And full-grown lambs loud bleat from hilly bourn;°   *region* 30
  Hedge-crickets sing; and now with treble soft
    The red-breast whistles from a garden-croft;
  And gathering swallows twitter in the skies.

[1820]

ELIZABETH BARRETT BROWNING   [1806–1861]

How do I love thee?
Let me count the ways

How do I love thee? Let me count the ways.
I love thee to the depth and breadth and height
My soul can reach, when feeling out of sight
For the ends of Being and ideal Grace.
I love thee to the level of everyday's   5
Most quiet need, by sun and candlelight.
I love thee freely, as men strive for Right;
I love thee purely, as they turn from Praise.
I love thee with the passion put to use
In my old griefs, and with my childhood's faith.   10
I love thee with a love I seemed to lose
With my lost saints—I love thee with the breath,
Smiles, tears, of all my life!—and, if God choose,
I shall but love thee better after death.

[1850]

EDGAR ALLAN POE   [1809–1849]

To Helen

Helen,° thy beauty is to me
    Like those Nicéan barks° of yore,
That gently, o'er a perfumed sea,
    The weary, way-worn wanderer bore
        To his own native shore.   5

On desperate seas long wont to roam,
    Thy hyacinth hair,° thy classic face,
Thy Naiad° airs have brought me home
    To the glory that was Greece
And the grandeur that was Rome.   10

1. **Helen:** Daughter of Leda and Zeus, the most beautiful woman in the world; her abduction by Paris gave rise to the Trojan war.
2. **barks:** Small sailing boats; Poe probably invented "Nicéan" for its sound and suggestiveness.
7. **hyacinth:** "Raven-black" and "naturally curling" (from Poe's story "Ligeia").
8. **Naiads:** Fresh-water nymphs in classical myths.

Lo! in yon brilliant window-niche
  How statue-like I see thee stand,
  The agate lamp within thy hand!
Ah! Psyche, from the regions which
  Are Holy Land!   15

                                      [*1823;* 1831]

EDGAR ALLAN POE   [1809–1849]

Annabel Lee

It was many and many a year ago,
  In a kingdom by the sea,
That a maiden there lived whom you may know
  By the name of Annabel Lee;
And this maiden she lived with no other thought   5
  Than to love and be loved by me.

She was a child and *I* was a child,
  In this kingdom by the sea,
But we loved with a love that was more than love—
  I and my Annabel Lee—   10
With a love that the wingèd seraphs° of Heaven   *angels of the highest order*
  Coveted her and me.

And this was the reason that, long ago,
  In this kingdom by the sea,
A wind blew out of a cloud by night   15
  Chilling my Annabel Lee;
So that her highborn kinsmen came
  And bore her away from me,
To shut her up in a sepulchre
  In this kingdom by the sea.   20

The angels, not half so happy in Heaven,
  Went envying her and me:
Yes! that was the reason (as all men know,
  In this kingdom by the sea)
That the wind came out of the cloud, chilling   25
  And killing my Annabel Lee.

But our love it was stronger by far than the love
  Of those who were older than we—

Of many far wiser than we —
And neither the angels in Heaven above   30
    Nor the demons down under the sea,
Can ever dissever my soul from the soul
    Of the beautiful Annabel Lee:

For the moon never beams without bringing me dreams
    Of the beautiful Annabel Lee;   35
And the stars never rise but I see the bright eyes
    Of the beautiful Annabel Lee;
And so, all the night-tide, I lie down by the side
Of my darling, my darling, my life and my bride,
    In her sepulchre there by the sea —   40
    In her tomb by the side of the sea.

                                                              [1849]

           ALFRED, LORD TENNYSON   [1809–1892]

                        Ulysses°

    It little profits that an idle king,
By this still hearth, among these barren crags,
Matched with an agèd wife, I mete and dole
Unequal laws° unto a savage race,
That hoard, and sleep, and feed, and know not me.   5

Ulysses (the Roman form of Odysseus): The hero of Homer's epic *The Odyssey*,
which tells the story of Odysseus's adventures on his voyage back to his home, the
little island of Ithaca, after he and the other Greek heroes had defeated Troy. It
took Odysseus ten years to reach Ithaca, the small, rocky island of which he was
king, where his wife (Penelope) and son (Telemachus) had been waiting for him.
Upon his return he defeated the suitors who had been trying to marry the faithful
Penelope, and he resumed the kingship and his old ways of life. Here Homer's
story ends, but in Canto 26 of the *Inferno* Dante extended the story: Odysseus
eventually became restless and dissatisfied with his settled life and decided to
return to the sea and sail west, into the unknown sea, and seek whatever adventures he might find there. Tennyson's poem amplifies the speech delivered
in Dante's poem as Ulysses challenges his men to accompany him on this new
voyage.
3–4. mete . . . race: Administer inadequate (unequal to what is needed) laws to a
still somewhat lawless race.

I cannot rest from travel; I will drink
Life to the lees. All times I have enjoyed
Greatly, have suffered greatly, both with those
That loved me, and alone; on shore, and when
Through scudding drifts° the rainy Hyades°   10
Vexed the dim sea. I am become a name;
For always roaming with a hungry heart
Much have I seen and known—cities of men
And manners, climates, councils, governments,
Myself not least, but honored of them all—   15
And drunk delight of battle with my peers,
Far on the ringing plains of windy Troy.
I am a part of all that I have met;
Yet all experience is an arch wherethrough
Gleams that untraveled world whose margin fades   20
Forever and forever when I move.
How dull it is to pause, to make an end,
To rust unburnished, not to shine in use!
As though to breathe were life! Life piled on life
Were all too little, and of one to me   25
Little remains; but every hour is saved
From that eternal silence, something more,
A bringer of new things; and vile it were
For some three suns° to store and hoard myself,   *years*
And this gray spirit yearning in desire   30
To follow knowledge like a sinking star,
Beyond the utmost bound of human thought.

    This is my son, mine own Telemachus,
To whom I leave the scepter and the isle—
Well-loved of me, discerning to fulfill   35
This labor, by slow prudence to make mild
A rugged people, and through soft degrees
Subdue them to the useful and the good.
Most blameless is he, centered in the sphere
Of common duties, decent not to fail   40
In offices of tenderness, and pay
Meet adoration to my household gods,
When I am gone. He works his work, I mine.

    There lies the port; the vessel puffs her sail;
There gloom the dark, broad seas. My mariners,   45

10. **scudding drifts:** Wind-driven spray; **Hyades:** Five stars in the constellation
Taurus whose rising was assumed would be followed by rain.

Souls that have toiled, and wrought, and thought with me—
That ever with a frolic welcome took
The thunder and the sunshine, and opposed
Free hearts, free foreheads—you and I are old;
Old age hath yet his honor and his toil.   50
Death closes all; but something ere the end,
Some work of noble note, may yet be done,
Not unbecoming men that strove with Gods.
The lights begin to twinkle from the rocks;
The long day wanes; the slow moon climbs; the deep   55
Moans round with many voices. Come, my friends,
'Tis not too late to seek a newer world.
Push off, and sitting well in order smite
The sounding furrows; for my purpose holds
To sail beyond the sunset, and the baths°   60
Of all the western stars, until I die.
It may be that the gulfs will wash us down;
It may be we shall touch the Happy Isles,°
And see the great Achilles,° whom we knew.
Though much is taken, much abides; and though   65
We are not now that strength which in old days
Moved earth and heaven, that which we are, we are—
One equal temper of heroic hearts,
Made weak by time and fate, but strong in will
To strive, to seek, to find, and not to yield.   70

                                                                                        [1833]

60. **baths:** The outer river or ocean surrounding the flat earth, in Greek cosmology, into which the stars descended upon setting.
63. **Happy Isles:** The Islands of the Blessed, or Elysian Fields, in Greek myth, which lay in the western seas beyond the Strait of Gibraltar and were the abode of heroes after death.
64. **Achilles:** The hero of the Greeks, and Odysseus's comrade, in Homer's *Iliad*.

ALFRED, LORD TENNYSON   [1809–1892]

Tears, idle tears

Tears, idle tears, I know not what they mean,
Tears from the depth of some divine despair
Rise in the heart, and gather to the eyes,
In looking on the happy Autumn-fields,
And thinking of the days that are no more.   5

Fresh as the first beam glittering on a sail,
That brings our friends up from the underworld,
Sad as the last which reddens over one
That sinks with all we love below the verge;
So sad, so fresh, the days that are no more.   10

   Ah, sad and strange as in dark summer dawns
The earliest pipe of half-awakened birds
To dying ears, when unto dying eyes
The casement slowly grows a glimmering square;
So sad, so strange, the days that are no more.   15

   Dear as remembered kisses after death,
And sweet as those by hopeless fancy feigned
On lips that are for others; deep as love,
Deep as first love, and wild with all regret;
O Death in Life, the days that are no more!   20

[1847]

ALFRED, LORD TENNYSON   [1809–1892]

Crossing the Bar

Sunset and evening star,
   And one clear call for me!
And may there be no moaning of the bar,
   When I put out to sea,

But such a tide as moving seems asleep,   5
   Too full for sound and foam,
When that which drew from out the boundless deep
   Turns again home.

Twilight and evening bell,
   And after that the dark!   10
And may there be no sadness of farewell,
   When I embark;

For though from out our bourne of Time and Place
   The flood may bear me far,
I hope to see my Pilot face to face   15
   When I have crossed the bar.

[1889]

ROBERT BROWNING   [1812–1889]

Home-Thoughts, from Abroad

1

Oh, to be in England
Now that April's there,
And whoever wakes in England
Sees, some morning, unaware,
That the lowest boughs and the brushwood sheaf   5
Round the elm-tree bole are in tiny leaf,
While the chaffinch sings on the orchard bough
In England—now!

2

And after April, when May follows,
And the whitethroat builds, and all the swallows!   10
Hark, where my blossomed pear-tree in the hedge
Leans to the field and scatters on the clover
Blossoms and dewdrops—at the bent spray's edge—
That's the wise thrush; he sings each song twice over,
Lest you should think he never could recapture   15
The first fine careless rapture!
And though the fields look rough with hoary dew
All will be gay when noontide wakes anew
The buttercups, the little children's dower
—Far brighter than this gaudy melon-flower!   20

[1845]

ROBERT BROWNING   [1812–1889]

My Last Duchess

Ferrara°

That's my last Duchess° painted on the wall,
Looking as if she were alive. I call

Ferrara: The poem is based on events that occurred in the life of Alfonso II, duke
of Ferrara in Italy, in the sixteenth century.
1. last Duchess: Ferrara's first wife, Lucrezia, died in 1561 at age seventeen after
three years of marriage.

That piece a wonder, now: Frà Pandolf's° hands
Worked busily a day, and there she stands.
Will't please you sit and look at her? I said   5
"Frà Pandolf" by design, for never read
Strangers like you that pictured countenance,
The depth and passion of its earnest glance,
But to myself they turned (since none puts by
The curtain I have drawn for you, but I)   10
And seemed as they would ask me, if they durst,
How such a glance came there; so, not the first
Are you to turn and ask thus. Sir, 'twas not
Her husband's presence only, called that spot
Of joy into the Duchess' cheek: perhaps   15
Frà Pandolf chanced to say "Her mantle laps
Over my lady's wrist too much," or "Paint
Must never hope to reproduce the faint
Half-flush that dies along her throat:" such stuff
Was courtesy, she thought, and cause enough   20
For calling up that spot of joy. She had
A heart—how shall I say?—too soon made glad,
Too easily impressed; she liked whate'er
She looked on, and her looks went everywhere.
Sir, 'twas all one! My favor at her breast,   25
The dropping of the daylight in the West,
The bough of cherries some officious fool
Broke in the orchard for her, the white mule
She rode with round the terrace—all and each
Would draw from her alike the approving speech,   30
Or blush, at least. She thanked men,—good! but thanked
Somehow—I know not how—as if she ranked
My gift of a nine-hundred-years-old name
With anybody's gift. Who'd stoop to blame
This sort of trifling? Even had you skill   35
In speech—(which I have not)—to make your will
Quite clear to such an one, and say, "Just this
Or that in you disgusts me; here you miss,
Or there exceed the mark"—and if she let
Herself be lessoned so, nor plainly set   40
Her wits to yours, forsooth, and made excuse,
—E'en then would be some stooping; and I choose
Never to stoop. Oh sir, she smiled, no doubt,

3. **Frà Pandolf:** Brother Pandolf, a fictional painter.

Whene'er I passed her; but who passed without
Much the same smile? This grew; I gave commands;   45
Then all smiles stopped together. There she stands
As if alive. Will't please you rise? We'll meet
The company below, then. I repeat,
The Count your master's known munificence
Is ample warrant that no just pretence   50
Of mine for dowry will be disallowed;
Though his fair daughter's self, as I avowed
At starting, is my object. Nay, we'll go
Together down, sir. Notice Neptune, though,
Taming a sea-horse, thought a rarity,   55
Which Claus of Innsbruck° cast in bronze for me!

[1842]

56. **Claus of Innsbruck:** A fictional sculptor.

EMILY BRONTË   [1818–1848]

Riches I hold in light esteem

Riches I hold in light esteem
And Love I laugh to scorn
And lust of Fame was but a dream
That vanished with the morn—

And if I pray, the only prayer   5
That moves my lips for me
Is—"Leave the heart that now I bear
And give me liberty."

Yes, as my swift days near their goal
'Tis all that I implore—   10
Through life and death, a chainless soul
With courage to endure!

[1846]

WALT WHITMAN   [1819–1892]

From Song of Myself

1

I celebrate myself, and sing myself,
And what I assume you shall assume,
For every atom belonging to me as good belongs to you.

I loafe and invite my soul,
I lean and loafe at my ease observing a spear of summer grass.   5

My tongue, every atom of my blood, form'd from this soil, this air,
Born here of parents born here from parents the same, and their parents
  the same,
I, now thirty-seven years old in perfect health begin,
Hoping to cease not till death.

Creeds and schools in abeyance,   10
Retiring back a while sufficed at what they are, but never forgotten,
I harbor for good or bad, I permit to speak at every hazard,
Nature without check with original energy.

2

Houses and rooms are full of perfumes, the shelves are crowded with
  perfumes,
I breathe the fragrance myself and know it and like it,   15
The distillation would intoxicate me also, but I shall not let it.

The atmosphere is not a perfume, it has no taste of the distillation, it is
  odorless,
It is for my mouth forever, I am in love with it,
I will go to the bank by the wood and become undisguised and naked,
I am mad for it to be in contact with me.   20

The smoke of my own breath,
Echoes, ripples, buzz'd whispers, love-root, silk-thread, crotch and
  vine,
My respiration and inspiration, the beating of my heart, the passing of
  blood and air through my lungs,
The sniff of green leaves and dry leaves, and of the shore and dark-
  color'd sea-rocks, and of hay in the barn,
The sound of the belch'd words of my voice loos'd to the eddies of the
  wind,   25
A few light kisses, a few embraces, a reaching around of arms,

The play of shine and shade on the trees as the supple boughs wag,
The delight alone or in the rush of the streets, or along the fields and
    hill-sides,
The feeling of health, the full-noon trill, the song of me rising from bed
    and meeting the sun.

Have you reckon'd a thousand acres much? have you reckon'd the earth
    much?   30
Have you practis'd so long to learn to read?
Have you felt so proud to get at the meaning of poems?

Stop this day and night with me and you shall possess the origin of all
    poems,
You shall possess the good of the earth and sun, (there are millions of
    suns left,)
You shall no longer take things at second or third hand, nor look
    through the eyes of the dead, nor feed on the spectres in books,   35
You shall not look through my eyes either, nor take things from me,
You shall listen to all sides and filter them from your self.

3

I have heard what the talkers were talking, the talk of the beginning and
    the end,
But I do not talk of the beginning or the end.

There was never any more inception than there is now,   40
Nor any more youth or age than there is now,
And will never be any more perfection than there is now,
Nor any more heaven or hell than there is now.
Urge and urge and urge,
Always the procreant urge of the world.   45

Out of the dimness opposite equals advance, always substance and
    increase, always sex,
Always a knit of identity, always distinction, always a breed of life.

To elaborate is no avail, learn'd and unlearn'd feel that it is so.

Sure as the most certain sure, plumb in the uprights, well entretied,°
    braced in the beams,
Stout as a horse, affectionate, haughty, electrical,   50
I and this mystery here we stand.

Clear and sweet is my soul, and clear and sweet is all that is not my soul.

---

49. entretied: Cross-braced, as between two joists in carpentry.

Lack one lacks both, and the unseen is proved by the seen,
Till that becomes unseen and receives proof in its turn.

Showing the best and dividing it from the worst age vexes age,   55
Knowing the perfect fitness and equanimity of things, while they discuss
   I am silent, and go bathe and admire myself.

Welcome is every organ and attribute of me, and of any man hearty and
   clean,
Not an inch nor a particle of an inch is vile, and none shall be less
   familiar than the rest.

I am satisfied—I see, dance, laugh, sing;
As the hugging and loving bed-fellow sleeps at my side through the
   night, and withdraws at the peep of the day with stealthy tread,   60
Leaving me baskets cover'd with white towels swelling the house with
   their plenty,
Shall I postpone my acceptation and realization and scream at my eyes,
That they turn from gazing after and down the road,
And forthwith cipher and show me to a cent,
Exactly the value of one and exactly the value of two, and which is
   ahead?   65

• • •

6

A child said *What is the grass?* fetching it to me with full hands;
How could I answer the child? I do not know what it is any more than
   he.   100

I guess it must be the flag of my disposition, out of hopeful green stuff
   woven.

Or I guess it is the handkerchief of the Lord,
A scented gift and remembrancer designedly dropt,
Bearing the owner's name someway in the corners, that we may see and
   remark, and say *Whose?*

Or I guess the grass is itself a child, the produced babe of the vegetation.   105

Or I guess it is a uniform hieroglyphic,
And it means, Sprouting alike in broad zones and narrow zones,
Growing among black folks as among white,
Kanuck, Tuckahoe, Congressman, Cuff,° I give them the same, I receive
   them the same.

109. **Kanuck:** A French Canadian; **Tuckahoe:** A Virginian living in the tidewater
region and eating tuckahoe, a fungus; **Cuff:** A black person.

And now it seems to me the beautiful uncut hair of graves.   110

Tenderly will I use you curling grass,
It may be you transpire from the breasts of young men,
It may be if I had known them I would have loved them,
It may be you are from old people, or from offspring taken soon out of
    their mothers' laps,
And here you are the mothers' laps.   115

This grass is very dark to be from the white heads of old mothers,
Darker than the colorless beards of old men,
Dark to come from under the faint red roofs of mouths.

O I perceive after all so many uttering tongues,
And I perceive they do not come from the roofs of mouths for nothing.   120

I wish I could translate the hints about the dead young men and women,
And the hints about old men and mothers, and the offspring taken soon
    out of their laps.
What do you think has become of the young and old men?
And what do you think has become of the women and children?

They are alive and well somewhere,   125
The smallest sprout shows there is really no death,
And if ever there was it led forward life, and does not wait at the end to
    arrest it,
And ceas'd the moment life appear'd.

All goes onward and outward, nothing collapses,
And to die is different from what any one supposed, and luckier.   130

7

Has any one supposed it lucky to be born?
I hasten to inform him or her it is just as lucky to die, and I know it.

I pass death with the dying and birth with the new-wash'd babe, and am
    not contain'd between my hat and boots,
And peruse manifold objects, no two alike and every one good,
The earth good and the stars good, and their adjuncts all good.   135

I am not an earth nor an adjunct of an earth,
I am the mate and companion of people, all just as immortal and
    fathomless as myself,
(They do not know how immortal, but I know.)

Every kind for itself and its own, for me mine male and female,
For me those that have been boys and that love women,   140
For me the man that is proud and feels how it stings to be slighted,

For me the sweet-heart and the old maid, for me mothers and the
    mothers of mothers,
For me lips that have smiled, eyes that have shed tears,
For me children and the begetters of children.

Undrape! you are not guilty to me, nor stale nor discarded,   145
I see through the broadcloth and gingham whether or no,
And am around, tenacious, acquisitive, tireless, and cannot be shaken
    away.

8

The little one sleeps in its cradle,
I lift the gauze and look a long time, and silently brush away flies with
    my hand.

The youngster and the red-faced girl turn aside up the bushy hill,   150
I peeringly view them from the top.

The suicide sprawls on the bloody floor of the bedroom,
I witness the corpse with its dabbled hair, I note where the pistol has
    fallen.

The blab of the pave, tires of carts, sluff of boot-soles, talk of the
    promenaders,
The heavy omnibus, the driver with his interrogating thumb, the clank
    of the shod horses on the granite floor,   155
The snow-sleighs, clinking, shouted jokes, pelts of snow-balls,
The hurrahs for popular favorites, the fury of rous'd mobs,
The flap of the curtain'd litter, a sick man inside borne to the hospital,
The meeting of enemies, the sudden oath, the blows and fall,
The excited crowd, the policeman with his star quickly working his
    passage to the centre of the crowd,   160
The impassive stones that receive and return so many echoes,
What groans of over-fed or half-starv'd who fall sunstruck or in fits,
What exclamations of women taken suddenly who hurry home and give
    birth to babes,
What living and buried speech is always vibrating here, what howls
    restrain'd by decorum,
Arrests of criminals, slights, adulterous offers made, acceptances,
    rejections with convex lips,   165
I mind them or the show or resonance of them—I come and I depart.

9

The big doors of the country barn stand open and ready,
The dried grass of the harvest-time loads the slow-drawn wagon,

The clear light plays on the brown gray and green intertinged,
The armfuls are pack'd to the sagging mow.   170

I am there, I help, I came stretch'd atop of the load,
I felt its soft jolts, one leg reclined on the other,
I jump from the cross-beams and seize the clover and timothy,
And roll head over heels and tangle my hair full of wisps.

10

Alone far in the wilds and mountains I hunt,   175
Wandering amazed at my own lightness and glee,
In the late afternoon choosing a safe spot to pass the night,
Kindling a fire and broiling the fresh-kill'd game,
Falling asleep on the gather'd leaves with my dog and gun by my side.

The Yankee clipper is under her sky-sails, she cuts the sparkle and scud,   180
My eyes settle the land, I bend at her prow or shout joyously from the
    deck.

The boatmen and clam-diggers arose early and stopt for me,
I tuck'd my trowser-ends in my boots and went and had a good time;
You should have been with us that day round the chowder-kettle.

I saw the marriage of the trapper in the open air in the far west, the
    bride was a red girl,   185
Her father and his friends sat near cross-legged and dumbly smoking,
    they had moccasins to their feet and large thick blankets hanging
    from their shoulders,
On a bank lounged the trapper, he was drest mostly in skins, his
    luxuriant beard and curls protected his neck, he held his bride by the
    hand,
She had long eyelashes, her head was bare, her coarse straight locks
    descended upon her voluptuous limbs and reach'd to her feet.

The runaway slave came to my house and stopt outside,
I heard his motions crackling the twigs of the woodpile,   190
Through the swung half-door of the kitchen I saw him limpsy and weak,
And went where he sat on a log and led him in and assured him,
And brought water and fill'd a tub for his sweated body and bruis'd feet,
And gave him a room that enter'd from my own, and gave him some
    coarse clean clothes,
And remember perfectly well his revolving eyes and his awkwardness,   195
And remember putting plasters on the galls of his neck and ankles;
He staid with me a week before he was recuperated and pass'd north,
I had him sit next me at table, my fire-lock lean'd in the corner.

14

The wild gander leads his flock through the cool night,   245
Ya-honk he says, and sounds it down to me like an invitation,
The pert may suppose it meaningless, but I listening close,
Find its purpose and place up there toward the wintry sky.

The sharp-hoof'd moose of the north, the cat on the house-sill, the
    chickadee, the prairie-dog,
The litter of the grunting sow as they tug at her teats,   250
The brood of the turkey-hen and she with her half-spread wings,
I see in them and myself the same old law.

The press of my foot to the earth springs a hundred affections,
They scorn the best I can do to relate them.

I am enamour'd of growing out-doors,   255
Of men that live among cattle or taste of the ocean or woods,
Of the builders and steerers of ships and the wielders of axes and mauls,
    and the drivers of horses,
I can eat and sleep with them week in and week out.

What is commonest, cheapest, nearest, easiest, is Me,
Me going in for my chances, spending for vast returns,   260
Adorning myself to bestow myself on the first that will take me,
Not asking the sky to come down to my good will,
Scattering it freely forever.

21

I am the poet of the Body and I am the poet of the Soul,
The pleasures of heaven are with me and the pains of hell are with me,
The first I graft and increase upon myself, the latter I translate into a
    new tongue.

I am the poet of the woman the same as the man,   425
And I say it is as great to be a woman as to be a man,
And I say there is nothing greater than the mother of men.

I chant the chant of dilation or pride,
We have had ducking and deprecating about enough,
I show that size is only development.   430

Have you outstript the rest? are you the President?
It is a trifle, they will more than arrive there every one, and still pass on.

I am he that walks with the tender and growing night,
I call to the earth and sea half-held by the night.

Press close bare-bosom'd night—press close magnetic nourishing night!   435
Night of south winds—night of the large few stars!
Still nodding night—mad naked summer night.

Smile O voluptuous cool-breath'd earth!
Earth of the slumbering and liquid trees!
Earth of departed sunset—earth of the mountains misty-topt!   440
Earth of the vitreous pour of the full moon just tinged with blue!
Earth of shine and dark mottling the tide of the river!
Earth of the limpid gray of clouds brighter and clearer for my sake!
Far-swooping elbow'd earth—rich apple-blossom'd earth!
Smile, for your lover comes.   445

Prodigal, you have given me love—therefore I to you give love!
O unspeakable passionate love.

24

Walt Whitman, a kosmos, of Manhattan the son,
Turbulent, fleshy, sensual, eating, drinking and breeding,
No sentimentalist, no stander above men and women or apart from
    them,
No more modest than immodest.   500

Unscrew the locks from the doors!
Unscrew the doors themselves from their jambs!

Whoever degrades another degrades me,
And whatever is done or said returns at last to me.

Through me the afflatus° surging and surging, through me the current
    and index.   505

I speak the pass-word primeval, I give the sign of democracy,
By God! I will accept nothing which all cannot have their counterpart of
    on the same terms.

Through me many long dumb voices,
Voices of the interminable generations of prisoners and slaves,
Voices of the diseas'd and despairing and of thieves and dwarfs,   510
Voices of cycles of preparation and accretion,
And of the threads that connect the stars, and of wombs and of the
    father-stuff,
And of the rights of them the others are down upon,
Of the deform'd, trivial, flat, foolish, despised,

---

505. afflatus: Inspiration (from the Latin for "to blow on").

Fog in the air, beetles rolling balls of dung.   515

Through me forbidden voices,
Voices of sexes and lusts, voices veil'd and I remove the veil,
Voices indecent by me clarified and transfigur'd.

I do not press my fingers across my mouth,
I keep as delicate around the bowels as around the head and heart,   520
Copulation is no more rank to me than death is.

I believe in the flesh and the appetites,
Seeing, hearing, feeling, are miracles, and each part and tag of me is a
    miracle.

Divine am I inside and out, and I make holy whatever I touch or am
    touch'd from,
The scent of these arm-pits aroma finer than prayer,   525
This head more than churches, bibles, and all the creeds.

If I worship one thing more than another it shall be the spread of my
    own body, or any part of it,
Translucent mould of me it shall be you!
Shaded ledges and rests it shall be you!
Firm masculine colter° it shall be you!   530
Whatever goes to the tilth° of me it shall be you!
You my rich blood! your milky stream pale strippings of my life!
Breast that presses against other breasts it shall be you!
My brain it shall be your occult convolutions!
Root of wash'd sweet-flag! timorous pond-snipe! nest of guarded
    duplicate eggs! it shall be you!   535
Mix'd tussled hay of head, beard, brawn, it shall be you!
Trickling sap of maple, fibre of manly wheat, it shall be you!
Sun so generous it shall be you!
Vapors lighting and shading my face it shall be you!
You sweaty brooks and dews it shall be you!   540
Winds whose soft-tickling genitals rub against me it shall be you!
Broad muscular fields, branches of live oak, loving lounger in my
    winding paths, it shall be you!
Hands I have taken, face I have kiss'd, mortal I have ever touch'd, it shall
    be you.

530. colter: Blade or disk on a plow for cutting the earth.
531. tilth: Cultivation of land.

46

I know I have the best of time and space, and was never measured and
    never will be measured.

I tramp a perpetual journey, (come listen all!)
My signs are a rain-proof coat, good shoes, and a staff cut from the woods,
No friend of mine takes his ease in my chair,
I have no chair, no church, no philosophy,   1205
I lead no man to a dinner-table, library, exchange,
But each man and each woman of you I lead upon a knoll,
My left hand hooking you round the waist,
My right hand pointing to landscapes of continents and the public road.

Not I, not any one else can travel that road for you,   1210
You must travel it for yourself.

It is not far, it is within reach,
Perhaps you have been on it since you were born and did not know,
Perhaps it is everywhere on water and on land.

Shoulder your duds dear son, and I will mine, and let us hasten forth,   1215
Wonderful cities and free nations we shall fetch as we go.

If you tire, give me both burdens, and rest the chuff° of your hand on
    my hip,
And in due time you shall repay the same service to me,
For after we start we never lie by again.

This day before dawn I ascended a hill and look'd at the crowded
    heaven,   1220
And I said to my spirit *When we become the enfolders of those orbs, and
    the pleasure and knowledge of every thing in them, shall we be fill'd and
    satisfied then?*
And my spirit said *No, we but level that lift to pass and continue beyond.*

You are also asking me questions and I hear you,
I answer that I cannot answer, you must find out for yourself.

Sit a while dear son,   1225
Here are biscuits to eat and here is milk to drink,
But as soon as you sleep and renew yourself in sweet clothes, I kiss you
    with a good-by kiss and open the gate for your egress hence.

Long enough have you dream'd contemptible dreams,
Now I wash the gum from your eyes,

1217. **chuff:** Weight.

You must habit yourself to the dazzle of the light and of every moment
   of your life.   1230

Long have you timidly waded holding a plank by the shore,
Now I will you to be a bold swimmer,
To jump off in the midst of the sea, rise again, nod to me, shout, and
   laughingly dash with your hair.

48

I have said that the soul is not more than the body,
And I have said that the body is not more than the soul,   1270
And nothing, not God, is greater to one than one's self is,
And whoever walks a furlong without sympathy walks to his own
   funeral drest in his shroud,
And I or you pocketless of a dime may purchase the pick of the earth,
And to glance with an eye or show a bean in its pod confounds the
   learning of all times,
And there is no trade or employment but the young man following it
   may become a hero,   1275
And there is no object so soft but it makes a hub for the wheel'd
   universe,
And I say to any man or woman, Let your soul stand cool and composed
   before a million universes.

And I say to mankind, Be not curious about God,
For I who am curious about each am not curious about God,
(No array of terms can say how much I am at peace about God and
   about death.)   1280

I hear and behold God in every object, yet understand God not in the
   least,
Nor do I understand who there can be more wonderful than myself.

Why should I wish to see God better than this day?
I see something of God each hour of the twenty-four, and each moment
   then,
In the faces of men and women I see God, and in my own face in the
   glass,   1285
I find letters from God dropt in the street, and every one is sign'd by
   God's name,
And I leave them where they are, for I know that wheresoe'er I go,
Others will punctually come for ever and ever.

51

The past and present wilt—I have fill'd them, emptied them,
And proceed to fill my next fold of the future.   1320

Listener up there! what have you to confide to me?
Look in my face while I snuff° the sidle° of evening,
(Talk honestly, no one else hears you, and I stay only a minute longer.)

Do I contradict myself?
Very well then I contradict myself,
(I am large, I contain multitudes.)   1325

I concentrate toward them that are nigh, I wait on the door-slab.

Who has done his day's work? who will soonest be through with his
    supper?
Who wishes to walk with me?

Will you speak before I am gone? will you prove already too late?
                                                                       1330
52

The spotted hawk swoops by and accuses me, he complains of my gab
    and my loitering.

I too am not a bit tamed, I too am untranslatable,
I sound my barbaric yawp over the roofs of the world.

The last scud of day holds back for me,
It flings my likeness after the rest and true as any on the shadow'd wilds,
It coaxes me to the vapor and the dusk.   1335

I depart as air, I shake my white locks at the runaway sun,
I effuse my flesh in eddies, and drift it in lacy jags.

I bequeath myself to the dirt to grow from the grass I love,
If you want me again look for me under your boot-soles.

You will hardly know who I am or what I mean,   1340
But I shall be good health to you nevertheless,
And filter and fibre your blood.

Failing to fetch me at first keep encouraged,
Missing me one place search another,
I stop somewhere waiting for you.   1345

                                        [*1855*/1891–1892]°

1322: **snuff:** Snuff out; **sidle:** Sidewise or stealthy movement.
Date: The poem was first published in 1855 as an untitled section of *Leaves
of Grass*. It was a rough, rude, and vigorous example of antebellum American
cultural politics and free verse experimentation. The version used here, from the
sixth edition (1891–1892), is much longer, more carefully crafted, and more con-
ventionally punctuated. Sections 1–3 introduce the persona and the scope and

WALT WHITMAN   [1819–1892]

When Lilacs Last in the Dooryard Bloom'd

1

When lilacs last in the dooryard bloom'd,
And the great star early droop'd in the western sky in the night,
I mourn'd, and yet shall mourn with ever-returning spring.

Ever-returning spring, trinity sure to me you bring,
Lilac blooming perennial and drooping star in the west,   5
And thought of him I love.

2

O powerful western fallen star!
O shades of night—O moody, tearful night!
O great star disappear'd—O the black murk that hides the star!
O cruel hands that hold me powerless—O helpless soul of me!   10
O harsh surrounding cloud that will not free my soul.

3

In the dooryard fronting an old farm-house near the white-wash'd
    palings,
Stands the lilac-bush tall-growing with heart-shaped leaves of rich
    green,
With many a pointed blossom rising delicate, with the perfume strong I
    love,
With every leaf a miracle—and from this bush in the dooryard,   15
With delicate-color'd blossoms and heart-shaped leaves of rich green,
A sprig with its flower I break.

4

In the swamp in secluded recesses,
A shy and hidden bird is warbling a song.

---

method of the poem; section 6 explains grass as a symbol; sections 7–10, examples
of Whitman's dynamic panoramic miniatures, are also of historical significance
regarding Native and African Americans; section 14 extends the outward sweep of
7–10; section 21 develops Whitman's theme of sex and nature; section 24 extends
the handling of the poem's persona; sections 46 and 48 offer a recapitulation of
the major themes of the poem; sections 51 and 52 deal with the absorption of the
poet's persona into the converted reader.

Solitary the thrush,   20
The hermit withdrawn to himself, avoiding the settlements,
Sings by himself a song.

Song of the bleeding throat,
Death's outlet song of life, (for well dear brother I know,
If thou wast not granted to sing thou would'st surely die.)   25

                                5

Over the breast of the spring, the land, amid cities,
Amid lanes and through old woods, where lately the violets peep'd from
    the ground, spotting the gray debris,
Amid the grass in the fields each side of the lanes, passing the endless
    grass,
Passing the yellow-spear'd wheat, every grain from its shroud in the
    dark-brown fields uprisen,
Passing the apple-tree blows of white and pink in the orchards,   30
Carrying a corpse to where it shall rest in the grave,
Night and day journeys a coffin.

                                6

Coffin that passes through lanes and streets,°
Through day and night with the great cloud darkening the land,
With the pomp of the inloop'd flags with the cities draped in black,   35
With the show of the States themselves as of crape-veil'd women
    standing,
With processions long and winding and the flambeaus° of the night,
With the countless torches lit, with the silent sea of faces and the
    unbared heads,
With the waiting depot, the arriving coffin, and the sombre faces,
With dirges through the night, with the thousand voices rising strong
    and solemn,   40
With all the mournful voices of the dirges pour'd around the coffin,
The dim-lit churches and the shuddering organs—where amid these
    you journey,
With the tolling tolling bells' perpetual clang,
Here, coffin that slowly passes,
I give you my sprig of lilac.   45

33. lanes and streets: President Lincoln's funeral procession traveled from
Washington to Springfield, Illinois, with stops at cities and towns to enable people
to honor their assassinated president.
37. flambeaus: Flaming torches.

7

(Nor for you, for one alone,
Blossoms and branches green to coffins all I bring,
For fresh as the morning, thus would I chant a song for you O sane and
    sacred death.

All over bouquets of roses,
O death, I cover you over with roses and early lilies,   50
But mostly and now the lilac that blooms the first,
Copious I break, I break the sprigs from the bushes,
With loaded arms I come, pouring for you,
For you and the coffins all of you O death.)

8

O western orb sailing the heaven,   55
Now I know what you must have meant as a month since I walk'd,
As I walk'd in silence the transparent shadowy night,
As I saw you had something to tell as you bent to me night after
    night,
As you droop'd from the sky low down as if to my side, (while the other
    stars all look'd on,)
As we wander'd together the solemn night, (for something I know not
    what kept me from sleep,)   60
As the night advanced, and I saw on the rim of the west how full you
    were of woe,
As I stood on the rising ground in the breeze in the cool transparent
    night,
As I watch'd where you pass'd and was lost in the netherward black of
    the night,
As my soul in its trouble dissatisfied sank, as where you sad orb,
Concluded, dropt in the night, and was gone.   65

9

Sing on there in the swamp,
O singer bashful and tender, I hear your notes, I hear your call,
I hear, I come presently, I understand you,
But a moment I linger, for the lustrous star has detain'd me,
The star my departing comrade holds and detains me.   70

10

O how shall I warble myself for the dead one there I loved?
And how shall I deck my song for the large sweet soul that has gone?
And what shall my perfume be for the grave of him I love?

Sea-winds blown from east and west,
Blown from the Eastern sea and blown from the Western sea, till there
  on the prairies meeting,   75
These and with these and the breath of my chant,
I'll perfume the grave of him I love.

11

O what shall I hang on the chamber walls?
And what shall the pictures be that I hang on the walls,
To adorn the burial-house of him I love?   80

Pictures of growing spring and farms and homes,
With the Fourth-month eve at sundown, and the gray smoke lucid and
  bright,
With floods of the yellow gold of the gorgeous, indolent, sinking sun,
  burning, expanding the air,
With the fresh sweet herbage under foot, and the pale green leaves of the
  trees prolific,
In the distance the flowing glaze, the breast of the river, with a wind-
  dapple here and there,   85
With ranging hills on the banks, with many a line against the sky, and
  shadows,
And the city at hand with dwellings so dense, and stacks of chimneys,
And all the scenes of life and the workshops, and the workmen
  homeward returning.

12

Lo, body and soul — this land,
My own Manhattan with spires, and the sparkling and hurrying tides,
  and the ships,   90
The varied and ample land, the South and the North in the light, Ohio's
  shores and flashing Missouri,
And ever the far-spreading prairies cover'd with grass and corn.

Lo, the most excellent sun so calm and haughty,
The violet and purple morn with just-felt breezes,
The gentle soft-born measureless light,   95
The miracle spreading, bathing all, the fulfill'd noon,
The coming eve delicious, the welcome night and the stars,
Over my cities shining all, enveloping man and land.

13

Sing on, sing on you gray-brown bird,
Sing from the swamps, the recesses, pour your chant from the bushes, 100
Limitless out of the dusk, out of the cedars and pines.

Sing on dearest brother, warble your reedy song,
Loud human song, with voice of uttermost woe.

O liquid and free and tender!
O wild and loose to my soul—O wondrous singer!   105
You only I hear—yet the star holds me, (but will soon depart,)
Yet the lilac with mastering odor holds me.

14

Now while I sat in the day and look'd forth,
In the close of the day with its light and the fields of spring, and the
    farmers preparing their crops,
In the large unconscious scenery of my land with its lakes and forests,   110
In the heavenly aerial beauty, (after the perturb'd winds and the storms,)
Under the arching heavens of the afternoon swift passing, and the voices
    of children and women,
The many-moving sea-tides, and I saw the ships how they sail'd,
And the summer approaching with richness, and the fields all busy with
    labor,
And the infinite separate houses, how they all went on, each with its
    meals and minutia of daily usages,   115
And the streets how their throbbings throbb'd, and the cities pent—lo,
    then and there,
Falling upon them all and among them all, enveloping me with the rest,
Appear'd the cloud, appear'd the long black trail,
And I knew death, its thought, and the sacred knowledge of death.

Then with the knowledge of death as walking one side of me,   120
And the thought of death close-walking the other side of me,
And I in the middle as with companions, and as holding the hands of
    companions,
I fled forth to the hiding receiving night that talks not,
Down to the shores of the water, the path by the swamp in the dimness,
To the solemn shadowy cedars and ghostly pines so still.   125

And the singer so shy to the rest receiv'd me,
The gray-brown bird I know receiv'd us comrades three,
And he sang the carol of death, and a verse for him I love.

From deep secluded recesses,
From the fragrant cedars and the ghostly pines so still,   130
Came the carol of the bird.

And the charm of the carol rapt me,
As I held as if by their hands my comrades in the night,
And the voice of my spirit tallied the song of the bird.

Come lovely and soothing death, 135
Undulate round the world, serenely arriving, arriving,
In the day, in the night, to all, to each,
Sooner or later delicate death.

Prais'd be the fathomless universe,
For life and joy, and for objects and knowledge curious, 140
And for love, sweet love—but praise! praise! praise!
For the sure-enwinding arms of cool-enfolding death.

Dark mother always gliding near with soft feet,
Have none chanted for thee a chant of fullest welcome?
Then I chant it for thee, I glorify thee above all, 145
I bring thee a song that when thou must indeed come, come unfalteringly.

Approach strong deliveress,
When it is so, when thou hast taken them I joyously sing the dead,
Lost in the loving floating ocean of thee,
Laved in the flood of thy bliss O death. 150

From me to thee glad serenades,
Dances for thee I propose saluting thee, adornments and feastings for thee,
And the sights of the open landscape and the high-spread sky are fitting,
And life and the fields, and the huge and thoughtful night.

The night in silence under many a star, 155
The ocean shore and the husky whispering wave whose voice I know,
And the soul turning to thee O vast and well-veil'd death,
And the body gratefully nestling close to thee.

Over the tree-tops I float thee a song,
Over the rising and sinking waves, over the myriad fields and the prairies
wide,
Over the dense-pack'd cities all and the teeming wharves and ways, 160
I float this carol with joy, with joy to thee O death.

15

To the tally of my soul,
Loud and strong kept up the gray-brown bird,
With pure deliberate notes spreading filling the night. 165

Loud in the pines and cedars dim,
Clear in the freshness moist and the swamp-perfume,
And I with my comrades there in the night.

While my sight that was bound in my eyes unclosed,
As to long panoramas of visions. 170

And I saw askant the armies,
I saw as in noiseless dreams hundreds of battle-flags,
Borne through the smoke of the battles and pierc'd with missiles I saw
    them,
And carried hither and yon through the smoke, and torn and bloody,
And at last but a few shreds left on the staffs, (and all in silence,)   175
And the staffs all splinter'd and broken.

I saw battle-corpses, myriads of them,
And the white skeletons of young men, I saw them,
I saw the debris and debris of all the slain soldiers of the war,
But I saw they were not as was thought,   180
They themselves were fully at rest, they suffer'd not,
The living remain'd and suffer'd, the mother suffer'd,
And the wife and the child and the musing comrade suffer'd,
And the armies that remain'd suffer'd.

16

Passing the visions, passing the night,   185
Passing, unloosing the hold of my comrades' hands,
Passing the song of the hermit bird and the tallying song of my soul,
Victorious song, death's outlet song, yet varying ever-altering song,
As low and wailing, yet clear the notes, rising and falling, flooding the
    night,
Sadly sinking and fainting, as warning and warning, and yet again
    bursting with joy,   190
Covering the earth and filling the spread of the heaven,
As that powerful psalm in the night I heard from recesses,
Passing, I leave thee lilac with heart-shaped leaves,
I leave thee there in the door-yard, blooming, returning with spring.

I cease from my song for thee,   195
From my gaze on thee in the west, fronting the west, communing with
    thee,
O comrade lustrous with silver face in the night.

Yet each to keep and all, retrievements out of the night,
The song, the wondrous chant of the gray-brown bird,
And the tallying chant, the echo arous'd in my soul,   200
With the lustrous and drooping star with the countenance full of woe,
With the holders holding my hand nearing the call of the bird,
Comrades mine and I in the midst, and their memory ever to keep, for
    the dead I loved so well,
For the sweetest, wisest soul of all my days and lands—and this for his
    dear sake,

Lilac and star and bird twined with the chant of my soul,   205
There in the fragrant pines and the cedars dusk and dim.

[1865 1891–92]°

Date: This is one of four elegies written by Whitman on the death of President
Abraham Lincoln, 14 April 1865, and first published as an addendum to *Drum-Taps* called "Sequel to *Drum-Taps*." Whitman later added the *Drum-Taps* volume
to *Leaves of Grass.* The version used here is from the sixth edition of *Leaves of
Grass* (1891–1892).

WALT WHITMAN   [1819–1892]

A Noiseless Patient Spider

A noiseless patient spider,
I mark'd where on a little promontory it stood isolated,
Mark'd how to explore the vacant vast surrounding,
It launch'd forth filament, filament, filament, out of itself,
Ever unreeling them, ever tirelessly speeding them.   5

And you O my soul where you stand,
Surrounded, detached, in measureless oceans of space,
Ceaselessly musing, venturing, throwing, seeking the spheres to connect
    them,
Till the bridge you will need be form'd, till the ductile anchor hold,
Till the gossamer thread you fling catch somewhere, O my soul.   10

[1868–1881]

MATTHEW ARNOLD   [1822–1888]

Dover Beach

The sea is calm tonight.
The tide is full, the moon lies fair
Upon the straits; on the French coast the light
Gleams and is gone; the cliffs of England stand,
Glimmering and vast, out in the tranquil bay.   5
Come to the window, sweet is the night-air!
Only, from the long line of spray
Where the sea meets the moon-blanched land,

Listen! you hear the grating roar
Of pebbles which the waves draw back, and fling,   10
At their return, up the high strand,
Begin, and cease, and then again begin,
With tremulous cadence slow, and bring
The eternal note of sadness in.

Sophocles long ago   15
Heard it on the Aegean, and it brought
Into his mind the turbid ebb and flow
Of human misery; we
Find also in the sound a thought,
Hearing it by this distant northern sea.   20

The Sea of Faith
Was once, too, at the full, and round earth's shore
Lay like the folds of a bright girdle furled.
But now I only hear
Its melancholy, long, withdrawing roar,   25
Retreating, to the breath
Of the night-wind, down the vast edges drear
And naked shingles° of the world.   *pebble-covered beaches*

Ah, love, let us be true
To one another! for the world, which seems   30
To lie before us like a land of dreams,
So various, so beautiful, so new,
Hath really neither joy, nor love, nor light,
Nor certitude, nor peace, nor help for pain;
And we are here as on a darkling plain   35
Swept with confused alarms of struggle and flight,
Where ignorant armies clash by night.

[*c. 1851;* 1867]

EMILY DICKINSON   [1830–1886]

I felt a Funeral, in my Brain

I felt a Funeral, in my Brain,
And Mourners to and fro
Kept treading—treading—till it seemed
That Sense was breaking through—

And when they all were seated,   5
A Service, like a Drum—
Kept beating—beating—till I thought
My Mind was going numb—

And then I heard them lift a Box
And creak across my Soul   10
With those same Boots of Lead, again,
Then Space—began to toll,

As all the Heavens were a Bell,
And Being, but an Ear,
And I, and Silence, some strange Race   15
Wrecked, solitary, here—

And then a Plank in Reason, broke,
And I dropped down, and down—
And hit a World, at every plunge,
And Finished knowing—then—   20

[*c. 1861;* 1896]

EMILY DICKINSON   [1830–1886]

Much Madness is divinest Sense

Much Madness is divinest Sense—
To a discerning Eye—
Much Sense—the starkest Madness—
'Tis the Majority
In this, as All, prevail—   5
Assent—and you are sane—
Demur—you're straightway dangerous—
And handled with a Chain—

[*c. 1862;* 1890]

EMILY DICKINSON   [1830–1886]

I heard a Fly buzz—when I died

I heard a Fly buzz—when I died—
The Stillness in the Room
Was like the Stillness in the Air—
Between the Heaves of Storm—

The Eyes around—had wrung them dry—   5
And Breaths were gathering firm
For that last Onset—when the King
Be witnessed—in the Room—

I willed my Keepsakes—Signed away
What portion of me be   10
Assignable—and then it was
There interposed a Fly—

With Blue—uncertain stumbling Buzz—
Between the light—and me—
And then the Windows failed—and then   15
I could not see to see—

[c. *1862;* 1890]

EMILY DICKINSON   [1830–1886]

Because I could not stop for Death

Because I could not stop for Death—
He kindly stopped for me—
The Carriage held but just Ourselves—
And Immortality.

We slowly drove—He knew no haste   5
And I had put away
My labor and my leisure too,
For His Civility—

We passed the School, where Children strove
At Recess—in the Ring—   10
We passed the Fields of Gazing Grain—
We passed the Setting Sun—

Or rather — He passed Us —
The Dews drew quivering and chill —
For only Gossamer, my Gown —   15
My Tippet° — only Tulle° —   *scarf/silk net*

We paused before a House that seemed
A Swelling of the Ground —
The Roof was scarcely visible —
The Cornice — in the Ground —   20

Since then — 'tis Centuries — and yet
Feels shorter than the Day
I first surmised the Horses' Heads
Were toward Eternity —

                                              [*c. 1863;* 1890]

CHRISTINA ROSSETTI   [1830–1894]

Song

When I am dead, my dearest,
  Sing no sad songs for me;
Plant thou no roses at my head,
  Nor shady cypress tree:
Be the green grass above me   5
  With showers and dewdrops wet;
And if thou wilt, remember,
  And if thou wilt, forget.

I shall not see the shadows,
  I shall not feel the rain;   10
I shall not hear the nightingale
  Sing on, as if in pain:
And dreaming through the twilight
  That doth not rise nor set,
Haply I may remember,   15
  And haply may forget.

                                                      [1862]

THOMAS HARDY   [1840–1928]

The Convergence of the Twain

Lines on the Loss of the Titanic°

1

In a solitude of the sea
Deep from human vanity,
And the Pride of Life that planned her, stilly couches she.

2

Steel chambers, late the pyres
Of her salamandrine° fires,   5
Cold currents thrid,° and turn to rhythmic tidal lyres.   *thread*

3

Over the mirrors meant
To glass the opulent
The sea-worm crawls — grotesque, slimed, dumb, indifferent.

4

Jewels in joy designed   10
To ravish the sensuous mind
Lie lightless, all their sparkles bleared and black and blind.

5

Dim moon-eyed fishes near
Gaze at the gilded gear
And query: "What does this vaingloriousness down here?"   15

6

Well: while was fashioning
This creature of cleaving wing,
The Immanent Will that stirs and urges everything

Titanic: A famous luxury ocean liner, largest of its time and considered unsinkable. It collided with an iceberg on its maiden voyage, 15 April 1912, and sank. Of some 2,200 people aboard, more than 1,500 were lost.
5. salamandrine: Fierce, inextinguishable (the lizardlike salamander supposedly is able to resist or live in fire).

7

Prepared a sinister mate
For her—so gaily great—   20
A Shape of Ice, for the time far and dissociate.

8

And as the smart ship grew
In stature, grace, and hue,
In shadowy silent distance grew the Iceberg too.

9

Alien they seemed to be: 25
No mortal eye could see
The intimate welding of their later history,

10

Or sign that they were bent
By paths coincident
On being anon twin halves of one august event,   30

11

Till the Spinner of the Years
Said "Now!" And each one hears,
And consummation comes, and jars two hemispheres.

[1912]

GERARD MANLEY HOPKINS   [1844–1889]

God's Grandeur

The world is charged with the grándeur of God.
  It will flame out, like shining from shook foil;°   *shaken gold foil*
  It gathers to a greatness, like the ooze of oil°   *(from olives)*
Crushed. Why do men then now not reck° his rod°?   *recognize/discipline*
Génerátions have trod, have trod, have trod;   5
  And all is seared with trade; bleared, smeared, with toil;
  And wears man's smudge and shares man's smell: the soil
Is bare now, nor can foot feel, being shod.

Ánd, for° all this, náture is never spent;   *despite*
  There lives the dearest freshness deep down things;   10
And though the last lights off the black West went
  Oh, morning, at the brown brink eastward, springs—
Because the Holy Ghost óver the bent
  World broods with warm breast and with ah! bright wings.

                                                              [*1877;* 1918]

GERARD MANLEY HOPKINS   [1844–1889]

The Windhover°

To Christ Our Lord

I caught this morning morning's minion,° king-   *darling, favorite*
  dom of daylight's dauphin,° dapple-dáwn-drawn Falcon,
    in his riding
Of the rólling level únderneath him steady air, and stríding
Hígh there, how he rung upon the rein of a wimpling° wing   *rippling*
In his ecstasy! then off, off forth on swing,   5
  As a skate's heel sweeps smooth on a bow-bend: the hurl and gliding
  Rebuffed the big wind. My heart in hiding
Stírred for a bird,—the achieve of, the mastery of the thing!

Brute beauty and valour and act, oh, air, pride, plume, here
  Buckle! AND the fire that breaks from thee then, a billion   10
Times told lovelier, more dangerous, O my chevalier!°   *knight, nobleman*
  Nó wonder of it: shéer plód makes plóugh down síllion°   *furrow*
Shíne, and blue-bleak embers, ah my dear,
  Fall, gáll themselves, and gásh gold-vermilion.

                                                              [*1877;* 1918]

Windhover: A kestrel (a species of small hawk), which seems to hover in the wind.
2. dauphin: Heir (eldest son of the king of France).

GERARD MANLEY HOPKINS   [1844–1889]

Pied° Beauty   *multicolored, variegated*

Glóry be to God for dappled things—
  For skies of couple-colour as a brinded° cow;   *streaked*
    For rose-moles all in stipple upon trout that swim;
Fresh-firecoal chestnut-fálls; fínches' wings;
  Lándscape plotted and pieced—fold, fallow, and plough;   5
    And áll trádes, their gear and tackle and trim.

All things counter, original, spáre, stránge;
  Whatever is fickle, freckled (who knows how?)
    With swift, slow; sweet, sour; adazzle, dim;
He fathers-forth whose beauty is pást chánge: 10
          Práise hím.

                    [*1877;* 1918]

GERARD MANLEY HOPKINS   [1844–1889]

Spring and Fall

to a young child

Márgarét, áre you gríeving
Over Goldengrove unleaving?
Leáves, líke the things of mán, you
With your fresh thoughts care for, can you?
Áh! ás the héart grows ólder   5
It will come to such sights colder
By and by, nor spare a sigh
Though worlds of wanwood leafmeal° lie;
And yet you *will* weep and know why.
Now no matter, child, the name: 10
Sórrow's springs áre the sáme.
Nor mouth had, no nor mind, expressed
What héart héard of, ghóst° guéssed: *spirit*
It ís the blíght man was bórn for,
It is Margaret you mourn for.   15

                    [*1880;* 1918]

8. **wanwood leafmeal:** Colorless forest with scattered leaves.

A. E. HOUSMAN   [1859–1936]

Loveliest of trees, the cherry now

Loveliest of trees, the cherry now
Is hung with bloom along the bough,
And stands about the woodland ride
Wearing white for Eastertide.

Now, of my threescore years and ten,   5
Twenty will not come again,
And take from seventy springs a score,
It only leaves me fifty more.

And since to look at things in bloom
Fifty springs are little room,   10
About the woodlands I will go
To see the cherry hung with snow.

[1896]

A. E. HOUSMAN   [1859–1936]

To an Athlete Dying Young

The time you won your town the race
We chaired you through the market-place;
Man and boy stood cheering by,
And home we brought you shoulder-high.

To-day, the road all runners come,   5
Shoulder-high we bring you home,
And set you at your threshold down,
Townsman of a stiller town.

Smart lad, to slip betimes away
From fields where glory does not stay   10
And early though the laurel grows
It withers quicker than the rose.

Eyes the shady night has shut
Cannot see the record cut,°   *broken*
And silence sounds no worse than cheers   15
After earth has stopped the ears:

Now you will not swell the rout
Of lads that wore their honours out,
Runners whom renown outran
And the name died before the man.   20

So set, before its echoes fade,
The fleet foot on the sill of shade,
And hold to the low lintel up
The still-defended challenge-cup.

And round that early-laurelled head   25
Will flock to gaze the strengthless dead,
And find unwithered on its curls
The garland briefer than a girl's.

[1896]

A. E. HOUSMAN   [1859–1936]

"Terence, this is stupid stuff"

"Terence,° this is stupid stuff:
You eat your victuals fast enough;
There can't be much amiss, 'tis clear,
To see the rate you drink your beer.
But oh, good Lord, the verse you make,   5
It gives a chap the belly-ache.
The cow, the old cow, she is dead;
It sleeps well, the horned head:
We poor lads, 'tis our turn now
To hear such tunes as killed the cow.   10
Pretty friendship 'tis to rhyme
Your friends to death before their time
Moping melancholy mad:
Come, pipe a tune to dance to, lad."

Why, if 'tis dancing you would be,   15
There's brisker pipes than poetry.
Say, for what were hop-yards meant,

---

1. **Terence:** *The Poems of Terence Hearsay* was the title Housman originally intended for the volume in which this poem was published. Later he changed it to *The Shropshire Lad.*

Or why was Burton° built on Trent?°   *famous brewing town/river in England*
Oh many a peer of England brews
Livelier liquor than the Muse,   20
And malt does more than Milton can
To justify God's ways to man.°
Ale, man, ale's the stuff to drink
For fellows whom it hurts to think:
Look into the pewter pot   25
To see the world as the world's not.
And faith, 'tis pleasant till 'tis past:
The mischief is that 'twill not last.
Oh I have been to Ludlow° fair   *market town in Shropshire*
And left my necktie God knows where,   30
And carried half-way home, or near,
Pints and quarts of Ludlow beer:
Then the world seemed none so bad,
And I myself a sterling lad;
And down in lovely muck I've lain,   35
Happy till I woke again.
Then I saw the morning sky:
Heigho, the tale was all a lie;
The world, it was the old world yet,
I was I, my things were wet,   40
And nothing now remained to do
But begin the game anew.

    Therefore, since the world has still
Much good, but much less good than ill,
And while the sun and moon endure   45
Luck's a chance, but trouble's sure,
I'd face it as a wise man would,
And train for ill and not for good.
'Tis true, the stuff I bring for sale
Is not so brisk a brew as ale: 50
Out of a stem that scored° the hand   *cut*
I wrung it in a weary land.
But take it: if the smack is sour,
The better for the embittered hour;
It should do good to heart and head   55
When your soul is in my soul's stead;
And I will friend you, if I may,
In the dark and cloudy day.

22. justify . . . man: See *Paradise Lost* 1.26.

There was a king reigned in the East:
There, when kings will sit to feast,   60
They get their fill before they think
With poisoned meat and poisoned drink.
He gathered all that springs to birth
From the many-venomed earth;
First a little, thence to more,   65
He sampled all her killing store;
And easy, smiling, seasoned sound,
Sate the king when healths went round.
They put arsenic in his meat
And stared aghast to watch him eat;   70
They poured strychnine in his cup
And shook to see him drink it up:
They shook, they stared as white's their shirt:
Them it was their poison hurt.
—I tell the tale that I heard told.   75
Mithridates,° he died old.

[1896]

76. **Mithridates:** King of Pontus, first century B.C.E., who according to Pliny's
Natural History made himself immune to poison by taking small doses daily.

WILLIAM BUTLER YEATS   [1865–1939]

The Second Coming°

Turning and turning in the widening gyre
The falcon cannot hear the falconer;
Things fall apart; the centre cannot hold;
Mere anarchy is loosed upon the world,

The Second Coming: Alludes to Matthew 24:3–44, on the return of Christ at the
end of the present age. Yeats viewed history as a series of 2,000-year cycles
(imaged as gyres, cone-shaped motions). The birth of Christ in Bethlehem
brought to an end the cycle that ran from the Babylonians through the Greeks and
Romans. The approach of the year 2000, then, anticipated for Yeats the end of
another era (the Christian age). Yeats wrote this poem shortly after the Russian
Revolution of 1917 (lines 4–8), which may have confirmed his sense of imminent
change and of a new beginning of an unpredictable nature (Yeats expected the
new era to be violent and despotic).

The blood-dimmed tide is loosed, and everywhere   5
The ceremony of innocence is drowned;
The best lack all conviction, while the worst
Are full of passionate intensity.

Surely some revelation is at hand;
Surely the Second Coming is at hand.   10
The Second Coming! Hardly are those words out
When a vast image out of *Spiritus Mundi*°
Troubles my sight: somewhere in sands of the desert
A shape with lion body and the head of a man,
A gaze blank and pitiless as the sun,   15
Is moving its slow thighs, while all about it
Reel shadows of the indignant desert birds.
The darkness drops again; but now I know
That twenty centuries of stony sleep
Were vexed to nightmare by a rocking cradle,   20
And what rough beast, its hour come round at last,
Slouches towards Bethlehem to be born?

[1921]

12. *Spiritus Mundi*: Latin, "the spirit of the universe." Yeats believed in a Great
Memory, a universal storehouse of symbolic images from the past. Individuals,
drawing on it for images, are put in touch with the soul of the universe.

WILLIAM BUTLER YEATS   [1865–1939]

Leda and the Swan°

A sudden blow: the great wings beating still
Above the staggering girl, her thighs caressed
By the dark webs, her nape caught in his bill,
He holds her helpless breast upon his breast.

How can those terrified vague fingers push   5
The feathered glory from her loosening thighs?
And how can body, laid in that white rush,
But feel the strange heart beating where it lies?

A shudder in the loins engenders there
The broken wall, the burning roof and tower   10
And Agamemnon dead.
               Being so caught up,

So mastered by the brute blood of the air,
Did she put on his knowledge with his power
Before the indifferent beak could let her drop?   15

[1928]

Leda and the Swan: In Greek mythology, Leda was seduced (or raped) by Zeus, who approached her in the form of a swan. She gave birth to Helen, whose abduction by Paris gave rise to the Trojan War (referred to in line 10). The Greek forces were headed by Agamemnon, who was killed (line 11) upon his return to Greece by his wife Clytemnestra, daughter of Leda by her husband, Tyndareus. Yeats regarded Zeus's visit as a "violent annunciation" of the founding of Greek civilization, with parallels to the annunciation to Mary (Luke 1:26–38), 2,000 years later, of the coming of the Christian age. See the note to "The Second Coming" for Yeats's view of historical eras (p. 123).

WILLIAM BUTLER YEATS   [1865–1939]

Among School Children°

1

I walk through the long schoolroom questioning;
A kind old nun in a white hood replies;
The children learn to cipher° and to sing,   *do arithmetic*
To study reading-books and history,
To cut and sew, be neat in everything   5
In the best modern way — the children's eyes
In momentary wonder stare upon
A sixty-year-old smiling public man.

2

I dream of a Ledaean° body, bent
Above a sinking fire, a tale that she   10
Told of a harsh reproof, or trivial event

Among School Children: In February 1926, Yeats visited a Montessori school as part of his duties as a senator. In March he wrote in his diary the following topic for a poem: "School children and the thought that life will waste them, perhaps that no possible life can fulfill their own dreams or even their teacher's hope. Bring in the old thought that life prepares for what never happens."
9. Ledaean: Helen-like (referring to Helen, daughter of Leda — see the note to "Leda and the Swan" above). Here and in lines 19–28 Yeats was thinking of Maud Gonne, a beautiful actress and Irish nationalist whom he loved desperately for many years but who refused to marry him.

That changed some childish day to tragedy—
Told, and it seemed that our two natures blent
Into a sphere from youthful sympathy,
Or else, to alter Plato's parable,   15
Into the yolk and white of the one shell.°

3

And thinking of that fit of grief or rage
I look upon one child or t'other there
And wonder if she stood so at that age—
For even daughters of the swan can share   20
Something of every paddler's heritage—
And had that colour upon cheek or hair,
And thereupon my heart is driven wild:
She stands before me as a living child.

4

Her present image floats into the mind—   25
Did Quattrocento° finger fashion it
Hollow of cheek as though it drank the wind
And took a mess of shadows for its meat?
And I though never of Ledaean kind
Had pretty plumage once—enough of that,   30
Better to smile on all that smile, and show
There is a comfortable kind of old scarecrow.

5

What youthful mother, a shape upon her lap
Honey of generation had betrayed,°

---

16. Into . . . shell: To explain love, in Plato's *Symposium*, Aristophanes describes
primeval humans as round with "four hands and four feet, back and sides forming
a circle, one head with two faces." Fearful of their power, Zeus cut them in two, as
one would divide an egg. After separation, each half desired to be reunited with its
opposite: "Each of us is . . . but the half of a human being, . . . forever seeking his
missing half."
26. Quattrocento: The fifteenth century, as a period in Italian art and literature.
34. Honey . . . betrayed: Yeats wrote in a note, "I have taken the 'honey of generation' from Porphyry's essay on 'The Cave of the Nymphs' but find no warrant in
Porphyry for considering it the 'drug' that destroys the 'recollection' of pre-natal
freedom." Porphyry (a third-century Neoplatonic philosopher) described the
sweetness of honey as allegorically representing "the pleasure arising from copulation." For Yeats, however, the honey of generation seems to blot out the memory
of prenatal happiness, thus "betraying" an infant into consenting to be born into
this world.

And that must sleep, shriek, struggle to escape   35
As recollection or the drug decide,
Would think her son, did she but see that shape
With sixty or more winters on its head,
A compensation for the pang of his birth,
Or the uncertainty of his setting forth?   40

6

Plato thought nature but a spume that plays
Upon a ghostly paradigm of things;°
Solider Aristotle played the taws
Upon the bottom of a king of kings;°
World-famous golden-thighed Pythagoras°   45
Fingered upon a fiddle-stick or strings
What a star sang and careless Muses heard:
Old clothes upon old sticks to scare a bird.°

7

Both nuns and mothers worship images,°
But those the candles light are not as those   50
That animate a mother's reveries,
But keep a marble or a bronze repose.
And yet they too break hearts—O Presences
That passion, piety or affection knows,
And that all heavenly glory symbolize—   55
O self-born mockers of man's enterprise;

8

Labour is blossoming or dancing where
The body is not bruised to pleasure soul,
Nor beauty born out of its own despair,
Nor blear-eyed wisdom out of midnight oil.   60

41–42. but . . . things: Plato thought that the world of nature is merely an appearance ("spume") that covers the world of ideal, spiritual and mathematical realities ("ghostly paradigm").
43–44. Solider . . . kings: Aristotle, who was tutor to Alexander the Great and presumably disciplined him by whippings ("played the taws"), was "solider" than Plato in that he believed that nature itself had reality.
45. Pythagoras: Greek philosopher (6th century B.C.E.) whose study of mathematics and music supposedly led to his discovery of the music of the spheres, the harmonies that hold the universe in order.
48. Old . . . bird: Yeats's dismissal of the three philosophers just named.
49. nuns . . . images: Nuns worship religious images; mothers worship mental images of their own children.

O chestnut-tree, great-rooted blossomer,
Are you the leaf, the blossom or the bole?°   *trunk*
O body swayed to music, O brightening glance,
How can we know the dancer from the dance?

[1928]

WILLIAM BUTLER YEATS   [1865–1939]

Sailing to Byzantium°

1

That is no country for old men. The young
In one another's arms, birds in the trees
— Those dying generations — at their song,
The salmon-falls, the mackerel-crowded seas,
Fish, flesh, or fowl, commend all summer long   5
Whatever is begotten, born, and dies.
Caught in that sensual music all neglect
Monuments of unaging intellect.

2

An aged man is but a paltry thing,
A tattered coat upon a stick, unless   10
Soul clap its hands and sing, and louder sing
For every tatter in its mortal dress,
Nor is there singing school but studying
Monuments of its own magnificence;
And therefore I have sailed the seas and come   15
To the holy city of Byzantium.

Sailing to Byzantium: Yeats wrote in *A Vision* (1925): "I think if I could be given a
month of Antiquity and leave to spend it where I chose, I would spend it in
Byzantium [modern Istanbul] a little before Justinian [ruled 527 to 565] opened
St. Sophia and closed the Academy of Plato. . . . I think that in early Byzantium,
and maybe never before or since in recorded history, religious, aesthetic and prac-
tical life were one, and that architect and artificers . . . spoke to the multitude and
the few alike. The painter and the mosaic worker, the worker in gold and silver, the
illuminator of Sacred Books were almost impersonal, almost perhaps without
the consciousness of individual design, absorbed in their subject matter and that
the vision of a whole people" (3.3). Byzantium becomes for Yeats a symbol of eternity, a place of perfection where the growth and change that characterize nature
and physical life do not occur.

3

O sages standing in God's holy fire
As in the gold mosaic of a wall,
Come from the holy fire, perne in a gyre,°
And be the singing-masters of my soul.   20
Consume my heart away; sick with desire
And fastened to a dying animal
It knows not what it is; and gather me
Into the artifice of eternity.

4

Once out of nature I shall never take   25
My bodily form from any natural thing,
But such a form as Grecian goldsmiths make
Of hammered gold and gold enamelling
To keep a drowsy Emperor awake;°
Or set upon a golden bough to sing   30
To lords and ladies of Byzantium
Of what is past, or passing, or to come.

[1928]

19. **gyre:** Whirl in a spiral motion (a *perne* is a spool or bobbin on which something is wound; a *gyre* is a spiral).
25–29. Yeats wrote in a note, "I have read somewhere that in the Emperor's
palace at Byzantium was a tree made of gold and silver, and artificial birds that
sang." He may have been thinking of Hans Christian Andersen's *The Emperor's
Nightingale.*

EDWIN ARLINGTON ROBINSON   [1869–1935]

Richard Cory

Whenever Richard Cory went down town,
We people on the pavement looked at him:
He was a gentleman from sole to crown,
Clean favored, and imperially slim.

And he was always quietly arrayed,   5
And he was always human when he talked;
But still he fluttered pulses when he said,
"Good-morning," and he glittered when he walked.

And he was rich—yes, richer than a king—
And admirably schooled in every grace: 10
In fine, we thought that he was everything
To make us wish that we were in his place.

So on we worked, and waited for the light,
And went without the meat, and cursed the bread;
And Richard Cory, one calm summer night,   15
Went home and put a bullet through his head.

[1897]

STEPHEN CRANE   [1871–1900]

Do not weep, maiden, for war is kind

Do not weep, maiden, for war is kind.
Because your lover threw wild hands toward the sky
And the affrighted steed ran on alone,
Do not weep.
War is kind.   5

    Hoarse, booming drums of the regiment,
    Little souls who thirst for fight,
    These men were born to drill and die.
    The unexplained glory flies above them,
    Great is the Battle-God, great, and his Kingdom—   10
    A field where a thousand corpses lie.

Do not weep, babe, for war is kind.
Because your father tumbled in the yellow trenches,
Raged at his breast, gulped and died,
Do not weep.   15
War is kind.

    Swift blazing flag of the regiment,
    Eagle with crest of red and gold,
    These men were born to drill and die.
    Point for them the virtue of slaughter,   20
    Make plain to them the excellence of killing
    And a field where a thousand corpses lie.

Mother whose heart hung humble as a button
On the bright splendid shroud of your son,

Do not weep.   25
War is kind.

[1899]

PAUL LAURENCE DUNBAR   [1872–1906]

We Wear the Mask

We wear the mask that grins and lies,
It hides our cheeks and shades our eyes, —
This debt we pay to human guile;
With torn and bleeding hearts we smile,
And mouth with myriad subtleties.   5

Why should the world be over-wise,
In counting all our tears and sighs?
Nay, let them only see us, while
    We wear the mask.

We smile, but, O great Christ, our cries   10
To thee from tortured souls arise.
We sing, but oh the clay is vile
Beneath our feet, and long the mile;
But let the world dream otherwise,
    We wear the mask!   15

[1896]

ROBERT FROST   [1874–1963]

After Apple-Picking

My long two-pointed ladder's sticking through a tree
Toward heaven still,
And there's a barrel that I didn't fill
Beside it, and there may be two or three
Apples I didn't pick upon some bough.   5
But I am done with apple-picking now.
Essence of winter sleep is on the night,
The scent of apples: I am drowsing off.
I cannot rub the strangeness from my sight

I got from looking through a pane of glass   10
I skimmed this morning from the drinking trough
And held against the world of hoary grass.
It melted, and I let it fall and break.
But I was well
Upon my way to sleep before it fell,   15
And I could tell
What form my dreaming was about to take.
Magnified apples appear and disappear,
Stem end and blossom end,
And every fleck of russet showing clear.   20
My instep arch not only keeps the ache,
It keeps the pressure of a ladder-round.
I feel the ladder sway as the boughs bend.
And I keep hearing from the cellar bin
The rumbling sound   25
Of load on load of apples coming in.
For I have had too much
Of apple-picking: I am overtired
Of the great harvest I myself desired.
There were ten thousand thousand fruit to touch,   30
Cherish in hand, lift down, and not let fall.
For all
That struck the earth,
No matter if not bruised or spiked with stubble,
Went surely to the cider-apple heap   35
As of no worth.
One can see what will trouble
This sleep of mine, whatever sleep it is.
Were he not gone,
The woodchuck could say whether it's like his   40
Long sleep, as I describe its coming on,
Or just some human sleep.

                                                                    [1914]

ROBERT FROST   [1874–1963]

The Road Not Taken

Two roads diverged in a yellow wood,
And sorry I could not travel both
And be one traveler, long I stood

And looked down one as far as I could
To where it bent in the undergrowth;   5

Then took the other, as just as fair,
And having perhaps the better claim,
Because it was grassy and wanted wear;
Though as for that, the passing there
Had worn them really about the same,   10

And both that morning equally lay
In leaves no step had trodden black.
Oh, I kept the first for another day!
Yet knowing how way leads on to way,
I doubted if I should ever come back.   15

I shall be telling this with a sigh
Somewhere ages and ages hence:
Two roads diverged in a wood, and I—
I took the one less traveled by,
And that has made all the difference.   20

[1916]

ROBERT FROST   [1874–1963]

Birches

When I see birches bend to left and right
Across the lines of straighter darker trees,
I like to think some boy's been swinging them.
But swinging doesn't bend them down to stay
As ice storms do. Often you must have seen them   5
Loaded with ice a sunny winter morning
After a rain. They click upon themselves
As the breeze rises, and turn many-colored
As the stir cracks and crazes their enamel.
Soon the sun's warmth makes them shed crystal shells   10
Shattering and avalanching on the snow crust—
Such heaps of broken glass to sweep away
You'd think the inner dome of heaven had fallen.
They are dragged to the withered bracken by the load,
And they seem not to break; though once they are bowed   15
So low for long, they never right themselves:
You may see their trunks arching in the woods

Years afterwards, trailing their leaves on the ground
Like girls on hands and knees that throw their hair
Before them over their heads to dry in the sun.   20
But I was going to say when Truth broke in
With all her matter of fact about the ice storm,
I should prefer to have some boy bend them
As he went out and in to fetch the cows—
Some boy too far from town to learn baseball,   25
Whose only play was what he found himself,
Summer or winter, and could play alone.
One by one he subdued his father's trees
By riding them down over and over again
Until he took the stiffness out of them,   30
And not one but hung limp, not one was left
For him to conquer. He learned all there was
To learn about not launching out too soon
And so not carrying the tree away
Clear to the ground. He always kept his poise   35
To the top branches, climbing carefully
With the same pains you use to fill a cup
Up to the brim, and even above the brim.
Then he flung outward, feet first, with a swish,
Kicking his way down through the air to the ground.   40
So was I once myself a swinger of birches.
And so I dream of going back to be.
It's when I'm weary of considerations,
And life is too much like a pathless wood
Where your face burns and tickles with the cobwebs   45
Broken across it, and one eye is weeping
From a twig's having lashed across it open.
I'd like to get away from earth awhile
And then come back to it and begin over.
May no fate willfully misunderstand me   50
And half grant what I wish and snatch me away
Not to return. Earth's the right place for love:
I don't know where it's likely to go better.
I'd like to go by climbing a birch tree,
And climb black branches up a snow-white trunk   55
Toward heaven, till the tree could bear no more,
But dipped its top and set me down again.
That would be good both going and coming back.
One could do worse than be a swinger of birches.

[1916]

ROBERT FROST   [1874–1963]

Stopping by Woods on a Snowy Evening

Whose woods these are I think I know.
His house is in the village, though;
He will not see me stopping here
To watch his woods fill up with snow.

My little horse must think it queer   5
To stop without a farmhouse near
Between the woods and frozen lake
The darkest evening of the year.

He gives his harness bells a shake
To ask if there is some mistake.   10
The only other sound's the sweep
Of easy wind and downy flake.

The woods are lovely, dark, and deep,
But I have promises to keep,
And miles to go before I sleep,   15
And miles to go before I sleep.

[1923]

GERTRUDE STEIN   [1874–1946]

Susie Asado

Sweet sweet sweet sweet sweet tea.
    Susie Asado.
Sweet sweet sweet sweet sweet tea.
    Susie Asado.
Susie Asado which is a told tray sure.   5
A lean on the shoe this means slips slips hers.
When the ancient light grey is clean it is yellow, it is a silver seller.
    This is a please this is a please there are the saids to jelly. These are
the wets these say the sets to leave a crown to Incy.
    Incy is short for incubus.   10
    A pot. A pot is a beginning of a rare bit of trees. Trees tremble, the
old vats are in bobbles, bobbles which shade and shove and render
clean, render clean must.

Drink pups.
Drink pups drink pups lease a sash hold, see it shine and a bobolink   15
has pins. It shows a nail.
What is a nail. A nail is unison.
Sweet sweet sweet sweet sweet tea.

[1913]

WALLACE STEVENS [1879–1955]

The Emperor of Ice-Cream

Call the roller of big cigars,
The muscular one, and bid him whip
In kitchen cups concupiscent curds.
Let the wenches dawdle in such dress
As they are used to wear, and let the boys   5
Bring flowers in last month's newspapers.
Let be be finale of seem.
The only emperor is the emperor of ice-cream.

Take from the dresser of deal.
Lacking the three glass knobs, that sheet   10
On which she embroidered fantails once
And spread it so as to cover her face.
If her horny feet protrude, they come
To show how cold she is, and dumb.
Let the lamp affix its beam.   15
The only emperor is the emperor of ice-cream.

[1923]

WALLACE STEVENS [1879–1955]

Disillusionment of Ten O'Clock

The houses are haunted
By white night-gowns.
None are green,
Or purple with green rings,
Or green with yellow rings,   5

Or yellow with blue rings.
None of them are strange,
With socks of lace
And beaded ceintures.°   *girdles*
People are not going   10
To dream of baboons and periwinkles.
Only, here and there, an old sailor,
Drunk and asleep in his boots,
Catches tigers
In red weather.   15

[1923]

WALLACE STEVENS   [1879–1955]

Sunday Morning

I

Complacencies of the peignoir,° and late   *negligee*
Coffee and oranges in a sunny chair,
And the green freedom of a cockatoo
Upon a rug mingle to dissipate
The holy hush of ancient sacrifice.   5
She dreams a little, and she feels the dark
Encroachment of that old catastrophe,
As a calm darkens among water-lights.
The pungent oranges and bright, green wings
Seem things in some procession of the dead,   10
Winding across wide water, without sound.
The day is like wide water, without sound,
Stilled for the passing of her dreaming feet
Over the seas, to silent Palestine,
Dominion of the blood and sepulchre.   15

II

Why should she give her bounty to the dead?
What is divinity if it can come
Only in silent shadows and in dreams?
Shall she not find in comforts of the sun,
In pungent fruit and bright, green wings, or else   20
In any balm or beauty of the earth,

Things to be cherished like the thought of heaven?
Divinity must live within herself:
Passions of rain, or moods in falling snow;
Grievings in loneliness, or unsubdued   25
Elations when the forest blooms; gusty
Emotions on wet roads on autumn nights;
All pleasures and all pains, remembering
The bough of summer and the winter branch.
These are the measures destined for her soul.   30

III

Jove in the clouds had his inhuman birth.
No mother suckled him, no sweet land gave
Large-mannered motions to his mythy mind
He moved among us, as a muttering king,
Magnificent, would move among his hinds,   35
Until our blood, commingling, virginal,
With heaven, brought such requital to desire
The very hinds discerned it, in a star.
Shall our blood fail? Or shall it come to be
The blood of paradise? And shall the earth   40
Seem all of paradise that we shall know?
The sky will be much friendlier then than now,
A part of labor and a part of pain,
And next in glory to enduring love,
Not this dividing and indifferent blue.   45

IV

She says, "I am content when wakened birds,
Before they fly, test the reality
Of misty fields, by their sweet questionings;
But when the birds are gone, and their warm fields
Return no more, where, then, is paradise?"   50
There is not any haunt of prophecy,
Nor any old chimera of the grave,
Neither the golden underground, nor isle
Melodious, where spirits gat° them home,   *got*
Nor visionary south, nor cloudy palm   55
Remote on heaven's hill, that has endured
As April's green endures; or will endure
Like her remembrance of awakened birds,
Or her desire for June and evening, tipped
By the consummation of the swallow's wings.   60

V

She says, "But in contentment I still feel
The need of some imperishable bliss."
Death is the mother of beauty; hence from her,
Alone, shall come fulfilment to our dreams
And our desires. Although she strews the leaves   65
Of sure obliteration on our paths,
The path sick sorrow took, the many paths
Where triumph rang its brassy phrase, or love
Whispered a little out of tenderness,
She makes the willow shiver in the sun   70
For maidens who were wont to sit and gaze
Upon the grass, relinquished to their feet.
She causes boys to pile new plums and pears
On disregarded plate. The maidens taste
And stray impassioned in the littering leaves.   75

VI

Is there no change of death in paradise?
Does ripe fruit never fall? Or do the boughs
Hang always heavy in that perfect sky,
Unchanging, yet so like our perishing earth,
With rivers like our own that seek for seas   80
They never find, the same receding shores
That never touch with inarticulate pang?
Why set the pear upon those river-banks
Or spice the shores with odors of the plum?
Alas, that they should wear our colors there,   85
The silken weavings of our afternoons,
And pick the strings of our insipid lutes!
Death is the mother of beauty, mystical,
Within whose burning bosom we devise
Our earthly mothers waiting, sleeplessly.   90

VII

Supple and turbulent, a ring of men
Shall chant in orgy on a summer morn
Their boisterous devotion to the sun,
Not as a god, but as a god might be,
Naked among them, like a savage source.   95
Their chant shall be a chant of paradise,
Out of their blood, returning to the sky;
And in their chant shall enter, voice by voice,

The windy lake wherein their lord delights,
The trees, like serafin,° and echoing hills,   *seraphim* 100
That choir among themselves long afterward.
They shall know well the heavenly fellowship
Of men that perish and of summer morn.
And whence they came and whither they shall go
The dew upon their feet shall manifest.   105

VIII

She hears, upon that water without sound,
A voice that cries, "The tomb in Palestine
Is not the porch of spirits lingering.
It is the grave of Jesus, where he lay."
We live in an old chaos of the sun,   110
Or old dependency of day and night,
Or island solitude, unsponsored, free,
Of that wide water, inescapable.
Deer walk upon our mountains, and the quail
Whistle about us their spontaneous cries;   115
Sweet berries ripen in the wilderness;
And, in the isolation of the sky,
At evening, casual flocks of pigeons make
Ambiguous undulations as they sink,
Downward to darkness, on extended wings.   120

[1923]

WILLIAM CARLOS WILLIAMS   [1883–1963]

The Red Wheelbarrow

so much depends
upon

a red wheel
barrow

glazed with rain   5
water

beside the white
chickens.

[1923]

WILLIAM CARLOS WILLIAMS   [1883–1963]

Spring and All

By the road to the contagious hospital
under the surge of the blue
mottled clouds driven from the
northeast—a cold wind. Beyond, the
waste of broad, muddy fields   5
brown with dried weeds, standing and fallen

patches of standing water
the scattering of tall trees

All along the road the reddish
purplish, forked, upstanding, twiggy   10
stuff of bushes and small trees
with dead, brown leaves under them
leafless vines—

Lifeless in appearance, sluggish
dazed spring approaches—   15

They enter the new world naked,
cold, uncertain of all
save that they enter. All about them
the cold, familiar wind—

Now the grass, tomorrow   20
the stiff curl of wildcarrot leaf

One by one objects are defined—
It quickens: clarity, outline of leaf

But now the stark dignity of
entrance—Still, the profound change   25
has come upon them: rooted, they
grip down and begin to awaken

[1923]

WILLIAM CARLOS WILLIAMS   [1883–1963]

This Is Just to Say

I have eaten
the plums
that were in
the icebox

and which   5
you were probably
saving
for breakfast

Forgive me
they were delicious   10
so sweet
and so cold

[1934]

EZRA POUND   [1885–1972]

The River-Merchant's Wife: A Letter

While my hair was still cut straight across my forehead
I played about the front gate, pulling flowers.
You came by on bamboo stilts, playing horse,
You walked about my seat, playing with blue plums.
And we went on living in the village of Chokan: 5
Two small people, without dislike or suspicion.

At fourteen I married My Lord you.
I never laughed, being bashful.
Lowering my head, I looked at the wall.
Called to, a thousand times, I never looked back.   10

At fifteen I stopped scowling,
I desired my dust to be mingled with yours
Forever and forever and forever.
Why should I climb the look out?

At sixteen you departed,   15
You went into far Ku-to-yen, by the river of swirling eddies,
And you have been gone five months.
The monkeys make sorrowful noise overhead.

You dragged your feet when you went out.
By the gate now, the moss is grown, the different mosses,   20
Too deep to clear them away!
The leaves fall early this autumn, in wind.
The paired butterflies are already yellow with August
Over the grass in the West garden;
They hurt me. I grow older.   25
If you are coming down through the narrows of the river Kiang,
Please let me know beforehand,
And I will come out to meet you
            As far as Cho-fu-Sa.

                                            By Rihaku°

                                            [1915]

By Rihaku: An adaptation of a Chinese poem by the famous poet Li Po (701–762
C.E.), whose Japanese name is Rihaku.

            H. D. [HILDA DOOLITTLE]   [1886–1961]

                        # Garden

I

You are clear
O rose, cut in rock,
hard as the descent of hail.

I could scrape the colour
from the petals   5
like spilt dye from a rock.

If I could break you
I could break a tree.

If I could stir
I could break a tree—   10
I could break you.

II

O wind, rend open the heat,
cut apart the heat,
rend it to tatters.

Fruit cannot drop   15
through this thick air—

fruit cannot fall into heat
that presses up and blunts
the points of pears
and rounds the grapes.   20

Cut the heat—
plough through it,
turning it on either side
of your path.

[1916]

MARIANNE MOORE [1887–1972]

Poetry

I, too, dislike it: there are things that are important beyond all this fiddle.
   Reading it, however, with a perfect contempt for it, one discovers in
   it after all, a place for the genuine.
      Hands that can grasp, eyes
      that can dilate, hair that can rise   5
         if it must, these things are important not because a

high-sounding interpretation can be put upon them but because they are
   useful. When they become so derivative as to become unintelligible,
   the same thing may be said for all of us, that we
      do not admire what   10
      we cannot understand: the bat
         holding on upside down or in quest of something to

eat, elephants pushing, a wild horse taking a roll, a tireless wolf under
   a tree, the immovable critic twitching his skin like a horse that feels a
                             flea, the base-
   ball fan, the statistician—   15
      nor is it valid
         to discriminate against "business documents and

school-books"; all these phenomena are important. One must make a
                            distinction
   however: when dragged into prominence by half poets, the result is
                            not poetry,
   nor till the poets among us can be   20
      "literalists of
      the imagination"—above
         insolence and triviality and can present

for inspection, "imaginary gardens with real toads in them," shall we
                                            have
    it. In the meantime, if you demand on the one hand,   25
    the raw material of poetry in
        all its rawness and
        that which is on the other hand
            genuine, you are interested in poetry.

[1921]

EDITH SITWELL   [1887–1964]

Lullaby

Though the world has slipped and gone,
Sounds my loud discordant cry
Like the steel birds' song on high:
"Still one thing is left—the Bone!"
Then out danced the Babioun.°   *baboon*   5

She sat in the hollow of the sea—
A socket whence the eye's put out—
She sang to the child a lullaby
(The steel birds' nest was thereabout).

"Do, do, do, do—   10
Thy mother's hied to the vaster race:
The Pterodactyl made its nest
And laid a steel egg in her breast—
Under the Judas-colored sun.
She'll work no more, nor dance, nor moan,   15
And I am come to take her place
Do, do.

There's nothing left but earth's low bed—
(The Pterodactyl fouls its nest):
But steel wings fan thee to thy rest,   20
And wingless truth and larvae lie
And eyeless hope and handless fear—
All these for thee as toys are spread,
Do—do—

Red is the bed of Poland, Spain,   25
And thy mother's breast, who has grown wise
In that fouled nest. If she could rise.

Give birth again,
In wolfish pelt she'd hide thy bones
To shield thee from the world's long cold,   30
And down on all fours shouldst thou crawl
For thus from no height canst thou fall—
Do, do.

She'd give no hands: there's nought to hold
And nought to make: there's dust to sift,   35
But no food for the hands to lift.
Do, do.

Heed my ragged lullaby,
Fear not living, fear not chance;
All is equal—blindness, sight,   40
There is no depth, there is no height:
Do, do.

The Judas-colored sun is gone,
And with the Ape thou art alone—
Do,   45
    Do."

[1942]

ROBINSON JEFFERS   [1887–1962]

Hurt Hawks

I

The broken pillar of the wing jags from the clotted shoulder,
The wing trails like a banner in defeat,
No more to use the sky forever but live with famine
And pain a few days: cat nor coyote
Will shorten the week of waiting for death, there is game without talons.   5
He stands under the oak-bush and waits
The lame feet of salvation; at night he remembers freedom
And flies in a dream, the dawns ruin it.
He is strong and pain is worse to the strong, incapacity is worse.
The curs of the day come and torment him   10
At distance, no one but death the redeemer will humble that head,
The intrepid readiness, the terrible eyes.
The wild God of the world is sometimes merciful to those
That ask mercy, not often to the arrogant.

You do not know him, you communal people, or you have forgotten him;   15
Intemperate and savage, the hawk remembers him;
Beautiful and wild, the hawks, and men that are dying, remember him.

II

I'd sooner, except the penalties, kill a man than a hawk; but the great
    redtail
Had nothing left but unable misery
From the bone too shattered for mending, the wing that trailed under
    his talons when he moved.   20
We had fed him six weeks, I gave him freedom,
He wandered over the foreland hill and returned in the evening, asking
    for death,
Not like a beggar, still eyed with the old
Implacable arrogance. I gave him the lead gift in the twilight. What fell
    was relaxed,   25
Owl-downy, soft feminine feathers; but what
Soared: the fierce rush: the night-herons by the flooded river cried fear
    at its rising
Before it was quite unsheathed from reality.

[1928]

T. S. ELIOT   [1888–1965]

The Love Song of J. Alfred Prufrock

S'io credesse che mia risposta fosse
A persona che mai tornasse al mondo,
Questa fiamma staria senza piu scosse.
Ma perciocche giammai di questo fondo
Non torno vivo alcun, s'i'odo il vero,
Senza tema d'infamia ti rispondo.°

Epigraph: "If I thought that my answer were being made to someone who would
ever return to earth, this flame would remain without further movement; but
since no one has ever returned alive from this depth, if what I hear is true, I
answer you without fear of infamy" (Dante, *Inferno* 27.61–66). Dante encounters
Guido de Montefeltro in the eighth circle of hell, where souls are trapped within
flames (tongues of fire) as punishment for giving evil counsel. Guido tells Dante
details about his evil life only because he assumes that Dante is on his way to an
even deeper circle in hell and will never return to earth and be able to repeat what
he has heard.

Let us go then, you and I,
When the evening is spread out against the sky
Like a patient etherised upon a table;
Let us go, through certain half-deserted streets,
The muttering retreats   5
Of restless nights in one-night cheap hotels
And sawdust restaurants with oyster-shells:
Streets that follow like a tedious argument
Of insidious intent
To lead you to an overwhelming question . . .   10
Oh, do not ask, "What is it?"
Let us go and make our visit.

  In the room the women come and go
Talking of Michelangelo.

  The yellow fog that rubs its back upon the window-panes,   15
The yellow smoke that rubs its muzzle on the window-panes
Licked its tongue into the corners of the evening,
Lingered upon the pools that stand in drains,
Let fall upon its back the soot that falls from chimneys,
Slipped by the terrace, made a sudden leap,   20
And seeing that it was a soft October night,
Curled once about the house, and fell asleep.

  And indeed there will be time
For the yellow smoke that slides along the street,
Rubbing its back upon the window-panes;   25
There will be time, there will be time
To prepare a face to meet the faces that you meet;
There will be time to murder and create,
And time for all the works and days° of hands
That lift and drop a question on your plate;   30
Time for you and time for me,
And time yet for a hundred indecisions,
And for a hundred visions and revisions,
Before the taking of a toast and tea.

  In the room the women come and go   35
Talking of Michelangelo.

  And indeed there will be time
To wonder, "Do I dare?" and, "Do I dare?"

29. works and days: *Works and Days* is the title of a didactic poem about farming
by the Greek poet Hesiod (eighth century B.C.E.) that includes instruction about
doing each task at the proper time.

Time to turn back and descend the stair,
With a bald spot in the middle of my hair—   40
[They will say: "How his hair is growing thin!"]
My morning coat, my collar mounting firmly to the chin,
My necktie rich and modest, but asserted by a simple pin—
[They will say: "But how his arms and legs are thin!"]
Do I dare   45
Disturb the universe?
In a minute there is time
For decisions and revisions which a minute will reverse.

    For I have known them all already, known them all:—
Have known the evenings, mornings, afternoons,   50
I have measured out my life with coffee spoons;
I know the voices dying with a dying fall°
Beneath the music from a farther room.
    So how should I presume?

    And I have known the eyes already, known them all—   55
The eyes that fix you in a formulated phrase,
And when I am formulated, sprawling on a pin,
When I am pinned and wriggling on the wall,
Then how should I begin
To spit out all the butt-ends of my days and ways?   60
    And how should I presume?

    And I have known the arms already, known them all—
Arms that are braceleted and white and bare
[But in the lamplight, downed with light brown hair!]
Is it perfume from a dress   65
That makes me so digress?
Arms that lie along a table, or wrap about a shawl.
    And should I then presume?
    And how should I begin?

          •   •   •

Shall I say, I have gone at dusk through narrow streets   70
And watched the smoke that rises from the pipes
Of lonely men in shirt-sleeves, leaning out of windows? . . .

    I should have been a pair of ragged claws
Scuttling across the floors of silent seas.

          •   •   •

52. a dying fall: An allusion to Shakespeare's *Twelfth Night* (1.1.4): "That strain
[of music] again! It had a dying fall" (a cadence that falls away).

And the afternoon, the evening, sleeps so peacefully!   75
Smoothed by long fingers,
Asleep . . . tired . . . or it malingers,
Stretched on the floor, here beside you and me.
Should I, after tea and cakes and ices,
Have the strength to force the moment to its crisis?   80
But though I have wept and fasted, wept and prayed,
Though I have seen my head [grown slightly bald] brought in upon a
      platter,°
I am no prophet—and here's no great matter;
I have seen the moment of my greatness flicker,
And I have seen the eternal Footman hold my coat, and snicker,   85
And in short, I was afraid.

And would it have been worth it, after all,
After the cups, the marmalade, the tea,
Among the porcelain, among some talk of you and me,
Would it have been worth while,   90
To have bitten off the matter with a smile,
To have squeezed the universe into a ball
To roll it toward some overwhelming question,
To say: "I am Lazarus,° come from the dead,
Come back to tell you all, I shall tell you all"—   95
If one, settling a pillow by her head,
    Should say: "That is not what I meant at all.
    That is not it, at all."

And would it have been worth it, after all,
Would it have been worth while,   100
After the sunsets and the dooryards and the sprinkled streets,
After the novels, after the teacups, after the skirts that trail along the
      floor—
And this, and so much more?—
It is impossible to say just what I mean!
But as if a magic lantern threw the nerves in patterns on a screen: 105
Would it have been worth while
If one, settling a pillow or throwing off a shawl,
And turning toward the window, should say:

---

82. head . . . platter: As a reward for dancing before King Herod, Salome, his
stepdaughter, asked for the head of John the Baptist to be presented to her on a
platter (Matthew 14:1–12; Mark 6:17–28).
94. Lazarus: Either the beggar Lazarus, who in Luke 16:19–31 did not return
from the dead, or Jesus' friend Lazarus, who did (John 11:1–44).

"That is not it at all,
That is not what I meant, at all."   110

· · ·

No! I am not Prince Hamlet, nor was meant to be;
Am an attendant lord, one that will do
To swell a progress,° start a scene or two,
Advise the prince; no doubt, an easy tool,
Deferential, glad to be of use,   115
Politic, cautious, and meticulous;
Full of high sentence,° but a bit obtuse;   *sententiousness*
At times, indeed, almost ridiculous—
Almost, at times, the Fool.

I grow old . . . I grow old . . .   120
I shall wear the bottoms of my trousers rolled.°   *turned up, with cuffs*

Shall I part my hair behind? Do I dare to eat a peach?
I shall wear white flannel trousers, and walk upon the beach.
I have heard the mermaids singing, each to each.

I do not think that they will sing to me.   125

I have seen them riding seaward on the waves
Combing the white hair of the waves blown back
When the wind blows the water white and black.

We have lingered in the chambers of the sea
By sea-girls wreathed with seaweed red and brown   130
Till human voices wake us, and we drown.

[1917]

113. **progress:** Ceremonial journey made by a royal court.

T. S. ELIOT   [1888–1965]

Preludes

I

The winter evening settles down
With smell of steaks in passageways.
Six o'clock.
The burnt-out ends of smoky days.

And now a gusty shower wraps   5
The grimy scraps
Of withered leaves about your feet
And newspapers from vacant lots;
The showers beat
On broken blinds and chimney-pots,   10
And at the corner of the street
A lonely cab-horse steams and stamps.
And then the lighting of the lamps.

II

The morning comes to consciousness
Of faint stale smells of beer   15
From the sawdust-trampled street
With all its muddy feet that press
To early coffee-stands.
With the other masquerades
That time resumes,   20
One thinks of all the hands
That are raising dingy shades
In a thousand furnished rooms.

III

You tossed a blanket from the bed,
You lay upon your back, and waited;   25
You dozed, and watched the night revealing
The thousand sordid images
Of which your soul was constituted;
They flickered against the ceiling.
And when all the world came back   30
And the light crept up between the shutters
And you heard the sparrows in the gutters,
You had such a vision of the street
As the street hardly understands;
Sitting along the bed's edge, where   35
You curled the papers from your hair,
Or clasped the yellow soles of feet
In the palms of both soiled hands.

IV

His soul stretched tight across the skies
That fade behind a city block,   40
Or trampled by insistent feet

At four and five and six o'clock;
And short square fingers stuffing pipes,
And evening newspapers, and eyes
Assured of certain certainties,   45
The conscience of a blackened street
Impatient to assume the world.

   I am moved by fancies that are curled
Around these images, and cling:
The notion of some infinitely gentle   50
Infinitely suffering thing.

   Wipe your hand across your mouth, and laugh;
The worlds revolve like ancient women
Gathering fuel in vacant lots.

                                 [1917]

JOHN CROWE RANSOM   [1888–1974]

Bells for John Whiteside's Daughter

There was such speed in her little body,
And such lightness in her footfall,
It is no wonder her brown study°
Astonishes us all.

Her wars were bruited in our high window.   5
We looked among orchard trees and beyond
Where she took arms against her shadow,
Or harried unto the pond

The lazy geese, like a snow cloud
Dripping their snow on the green grass,   10
Tricking and stopping, sleepy and proud,
Who cried in goose, Alas,

For the tireless heart within the little
Lady with rod that made them rise
From their noon apple-dreams and scuttle   15
Goose-fashion under the skies!

---

3. **brown study:** Being deeply absorbed in one's thoughts; reverie.

But now go the bells, and we are ready,
In one house we are sternly stopped   20
To say we are vexed at her brown study,
Lying so primly propped.

                                                    [1924]

CLAUDE McKAY   [1890–1948]

America

Although she feeds me bread of bitterness,
And sinks into my throat her tiger's tooth,
Stealing my breath of life, I will confess
I love this cultured hell that tests my youth!
Her vigor flows like tides into my blood,   5
Giving me strength erect against her hate.
Her bigness sweeps my being like a flood.
Yet as a rebel fronts a king in state,
I stand within her walls with not a shred
Of terror, malice, not a word of jeer.   10
Darkly I gaze into the days ahead,
And see her might and granite wonders there,
Beneath the touch of Time's unerring hand,
Like priceless treasures sinking in the sand.

                                                    [1922]

EDNA ST. VINCENT MILLAY   [1892–1950]

Wild Swans

I looked in my heart while the wild swans went over.
And what did I see I had not seen before?
Only a question less or a question more;
Nothing to match the flight of wild birds flying.
Tiresome heart, forever living and dying,   5
House without air, I leave you and lock your door.
Wild swans, come over the town, come over
The town again, trailing your legs and crying!

                                                    [1921]

WILFRED OWEN   [1893–1918]

Dulce et Decorum Est

Bent double, like old beggars under sacks,
Knock-kneed, coughing like hags, we cursed through sludge,
Till on the haunting flares we turned our backs
And towards our distant rest began to trudge.
Men marched asleep. Many had lost their boots   5
But limped on, blood-shod. All went lame; all blind;
Drunk with fatigue; deaf even to the hoots
Of tired, outstripped Five-Nines° that dropped behind.

Gas! GAS! Quick, boys!—An ecstasy of fumbling,
Fitting the clumsy helmets just in time;   10
But someone still was yelling out and stumbling
And flound'ring like a man in fire or lime . . .
Dim, through the misty panes° and thick green light,   *of a gas mask*
As under a green sea, I saw him drowning.

In all my dreams, before my helpless sight,   15
He plunges at me, guttering, choking, drowning.

If in some smothering dreams you too could pace
Behind the wagon that we flung him in,
And watch the white eyes writhing in his face,
His hanging face, like a devil's sick of sin;   20
If you could hear, at every jolt, the blood
Come gargling from the froth-corrupted lungs,
Obscene as cancer, bitter as the cud
Of vile, incurable sores on innocent tongues,—
My friend, you would not tell with such high zest   25
To children ardent for some desperate glory,
The old Lie: Dulce et decorum est
Pro patria mori.°

[1920]

8. **Five-Nines:** 5.9-inch caliber shells.
27–28. **Dulce . . . mori:** It is sweet and fitting / to die for one's country (Horace, *Odes* 3.12.13).

E. E. CUMMINGS [1894–1962]

in Just-

in Just-
spring   when the world is mud-
luscious the little
lame balloonman

whistles   far   and wee   5

and eddieandbill come
running from marbles and
piracies and it's
spring

when the world is puddle-wonderful   10

the queer
old balloonman whistles
far   and   wee
and bettyandisbel come dancing

from hop-scotch and jump-rope and   15

it's
spring
and
  the

    goat-footed   20

balloonMan   whistles
far
and
wee

[1923]

E. E. CUMMINGS [1894–1962]

pity this busy monster,manunkind

pity this busy monster,manunkind,

not. Progress is a comfortable disease:
your victim(death and life safely beyond)

plays with the bigness of his littleness
—electrons deify one razorblade   5
into a mountainrange;lenses extend

unwish through curving wherewhen till unwish
returns on its unself.

A world of made
is not a world of born—pity poor flesh   10

and trees,poor stars and stones,but never this
fine specimen of hypermagical

ultraomnipotence. We doctors know

a hopeless case if—listen:there's a hell
of a good universe next door;let's go   15

[1944]

JEAN TOOMER   [1894–1967]

Reapers

Black reapers with the sound of steel on stones
Are sharpening scythes. I see them place the hones
In their hip-pockets as a thing that's done.
And start their silent swinging, one by one.
Black horses drive a mower through the weeds.   5
And there, a field rat, startled, squealing bleeds.
His belly close to ground. I see the blade,
Blood-stained, continue cutting weeds and shade.

[1923]

LOUISE BOGAN   [1897–1970]

Women

Women have no wilderness in them,
They are provident instead,
Content in the tight hot cell of their hearts
To eat dusty bread.

They do not see cattle cropping red winter grass,   5
They do not hear
Snow water going down under culverts
Shallow and clear.

They wait, when they should turn to journeys,
They stiffen, when they should bend.   10
They use against themselves that benevolence
To which no man is friend.

They cannot think of so many crops to a field
Or of clean wood cleft by an axe.
Their love is an eager meaninglessness   15
Too tense, or too lax.

They hear in every whisper that speaks to them
A shout and a cry.
As like as not, when they take life over their door-sills
They should let it go by.   20

[1923]

HART CRANE   [1899–1932]

My Grandmother's Love Letters

There are no stars tonight
But those of memory.
Yet how much room for memory there is
In the loose girdle of soft rain.

There is even room enough   5
For the letters of my mother's mother,
Elizabeth,
That have been pressed so long
Into a corner of the roof
That they are brown and soft,   10
And liable to melt as snow.

Over the greatness of such space
Steps must be gentle.
It is all hung by an invisible white hair.
It trembles as birch limbs webbing the air.   15

And I ask myself:

"Are your fingers long enough to play
Old keys that are but echoes:
Is the silence strong enough
To carry back the music to its source   20
And back to you again
As though to her?"

Yet I would lead my grandmother by the hand
Through much of what she would not understand;
And so I stumble. And the rain continues on the roof   25
With such a sound of gently pitying laughter.

[1926]

STERLING A. BROWN   [1901–1989]

Riverbank Blues

A man git his feet set in a sticky mudbank,
A man git dis yellow water in his blood,
No need for hopin', no need for doin',
Muddy streams keep him fixed for good.

Little Muddy, Big Muddy, Moreau and Osage,   5
Little Mary's, Big Mary's, Cedar Creek,
Flood deir muddy water roundabout a man's roots,
Keep him soaked and stranded and git him weak.

Lazy sun shinin' on a little cabin,
Lazy moon glistenin' over river trees;   10
Ole river whisperin', lappin' 'gainst de long roots:
"Plenty of rest and peace in these. . . ."

Big mules, black loam, apple and peach trees,
But seems lak de river washes us down
Past de rich farms, away from de fat lands,   15
Dumps us in some ornery riverbank town.

Went down to the river, sot me down an' listened,
Heard de water talkin' quiet, quiet lak an' slow:
"Ain' no need fo' hurry, take yo' time, take yo' time. . . ."
Heard it sayin'—*"Baby, hyeahs de way life go. . . ."*   20

Dat is what it tole me as I watched it slowly rollin',
But somp'n way inside me rared up an' say,
"Better be movin'. . . better be travelin'. . .
Riverbank'll git you ef you stay. . . ."

Towns are sinkin' deeper, deeper in de riverbank,   25
Takin' on de ways of deir sulky Ole Man—
Takin' on his creepy ways, takin' on his evil ways,
"Bes' git way, a long way . . . whiles you can.

"Man got his sea too lak de Mississippi
Ain't got so long for a whole lot longer way,   30
Man better move some, better not git rooted
Muddy water fool you, ef you stay. . . ."

[1932]

LANGSTON HUGHES   [1902–1967]

The Negro Speaks of Rivers

I've known rivers:
I've known rivers ancient as the world and older than the flow of human
    blood in human veins.

My soul has grown deep like the rivers.

I bathed in the Euphrates when dawns were young.
I built my hut near the Congo and it lulled me to sleep.   5
I looked upon the Nile and raised the pyramids above it.
I heard the singing of the Mississippi when Abe Lincoln went down to
    New Orleans, and I've seen its muddy bosom turn all golden in the
    sunset.

I've known rivers:
Ancient, dusky rivers.

My soul has grown deep like the rivers.   10

[1926]

LANGSTON HUGHES   [1902–1967]

Harlem

What happens to a dream deferred?

Does it dry up
like a raisin in the sun?
Or fester like a sore —
And then run?   5
Does it stink like rotten meat?
Or crust and sugar over —
like a syrupy sweet?

Maybe it just sags
like a heavy load.   10

Or does it explode?

[1951]

COUNTEE CULLEN   [1903–1946]

Incident

for Eric Walrond

Once riding in old Baltimore,
    Heart-filled, head-filled with glee,
I saw a Baltimorean
    Keep looking straight at me.

Now I was eight and very small,   5
    And he was no whit bigger,
And so I smiled, but he poked out
    His tongue, and called me, "Nigger."

I saw the whole of Baltimore
    From May until December;   10
Of all the things that happened there
    That's all that I remember.

[1925]

LOUIS ZUKOFSKY   [1904–1978]

From "A" 15

An
  hinny
by
  stallion
out of   5
  she-ass

He neigh ha lie low h'who y'he gall mood
So roar cruel hire
Lo to achieve an eye leer rot off
Mass th'lo low o loam echo   10
How deal me many coeval yammer
Naked on face of white rock — sea.
Then I said: Liveforever my nest
Is arable hymn
Shore she root to water   15
Dew anew to branch.

Wind: Yahweh° at Iyyob°   *Israel's deity/Job*
Mien His roar "Why yammer
Measly make short hates oh
By milling bleat doubt?   20
Eye sore gnaw key heaver haul its core
Weigh as I lug where hide any?
If you — had you towed beside the roots?
How goad Him — you'd do it by now —
My sum My made day a key to daw?   25
O Me not there allheal — a cave.

All mouth deny hot bough?
O Me you're raw — Heaven pinned Dawn stars
Brine I heard choir and weigh by care —
Why your ear would call by now Elohim:°   *Hebrew for God* 30
Where was soak — bid lot tie in hum —
How would you have known to hum
How would you all oats rose snow lay
Assáy how'd a rock light rollick ore
Had the rush in you curb, ah bay,   35
Bay the shophar yammer *heigh horse*"

Wind: Yahweh at Iyyob "Why yammer,"
Wind: Iyyob at Yahweh, "Why yammer
How cold the mouth achieved echo."
Wind: Yahweh at Iyyob "Why yammer   40
Ha neigh now behēmoth° and share I see see your make   *beast*
Giddy pair—stones—whose rages go
Weigh raw all gay where how spill lay who"
Wind: Iyyob
"Rain without sun hated? *hurt no one*   45
In two we shadow, how hide any."

The traffic below,
sound of it a wind
eleven stories
below: *The Parkway*   50
no parking there ever:
the deaths as
after it might be said
"ordered," the one
the two old   55
songsters would not
live to see—
the death of
the young man,
who had possibly   60
alleviated
the death of
the oldest
vagrantly back he
might have thought   65
from vying culturally
with the Russian
Puritan Bear—
to vagary of
Bear hug and King   70
Charles° losing his head—   *Charles I of England*
and the other
a decade younger
never international
emissary   75
at least not
for his President,
aged in a suburb

dying maundering
the language—   80
American—impatient now
sometimes extreme clarity—
to hurrȳ
his compost
to the hill   85
his grave—
(distance
   a gastank)

he would
miss   90
living thru the
assassination

[1978]

STANLEY KUNITZ   [b. 1905]

Father and Son

Now in the suburbs and the falling light
I followed him, and now down sandy road
Whiter than bone-dust, through the sweet
Curdle of fields, where the plums
Dropped with their load of ripeness, one by one.   5
Mile after mile I followed, with skimming feet,
After the secret master of my blood,
Him, steeped in the odor of ponds, whose indomitable love
Kept me in chains. Strode years; stretched into bird;
Raced through the sleeping country where I was young,   10
The silence unrolling before me as I came,
The night nailed like an orange to my brow.

How should I tell him my fable and the fears,
How bridge the chasm in a casual tone,
Saying, "The house, the stucco one you built,   15
We lost. Sister married and went from home,
And nothing comes back, it's strange, from where she goes.
I lived on a hill that had too many rooms:
Light we could make, but not enough of warmth,

And when the light failed, I climbed under the hill.   20
The papers are delivered every day;
I am alone and never shed a tear."

At the water's edge, where the smothering ferns lifted
Their arms, "Father!" I cried, "Return! You know
The way. I'll wipe the mudstains from your clothes;   25
No trace, I promise, will remain. Instruct
Your son, whirling between two wars,
In the Gemara° of your gentleness,
For I would be a child to those who mourn
And brother to the foundlings of the field   30
And friend of innocence and all bright eyes.
O teach me how to work and keep me kind."

Among the turtles and the lilies he turned to me
The white ignorant hollow of his face.

[1944]

28. **Gemara:** The second division of the Talmud; it is a commentary on Jewish
civil and religious laws.

W. H. AUDEN   [1907–1973]

As I Walked Out One Evening

As I walked out one evening,
  Walking down Bristol Street,
The crowds upon the pavement
  Were fields of harvest wheat.

And down by the brimming river   5
  I heard a lover sing
Under an arch of the railway:
  "Love has no ending.

"I'll love you, dear, I'll love you
  Till China and Africa meet,   10
And the river jumps over the mountain
  And the salmon sing in the street,

"I'll love you till the ocean
  Is folded and hung up to dry

And the seven stars° go squawking   15
   Like geese about the sky.

The years shall run like rabbits,
   For in my arms I hold
The Flower of the Ages,
   And the first love of the world."   20

But all the clocks in the city
   Began to whirr and chime:
"O let not Time deceive you,
   You cannot conquer Time.

"In the burrows of the Nightmare   25
   Where Justice naked is,
Time watches from the shadow
   And coughs when you would kiss.

"In headaches and in worry
   Vaguely life leaks away,   30
And Time will have his fancy
   To-morrow or to-day.

"Into many a green valley
   Drifts the appalling snow;
Time breaks the threaded dances   35
   And the diver's brilliant bow.

"O plunge your hands in water,
   Plunge them in up to the wrist;
Stare, stare in the basin
   And wonder what you've missed.   40

"The glacier knocks in the cupboard,
   The desert sighs in the bed,
And the crack in the tea-cup opens
   A lane to the land of the dead.

"Where the beggars raffle the banknotes°   45
   And the Giant° is enchanting to Jack,

---

15. **the seven stars:** An echo of the traditional counting song "Green Grow the Rushes, O": "What are your seven, O? / Seven for the seven stars in the sky."
45–48. **"Where the beggars . . .":** This stanza alludes to and—through social satire and sexual innuendo—inverts the milieu of nursery rhymes and a counting song.
46. **Giant:** From the fairy tale "Jack the Giant-Killer."

And the Lily-white Boy° is a Roarer,°
And Jill° goes down on her back.

"O look, look in the mirror,
  O look in your distress;   50
Life remains a blessing
  Although you cannot bless.

"O stand, stand at the window
  As the tears scald and start;
You shall love your crooked neighbour   55
  With your crooked heart."°

It was late, late in the evening,
  The lovers they were gone;
The clocks had ceased their chiming,
  And the deep river ran on.   60

[1937]

47. Lily-white Boy: Echoing "Green Grow the Rushes, O": "What are your two,
O? / Two, two the lily-white boys / Clothed all in green, O"; **Roarer:** Hell raiser.
48. Jill: From the nursery rhyme "Jack and Jill."
55–56. "You . . . heart.": Perhaps a distorted conflation of Matthew 22:37 and
22:39: "Thou shalt love the Lord thy God with all thy heart . . . [and] thy neighbor
as thyself."

W. H. AUDEN   [1907–1973]

Musée des Beaux Arts°

About suffering they were never wrong,
The Old Masters: how well they understood
Its human position; how it takes place
While someone else is eating or opening a window or just walking dully
  along;
How, when the aged are reverently, passionately waiting   5
For the miraculous birth, there always must be

Musée des Beaux Arts: The painting *Landscape with the Fall of Icarus* by Pieter
Brueghel the Elder, on which the poem is based, is in the Musées Royaux des
Beaux-Arts in Brussels.

Brueghel, *Landscape with the Fall of Icarus*

Children who did not specially want it to happen, skating
On a pond at the edge of the wood:
They never forgot
That even the dreadful martyrdom must run its course   10
Anyhow in a corner, some untidy spot
Where the dogs go on with their doggy life and the torturer's horse
Scratches its innocent behind on a tree.

In Breughel's *Icarus,* for instance: how everything turns away
Quite leisurely from the disaster; the ploughman may   15
Have heard the splash, the forsaken cry,
But for him it was not an important failure; the sun shone
As it had to on the white legs disappearing into the green
Water; and the expensive delicate ship that must have seen
Something amazing, a boy falling out of the sky,   20
Had somewhere to get to and sailed calmly on.

[1940]

THEODORE ROETHKE   [1908–1963]

My Papa's Waltz

The whiskey on your breath
Could make a small boy dizzy;
But I hung on like death:
Such waltzing was not easy.

We romped until the pans   5
Slid from the kitchen shelf;
My mother's countenance
Could not unfrown itself.

The hand that held my wrist
Was battered on one knuckle;   10
At every step you missed
My right ear scraped a buckle.

You beat time on my head
With a palm caked hard by dirt,
Then waltzed me off to bed   15
Still clinging to your shirt.

[1948]

GEORGE OPPEN   [1908–1984]

The Forms of Love

Parked in the fields
All night
So many years ago,
We saw
A lake beside us   5
When the moon rose.
I remember

Leaving that ancient car
Together. I remember
Standing in the white grass   10
Beside it. We groped
Our way together

Downhill in the bright
Incredible light

Beginning to wonder   15
Whether it could be lake
Or fog
We saw, our heads
Ringing under the stars. We walked
To where it would have wet our feet   20
Had it been water

[1965]

ELIZABETH BISHOP   [1911–1979]

The Fish

I caught a tremendous fish
and held him beside the boat
half out of water, with my hook
fast in a corner of his mouth.
He didn't fight.   5
He hadn't fought at all.
He hung a grunting weight,
battered and venerable
and homely. Here and there
his brown skin hung in strips   10
like ancient wallpaper,
and its pattern of darker brown
was like wallpaper:
shapes like full-blown roses
stained and lost through age.   15
He was speckled with barnacles,
fine rosettes of lime,
and infested
with tiny white sea-lice,
and underneath two or three   20
rags of green weed hung down.
While his gills were breathing in
the terrible oxygen
—the frightening gills,
fresh and crisp with blood,   25

that can cut so badly—
I thought of the coarse white flesh
packed in like feathers,
the big bones and the little bones,
the dramatic reds and blacks   30
of his shiny entrails,
and the pink swim-bladder
like a big peony.
I looked into his eyes
which were far larger than mine   35
but shallower, and yellowed,
the irises backed and packed
with tarnished tinfoil
seen through the lenses
of old scratched isinglass.°   *transparent sheet of mica* 40
They shifted a little, but not
to return my stare.
—It was more like the tipping
of an object toward the light.
I admired his sullen face,   45
the mechanism of his jaw,
and then I saw
that from his lower lip
—if you could call it a lip—
grim, wet, and weaponlike,   50
hung five old pieces of fish-line,
or four and a wire leader
with the swivel still attached,
with all their five big hooks
grown firmly in his mouth.   55
A green line, frayed at the end
where he broke it, two heavier lines,
and a fine black thread
still crimped from the strain and snap
when it broke and he got away.   60
Like medals with their ribbons
frayed and wavering,
a five-haired beard of wisdom
trailing from his aching jaw.
I stared and stared   65
and victory filled up
the little rented boat,
from the pool of bilge

where oil had spread a rainbow
around the rusted engine   70
to the bailer rusted orange,
the sun-cracked thwarts,
the oarlocks on their strings,
the gunnels—until everything
was rainbow, rainbow, rainbow!   75
And I let the fish go.

[1946]

ELIZABETH BISHOP   [1911–1979]

One Art

The art of losing isn't hard to master;
so many things seem filled with the intent
to be lost that their loss is no disaster.

Lose something every day. Accept the fluster
of lost door keys, the hour badly spent.   5
The art of losing isn't hard to master.

Then practice losing farther, losing faster:
places, and names, and where it was you meant
to travel. None of these will bring disaster.

I lost my mother's watch. And look! my last, or   10
next-to-last, of three loved houses went.
The art of losing isn't hard to master.

I lost two cities, lovely ones. And, vaster,
some realms I owned, two rivers, a continent.
I miss them, but it wasn't a disaster.   15

—Even losing you (the joking voice, a gesture
I love) I shan't have lied. It's evident
the art of losing's not too hard to master
though it may look like (*Write* it!) like disaster.

[1976]

JOHN FREDERICK NIMS   [1913–1999]

Love Poem

My clumsiest dear, whose hands shipwreck vases,
At whose quick touch all glasses chip and ring,
Whose palms are bulls in china, burs in linen,
And have no cunning with any soft thing

Except all ill-at-ease fidgeting people: 5
The refugee uncertain at the door
You make at home; deftly you steady
The drunk clambering on his undulant floor.

Unpredictable dear, the taxi drivers' terror,
Shrinking from far headlights pale as a dime   10
Yet leaping before red apoplectic streetcars—
Misfit in any space. And never on time.

A wrench in clocks and the solar system. Only
With words and people and love you move at ease;
In traffic of wit expertly maneuver   15
And keep us, all devotion, at your knees.

Forgetting your coffee spreading on our flannel,
Your lipstick grinning on our coat,
So gaily in love's unbreakable heaven
Our souls on glory of spilt bourbon float.   20

Be with me, darling, early and late. Smash glasses—
I will study wry music for your sake.
For should your hands drop white and empty
All the toys of the world would break.

[1947]

ROBERT HAYDEN   [1913–1980]

Those Winter Sundays

Sundays too my father got up early
and put his clothes on in the blueblack cold,
then with cracked hands that ached
from labor in the weekday weather made
banked fires blaze. No one ever thanked him.   5

I'd wake and hear the cold splintering, breaking.
When the rooms were warm, he'd call,
and slowly I would rise and dress,
fearing the chronic angers of that house,

Speaking indifferently to him,   10
who had driven out the cold
and polished my good shoes as well.
What did I know, what did I know
of love's austere and lonely offices?

[1962]

DUDLEY RANDALL   [1914–2000]

Ballad of Birmingham

On the bombing of a church in Birmingham, Alabama, 1963

"Mother dear, may I go downtown
Instead of out to play,
And march the streets of Birmingham
In a Freedom March today?"

"No, baby, no, you may not go,   5
For the dogs are fierce and wild,
And clubs and hoses, guns and jails
Aren't good for a little child."

"But, mother, I won't be alone.
Other children will go with me,   10
And march the streets of Birmingham
To make our country free."

"No, baby, no, you may not go,
For I fear those guns will fire.
But you may go to church instead   15
And sing in the children's choir."

She has combed and brushed her night-dark hair,
And bathed rose petal sweet,
And drawn white gloves on her small brown hands,
And white shoes on her feet.   20

The mother smiled to know her child
Was in the sacred place,
But that smile was the last smile
To come upon her face.

For when she heard the explosion,   25
Her eyes grew wet and wild.
She raced through the streets of Birmingham
Calling for her child.

She clawed through bits of glass and brick,
Then lifted out a shoe.   30
"Oh, here's the shoe my baby wore,
But, baby, where are you?"

[1969]

JOHN BERRYMAN   [1914–1972]

Henry's Confession

from *The Dream Songs* 76

Nothin very bad happen to me lately.
How you explain that? — I explain that, Mr Bones,°   *minstrel figure*
terms o' your bafflin odd sobriety.
Sober as man can get, no girls, no telephones,
what could happen bad to Mr Bones?   5
— *If* life is a handkerchief sandwich,

in a modesty of death I join my father
who dared so long agone leave me.
A bullet on a concrete stoop
close by a smothering southern sea   10
spreadeagled on an island, by my knee.
— You is from hunger, Mr Bones,

I offers you this handkerchief, now set
your left foot by my right foot,
shoulder to shoulder, all that jazz,   15
arm in arm, by the beautiful sea,
hum a little, Mr Bones.
— I saw nobody coming, so I went instead.

[1964]

WILLIAM STAFFORD   [1914–1995]

Traveling through the Dark

Traveling through the dark I found a deer
dead on the edge of the Wilson River road.
It is usually best to roll them into the canyon:
that road is narrow; to swerve might make more dead.

By glow of the tail-light I stumbled back of the car   5
and stood by the heap, a doe, a recent killing;
she had stiffened already, almost cold.
I dragged her off; she was large in the belly.

My fingers touching her side brought me the reason—
her side was warm; her fawn lay there waiting,   10
alive, still, never to be born.
Beside that mountain road I hesitated.

The car aimed ahead its lowered parking lights;
under the hood purred the steady engine.
I stood in the glare of the warm exhaust turning red;   15
around our group I could hear the wilderness listen.

I thought hard for us all—my only swerving—,
then pushed her over the edge into the river.

[1962]

DYLAN THOMAS   [1914–1953]

Fern Hill

Now as I was young and easy under the apple boughs
About the lilting house and happy as the grass was green,
   The night above the dingle° starry,   *small wooded valley*
    Time let me hail and climb
   Golden in the heydays of his eyes,   5
And honoured among wagons I was prince of the apple towns
And once below a time I lordly had the trees and leaves
   Trail with daisies and barley
   Down the rivers of the windfall light.

And as I was green and carefree, famous among the barns   10
About the happy yard and singing as the farm was home,
 In the sun that is young once only,
  Time let me play and be
 Golden in the mercy of his means,
And green and golden I was huntsman and herdsman, the calves   15
Sang to my horn, the foxes on the hills barked clear and cold,
  And the sabbath rang slowly
 In the pebbles of the holy streams.

All the sun long it was running, it was lovely, the hay
Fields high as the house, the tunes from the chimneys, it was air   20
 And playing, lovely and watery
  And fire green as grass.
 And nightly under the simple stars
As I rode to sleep the owls were bearing the farm away,
All the moon long I heard, blessed among stables, the nightjars   25
 Flying with the ricks, and the horses
  Flashing into the dark.

And then to awake, and the farm, like a wanderer white
With the dew, come back, the cock on his shoulder: it was all
 Shining, it was Adam and maiden,   30
  The sky gathered again
 And the sun grew round that very day.
So it must have been after the birth of the simple light
In the first, spinning place, the spellbound horses walking warm
 Out of the whinnying green stable   35
  On to the fields of praise.

And honoured among foxes and pheasants by the gay house
Under the new made clouds and happy as the heart was long,
 In the sun born over and over,
  I ran my heedless ways,   40
 My wishes raced through the house high hay
And nothing I cared, at my sky blue trades, that time allows
In all his tuneful turning so few and such morning songs
 Before the children green and golden
  Follow him out of grace,   45

Nothing I cared, in the lamb white days, that time would take me
Up to the swallow thronged loft by the shadow of my hand,
 In the moon that is always rising,
  Nor that riding to sleep

I should hear him fly with the high fields   50
And wake to the farm forever fled from the childless land.
Oh as I was young and easy in the mercy of his means,
 Time held me green and dying
Though I sang in my chains like the sea.

[1946]

DYLAN THOMAS [1914–1953]

Do not go gentle into that good night

Do not go gentle into that good night,
Old age should burn and rave at close of day;
Rage, rage against the dying of the light.

Though wise men at their end know dark is right,
Because their words had forked no lightning they   5
Do not go gentle into that good night.

Good men, the last wave by, crying how bright
Their frail deeds might have danced in a green bay,
Rage, rage against the dying of the light.

Wild men who caught and sang the sun in flight,   10
And learn, too late, they grieved it on its way,
Do not go gentle into that good night.

Grave men, near death, who see with blinding sight
Blind eyes could blaze like meteors and be gay,
Rage, rage against the dying of the light.   15

And you, my father, there on the sad height,
Curse, bless, me now with your fierce tears, I pray.
Do not go gentle into that good night.
Rage, rage against the dying of the light.

[1952]

HENRY REED   [1914–1986]

Naming of Parts

Today we have naming of parts. Yesterday,
We had daily cleaning. And tomorrow morning,
We shall have what to do after firing. But today,
Today we have naming of parts. Japonica
Glistens like coral in all of the neighbouring gardens,   5
    And today we have naming of parts.

This is the lower sling swivel. And this
Is the upper sling swivel, whose use you will see,
When you are given your slings. And this is the piling swivel,
Which in your case you have not got. The branches   10
Hold in the gardens their silent, eloquent gestures,
    Which in our case we have not got.

This is the safety-catch, which is always released
With an easy flick of the thumb. And please do not let me
See anyone using his finger. You can do it quite easy   15
If you have any strength in your thumb. The blossoms
Are fragile and motionless, never letting anyone see
    Any of them using their finger.

And this you can see is the bolt. The purpose of this
Is to open the breech, as you see. We can slide it   20
Rapidly backwards and forwards: we call this
Easing the spring. And rapidly backwards and forwards
The early bees are assaulting and fumbling the flowers:
    They call it easing the Spring.

They call it easing the Spring: it is perfectly easy   25
If you have any strength in your thumb: like the bolt,
And the breech, and the cocking-piece, and the point of balance,
Which in our case we have not got; and the almond-blossom
Silent in all of the gardens and the bees going backwards and forwards,
    For today we have naming of parts.   30

[1946]

RANDALL JARRELL   [1914–1965]

The Woman at the Washington Zoo

The saris go by me from the embassies.

Cloth from the moon. Cloth from another planet.
They look back at the leopard like the leopard.

And I. . . .
                    this print of mine, that has kept its color   5
Alive through so many cleanings; this dull null
Navy I wear to work, and wear from work, and so
To my bed, so to my grave, with no
Complaints, no comment: neither from my chief,
The Deputy Chief Assistant, nor his chief—   10
Only I complain. . . . this serviceable
Body that no sunlight dyes, no hand suffuses
But, dome-shadowed, withering among columns,
Wavy beneath fountains—small, far-off, shining
In the eyes of animals, these beings trapped   15
As I am trapped but not, themselves, the trap,
Aging, but without knowledge of their age,
Kept safe here, knowing not of death, for death—
Oh, bars of my own body, open, open!

The world goes by my cage and never sees me.   20
And there come not to me, as come to these,
The wild beasts, sparrows pecking the llamas' grain,
Pigeons settling on the bears' bread, buzzards
Tearing the meat the flies have clouded. . . .
                                            Vulture,   25
When you come for the white rat that the foxes left,
Take off the red helmet of your head, the black
Wings that have shadowed me, and step to me as man:
The wild brother at whose feet the white wolves fawn,
To whose hand of power the great lioness   30
Stalks, purring. . . .
                    You know what I was,
You see what I am: change me, change me!

                                                            [1960]

GWENDOLYN BROOKS   [1917–2000]

We Real Cool

The Pool Players.
Seven at the Golden Shovel.

We real cool. We
Left school. We

Lurk late. We
Strike straight. We

Sing sin. We   5
Thin gin. We

Jazz June.° We   *sexual intercourse*
Die soon.

[1960]

GWENDOLYN BROOKS   [1917–2000]

The Bean Eaters

They eat beans mostly, this old yellow pair.
Dinner is a casual affair.
Plain chipware on a plain and creaking wood,
Tin flatware.

Two who are Mostly Good.   5
Two who have lived their day,
But keep on putting on their clothes
and putting things away.

And remembering . . .
Remembering, with twinklings and twinges,   10
As they lean over the beans in their rented back room that
    is full of beads and receipts and dolls and cloths,
    tobacco crumbs, vases and fringes.

[1960]

ROBERT LOWELL   [1917–1978]

Skunk Hour

for Elizabeth Bishop

Nautilus Island's hermit
heiress still lives through winter in her Spartan cottage;
her sheep still graze above the sea.
Her son's a bishop. Her farmer
is first selectman in our village;   5
she's in her dotage.

Thirsting for
the hierarchic privacy
of Queen Victoria's century,
she buys up all   10
the eyesores facing her shore,
and lets them fall.

The season's ill—
we've lost our summer millionaire,
who seemed to leap from an L. L. Bean   15
catalogue. His nine-knot yawl
was auctioned off to lobstermen.
A red fox stain covers Blue Hill.

And now our fairy
decorator brightens his shop for fall;   20
his fishnet's filled with orange cork,
orange, his cobbler's bench and awl;
there is no money in his work,
he'd rather marry.

One dark night,   25
my Tudor Ford climbed the hill's skull;
I watched for love-cars. Lights turned down,
they lay together, hull to hull,
where the graveyard shelves on the town. . . .
My mind's not right.   30

A car radio bleats,
"Love, O careless Love. . . ." I hear
my ill-spirit sob in each blood cell,
as if my hand were at its throat. . . .

I myself am hell;   35
nobody's here—

only skunks, that search
in the moonlight for a bite to eat.
They march on their soles up Main Street:
white stripes, moonstruck eyes' red fire   40
under the chalk-dry and spar spire
of the Trinitarian Church.

I stand on top
of our back steps and breathe the rich air—
a mother skunk with her column of kittens swills the garbage pail.   45
She jabs her wedge-head in a cup
of sour cream, drops her ostrich tail,
and will not scare.

[1963]

ROBERT DUNCAN   [1919–1988]

The Torso

Passages 18

Most beautiful!   the red-flowering eucalyptus,
        the madrone, the yew

Is he . . .

So thou wouldst smile, and take me in thine arms
The sight of London to my exiled eyes   5
Is as Elysium° to a new-come soul   *paradise*

If he be Truth
I would dwell in the illusion of him

His hands unlocking from chambers of my male body

such an idea in man's image   10

rising tides that sweep me towards him

. . . *homosexual?*

and at the treasure of his mouth

pour forth my soul

        his soul   commingling   15

I thought a Being more than vast, His body leading
    into Paradise,   his eyes
        quickening a fire in me,   a trembling

hieroglyph:°   At the root of the neck

the clavicle, for the neck is the stem of the great artery   20
    upward into his head that is beautiful

        At the rise of the pectoral muscle,

the nipples, for the breasts are like sleeping fountains
    of feeling in man, waiting above the beat of his heart,
    shielding the rise and fall of his breath, to be   25
    awakend

        At the axis of his mid hriff

the navel, for in the pit of his stomach the chord from
    which first he was fed has its temple

        At the root of the groin   30

the pubic hair, for the torso is the stem in which the man
    flowers forth and leads to the stamen of flesh in which
    his seed rises

a wave of need and desire over   taking me

        cried out my name   35

    (This was long ago.   It was another life)

        and said,

    What do you want of me?

I do not know, I said.   I have fallen in love.   He
    has brought me into heights and depths my heart   40
        would fear   without him.   His look

pierces my side • fire eyes •

    I have been waiting for you, he said:
        I know what you desire

    you do not yet know   but through me •   45

---

19. **hieroglyph:** A picture or symbol representing a word or sound.

And I am with you everywhere.   In your falling

I have fallen from a high place.   I have raised myself

from darkness in your   rising

wherever you are

my hand in your hand   seeking   the locks, the keys   50

I am there.   Gathering me, you gather

your Self   •

For my Other is not a woman but a man

the King upon whose bosom let me lie.

[1968]

CHARLES BUKOWSKI   [1920–1994]

my old man

16 years old
during the depression
I'd come home drunk
and all my clothing—
shorts, shirts, stockings—   5
suitcase, and pages of
short stories
would be thrown out on the
front lawn and about the
street.   10

my mother would be
waiting behind a tree:
"Henry, Henry, don't
go in . . . he'll
kill you, he's read   15
your stories . . ."

"I can whip his
ass . . ."

"Henry, please take
this . . . and   20
find yourself a room."

but it worried him
that I might not
finish high school
so I'd be back   25
again.

one evening he walked in
with the pages of
one of my short stories
(which I had never submitted   30
to him)
and he said, "this is
a great short story."
I said, "o.k.,"
and he handed it to me   35
and I read it.
it was a story about
a rich man
who had a fight with
his wife and had   40
gone out into the night
for a cup of coffee
and had observed
the waitress and the spoons
and forks and the   45
salt and pepper shakers
and the neon sign
in the window
and then had gone back
to his stable   50
to see and touch his
favorite horse
who then
kicked him in the head
and killed him.   55

somehow
the story held
meaning for him
though
when I had written it   60
I had no idea
of what I was
writing about.

so I told him,
"o.k., old man, you can   65
have it."
and he took it
and walked out
and closed the door.
I guess that's   70
as close
as we ever got.

[1977]

RICHARD WILBUR   [b. 1921]

Love Calls Us to the Things of This World

The eyes open to a cry of pulleys,
And spirited from sleep, the astounded soul
Hangs for a moment bodiless and simple
As false dawn.
               Outside the open window
The morning air is all awash with angels.   5

Some are in bed-sheets, some are in blouses,
Some are in smocks: but truly there they are.
Now they are rising together in calm swells
Of halcyon feeling, filling whatever they wear
With the deep joy of their impersonal breathing;   10

Now they are flying in place, conveying
The terrible speed of their omnipresence, moving
And staying like white water; and now of a sudden
They swoon down into so rapt a quiet
That nobody seems to be there.
               The soul shrinks   15

From all that it is about to remember,
From the punctual rape of every blessèd day,
And cries,
        "Oh, let there be nothing on earth but laundry,
Nothing but rosy hands in the rising steam
And clear dances done in the sight of heaven."   20

Yet, as the sun acknowledges
With a warm look the world's hunks and colors,
The soul descends once more in bitter love
To accept the waking body, saying now
In a changed voice as the man yawns and rises,   25

"Bring them down from their ruddy gallows;
Let there be clean linen for the backs of thieves;
Let lovers go fresh and sweet to be undone,
And the heaviest nuns walk in a pure floating
Of dark habits,
          keeping their difficult balance."   30

[1956]

HAYDEN CARRUTH   [b. 1921]

Regarding Chainsaws

The first chainsaw I owned was years ago,
an old yellow McCulloch that wouldn't start.
Bo Bremmer give it to me that was my friend,
though I've had enemies couldn't of done
no worse. I took it to Ward's over to Morrisville,   5
and no doubt they tinkered it as best they could,
but it still wouldn't start. One time later
I took it down to the last bolt and gasket
and put it together again, hoping somehow
I'd do something accidental-like that would   10
make it go, and then I yanked on it
450 times, as I figured afterwards,
and give myself a bursitis in the elbow
that went five years even after
Doc Arrowsmith shot it full of cortisone   15
and near killed me when he hit a nerve
dead on. Old Stan wanted that saw, wanted it bad.
Figured I was a greenhorn that didn't know
nothing and he could fix it. Well, I was,
you could say, being only forty at the time,   20
but a fair hand at tinkering. "Stan," I said,
"you're a neighbor. I like you. I wouldn't
sell that thing to nobody, except maybe

Vice-President Nixon." But Stan persisted.
He always did. One time we was loafing and   25
gabbing in his front dooryard, and he spied
that saw in the back of my pickup. He run
quick inside, then come out and stuck a double
sawbuck° in my shirt pocket, and he grabbed   *twenty dollar bill*
that saw and lugged it off. Next day, when I   30
drove past, I seen he had it snugged down tight
with a tow-chain on the bed of his old Dodge
Powerwagon, and he was yanking on it
with both hands. Two or three days after,
I asked him, "How you getting along with that   35
McCulloch, Stan?" "Well," he says, "I tooken
it down to scrap, and I buried it in three
separate places yonder on the upper side
of the potato piece. You can't be too careful,"
he says, "when you're disposing of a hex."   40
The next saw I had was a godawful ancient
Homelite that I give Dry Dryden thirty bucks for,
temperamental as a ram too, but I liked it.
It used to remind me of Dry and how he'd
clap that saw a couple times with the flat   45
of his double-blade axe to make it go
and how he honed the chain with a worn-down
file stuck in an old baseball. I worked
that saw for years. I put up forty-five
run them days each summer and fall to keep   50
my stoves het through the winter. I couldn't now.
It'd kill me. Of course they got these here
modern Swedish saws now that can take
all the worry out of it. What's the good
of that? Takes all the fun out too, don't it?   55
Why, I reckon. I mind when Gilles Boivin snagged
an old sap spout buried in a chunk of maple
and it tore up his mouth so bad he couldn't play
"Tea for Two" on his cornet in the town band
no more, and then when Toby Fox was holding   60
a beech limb that Rob Bowen was bucking up
and the saw skidded crossways and nipped off
one of Toby's fingers. Ain't that more like it?
Makes you know you're living. But mostly they wan't
dangerous, and the only thing they broke was your   65
back. Old Stan, he was a buller and a jammer

in his time, no two ways about that, but he
never sawed himself. Stan had the sugar
all his life, and he wan't always too careful
about his diet and the injections. He lost   70
all the feeling in his legs from the knees down.
One time he started up his Powerwagon
out in the barn, and his foot slipped off the clutch,
and she jumped forwards right through the wall
and into the manure pit. He just set there,   75
swearing like you could of heard it in St.
Johnsbury, till his wife come out and said,
"Stan, what's got into you?" "Missus," he says,
"ain't nothing got into me. Can't you see?
It's me that's got into this here pile of shit."   80
Not much later they took away one of his
legs, and six months after that they took
the other and left him sitting in his old chair
with a tank of oxygen to sip at whenever
he felt himself sinking. I remember that chair.   85
Stan reupholstered it with an old bearskin
that must of come down from his great-great-
grandfather and had grit in it left over
from the Civil War and a bullet-hole as big
as a yawning cat. Stan latched the pieces together   90
with rawhide, cross fashion, but the stitches was
always breaking and coming undone. About then
I quit stopping by to see old Stan, and I
don't feel so good about that neither. But my mother
was having her strokes then. I figured   95
one person coming apart was as much
as a man can stand. Then Stan was taken away
to the nursing home, and then he died. I always
remember how he planted them pieces of spooked
McCulloch up above the potatoes. One time   100
I went up and dug, and I took the old
sprocket, all pitted and et away, and set it
on the windowsill right there next to the
butter mold. But I'm damned if I know why.

[1983]

PHILIP LARKIN   [1922–1985]

High Windows

When I see a couple of kids
And guess he's fucking her and she's
Taking pills or wearing a diaphragm,
I know this is paradise

Everyone old has dreamed of all their lives —   5
Bonds and gestures pushed to one side
Like an outdated combine harvester,
And everyone young going down the long slide

To happiness, endlessly. I wonder if
Anyone looked at me, forty years back,   10
And thought, *That'll be the life;*
No God any more, or sweating in the dark

About hell and that, or having to hide
What you think of the priest. He
And his lot will all go down the long slide   15
Like free bloody birds. And immediately

Rather than words comes the thought of high windows:
The sun-comprehending glass,
And beyond it, the deep blue air, that shows
Nothing, and is nowhere, and is endless.   20

[1974]

DENISE LEVERTOV   [1923–1997]

February Evening in New York

As the stores close, a winter light
    opens air to iris blue,
    glint of frost through the smoke
    grains of mica, salt of the sidewalk.
As the buildings close, released autonomous   5
    feet pattern the streets
    in hurry and stroll; balloon heads
    drift and dive above them; the bodies
    aren't really there.

As the lights brighten, as the sky darkens,   10
    a woman with crooked heels says to another woman
    while they step along at a fair pace,
    "You know, I'm telling you, what I love best
    is life. I love life! Even if I ever get
    to be old and wheezy—or limp! You know?   15
    Limping along?—I'd still . . ." Out of hearing.
To the multiple disordered tones
    of gears changing, a dance
    to the compass points, out, four-way river.
    Prospect of sky   20
    wedged into avenues, left at the ends of streets,
    west sky, east sky: more life tonight! A range
    of open time at winter's outskirts.

                                                                    [1959]

MAXINE KUMIN   [b. 1925]

The Excrement Poem

It is done by us all, as God disposes, from
the least cast of worm to what must have been
in the case of the brontosaur, say, spoor
of considerable heft, something awesome.

We eat, we evacuate, survivors that we are.   5
I think these things each morning with shovel
and rake, drawing the risen brown buns
toward me, fresh from the horse oven, as it were,

or culling the alfalfa-green ones, expelled
in a state of ooze, through the sawdust bed   10
to take a serviceable form, as putty does,
so as to lift out entire from the stall.

And wheeling to it, storming up the slope,
I think of the angle of repose the manure
pile assumes, how sparrows come to pick   15
the redelivered grain, how inky-cap

coprinus mushrooms spring up in a downpour.
I think of what drops from us and must then

be moved to make way for the next and next.
However much we stain the world, spatter   20

it with our leavings, make stenches, defile
the great formal oceans with what leaks down,
trundling off today's last barrowful,
I honor shit for saying: We go on.

[1978]

KENNETH KOCH   [1925–2002]

The History of Jazz

1

The leaves of blue came drifting down.
In the corner Madeleine Reierbacher was reading *Lorna Doone.*°
The bay's water helped to implement the structuring of the garden hose.
The envelope fell. Was it pink or was it red? Consult *Lorna Doone.*
There, voyager, you will find your answer. The savant grapeade stands   5
Remember Madeleine Reierbacher. Madeleine Reierbacher says,
"If you are happy, there is no one to keep you from being happy;
Don't let them!" Madeleine Reierbacher went into the racing car.
The racing car was orange and red. Madeleine Reierbacher drove to
    Beale Street.
There Maddy doffed her garments to get into some more comfortable
    clothes.   10
Jazz was already playing in Beale Street when Madeleine Reierbacher
    arrived there.
Madeleine Reierbacher picked up the yellow horn and began to play.
No one had ever heard anything comparable to the playing of Madeleine
    Reierbacher.
What a jazz musician! The pianist missed his beats because he was so
    excited.
The drummer stared out the window in ecstasy at the yellow wooden
    trees.   15
The orchestra played "September in the Rain," "Mugging," and "I'm Full
    of Love."
Madeleine Reierbacher rolled up her sleeves; she picked up her horn;
    she played "Blues in the Rain."

2. *Lorna Doone*: Romance novel (1869) by Richard Doddridge Blackmore.

It was the best jazz anyone had ever heard. It was mentioned in the
    newspapers. St. Louis!
Madeleine Reierbacher became a celebrity. She played with Pesky
    Summerton and Muggsy Pierce.
Madeleine cut numerous disks. Her best waxings are "Alpha Beta and
    Gamma"   20
And "Wing Song." One day Madeleine was riding on a donkey
When she came to a yellow light; the yellow light did not change.
Madeleine kept hoping it would change to green or red. She said, "As
    long as you have confidence,
You need be afraid of nothing." Madeleine saw the red smokestacks, she
    looked at the thin trees,
And she regarded the railroad tracks. The yellow light was unchanging.
    Madeleine's donkey dropped dead   25
From his mortal load. Madeleine Reierbacher, when she fell to earth,
Picked up a blade of grass and began to play. "The Blues!" cried the
    workmen of the vicinity.
And they ran and came in great numbers to where Madeleine
    Reierbacher was.
They saw her standing in that simple field beside the railroad track
Playing, and they saw that light changing to green and red, and they saw
    that donkey stand up   30
And rise into the sky; and Madeleine Reierbacher was like a clot of blue
In the midst of the blue of all that sky, and the young farmers screamed
In excitement, and the workmen dropped their heavy boards and stones
    in their excitement,
And they cried, "O Madeleine Reierbacher, play us the 'Lead Flint Blues'
    once again!"

O railroad stations, pennants, evenings, and lumberyards!   35
When will you ever bring us such a beautiful soloist again?
An argent strain shows on the reddish face of the sun.
Madeleine Reierbacher stands up and screams, "I am getting wet! You
    are all egotists!"
Her brain floats up into the lyric atmosphere of the sky.
We must figure out a way to keep our best musicians with us.   40
The finest we have always melt into the light blue sky!
In the middle of a concert, sometimes, they disappear, like anvils.
(The music comes down to us with sweet white hands on our
    shoulders.)
We stare up in surprise; and we hear Madeleine's best-known tune once
    again,
"If you ain't afraid of life, life can't be afraid for you."   45
Madeleine! Come back and sing to us!

2

Dick looked up from his blackboard.
Had he really written a history of the jazz age?
He stared at his television set; the technicolor jazz program was
    coming on.
The program that day was devoted to pictures of Madeleine Reierbacher   50
Playing her saxophone in the golden age of jazz.
Dick looked at his blackboard. It was a mass of green and orange lines.
Here and there a red chalk line interlaced with the others.
He stared attentively at the program.

It was a clear and blue white day. Amos said, "The calibration is
    finished. Now there need be no more jazz."   55

In his mountain home old Lucas Dog laughed when he heard what
    Amos had said.
He smilingly picked up his yellow horn to play, but all that came out of
    it was steam.

[1961]

GERALD STERN   [b. 1925]

Cow Worship

I love the cows best when they are a few feet away
from my dining-room window and my pine floor,
when they reach in to kiss me with their wet
mouths and their white noses.
I love them when they walk over the garbage cans   5
and across the cellar doors,
over the sidewalk and through the metal chairs
and the birdseed.
—Let me reach out through the thin curtains
and feel the warm air of May.   10
It is the temperature of the whole galaxy,
all the bright clouds and clusters,
beasts and heroes,
glittering singers and isolated thinkers
at pasture.   15

[1981]

JACK GILBERT   [b. 1925]

Michiko Dead

He manages like somebody carrying a box
that is too heavy, first with his arms
underneath. When their strength gives out,
he moves the hands forward, hooking them
on the corners, pulling the weight against   5
his chest. He moves his thumbs slightly
when the fingers begin to tire, and it makes
different muscles take over. Afterward,
he carries it on his shoulder, until the blood
drains out of the arm that is stretched up   10
to steady the box and the arm goes numb. But now
the man can hold underneath again, so that
he can go on without ever putting the box down.

[1994]

FRANK O'HARA   [1926–1966]

The Day Lady° Died   *jazz singer*
                                            Billie Holliday

It is 12:20 in New York a Friday
three days after Bastille day,° yes   *(July 14)*
it is 1959 and I go get a shoeshine
because I will get off the 4:19 in Easthampton
at 7:15 and then go straight to dinner   5
and I don't know the people who will feed me

I walk up the muggy street beginning to sun
and have a hamburger and a malted and buy
an ugly NEW WORLD WRITING to see what the poets
in Ghana are doing these days   10
                    I go on to the bank
and Miss Stillwagon (first name Linda I once heard)
doesn't even look up my balance for once in her life
and in the GOLDEN GRIFFIN I get a little Verlaine°   *French poet*
for Patsy with drawings by Bonnard° although I do   15

---

15. **Bonnard:** French modernist painter.

think of Hesiod,° trans. Richmond Lattimore or   *Greek poet*
Brendan Behan's° new play or *Le Balcon* or *Les Nègres*   *Irish playwright*
of Genet,° but I don't, I stick with Verlaine   *French playwright and novelist*
after practically going to sleep with quandariness

and for Mike I just stroll into the PARK LANE   20
Liquor Store and ask for a bottle of Strega and
then I go back where I came from to 6th Avenue
and the tobacconist in the Ziegfeld Theatre and
casually ask for a carton of Gauloises° and a carton   *French cigarettes*
of Picayunes,° and a NEW YORK POST with her face on it   *Southern cigarettes* 25

and I am sweating a lot by now and thinking of
leaning on the john door in the 5 SPOT
while she whispered a song along the keyboard
to Mal Waldron and everyone and I stopped breathing

[1964]

ALLEN GINSBERG   [1926–1997]

A Supermarket in California

What thoughts I have of you tonight, Walt Whitman, for I walked down
the sidestreets under the trees with a headache self-conscious looking at
the full moon.

In my hungry fatigue, and shopping for images, I went into the neon
fruit supermarket, dreaming of your enumerations!

What peaches and what penumbras! Whole families shopping at
night! Aisles full of husbands! Wives in the avocados, babies in the tomatoes! — and you, García Lorca,° what were you doing down by the water-
melons?

I saw you, Walt Whitman, childless, lonely old grubber, poking among
the meats in the refrigerator and eyeing the grocery boys.

I heard you asking questions of each: Who killed the pork chops? What
price bananas? Are you my Angel?   5

I wandered in and out of the brilliant stacks of cans following you, and
followed in my imagination by the store detective.

We strode down the open corridors together in our solitary fancy tasting
artichokes, possessing every frozen delicacy, and never passing the cashier.

---

3. **García Lorca:** (1899–1936), Spanish surrealist poet and playwright.

Where are we going, Walt Whitman? The doors close in an hour.
Which way does your beard point tonight?
   (I touch your book and dream of our odyssey in the supermarket and
feel absurd.)
   Will we walk all night through solitary streets? The trees add shade to
shade, lights out in the houses, we'll both be lonely.   10
   Will we stroll dreaming of the lost America of love past blue automo-
biles in driveways, home to our silent cottage?
   Ah, dear father, graybeard, lonely old courage-teacher, what America did
you have when Charon° quit poling his ferry and you got out on a smoking
bank and stood watching the boat disappear on the black waters of Lethe?°
Berkeley, 1955

[1956]

12. Charon: The boatman in Greek mythology who carried the dead across the
river Styx to Hades. **Lethe:** River of Forgetfullness in Hades.

ROBERT CREELEY   [b. 1926]

Time

Moment to
moment the
body seems

to me to
be there: a   5
catch of

air, pattern
of space— Let's
walk today

all the way   10
to the beach,
let's think

of where we'll be
in two years'
time, of where   15

we *were.* Let
the days go.
Each moment is

of such paradoxical
definition—a
waterfall that would   20

flow backward
if it could. It
can? My time,

one thinks,   25
is drawing to
some close. This

feeling comes
and goes. No
measure ever serves   30

enough, enough—
so "finish it"
gets done, alone.

[1972]

JAMES MERRILL   [1926–1995]

The Pier: Under Pisces

The shallows, brighter,
Wetter than water,
Tepidly glitter with the fingerprint-
Obliterating feel of kerosene.

Each piling like a totem   5
Rises from rock bottom
Straight through the ceiling
Aswirl with suns, clear ones or pale bluegreen,

And beyond! where bubbles burst,
Sphere of their worst dreams,   10
If dream is what they do,
These floozy fish—

Ceramic-lipped in filmy
Peekaboo blouses,
Fluorescent body   15
Stockings, hot stripes,

Swayed by the hypnotic ebb and flow
Of supermarket Muzak,
Bolero° beat the undertow's   *a Spanish dance*
Pebble-filled gourds repeat;   20

Jailbait consumers of subliminal
Hints dropped from on high
In gobbets° none   *fragments, bits*
Eschews as minced kin;

Who, hooked themselves—bamboo diviner   25
Bent their way
Vigorously nodding
Encouragement—

Are one by one hauled kisswise, oh
Into some blinding hell   30
Policed by leathery ex-
Justices each

Minding his catch, if catch is what he can,
If mind is what one means—
The torn mouth   35
Stifled by newsprint, working still. If . . . if . . .

The little scales
Grow stiff. Dusk plugs her dryer in,
Buffs her nails, riffles through magazines,
While far and wide and deep   40

Rover the great sharkskin-suited criminals
And safe in this lit shrine
A boy sits. He'll be eight.
We've drunk our milk, we've eaten our stringbeans,

But left untasted on the plate   45
The fish. An eye, a broiled pearl, meeting mine,
I lift his fork . . .
The bite. The tug of fate.

[1985]

ROBERT BLY   [b. 1926]

Driving to Town Late to Mail a Letter

It is a cold and snowy night. The main street is deserted.
The only things moving are swirls of snow.
As I lift the mailbox door, I feel its cold iron.
There is a privacy I love in this snowy night.
Driving around, I will waste more time.   5

[1962]

W. S. MERWIN   [b. 1927]

Yesterday

My friend says I was not a good son
you understand
I say yes I understand

he says I did not go
to see my parents very often you know   5
and I say yes I know

even when I was living in the same city he says
maybe I would go there once
a month or maybe even less
I say oh yes   10

he says the last time I went to see my father
I say the last time I saw my father

he says the last time I saw my father
he was asking me about my life
how I was making out and he   15
went into the next room
to get something to give me

oh I say
feeling again the cold
of my father's hand the last time   20

he says and my father turned
in the doorway and saw me
look at my wristwatch and he

said you know I would like you to stay
and talk with me   25

oh yes I say

but if you are busy he said
I don't want you to feel that you
have to
just because I'm here   30

I say nothing

he says my father
said maybe
you have important work you are doing
or maybe you should be seeing   35
somebody I don't want to keep you

I look out the window
my friend is older than I am
he says and I told my father it was so
and I got up and left him then   40
you know

though there was nowhere I had to go
and nothing I had to do

                                                    [1983]

JOHN ASHBERY   [b. 1927]

One Coat of Paint

We will all have to just hang on for a while,
It seems, now. This could mean "early retirement"
For some, if only for an afternoon of pottering around
Buying shoelaces and the like. Or it could mean a spell
In some enchanter's cave, after several centuries of which   5
You wake up curiously refreshed, eager to get back
To the crossword puzzle, only no one knows your name
Or who you are, really, or cares much either. To seduce
A fact into becoming an object, a pleasing one, with some
Kind of esthetic quality, which would also add to the store   10
Of knowledge and even extend through several strata

Of history, like a pin through a cracked wrist bone,
Connecting these in such a dynamic way that one would be forced
To acknowledge a new kind of superiority without which the world
Could no longer conduct its business, even simple stuff like bringing   15
Water home from wells, coals to hearths, would of course be
An optimal form of it but in any case the thing's got to
Come into being, something has to happen, or all
We'll have left is disagreements, *désagréments*,° to name a few.
O don't you see how necessary it is to be around,
To be ferried from here to that near, smiling shore   20
And back again into the arms of those that love us,
Not many, but of such infinite, superior sweetness
That their lie is for us and it becomes stained, encrusted,
Finally gilded in some exasperating way that turns it
To a truth plus something, delicate and dismal as a star,   25
Cautious as a drop of milk, so that they let us
Get away with it, some do at any rate?

[1987]

19. **désagréments:** Unpleasantness, difficulties.

GALWAY KINNELL   [b. 1927]

The Bear

1

In late winter
I sometimes glimpse bits of steam
coming up from
some fault in the old snow
and bend close and see it is lung-colored   5
and put down my nose
and know
the chilly, enduring odor of bear.

2

I take a wolf's rib and whittle
it sharp at both ends   10
and coil it up
and freeze it in blubber and place it out
on the fairway of the bears.

And when it has vanished
I move out on the bear tracks,   15
roaming in circles
until I come to the first, tentative, dark
splash on the earth.

And I set out
running, following the splashes   20
of blood wandering over the world.
At the cut, gashed resting places
I stop and rest,
at the crawl-marks
where he lay out on his belly   25
to overpass some stretch of bauchy ice
I lie out
dragging myself forward with bear-knives in my fists.

3

On the third day I begin to starve,
at nightfall I bend down as I knew I would   30
at a turd sopped in blood,
and hesitate, and pick it up,
and thrust it in my mouth, and gnash it down,
and rise
and go on running.   35

4

On the seventh day,
living by now on bear blood alone,
I can see his upturned carcass far out ahead, a scraggled,
steamy hulk,
the heavy fur riffling in the wind.   40

I come up to him
and stare at the narrow-spaced, petty eyes,
the dismayed
face laid back on the shoulder, the nostrils
flared, catching   45
perhaps the first taint of me as he
died.

I hack
a ravine in his thigh, and eat and drink,
and tear him down his whole length   50

and open him and climb in
and close him up after me, against the wind,
and sleep.

5

And dream
of lumbering flatfooted   55
over the tundra,
stabbed twice from within,
splattering a trail behind me,
splattering it out no matter which way I lurch,
no matter which parabola of bear-transcendence,   60
which dance of solitude I attempt,
which gravity-clutched leap,
which trudge, which groan.

6

Until one day I totter and fall—
fall on this   65
stomach that has tried so hard to keep up,
to digest the blood as it leaked in,
to break up
and digest the bone itself: and now the breeze
blows over me, blows off   70
the hideous belches of ill-digested bear blood
and rotted stomach
and the ordinary, wretched odor of bear,

blows across
my sore, lolled tongue a song   75
or screech, until I think I must rise up
and dance. And I lie still.

7

I awaken I think. Marshlights
reappear, geese
come trailing again up the flyway.   80
In her ravine under old snow the dam-bear
lies, licking
lumps of smeared fur
and drizzly eyes into shapes
with her tongue. And one   85
hairy-soled trudge stuck out before me,

the next groaned out,
the next,
the next,
the rest of my days I spend   90
wandering: wondering
what, anyway,
was that sticky infusion, that rank flavor of blood, that poetry, by which
    I lived?

[1967]

JAMES WRIGHT   [1927–1980]

A Blessing

Just off the highway to Rochester, Minnesota,
Twilight bounds softly forth on the grass.
And the eyes of those two Indian ponies
Darken with kindness.
They have come gladly out of the willows   5
To welcome my friend and me.
We step over the barbed wire into the pasture
Where they have been grazing all day, alone.

They ripple tensely, they can hardly contain their happiness
That we have come.   10
They bow shyly as wet swans. They love each other.
There is no loneliness like theirs.
At home once more,
They begin munching the young tufts of spring in the darkness.
I would like to hold the slenderer one in my arms,   15
For she has walked over to me
And nuzzled my left hand.
She is black and white,
Her mane falls wild on her forehead,
And the light breeze moves me to caress her long ear   20
That is delicate as the skin over a girl's wrist.
Suddenly I realize
That if I stepped out of my body I would break
Into blossom.

[1963]

PHILIP LEVINE   [b. 1928]

What Work Is

We stand in the rain in a long line
waiting at Ford Highland Park. For work.
You know what work is—if you're
old enough to read this you know what
work is, although you may not do it.   5
Forget you. This is about waiting,
shifting from one foot to another.
Feeling the light rain falling like mist
into your hair, blurring your vision
until you think you see your own brother   10
ahead of you, maybe ten places.
You rub your glasses with your fingers,
and of course it's someone else's brother,
narrower across the shoulders than
yours but with the same sad slouch, the grin   15
that does not hide the stubbornness,
the sad refusal to give in to
rain, to the hours wasted waiting,
to the knowledge that somewhere ahead
a man is waiting who will say, "No,   20
we're not hiring today," for any
reason he wants. You love your brother,
now suddenly you can hardly stand
the love flooding you for your brother,
who's not beside you or behind or   25
ahead because he's home trying to
sleep off a miserable night shift
at Cadillac so he can get up
before noon to study his German.
Works eight hours a night so he can sing   30
Wagner, the opera you hate most,
the worst music ever invented.
How long has it been since you told him
you loved him, held his wide shoulders,
opened your eyes wide and said those words,   35
and maybe kissed his cheek? You've never
done something so simple, so obvious,
not because you're too young or too dumb,
not because you're jealous or even mean

or incapable of crying in   40
the presence of another man, no,
just because you don't know what work is.

[1991]

CONRAD HILBERRY   [b. 1928]

Player Piano

She was right: basement was the place for it.
Who wants a Pianola in the dining room?
It's not an instrument, not a household
object even, more a curiosity.

So with a rented dolly and four big friends   5
from work, he eased it down the cellar stairs,
across the concrete to its place against
the wall. Now he leans back on the bench

and pumps the Basement Rag. His youngest daughter
sits beside him on the bench within   10
the light of the gooseneck lamp, the dog curls
on the rug, and always the ghostly fingers move,

the left hand striding and the right hand climbing
down out of the high notes. Four of them,
father, daughter, dog, and piano player,   15
all in a circle of light, the roll unwinding

its dots and dashes, music clattering out,
and no one saying anything. "Hey,
Cosby's on,"° his wife calls down the stairs.
"Why not come on up?" And so they sit   20

in the kitchen, laughing at Rudy and the Cos.
Afterwards, homework and bed—and he drifts
back to the basement, back to the wooden music.
Gradually, his wife becomes sarcastic,

as if he were counterfeiting bills down there,   25
or dissecting cats. His daughter says she isn't

19. **Cosby's on:** *The Cosby Show* was a popular television situation comedy
(1984–1992) starring Bill Cosby and Phylicia Rashad.

coming down. But he believes the piano
brings him closer to them all. It's something

he can count on, almost like a law
of nature, not needing praise or inspiration,   30
sticking to its version of the story.
The roll scrolling in front of him is

Morse code talking to people in other basements
or in huts or lean-to's—Sarasota, Caracas,
up-country Liberia. The key taps out   35
news of high winds, the river rising, families

sheltered in the local school, news
of people he's never met, clicking in a voice
without inflection, neither speech
nor silence. The longs and shorts, the steady   40

white keys and the black must carry
through the studs of the house, he thinks,
easing the children into sleep.
He hears a pipe muttering

and knows his wife is drawing water for   45
a bath. It stops. She must be in the tub.
He taps a message on the pipe, binary,
the way nerves talk, signaling across

the gaps, need and love condensed to dots
and dashes. She must hear it as she steams   50
and lathers in the bath, metallic music
played by no one's fingers on the pipes.

[1999]

SAMUEL HAZO   [b. 1928]

For Fawzi in Jerusalem

Leaving a world too old to name
and too undying to forsake,
I flew the cold, expensive sea
toward Columbus' mistake
where life could never be the same   5

for me. In Jerash° on the sand
I saw the colonnades of Rome
bleach in the sun like skeletons.
Behind a convalescent home,
armed soldiers guarded no man's land   10

between Jordanians and Jews.
Opposing sentries frowned and spat.
Fawzi, you mocked in Arabic
this justice from Jehoshophat°
before you shined my Pittsburgh shoes   15

for nothing. Why you never kept
the coins I offered you is still
your secret and your victory.
Saying you saw marauders kill
your father while Beershebans° wept   20

for mercy in their holy war,
you told me how you stole to stay
alive. You must have thought I thought
your history would make me pay
a couple of piastres more   25

than any shine was worth—and I
was ready to—when you said, "No,
I never take. I never want
America to think I throw
myself on you. I never lie."   30

I watched your young but old man's stare
demand the sword to flash again
in blood and flame from Jericho°
and leave the bones of these new men
of Judah bleaching in the air   35

6. **Jerash:** The ancient city of Gerasa, twenty-two miles north of Amman in present-day Jordan. Called Jerash by the Romans who rebuilt it in 65 C.E., it is the best-preserved Palestinian city of Roman times.

14. **Jehoshophat:** Hebrew king of Judah (c. 873–849 B.C.E.), the first to make a treaty with the neighboring kingdom of Israel.

20. **Beershebans:** Inhabitants of Beersheba, a city in southern Israel. Given to the Arabs in the partition of Palestine (1948), it was retaken by Israel in the Arab-Israeli war of 1948.

33. **Jericho:** Ancient city in biblical Palestine, in the Jordan valley north of the Dead Sea, captured from the Canaanites by Joshua and destroyed (Joshua 6:1–21).

like Roman stones upon the plain
of Jerash. Then you faced away.
Jerusalem, Jerusalem,
I asked myself if I could pray
for peace and not recall the pain   40

you spoke. But what could praying do?
Today I live your loss in no
man's land but mine, and every time
I talk of fates not just but so,
Fawzi, my friend, I think of you.   45

[1968]

ANNE SEXTON   [1928–1974]

Cinderella

You always read about it:
the plumber with twelve children
who wins the Irish Sweepstakes.
From toilets to riches.
That story.   5

Or the nursemaid,
some luscious sweet from Denmark
who captures the oldest son's heart.
From diapers to Dior.°
That story.   10

Or a milkman who serves the wealthy,
eggs, cream, butter, yogurt, milk,
the white truck like an ambulance
who goes into real estate
and makes a pile.   15
From homogenized to martinis at lunch.

Or the charwoman
who is on the bus when it cracks up
and collects enough from the insurance.
   From mops to Bonwit Teller.°   20
   That story.

9. **Dior:** Fashions designed by the French house of Dior, established by Christian
Dior (1905–1957).
20. **Bonwit Teller:** A fashionable and expensive department store.

Once
the wife of a rich man was on her deathbed
and she said to her daughter Cinderella:
Be devout. Be good. Then I will smile   25
down from heaven in the seam of a cloud.
The man took another wife who had
two daughters, pretty enough
but with hearts like blackjacks.
Cinderella was their maid.   30
She slept on the sooty hearth each night
and walked around looking like Al Jolson.°
Her father brought presents home from town,
jewels and gowns for the other women
but the twig of a tree for Cinderella.   35
She planted that twig on her mother's grave
and it grew to a tree where a white dove sat.
Whenever she wished for anything the dove
would drop it like an egg upon the ground.
The bird is important, my dears, so heed him.   40

Next came the ball, as you all know.
It was a marriage market.
The prince was looking for a wife.
All but Cinderella were preparing
and gussying up for the big event.   45
Cinderella begged to go too.
Her stepmother threw a dish of lentils
into the cinders and said: Pick them
up in an hour and you shall go.
The white dove brought all his friends;   50
all the warm wings of the fatherland came,
and picked up the lentils in a jiffy.
No, Cinderella, said the stepmother,
you have no clothes and cannot dance.
That's the way with stepmothers.   55

Cinderella went to the tree at the grave
and cried forth like a gospel singer:
Mama! Mama! My turtledove,
send me to the prince's ball!
The bird dropped down a golden dress   60

32. **Al Jolson:** American entertainer (1888–1950), known particularly for singing
in blackface.

and delicate little gold slippers.
Rather a large package for a simple bird.
So she went. Which is no surprise.
Her stepmother and sisters didn't
recognize her without her cinder face   65
and the prince took her hand on the spot
and danced with no other the whole day.

As nightfall came she thought she'd better
get home. The prince walked her home
and she disappeared into the pigeon house   70
and although the prince took an axe and broke
it open she was gone. Back to her cinders.
These events repeated themselves for three days.
However on the third day the prince
covered the palace steps with cobbler's wax   75
and Cinderella's gold shoe stuck upon it.

Now he would find whom the shoe fit
and find his strange dancing girl for keeps.
He went to their house and the two sisters
were delighted because they had lovely feet.   80
The eldest went into a room to try the slipper on
but her big toe got in the way so she simply
sliced it off and put on the slipper.
The prince rode away with her until the white dove
told him to look at the blood pouring forth.   85
That is the way with amputations.
They don't just heal up like a wish.
The other sister cut off her heel
but the blood told as blood will.
The prince was getting tired.   90
He began to feel like a shoe salesman.
But he gave it one last try.
This time Cinderella fit into the shoe
like a love letter into its envelope.

At the wedding ceremony   95
the two sisters came to curry favor
and the white dove pecked their eyes out.
Two hollow spots were left
like soup spoons.

Cinderella and the prince   100
lived, they say, happily ever after,

like two dolls in a museum case
never bothered by diapers or dust,
never arguing over the timing of an egg,
never telling the same story twice,   105
never getting a middle-aged spread,
their darling smiles pasted on for eternity.
Regular Bobbsey Twins.
That story.

[1971]

ADRIENNE RICH   [b. 1929]

Diving into the Wreck

First having read the book of myths,
and loaded the camera,
and checked the edge of the knife-blade,
I put on
the body-armor of black rubber   5
the absurd flippers
the grave and awkward mask.
I am having to do this
not like Cousteau° with his
assiduous team   10
aboard the sun-flooded schooner
but here alone.

There is a ladder.
The ladder is always there
hanging innocently   15
close to the side of the schooner.
We know what it is for,
we who have used it.
Otherwise
it's a piece of maritime floss   20
some sundry equipment.

I go down.
Rung after rung and still
the oxygen immerses me

9. **Cousteau:** Jacques-Yves Cousteau (1910–1997), French underwater explorer,
photographer, and author.

the blue light   25
the clear atoms
of our human air.
I go down.
My flippers cripple me,
I crawl like an insect down the ladder   30
and there is no one
to tell me when the ocean
will begin.

First the air is blue and then
it is bluer and then green and then   35
black I am blacking out and yet
my mask is powerful
it pumps my blood with power
the sea is another story
the sea is not a question of power   40
I have to learn alone
to turn my body without force
in the deep element.

And now: it is easy to forget
what I came for   45
among so many who have always
lived here
swaying their crenellated° fans
between the reefs
and besides   50
you breathe differently down here.

I came to explore the wreck.
The words are purposes.
The words are maps.
I came to see the damage that was done   55
and the treasures that prevail.
I stroke the beam of my lamp
slowly along the flank
of something more permanent
than fish or weed   60

the thing I came for:
the wreck and not the story of the wreck
the thing itself and not the myth

48. crenellated: Notched; *crenels* are the open spaces between the solid portions
of a battlement.

the drowned face° always staring
toward the sun   65
the evidence of damage
worn by salt and sway into this threadbare beauty
the ribs of the disaster
curving their assertion
among the tentative haunters.   70

This is the place.
And I am here, the mermaid whose dark hair
streams black, the merman in his armored body
We circle silently
about the wreck   75
we dive into the hold.
I am she: I am he

whose drowned face sleeps with open eyes
whose breasts still bear the stress
whose silver, copper, vermeil° cargo lies   80
obscurely inside barrels
half-wedged and left to rot
we are the half-destroyed instruments
that once held to a course
the water-eaten log   85
the fouled compass

We are, I am, you are
by cowardice or courage
the one who find our way
back to this scene   90
carrying a knife, a camera
a book of myths
in which
our names do not appear.

[1973]

---

64. drowned face: The ornamental female figurehead on the prow of an old sailing ship.
80. vermeil: Gilded silver, bronze, or copper.

GARY SNYDER   [b. 1930]

Hitch Haiku

They didn't hire him
        so he ate his lunch alone:
the noon whistle
       • • •

Cats shut down
         deer thread through   5
men all eating lunch
       • • •

Frying hotcakes in a dripping shelter
      Fu Manchu°
Queets Indian Reservation in the rain
       • • •

A truck went by   10
        three hours ago:
Smoke Creek desert
       • • •

Jackrabbit eyes all night
  breakfast in Elko.
       • • •

Old kanji hid by dirt   15
on skidroad Jap town walls
       down the hill
to the Wobbly hall

Seattle
       • • •

Spray drips from the cargo-booms
a fresh-chipped winch   20
      spotted with red lead
young fir—
      soaking in summer rain
       • • •

Over the Mindanao Deep

Scrap bass
      dumpt off the fantail   25
falling six miles

8. **Fu Manchu:** Master criminal in a series of "Yellow Peril Thrillers" by Sax Rohmer (pen name of Arthur Henry Sarsfield Ward, 1883–1959) that were immensely popular in the first half of the twentieth century.

• • •

[The following two were written on classical
themes while traveling through Sappho, Washington.
The first is by Thomas L. Hoodlatch.]

Moonlight on the burned-out temple —
                wooden horse shit.

Sunday dinner in Ithaca —
                the twang of a bowstring   30

• • •

After weeks of watching the roof leak
                I fixed it tonight
by moving a single board

• • •

A freezing morning in October in the high
Sierra crossing Five Lakes Basin to the
Kaweahs with Bob Greensfelder and Claude Dalenburg

Stray white mare
                neck rope dangling   35
forty miles from farms.

• • •

Back from the Kaweahs

Sundown, Timber Gap
                — sat down —
                        dark firs.
    dirty;   cold;   40
too tired to talk

• • •

Cherry blossoms at Hood river
                rusty sand near Tucson
mudflats of Willapa Bay

• • •

Pronghorn country

Steering into the sun   45
                glittering jewel-road
shattered obsidian

• • •

The mountain walks over the water!
Rain down from the mountain!
                high bleat of a   50
cow elk
                over blackberries

• • •

A great freight truck
        lit like a town
through the dark stony desert   55

• • •

Drinking hot saké
                toasting fish on coals
    the motorcycle
out   parked in the rain.

• • •

Switchback

turn, turn,   60
and again,   hard-
scrabble
steep travel a-
head.

[1968]

DEREK WALCOTT   [b. 1930]

Sea Grapes

That sail which leans on light,
tired of islands,
a schooner beating up the Caribbean

for home, could be Odysseus,°
home-bound on the Aegean;   5
that father and husband's

longing, under gnarled sour grapes, is
like the adulterer hearing Nausicaa's name
in every gull's outcry.

4. **Odysseus:** For background, see page 85. Princess Nausicaa (line 8) fell in love
with Odysseus when he was carried by a storm to Phaiacia; he could have married
her and stayed there, but he chose to go home (responsibility) rather than to enjoy
an indulgent life with her (obsession). Odysseus blinded Polyphemus (line 16), a
giant one-eyed Cyclops, who held him prisoner; as Odysseus escaped, Polyphemus threw great rocks in front of his boat to wash it back to shore. The *Odyssey*
was written in hexameter verse (line 17).

This brings nobody peace. The ancient war   10
between obsession and responsibility
will never finish and has been the same

for the sea-wanderer or the one on shore
now wriggling on his sandals to walk home,
since Troy sighed its last flame,   15

and the blind giant's boulder heaved the trough
from whose groundswell the great hexameters come
to the conclusions of exhausted surf.

The classics can console. But not enough.

[1976]

GEOFFREY HILL   [b. 1932]

In Memory of Jane Fraser

When snow like sheep lay in the fold
And winds went begging at each door,
And the far hills were blue with cold,
And a cold shroud lay on the moor,

She kept the siege. And every day   5
We watched her brooding over death
Like a strong bird above its prey.
The room filled with the kettle's breath.

Damp curtains glued against the pane
Sealed time away. Her body froze   10
As if to freeze us all, and chain
Creation to a stunned repose.

She died before the world could stir.
In March the ice unloosed the brook
And water ruffled the sun's hair.   15
Dead cones upon the alder shook.

[1959]

LINDA PASTAN   [b. 1932]

An Early Afterlife

. . . a wise man in time of peace, shall
make the necessary preparations for war.
                              —Horace

Why don't we say goodbye right now
in the fallacy of perfect health
before whatever is going to happen
happens. We could perfect our parting,
like those characters in *On the Beach*   5
who said farewell in the shadow
of the bomb as we sat watching,
young and holding hands at the movies.
We could use the loving words
we otherwise might not have time to say.   10
We could hold each other for hours
in a quintessential dress rehearsal.

Then we would just continue
for however many years were left.
The ragged things that are coming next—   15
arteries closing like rivers silting over,
or rampant cells stampeding us to the exit—
would be like postscripts to our lives
and wouldn't matter. And we would bask
in an early afterlife of ordinary days,   20
impervious to the inclement weather
already in our long-range forecast.
Nothing could touch us. We'd never
have to say goodbye again.

                                                    [1995]

SYLVIA PLATH   [1932–1963]

Metaphors

I'm a riddle in nine syllables,
An elephant, a ponderous house,
A melon strolling on two tendrils.

O red fruit, ivory, fine timbers!
This loaf's big with its yeasty rising.   5
Money's new-minted in this fat purse.
I'm a means, a stage, a cow in calf.
I've eaten a bag of green apples,
Boarded the train there's no getting off.

[1960]

SYLVIA PLATH   [1932–1963]

Daddy

You do not do, you do not do
Any more, black shoe
In which I have lived like a foot
For thirty years, poor and white,
Barely daring to breathe or Achoo.   5

Daddy, I have had to kill you.
You died before I had time—
Marble-heavy, a bag full of God,
Ghastly statue with one grey toe
Big as a Frisco seal   10

And a head in the freakish Atlantic
Where it pours bean green over blue
In the waters off beautiful Nauset.
I used to pray to recover you.
Ach, du.°   *Oh, you (German)* 15

In the German tongue, in the Polish town
Scraped flat by the roller
Of wars, wars, wars.
But the name of the town is common.
My Polack friend   20

Says there are a dozen or two.
So I never could tell where you
Put your foot, your root,
I never could talk to you.
The tongue stuck in my jaw.   25

It stuck in a barb wire snare.
Ich, ich, ich, ich,°   *I (German)*

I could hardly speak.
I thought every German was you.
And the language obscene   30

An engine, an engine
Chuffing me off like a Jew.
A Jew to Dachau, Auschwitz, Belsen.°
I began to talk like a Jew.
I think I may well be a Jew.   35

The snows of the Tyrol,° the clear beer of Vienna
Are not very pure or true.
With my gypsy ancestress and my weird luck
And my Taroc pack and my Taroc pack
I may be a bit of a Jew.   40

I have always been scared of *you,*
With your Luftwaffe,° your gobbledygoo.
And your neat moustache
And your Aryan eye, bright blue.
Panzer°-man, panzer-man, O You—   45

Not God but a swastika
So black no sky could squeak through.
Every woman adores a Fascist,
The boot in the face, the brute
Brute heart of a brute like you.   50

You stand at the blackboard, daddy,
In the picture I have of you,
A cleft in your chin instead of your foot
But no less a devil for that, no not
Any less the black man who   55

Bit my pretty red heart in two.
I was ten when they buried you.
At twenty I tried to die
And get back, back, back to you.
I thought even the bones would do.   60

But they pulled me out of the sack,
And they stuck me together with glue.
And then I knew what to do.

33. **Dachau, Auschwitz, Belsen:** Nazi concentration camps.
36. **the Tyrol:** An alpine region in western Austria and northern Italy.
42. **Luftwaffe:** The Nazi air force in World War II.
45. **Panzer:** An armored unit in the German army in World War II.

I made a model of you,
A man in black with a Meinkampf° look   65

And a love of the rack and the screw.
And I said I do, I do.
So daddy, I'm finally through.
The black telephone's off at the root,
The voices just can't worm through.   70

If I've killed one man, I've killed two—
The vampire who said he was you
And drank my blood for a year,
Seven years, if you want to know.
Daddy, you can lie back now.   75

There's a stake in your fat black heart
And the villagers never liked you.
They are dancing and stamping on you.
They always *knew* it was you.
Daddy, daddy, you bastard, I'm through.   80

[1962]

65. *Mein Kampf*: *My Struggle*, the title of Adolf Hitler's autobiography.

ETHERIDGE KNIGHT   [1933–1991]

Hard Rock Returns to Prison from the Hospital for the Criminal Insane

Hard Rock / was / "known not to take no shit
From nobody," and he had the scars to prove it:
Split purple lips, lumbed ears, welts above
His yellow eyes, and one long scar that cut
Across his temple and plowed through a thick   5
Canopy of kinky hair.

The WORD / was / that Hard Rock wasn't a mean nigger
Anymore, that the doctors had bored a hole in his head,
Cut out part of his brain, and shot electricity
Through the rest. When they brought Hard Rock back,   10
Handcuffed and chained, he was turned loose,
Like a freshly gelded stallion, to try his new status.

And we all waited and watched, like a herd of sheep,
To see if the WORD was true.

As we waited we wrapped ourselves in the cloak   15
Of his exploits: "Man, the last time, it took eight
Screws° to put him in the Hole."° "Yeah, remember when he
Smacked the captain with his dinner tray?" "He set
The record for time in the Hole—67 straight days!"
"Ol Hard Rock! man, that's one crazy nigger."   20
And then the jewel of a myth that Hard Rock had once bit
A screw on the thumb and poisoned him with syphilitic spit.

The testing came, to see if Hard Rock was really tame.
A hillbilly called him a black son of a bitch
And didn't lose his teeth, a screw who knew Hard Rock   25
From before shook him down and barked in his face.
And Hard Rock did *nothing*. Just grinned and looked silly,
His eyes empty like knot holes in a fence.

And even after we discovered that it took Hard Rock
Exactly 3 minutes to tell you his first name,   30
We told ourselves that he had just wised up,
Was being cool; but we could not fool ourselves for long,
And we turned away, our eyes on the ground. Crushed.
He had been our Destroyer, the doer of things
We dreamed of doing but could not bring ourselves to do,   35
The fears of years, like a biting whip,
Had cut deep bloody grooves
Across our backs.

                                                           [1968]

17. **Screws:** Guards; **Hole:** Solitary confinement.

JIM BARNES   [b. 1933]

Return to La Plata, Missouri

The warping bandstand reminds you of the hard rage
you felt in the heart of the town the day you said goodbye
to the park, silver jet, and cicadas dead in the sage.

The town is basic red, although it browns. A cry
of murder, rape, or wrong will always bend the night   5
hard into the broken grass. You listen close for sighs

of lovers on the ground. The darkness gathers light
and throws it down: something glows that you cannot name,
something fierce, abstract, given time and space you might

on a journey leave behind, a stone to carve your fame   10
on, or a simple word like *love*. The sun is down
or always going down in La Plata, the same

sun. Same too the child's cry that turns the mother's frown
brittle as chalk or the town's face against the moon.
Same too the moan of dog and diesel circling the town   15

in an air so heavy with cloud that there is little room
for breath or moon. Strange: in a town so country, so
foreign, you never hear a song nor see a loom

pattern dark threads into a history you would know
and would not know. You think you see one silver star.   20
But the town offers only itself, and you must go.

[1982]

JEAN VALENTINE   [b. 1934]

December 21st

How will I think of you
"God-with-us"
a name: a word

and trees paths stars this earth
how will I think of them   5

and the dead I love   and all absent friends
here-with-me

and table: hand: white coffee mug:
a northern still life:

and you   10
without a body

quietness

and the infant's red-brown mouth   a star
at the star of a girl's nipple . . .

[1979]

SONIA SANCHEZ   [b. 1934]

An Anthem

for the anc and brandywine peace community

Our vision is our voice
we cut through the country
where madmen goosestep in tune to Guernica.°

we are people made of fire
we walk with ceremonial breaths   5
we have condemned talking mouths.

we run without legs
we see without eyes
loud laughter breaks over our heads.

give me courage so I can spread   10
it over my face and mouth.

we are secret rivers
with shaking hips and crests
come awake in our thunder
so that our eyes can see behind trees.   15

for the world is split wide open
and you hide your hands behind your backs
for the world is broken into little pieces
and you beg with tin cups for life.

are we not more than hunger and music?   20
are we not more than harlequins and horns?
are we not more than color and drums?
are we not more than anger and dance?
give me courage so I can spread it
over my face and mouth.   25

we are the shakers
walking from top to bottom in a day
we are like Shango°

3. **Guernica:** A town in northern Spain that was destroyed in 1937 by insurgents in the Spanish civil war, aided by German planes; the indiscriminate killing of women and children aroused world opinion, and the bombing of Guernica made it a symbol of fascist brutality.
28. **Shango:** One of the orishas, or gods, of the Yoruba tribe of western Nigeria. The legendary fourth king of the ancient kingdom of Oyo, he is lord of lightning, thunder, rain, and testicular fertility.

involving ourselves in acts
that bring life to the middle   30
of our stomachs

we are coming towards you madmen
shredding your death talk
standing in front with mornings around our waist
we have inherited our prayers from   35
the rain
our eyes from the children of Soweto.°

red rain pours over the land
and our fire mixes with the water.

give me courage so I can spread   40
it over my face and mouth.

[1987]

37. **Soweto:** A group of segregated townships inhabited by blacks near Johannesburg, South Africa. It was the scene of a massive uprising in 1976 against the policies of apartheid.

PAUL ZIMMER   [b. 1934]

Zimmer Imagines Heaven

for Merrill Leffler

I sit with Joseph Conrad in Monet's garden.
We are listening to Yeats chant his poems,
A breeze stirs through Thomas Hardy's moustache,
John Skelton has gone to the house for beer,
Wanda Landowska lightly fingers a harpsichord,   5
Along the spruce tree walk Roberto Clemente and
Thurman Munson whistle a baseball back and forth.
Mozart chats with Ellington in the roses.

Monet smokes and dabs his canvas in the sun,
Brueghel and Turner set easels behind the wisteria.   10
The band is warming up in the Big Studio:
Bean, Brute, Bird, and Serge on saxes,
Kai, Bill Harris, Lawrence Brown trombones,
Little Jazz, Clifford, Fats, Diz on trumpets,
Klook plays drums, Mingus bass, Bud the piano.   15

Later Madam Schuman-Heink will sing Schubert,
The monks of Benedictine Abbey will chant.
There will be more poems from Emily Dickinson,
James Wright, John Clare, Walt Whitman.
Shakespeare rehearses players for *King Lear.*   20

At dusk Alice Toklas brings out platters
Of sweetbreads, Salad Livonière,
And a tureen of Gazpacho of Málaga.
After the meal Brahms passes fine cigars.
God comes then, radiant with a bottle of cognac,   25
She pours generously into the snifters,
I tell Her I have begun to learn what
Heaven is about. She wants to hear.
It is, I say, being thankful for eternity.
Her smile is the best part of the day.   30

[1996]

AUDRE LORDE   [1934–1992]

Coal

I   is the total black
being spoken
from the earth's inside.

There are many kinds of open
how a diamond comes   5
into a knot of flame
how sound comes into a word
colored
by who pays what for speaking.

Some words are open   10
diamonds on a glass window
singing out within the crash
of passing sun
other words are stapled wagers
in a perforated book   15
buy and sign and tear apart
and come whatever wills all chances
the stub remains
an ill-pulled tooth
with a ragged edge.   20

Some words live in my throat
breeding like adders
others
know sun
seeking like gypsies   25
over my tongue
to explode through my lips
like young sparrows
bursting from shell.

Some words   30
bedevil me.

Love is a word, another kind of open.
As the diamond comes
into a knot of flame
I am Black   35
because I come from the earth's inside
take my word for jewel
in the open light.

[1962; rev. 1992]

CHARLES WRIGHT   [b. 1935]

March Journal

—After the Rapture comes, and everyone goes away
Quicker than cream in a cat's mouth,
                              all of them gone
In an endless slipknot down the sky
                              and its pink tongue   5
Into the black hole of Somewhere Else,

What will we do, left with the empty spaces of our lives
Intact,
       the radio frequencies still unchanged,
The same houses up for sale,   10
Same books unread,
                 all comfort gone and its comforting . . .

For us, the earth is a turbulent rest,
                     a different bed

Altogether, and kinder than that—   15
After the first death is the second,
A little fire in the afterglow,
                    somewhere to warm your hands.

—The clean, clear line, incised, unbleeding,
Sharp and declarative as a cut   20
                    the instant before the blood wells out . . .

—*March Blues*
The insides were blue, the color of Power Putty,
When Luke dissected the dogfish,
                    a plastic blue   25
In the whey
            sharkskin infenestrated:
Its severed tailfin bobbed like a wing nut in another pan
As he explained the dye job
                    and what connected with what,   30
Its pursed lips skewed and pointed straight-lined at the ceiling,
The insides so blue, so blue . . .

March gets its second wind,
                    starlings high shine in the trees
As dread puts its left foot down and then the other.   35
Buds hold their breaths and sit tight.
The weeping cherries
            lower their languorous necks and nibble the grass
Sprout ends that jump headfirst from the ground,
Magnolia drums blue weight   40
                    next door when the sun is right.

—Rhythm comes from the roots of the world,
                    rehearsed and expandable.

—After the ice storm a shower of crystal down from the trees
Shattering over the ground   45
                    like cut glass twirling its rainbows,
Sunlight in flushed layers under the clouds,
Twirling and disappearing into the clenched March grass.

—Structure is binary, intent on a resolution,
Its parts tight but the whole loose   50
                    and endlessly repetitious.

—And here we stand, caught
In the crucifixal noon
            with its bled, attendant bells,

And nothing to answer back with.   55
Forsythia purrs in its burning shell,
Jonquils, like Dante's angels, appear from their blue shoots.

How can we think to know of another's desire for darkness,
That low coo like a dove's
                          insistent outside the heart's window?   60
How can we think to think this?
How can we sit here, crossing out line after line,
Such five-finger exercises
                          up and down, learning our scales,

And say that all quartets are eschatological°   *pertaining to the end times* 65
Heuristically
          when the willows swim like medusas through the trees,
Their skins beginning to blister into a thousand green welts?
How can we think to know these things,
Clouds like full suds in the sky   70
                          keeping away, keeping away?

—Form is finite, an undestroyable hush over all things.

                                                                       [1988]

MARY OLIVER   [b. 1935]

August

When the blackberries hang
swollen in the woods, in the brambles
nobody owns, I spend

all day among the high
branches, reaching   5
my ripped arms, thinking

of nothing, cramming
the black honey of summer
into my mouth; all day my body

accepts what it is. In the dark   10
creeks that run by there is
this thick paw of my life darting among

the black bells, the leaves; there is
this happy tongue.

                                                                       [1983]

JAYNE CORTEZ   [b. 1936]

Into This Time

for Charles Mingus°

Into this time
of steel feathers blowing from hearts
into this turquoise flame time in the mouth
into this sonic boom time in the conch
into this musty stone-fly time sinking into   5
the melancholy buttocks of dawn
sinking into lacerated whelps
into gun holsters
into breast bones
into a manganese field of uranium nozzles   10
into a nuclear tube full of drunk rodents
into the massive vein of one interval
into one moment's hair plucked down into
the timeless droning fixed into
long pauses   15
fixed into a lash of ninety-eight minutes screeching into
the internal heat of an ice ball melting time into
a configuration of commas on strike
into a work force armed with a calendar of green wings
into a collection of nerves   20
into magnetic mucus
into tongueless shrines
into water pus of a silver volcano
into the black granite face of Morelos°
into the pigeon toed dance of Mingus   25
into a refuge of air bubbles
into a cylinder of snake whistles
into clusters of slow spiders
into spade fish skulls
into rosin coated shadows of women wrapped in live iguanas   30
into coins into crosses into St. Martin De Porres°
into the pain of this place changing pitches beneath
fingers swelling into
night shouts

Charles Mingus: An innovative American jazz bassist (1929–1979).
24. Morelos: José Maria Morelos (1765–1815), a Mexican revolutionary leader.
31. Martin De Porres: A seventeenth-century Peruvian saint.

into day trembles   35
into month of precious bloods flowing into
this fiesta of sadness year
into this city of eternal spring
into this solo
on the road of young bulls   40
on the street of lost children
on the avenue of dead warriors
on the frisky horse tail fuzz zooming
into ears of every madman
stomping into every new composition   45
everyday of the blues
penetrating into this time

This time of loose strings in low tones
pulling boulders of Olmec heads into the sun
into tight wires uncoiling from body of a strip teaser on the table   50
into half-tones wailing between snap and click
of two castanets smoking into
scales jumping from tips of sacrificial flints
into frogs yodeling across grieving cults
yodeling up into word stuffed smell of flamingo stew   55
into wind packed fuel of howling dog throats slit into
this January flare of aluminum dust falling into
laminated stomach of a bass violin rubbed into red ashes
rubbed into the time sequence of
this time of salmonella leaking from eyeballs of a pope   60
into this lavender vomit time in the chest into
this time plumage of dried bats in the brain into
this wallowing time weed of invisible wakes on cassettes into
this off-beat time syncopation in a leopard skin suit
into this radiated protrusion of time in the desert into   65
this frozen cheek time of dead infants in the cellar
into this time flying with the rotten bottoms of used tuxedos
into this purple   brown   grey   gold minus zero time trilling into
a lime stone crusted Yucatan belching
into fifty six medallions shaking   70
into armadillo drums thumping
into tambourines of fetishes rattling
into an oil slick of poverty symbols flapping
into flat-footed shuffle of two birds advancing
into back spine of luminous impulses tumbling   75
into metronomes of colossal lips ticking

into a double zigzag of callouses splitting
into foam of electric snow flashing into this time
of steel feathers blowing from hearts
into this turquoise flame time in the mouth into   80
this sonic boom time in the conch
into this musty stone fly time sinking into
the melancholy buttocks of dawn

[1991]

LUCILLE CLIFTON   [b. 1936]

at the cemetery,
walnut grove plantation,
south carolina, 1989

among the rocks
at walnut grove
your silence drumming
in my bones,
tell me your names.   5

nobody mentioned slaves
and yet the curious tools
shine with your fingerprints.
nobody mentioned slaves
but somebody did this work   10
who had no guide, no stone,
who moulders under rock.

tell me your names,
tell me your bashful names
and i will testify.   15

the inventory lists ten slaves
but only men were recognized.

among the rocks
at walnut grove
some of these honored dead   20
were dark
some of these dark
were slaves

some of these slaves
were women   25
some of them did this
honored work.
tell me your names
foremothers, brothers,
tell me your dishonored names.   30
here lies
here lies
here lies
here lies
hear   35

[1991]

NANCY WILLARD   [b. 1936]

Questions My Son Asked Me,
Answers I Never Gave Him

1. Do gorillas have birthdays?
   Yes. Like the rainbow, they happen.
   Like the air, they are not observed.

2. Do butterflies make a noise?
   The wire in the butterfly's tongue
   hums gold. Some men hear butterflies
   even in winter.

3. Are they part of our family?
   They forgot us, who forgot how to fly.

4. Who tied my navel? Did God tie it?
   God made the thread: O man, live forever!
   Man made the knot: enough is enough.

5. If I drop my tooth in the telephone
   will it go through the wires and bite someone's ear?
   I have seen earlobes pierced by a tooth of steel.
   It loves what lasts.
   It does not love flesh.
   It leaves a ring of gold in the wound.

6. If I stand on my head
   will the sleep in my eye roll up into my head?

Does the dream know its own father?
Can bread go back to the field of its birth?

7. Can I eat a star?
   Yes, with the mouth of time
   that enjoys everything.

8. Could we Xerox the moon?
   This is the first commandment:
   I am the moon, thy moon.
   Thou shalt have no other moons before thee.

9. Who invented water?
   The hands of the air, that wanted to wash each other.

10. What happens at the end of numbers?
    I see three men running toward a field.
    At the edge of the tall grass, they turn into light.

11. Do the years ever run out?
    God said, I will break time's heart.
    Time ran down like an old phonograph.
    It lay flat as a carpet.
    At rest on its threads, I am learning to fly.

[1982]

DAVID YOUNG   [b. 1936]

The Portable Earth-Lamp

The planet on the desk, illuminated globe
we ordered for Bo's birthday,
sits in its Lucite crescent, a medicine ball
of Rand McNally plastic. A brown cord   5
runs from the South Pole toward a socket.

It's mostly a night-light for the boys
and it blanches their dreaming faces
a blue sphere patched with continents
mottled by deeps and patterned currents,   10
its capital cities bright white dots.

Our models: they're touching and absurd,
magical for both their truth and falsehood.

I like its shine at night. Moth-light.
I sleepwalk toward it, musing.
This globe's a bible, a bubble of myth-   15
light, a blue eye, a double
bowl: empty of all but its bulb and clever skin,
full of whatever we choose to lodge there.

I haven't been able to shake off all my grief,
my globe's cold poles and arid wastes,   20
the weight of death, disease and history.
But see how the oceans heave and shine,
see how the clouds and mountains glisten!

We float through space. Days pass.
Sometimes we know we are part of a crystal   25
where light is sorted and stored,
sharing an iridescence
cobbled and million-featured.

Oh, tiny beacon in the hurting dark.
Oh, soft blue glow.   30

[1988]

MARGE PIERCY   [b. 1936]

Barbie Doll

This girlchild was born as usual
and presented dolls that did pee-pee
and miniature GE stoves and irons
and wee lipsticks the color of cherry candy.
Then in the magic of puberty, a classmate said: 5
You have a great big nose and fat legs.

She was healthy, tested intelligent,
possessed strong arms and back,
abundant sexual drive and manual dexterity.
She went to and fro apologizing.   10
Everyone saw a fat nose on thick legs.

She was advised to play coy,
exhorted to come on hearty,
exercise, diet, smile and wheedle.

Her good nature wore out   15
like a fan belt.
So she cut off her nose and her legs
and offered them up.

In the casket displayed on satin she lay
with the undertaker's cosmetics painted on,   20
a turned-up putty nose,
dressed in a pink and white nightie.
Doesn't she look pretty? everyone said.
Consummation at last.
To every woman a happy ending.   25

[1973]

SUSAN HOWE   [b. 1937]

From Speeches at the Barriers

2.

Right or ruth
rent

to the winds shall be thrown

words being wind or web

What (pine-cone wheat-ear   35
sea-shell) what

volume of secrets to teach
Socrates

Banks of wild bees in story
sing in no wood so on   40

cornstalk and cornsheaf

prodigal benevolence
wealth washed up by the sea

What I find
signal seen by my eye   45

This winter falls froward
forever

sound and suggestion speared
open

Free will in blind duel   50

sees in secret houses in sand

each day's last purpose
each day's firm progress

schoolgirls sleeping
schoolboys sleeping and stemmed   55

I will dream you
Draw you

dawn and horses of the sun
dawn galloped in greek before flame

fugitive dialogue of masterwork   60

[1983]

CHARLES SIMIC   [b. 1938]

Begotten of the Spleen°

The Virgin Mother° walked barefoot
Among the land mines.
She carried an old man in her arms
Like a howling babe.

The earth was an old people's home.   5
Judas was the night nurse,
Emptying bedpans into the river Jordan,
Tying people on a dog chain.

The old man had two stumps for legs.
St. Peter came pushing a cart   10
Loaded with flying carpets.
They were not flying carpets.

They were piles of bloody diapers.
The Magi° stood around

Spleen: The seat or source in a person either of high spirit, courage, and resolute
mind or of ill-nature, ill-humor, and irritable or peevish temper.
1. The Virgin Mother: Mary, the mother of Jesus.

Cleaning their nails with bayonets.   15
The old man gave little Mary Magdalene°

A broke piece of a mirror.
She hid in the church outhouse.
When she got thirsty she licked
the steam off the glass.   20

That leaves Joseph.° Poor Joseph,
Standing naked in the snow.
He only had a rat
To load his suitcases on.

The rat wouldn't run into its hole.   25
Even when the lights came on—
And the lights came on:
The floodlights in the guard towers.

[1980; 1999]

15. **Magi:** The wise men from the East who visited the baby Jesus.
17. **Mary Magdalene:** A follower of Jesus who was present at his crucifixion and burial and who went to the tomb on Easter Sunday to anoint his body.
21. **Joseph:** The husband of Mary, the mother of Jesus.

MICHAEL S. HARPER   [b. 1938]

Nightmare Begins Responsibility

I place these numbed wrists to the pane
watching white uniforms whisk over
him in the tube-kept
prison
fear what they will do in experiment
watch my gloved stickshifting gasolined hands   5
breathe *boxcar-information-please* infirmary tubes
distrusting white-pink mending paperthin
silkened end hairs, distrusting tubes
shrunk in his *trunk-skincapped*
shaven head, in thighs   10
distrusting-white-hands-picking-baboon-light
on this son who will not make his second night
of this wardstrewn intensive airpocket

where his father's asthmatic   15
hymns of *night-train,* train done gone
his mother can only know that he has flown
up into essential calm unseen corridor
going boxscarred home, *mamaborn, sweetsonchild*
gonedowntown into *researchtestingwarehousebatteryacid*   20
mama-son-done-gone/me telling her 'nother
train tonight, no music, no breathstroked
heartbeat in my infinite distrust of them:

and of my distrusting self
white-doctor-who-breathed-for-him-all-night   25
say it for two sons gone,
say nightmare, say it loud
panebreaking heartmadness:
nightmare begins responsibility.

[1975]

SEAMUS HEANEY   [b. 1939]

Digging

Between my finger and my thumb
The squat pen rests; snug as a gun.

Under my window, a clean rasping sound
When the spade sinks into gravelly ground:
My father, digging. I look down   5

Till his straining rump among the flowerbeds
Bends low, comes up twenty years away
Stooping in rhythm through potato drills
Where he was digging.

The coarse boot nestled on the lug, the shaft   10
Against the inside knee was levered firmly.
He rooted out tall tops, buried the bright edge deep
To scatter new potatoes that we picked
Loving their cool hardness in our hands.

By God, the old man could handle a spade.   15
Just like his old man.

My grandfather cut more turf in a day
Than any other man on Toner's bog.
Once I carried him milk in a bottle
Corked sloppily with paper. He straightened up   20
To drink it, then fell to right away
Nicking and slicing neatly, heaving sods
Over his shoulder, going down and down
For the good turf. Digging.

The cold smell of potato mould, the squelch and slap   25
Of soggy peat, the curt cuts of an edge
Through living roots awaken in my head.
But I've no spade to follow men like them.

Between my finger and my thumb
The squat pen rests.   30
I'll dig with it.

[1966]

MARGARET ATWOOD   [b. 1939]

The Woman Who Could Not Live
with Her Faulty Heart

I do not mean the symbol
of love, a candy shape
to decorate cakes with,
the heart that is supposed
to belong or break;   5

I mean this lump of muscle
that contracts like a flayed biceps,
purple-blue, with its skin of suet,
its skin of gristle, this isolate,
this caved hermit, unshelled   10
turtle, this one lungful of blood,
no happy plateful.

All hearts float in their own
deep oceans of no light,
wetblack and glimmering,   15

their four mouths gulping like fish.
Hearts are said to pound:
this is to be expected, the heart's
regular struggle against being drowned.

But most hearts say, I want, I want,   20
I want, I want. My heart
is more duplicitous,
though no twin as I once thought.
It says, I want, I don't want, I
want, and then a pause.   25
It forces me to listen,

and at night it is the infra-red
third eye that remains open
while the other two are sleeping
but refuses to say what it has seen.   30

It is a constant pestering
in my ears, a caught moth, limping drum,
a child's first beating
itself against the bedsprings:
I want, I don't want.   35
How can one live with such a heart?

Long ago I gave up singing
to it, it will never be satisfied or lulled.
One night I will say to it:
Heart, be still,   40
and it will.

[1978]

AL YOUNG   [b. 1939]

A Dance for Ma Rainey

I'm going to be just like you, Ma
Rainey this monday morning
clouds puffing up out of my head
like those balloons
that float above the faces of white people   5
in the funnypapers

I'm going to hover in the corners
of the world, Ma
& sing from the bottom of hell
up to the tops of high heaven   10
& send out scratchless waves of yellow
& brown & that basic black honey
misery

I'm going to cry so sweet
& so low   15
& so dangerous,
Ma,
that the message is going to reach you
back in 1922
where you shimmer   20
snaggle-toothed
perfumed &
powdered
in your bauble beads

hair pressed & tied back   25
throbbing with that sick pain
I know
& hide so well
that pain that blues
jives the world with   30
aching to be heard
that downness
that bottomlessness
first felt by some stolen delta nigger
swamped under with redblooded american agony;   35
reduced to the sheer shit
of existence
that bred
& battered us all,
Ma,   40
the beautiful people
our beautiful brave black people
who no longer need to jazz
or sing to themselves in murderous vibrations
or play the veins of their strong tender arms   45
with needles
to prove we're still here

                                                        [1969]

JAMES WELCH   [b. 1940]

Christmas Comes to Moccasin Flat

Christmas comes like this: Wise men
unhurried, candles bought on credit (poor price
for calves), warriors face down in wine sleep.
Winds cheat to pull heat from smoke.

Friends sit in chinked cabins, stare out   5
plastic windows and wait for commodities.
Charlie Blackbird, twenty miles from church
and bar, stabs his fire with flint.

When drunks drain radiators for love
or need, chiefs eat snow and talk of change,   10
an urge to laugh pounding their ribs.
Elk play games in high country.

Medicine Woman, clay pipe and twist tobacco,
calls each blizzard by name and predicts
five o'clock by spitting at her television.   15
Children lean into her breath to beg a story:

Something about honor and passion,
warriors back with meat and song,
a peculiar evening star, quick vision of birth.
Blackbird feeds his fire. Outside, a quick 30 below.   20

[1976]

NELLIE WONG   [b. 1940]

Grandmother's Song

Grandmothers sing their song
Blinded by the suns' rays
Grandchildren for whom they long
For pomelo°-golden days   *grapefruit*

Blinded by the sun's rays   5
Gold bracelets, opal rings
For pomelo-golden days
Tiny fingers, ancient things

Gold bracelets, opal rings
Sprinkled with Peking dust   10
Tiny fingers, ancient things
So young they'll never rust

Sprinkled with Peking dust
To dance in fields of mud
So young they'll never rust   15
Proud as if of royal blood

To dance in fields of mud
Or peel shrimp for pennies a day
Proud as if of royal blood
Coins and jade to put away   20

Or peel shrimp for pennies a day
Seaweed washes up the shore
Coins and jade to put away
A camphor chest is home no more

Seaweed washes up the shore   25
Bound feet struggle to loosen free
A camphor chest is home no more
A foreign tongue is learned at three

Bound feet struggle to loosen free
Grandchildren for whom they long   30
A foreign tongue is learned at three
Grandmothers sing their song

[1977]

ROBERT PINSKY   [b. 1940]

Shirt

The back, the yoke, the yardage. Lapped seams,
The nearly invisible stitches along the collar
Turned in a sweatshop by Koreans or Malaysians

Gossiping over tea and noodles on their break
Or talking money or politics while one fitted   5
This armpiece with its overseam to the band

Of cuff I button at my wrist. The presser, the cutter,
The wringer, the mangle. The needle, the union,
The treadle, the bobbin. The code. The infamous blaze

At the Triangle Factory° in nineteen-eleven.   *(in New York City)*   10
One hundred and forty-six died in the flames
On the ninth floor, no hydrants, no fire escapes —

The witness in a building across the street
Who watched how a young man helped a girl to step
Up to the windowsill, then held her out   15

Away from the masonry wall and let her drop.
And then another. As if he were helping them up
To enter a streetcar, and not eternity.

A third before he dropped her put her arms
Around his neck and kissed him. Then he held   20
Her into space, and dropped her. Almost at once

He stepped to the sill himself, his jacket flared
And fluttered up from his shirt as he came down,
Air filling up the legs of his gray trousers —

Like Hart Crane's Bedlamite, "shrill shirt ballooning."   25
Wonderful how the pattern matches perfectly
Across the placket and over the twin bar-tacked

Corners of both pockets, like a strict rhyme
Or a major chord. Prints, plaids, checks,
Houndstooth, Tattersall, Madras. The clan tartans   30

Invented by mill-owners inspired by the hoax of Ossian,°
To control their savage Scottish workers, tamed
By a fabricated heraldry: MacGregor,

Bailey, MacMartin. The kilt, devised for workers
To wear among the dusty clattering looms.   35
Weavers, carders, spinners. The loader,

The docker, the navvy. The planter, the picker, the sorter
Sweating at her machine in a litter of cotton
As slaves in calico headrags sweated in fields:

---

31. Ossian: Legendary Gaelic poet, hero of a cycle of traditional tales and poems
that place him in the third century c.e. The hoax involved Scottish author James
Macpherson (1736–1796), who published two epic poems that he said were translations of works written by Ossian but were in fact mostly composed by
Macpherson himself.

George Herbert,° your descendant is a Black   40
Lady in South Carolina, her name is Irma
And she inspected my shirt. Its color and fit

And feel and its clean smell have satisfied
Both her and me. We have culled its cost and quality
Down to the buttons of simulated bone,   45

The buttonholes, the sizing, the facing, the characters
Printed in black on neckband and tail. The shape,
The label, the labor, the color, the shade. The shirt.

[1990]

40. George Herbert: (1593–1633), English metaphysical poet. See Biographical
Notes (pp. 351–52).

ROBERT HASS   [b. 1941]

Late Spring

And then in mid-May the first morning of steady heat,

the morning, Leif says, when you wake up, put on shorts, and that's it for
the day,

when you pour coffee and walk outside, blinking in the sun.

Strawberries have appeared in the markets, and peaches will soon;

squid is so cheap in the fishstores you begin to consult Japanese and
Italian cookbooks for the various and ingenious ways of preparing *ika*
and *calamari*;°   5

and because the light will enlarge your days, your dreams at night will be
as strange as the jars of octopus you saw once in a fisherman's boat
under the summer moon;

and after swimming, white wine; and the sharing of stories before dinner
is prolonged because the relations of the children in the neighborhood
have acquired village intensity and the stories take longer telling;

and there are the nights when the fog rolls in that nobody likes—hey,
fog, the Miwok° sang, who lived here first, you better go home, pelican is
beating your wife—

5. *ika* and *calamari*: Squid, in Japanese and Italian.
8. Miwoks: Native American people formerly living in California.

and after dark in the first cool hour, your children sleep so heavily in
their beds exhausted from play, it is a pleasure to watch them,

Leif does not move a muscle as he lies there; no, wait; it is Luke who lies
there in his eight-year-old body,   10

Leif is taller than you are and he isn't home; when he is, his feet will
extend past the end of the mattress, and Kristin is at the corner in the
dark, talking to neighborhood boys;

things change; there is no need for this dream-compelled narration; the
rhythm will keep me awake, changing.

[1989]

BILLY COLLINS   [b. 1941]

Aristotle

This is the beginning.
Almost anything can happen.
This is where you find
the creation of light, a fish wriggling onto land,
the first word of *Paradise Lost* on an empty page.   5
Think of an egg, the letter *A*,
a woman ironing on a bare stage
as the heavy curtain rises.
This is the very beginning.
The first-person narrator introduces himself,   10
tells us about his lineage.
The mezzo-soprano stands in the wings.
Here the climbers are studying a map
or pulling on their long woolen socks.
This is early on, years before the Ark, dawn.   15
The profile of an animal is being smeared
on the wall of a cave,
and you have not yet learned to crawl.
This is the opening, the gambit,
a pawn moving forward an inch.   20
This is your first night with her,
your first night without her.
This is the first part
where the wheels begin to turn,

where the elevator begins its ascent,   25
before the doors lurch apart.

This is the middle.
Things have had time to get complicated,
messy, really. Nothing is simple anymore.
Cities have sprouted up along the rivers   30
teeming with people at cross-purposes —
a million schemes, a million wild looks.
Disappointment unshoulders his knapsack
here and pitches his ragged tent.
This is the sticky part where the plot congeals,   35
where the action suddenly reverses
or swerves off in an outrageous direction.
Here the narrator devotes a long paragraph
to why Miriam does not want Edward's child.
Someone hides a letter under a pillow.   40
Here the aria rises to a pitch,
a song of betrayal, salted with revenge.
And the climbing party is stuck on a ledge
halfway up the mountain.
This is the bridge, the painful modulation.   45
This is the thick of things.
So much is crowded into the middle —
the guitars of Spain, piles of ripe avocados,
Russian uniforms, noisy parties,
lakeside kisses, arguments heard through a wall —   50
too much to name, too much to think about.

And this is the end,
the car running out of road,
the river losing its name in an ocean,
the long nose of the photographed horse   55
touching the white electronic line.
This is the colophon, the last elephant in the parade,
the empty wheelchair,
and pigeons floating down in the evening.

[1998]

RICHARD GARCIA   [b. 1941]

Why I Left the Church

Maybe it was
because the only time
I hit a baseball
it smashed the neon cross
on the church across   5
the street. Even
twenty-five years later
when I saw Father Harris
I would wonder
if he knew it was me.   10
Maybe it was the demon-stoked
rotisseries of purgatory
where we would roast
hundreds of years
for the smallest of sins.   15
Or was it the day
I wore my space helmet
to catechism? Clear plastic
with a red-and-white
inflatable rim.   20
Sister Mary Bernadette
pointed toward the door
and said, "Out! Come back
when you're ready."
I rose from my chair   25
and kept rising
toward the ceiling
while the children
screamed and Sister
kept crossing herself.   30
The last she saw of me
was my shoes disappearing
through cracked plaster.
I rose into the sky and beyond.
It is a good thing   35
I am wearing my helmet,
I thought as I floated
and turned in the blackness
and brightness of outer space,

my body cold on one side and hot   40
on the other. It would
have been very quiet
if my blood had not been
rumbling in my ears so loud.
I remember thinking,   45
Maybe I will come back
when I'm ready.
But I won't tell
the other children
what it was like.   50
I'll have to make something up.

[1993]

SIMON J. ORTIZ   [b. 1941]

Speaking

I take him outside
under the trees,
have him stand on the ground.
We listen to the crickets,
cicadas, million years old sound.   5
Ants come by us.
I tell them,
"This is he, my son.
This boy is looking at you.
I am speaking for him."   10

The crickets, cicadas,
the ants, the millions of years
are watching us,
hearing us.
My son murmurs infant words,   15
speaking, small laughter
bubbles from him.
Tree leaves tremble.
They listen to this boy
speaking for me.   20

[1977]

TOI DERRICOTTE   [b. 1941]

A Note on My Son's Face

I

Tonight, I look, thunderstruck
at the gold head of my grandchild.
Almost asleep, he buries his feet
between my thighs;
his little straw eyes   5
close in the near dark.
I smell the warmth of his raw
slightly foul breath, the new death
waiting to rot inside him.
Our breaths equalize our heartbeats;   10
every muscle of the chest uncoils,
the arm bones loosen in the nest
of nerves. I think of the peace
of walking through the house,
pointing to the name of this, the name of that,   15
an educator of a new man.

Mother. Grandmother. Wise
Snake-woman who will show the way;
Spider-woman whose black tentacles
hold him precious. Or will tear off his head,   20
her teeth over the little husband,
the small fist clotted in trust at her breast.

This morning, looking at the face of his father,
I remembered how, an infant, his face was too dark,
nose too broad, mouth too wide.   25
I did not look in that mirror
and see the face that could save me
from my own darkness.
Did he, looking in my eye, see
what I turned from: 30
my own dark grandmother
bending over gladioli in the field,
her shaking black hand defenseless
at the shining cock of flower?

I wanted that face to die,   35
to be reborn in the face of a white child.

I wanted the soul to stay the same,
for I loved to death,
to damnation and God-death,
the soul that broke out of me.   40
I crowed: My Son! My Beautiful!
But when I peeked in the basket,
I saw the face of a black man.

Did I bend over his nose
and straighten it with my fingers   45
like a vine growing the wrong way?
Did he feel my hand in malice?

Generations we prayed and fucked
for this light child,
the shining god of the second coming;   50
we bow down in shame
and carry the children of the past
in our wallets, begging forgiveness.

II

A picture in a book,
a lynching.   55
The bland faces of men who watch
a Christ go up in flames, smiling,
as if he were a hooked
fish, a felled antelope, some
wild thing tied to boards and burned.   60
His charring body
gives off light — a halo
burns out of him.
His face scorched featureless;
the hair matted to the scalp   65
like feathers.
One man stands with his hand on his hip,
another with his arm
slung over the shoulder of a friend,
as if this moment were large enough   70
to hold affection.

III

How can we wake
from a dream
we are born into,

that shines around us,   75
the terrible bright air?

Having awakened,
having seen our own bloody hands,
how can we ask forgiveness,
bring before our children the real   80
monster of their nightmares?

The worst is true.
Everything you did not want to know.

[1989]

LYN HEJINIAN   [b. 1941]

A Mask of Anger

he said I should try something harder
a mask of rage

says of snakes
says of broken glass
says of aged foundations   5
unconsolable wildness,
an imagination uncomforted,
says without comfort

where are the gods who support the event

crashed into the circle   10

took the blue out of the sky

walled the warbler; turned the walker

wrong and wrong

there's no song but what's said
felt it   15
and no thought but what's bitten

[1977]

SHARON OLDS   [b. 1942]

I Go Back to May 1937

I see them standing at the formal gates of their colleges,
I see my father strolling out
under the ochre sandstone arch, the
red tiles glinting like bent
plates of blood behind his head, I   5
see my mother with a few light books at her hip
standing at the pillar made of tiny bricks with the
wrought-iron gate still open behind her, its
sword-tips black in the May air,
they are about to graduate, they are about to get married,   10
they are kids, they are dumb, all they know is they are
innocent, they would never hurt anybody.
I want to go up to them and say Stop,
don't do it—she's the wrong woman,
he's the wrong man, you are going to do things   15
you cannot imagine you would ever do,
you are going to do bad things to children,
you are going to suffer in ways you never heard of,
you are going to want to die. I want to go
up to them there in the late May sunlight and say it,   20
her hungry pretty blank face turning to me,
her pitiful beautiful untouched body,
his arrogant handsome blind face turning to me,
his pitiful beautiful untouched body,
but I don't do it. I want to live. I   25
take them up like the male and female
paper dolls and bang them together
at the hips like chips of flint as if to
strike sparks from them, I say
Do what you are going to do, and I will tell about it.   30

[1987]

MARILYN HACKER   [b. 1942]

Villanelle

Every day our bodies separate,
explode torn and dazed.
Not understanding what we celebrate

we grope through languages and hesitate
and touch each other, speechless and amazed;   5
and every day our bodies separate

us further from our planned, deliberate
ironic lives. I am afraid, disphased,
not understanding what we celebrate

when our fused limbs and lips communicate   10
the unlettered power we have raised.
Every day our bodies' separate

routines are harder to perpetuate.
In wordless darkness we learn wordless praise,
not understanding what we celebrate;   15

wake to ourselves, exhausted, in the late
morning as the wind tears off the haze,
not understanding how we celebrate
our bodies. Every day we separate.

[1974]

ELLEN BRYANT VOIGT   [b. 1943]

Woman Who Weeps

Up from the valley, ten children working the fields
and three in the ground, plus four who'd slipped like fish
from a faulty seine, she wept to the priest:
        Father, I saw the Virgin on a hill,
        she was a lion, lying on her side,   5
        grooming her blond shoulders with her tongue.

Six months weeping as she hulled the corn,
gathered late fruit and milked the goats,
planted grain and watched the hillside blossom,

before she went to the Bishop, kissed his ring.   10
    Father, I saw Our Lady in a tree,
    swaddled in black, she was a raven,
    on one leg, on one bent claw
    she hunched in the tree but she was the tree,
    charred trunk in a thicket of green.   15

After seven years of weeping,
not as other stunned old women weep,
she baked flat bread, washed the cooking stones,
cut a staff from a sapling by the road.
The Holy Father sat in a gilded chair: 20
    Father, I saw Christ's Mother in a stream,
    she was a rock, the water
    parted on either side of her,
    from one stream she made two—
    two tresses loosened across her collarbone—   25
    until the pouring water met at her breast
    and made a single stream again—

Then from the marketplace, from the busiest stall
she stole five ripened figs
and carried her weeping back to the countryside,   30
with a cloth sack, with a beggar's cup,
village to village and into the smoky huts,
her soul a well, an eye, an open door.

[1992]

LOUISE GLÜCK   [b. 1943]

Parable of Flight

A flock of birds leaving the side of the mountain.
Black against the spring evening, bronze in early summer,
rising over blank lake water.

Why is the young man disturbed suddenly,
his attention slipping from his companion?   5
His heart is no longer wholly divided; he's trying to think
how to say this compassionately.

Now we hear the voices of the others, moving through the library
toward the veranda, the summer porch; we see them

taking their usual places on the various hammocks and chairs,   10
the white wood chairs of the old house, rearranging
the striped cushions.

Does it matter where the birds go? Does it even matter
what species they are?
They leave here, that's the point,   15
first their bodies, then their sad cries.
And from that moment, cease to exist for us.

You must learn to think of our passion that way.
Each kiss was real, then
each kiss left the face of the earth.   20

[1996]

JAMES TATE   [b. 1943]

The Wheelchair Butterfly

O sleepy city of reeling wheelchairs
where a mouse can commit suicide if he can

concentrate long enough
on the history book of rodents
in this underground town   5

of electrical wheelchairs!
The girl who is always pregnant and bruised
like a pear

rides her many-stickered bicycle
backward up the staircase   10
of the abandoned trolleybarn.

Yesterday was warm. Today a butterfly froze
in midair; and was plucked like a grape
by a child who swore he could take care

of it. O confident city where   15
the seeds of poppies pass for carfare,

where the ordinary hornets in a human's heart
may slumber and snore, where bifocals bulge

in an orange garage of daydreams,
we wait in our loose attics for a new season   20

as if for an ice-cream truck.
An Indian pony crosses the plains

whispering Sanskrit prayers to a crater of fleas.
Honeysuckle says: I thought I could swim.

The Mayor is urinating on the wrong side   25
of the street! A dandelion sends off sparks:
beware your hair is locked!

Beware the trumpet wants a glass of water!
Beware a velvet tabernacle!

Beware the Warden of Light has married   30
an old piece of string!

[1969]

QUINCY TROUPE   [b. 1943]

Snake-Back Solo 2

for Louis Armstrong, Steve Cannon, Miles Davis,
& Eugene Redmond

with the music up high, boogalooin
bass down way way low
up & under, eye come slidin on in, mojoin
on in, spacin on in on a riff full of rain
riffin on in full of rain & pain   5
spacin on in on a sound
like coltrane°

& my metaphor is a blues
hot pain dealin blues, is a blues
axin guitar voices, whiskey broken, niggah   10
deep in the heart, is a blues in a glass filled with rain
is a blues in the dark
slurred voices of straight bourbon
is a blues, dagger stuck off in the heart
of night, moanin like bessie smith°   15

---

7. coltrane: John Coltrane (1926–1967), a well-known jazz saxophonist.
15. bessie smith: Bessie Smith (1894–1937), an influential classic blues singer of
the 1920s.

is a blues filling up, glooming under
the wings of darkness, is a blues
is a blues, a blues

& looking through the heart
a dream can become a raindrop window to see through   20
can become a window, to see through this moment
to see yourself hanging around the dark
to see through this moment
& see yourself as a river catching rain there
feeding time there with your movement   25
to wash time clean as a window
to see through to the other side
while outside windows, flames trigger
the deep explosion, time steals rivers that move on
& stay where they are, inside yourself, moving   30
soon there will be daylight
breaking the darkness
to point the way home, soon there will be
voices breaking music, to come on home by
down & up river, breaking the darkness   35
to come on home by, stroking with the music
swimming up river
the sound of louie armstrong
swinging up river, carrying river boats
upstream, on the back of his honky-tonk jazz rhythms   40
licks of vibratos climbing up from new orleans, close heat & rain
swimming up river, up the river of mud & rain
satchmo° breaking the darkness, his cornet speaking
flames bouncing off the river's back
at sunset, snake river's back, big muddy, mississippi   45
up from naw leans, to east st. louis, illinois
cross river from st. louis
to come on home by, up river now
the music swims, breaking silence to land
in miles dewey davis's° horn, then leap off again   50
& fly up in space to create
new music in time with place
to create new music in time with this place

43. satchmo: Louis "Satchmo" Armstrong (1901–1971), American jazz trumpeter.
50. miles dewey davis: Miles Davis (1926–1991), jazz trumpet player, composer, and bandleader.

to pass it on, pass it on
pass it on, into space   55

where eye catch it now, inside myself
inside this poem eye am (w)riting here
where eye am soloing, now
soloing of rivers catching rains & dreams & sunsets
solo of trane tracks screaming through the night, stark   60
a dagger in the heart
solo of bird° spreading wings for the wind
to lift up by, solo of miles, pied piper, prince of darkness
river rain voice now, eye solo at the root of the flower
leaning against promises of shadows   65
solo of bones leering beneath the river's snake-back
solo of trees cut down by double-bladed axes
river rain voice now eye solo
of the human condition, solo of the matrix
mojoin new blues, river rain voice   70
now, eye solo   solo
solo now to become the wings & eyes of an owl
to see through this darkness, eye solo now
to become a simple skybreak shattering darkness
to become lightning's jagged-sword-like thunder   75
eye solo now to become, to become
eye solo now to become

with the music up high
up way, way high, boogalooin bass down
way, way low   80
up & under, eye come slidin on in, mojoin on in
spacin on in on a poetic riff full of rain
river riff full of rain & trains & dreams
lookin through ajax° clean windows
eye come slidin on through   85
these blues metaphors
riffin on in through rain & pain
ridin on a tongue of poetic flame
leanin & glidin, eye solo   solo
loopin & flyin eye solo now   solo   90

[1979]

---

62. bird: Charlie Parker (1920–1955), jazz saxophonist and composer.
84. ajax: A brand name for household cleaning products.

EAVAN BOLAND   [b. 1944]

The Pomegranate

The only legend I have ever loved is
The story of a daughter lost in hell,
And found and rescued there.
Love and blackmail are the gist of it.
Ceres° and Persephone the names.   5
And the best thing about the legend is
I can enter it anywhere. And have.
As a child in exile in
A city of fogs and strange consonants,
I read it first and at first I was   10
An exiled child in the crackling dusk of
The underworld, the stars blighted. Later
I walked out in a summer twilight
Searching for my daughter at bedtime.
When she came running I was ready   15
To make any bargain to keep her.
I carried her back past whitebeams.
And wasps and honey-scented buddleias.
But I was Ceres then and I knew
Winter was in store for every leaf   20
On every tree on that road.
Was inescapable for each one we passed.
And for me.
It is winter
And the stars are hidden.   25
I climb the stairs and stand where I can see
My child asleep beside her teen magazines,
Her can of Coke, her plate of uncut fruit.
The pomegranate! How did I forget it?
She could have come home and been safe   30

5. **Ceres:** Roman name of Demeter, the goddess of crops and harvest. Her daughter Persephone was kidnapped by Pluto (or Hades) and taken to the underworld. Demeter, grieving and angry, refused to let seeds germinate or crops grow. To save the human race from extinction, Zeus finally ordered Pluto to release Persephone. Pluto told her she was free to leave but tricked her by offering a pomegranate seed; anyone who eats food in the underworld must return there. Zeus therefore arranged a compromise: Persephone would spend a third of each year in the land of the dead with Pluto (winter, when Demeter went into mourning); but she would be with her mother for the other two-thirds of each year (spring and summer).

And ended the story and all
Our heartbroken searching but she reached
Out a hand and plucked a pomegranate.
She put out her hand and pulled down
The French sound for apple° and   *pomme*   35
The noise of stone° and the proof   *granite*
That even in the place of death,
At the heart of legend, in the midst
Of rocks full of unshed tears
Ready to be diamonds by the time   40
The story was told, a child can be
Hungry. I could warn her. There is still a chance.
The rain is cold. The road is flint-coloured.
The suburb has cars and cable television.
The veiled stars are above ground.   45
It is another world. But what else
Can a mother give her daughter but such
Beautiful rifts in time?
If I defer the grief I will diminish the gift.
The legend must be hers as well as mine.   50
She will enter it. As I have.
She will wake up. She will hold
The papery, flushed skin in her hand.
And to her lips. I will say nothing.

[1994]

ROBERT MORGAN   [b. 1944]

Mountain Bride

They say Revis found a flatrock
on the ridge just
perfect for a natural hearth,
and built his cabin with a stick

and clay chimney right over it.   5
On their wedding night he lit
the fireplace to dry away the mountain
chill of late spring, and flung on

applewood to dye
the room with molten color while   10

he and Martha that was a Parrish
warmed the sheets between the tick

stuffed with leaves and its feather
cover. Under that wide hearth
a nest of rattlers,   15
they'll knot a hundred together,

had wintered and were coming awake.
The warming rock
flushed them out early.
It was she   20

who wakened to their singing near
the embers and roused him to go look.
Before he reached the fire
more than a dozen struck

and he died yelling her to stay   25
on the big four-poster.
Her uncle coming up the hollow
with a gift bearham two days later

found her shivering there
marooned above a pool   30
of hungry snakes,
and the body beginning to swell.

[1979]

ANNE WALDMAN   [b. 1945]

Makeup on Empty Space

I am putting makeup on empty space
all patinas convening on empty space
rouge blushing on empty space
I am putting makeup on empty space
pasting eyelashes on empty space   5
painting the eyebrows of empty space
piling creams on empty space
painting the phenomenal world
I am hanging ornaments on empty space

gold clips, lacquer combs, plastic hairpins on empty space   10
I am sticking wire pins into empty space
I pour words over empty space, enthrall the empty space
packing, stuffing jamming empty space
spinning necklaces around empty space
Fancy this, imagine this: painting the phenomenal world   15
bangles on wrists
pendants hung on empty space
I am putting my memory into empty space
undressing you
hanging the wrinkled clothes on a nail   20
hanging the green coat on a nail
dancing in the evening it ended with dancing in the evening
I am still thinking about putting makeup on empty space
I want to scare you: the hanging night, the drifting night,
the moaning night, daughter of troubled sleep I want to scare you   25
you
I bind as far as cold day goes
I bind the power of 20 husky men
I bind the seductive colorful women, all of them
I bind the massive rock   30
I bind the hanging night, the drifting night, the
moaning night, daughter of troubled sleep
I am binding my debts, I magnetize the phone bill
bind the root of my pointed tongue
I cup my hands in water, splash water on empty space   35
water drunk by empty space
Look what thoughts will do   Look what words will do
from nothing to the face
from nothing to the root of the tongue
from nothing to speaking of empty space   40
I bind the ash tree
I bind the yew
I bind the willow
I bind uranium
I bind the uneconomical unrenewable energy of uranium   45
dash uranium to empty space
I bind the color red I seduce the color red to empty space
I put the sunset in empty space
I take the blue of his eyes and make an offering to empty space
renewable blue   50
I take the green of everything coming to life, it grows &

climbs into empty space
I put the white of the snow at the foot of empty space
I clasp the yellow of the cat's eyes sitting in the
black space I clasp them to my heart, empty space   55
I want the brown of this floor to rise up into empty space
Take the floor apart to find the brown,
bind it up again under spell of empty space
I want to take this old wall apart I am rich in my mind thinking
of this, I am thinking of putting makeup on empty space   60
Everything crumbles around empty space
the thin dry weed crumbles, the milkweed is blown into empty space
I bind the stars reflected in your eye
from nothing to these typing fingers
from nothing to the legs of the elk   65
from nothing to the neck of the deer
from nothing to porcelain teeth
from nothing to the fine stand of pine in the forest
I kept it going when I put the water on
when I let the water run   70
sweeping together in empty space
There is a better way to say empty space
Turn yourself inside out and you might disappear
you have a new definition in empty space
What I like about impermanence is the clash   75
of my big body with empty space
I am putting the floor back together again
I am rebuilding the wall
I am slapping mortar on bricks
I am fastening the machine together with delicate wire   80
There is no eternal thread, maybe there is thread of pure gold
I am starting to sing inside about the empty space
there is some new detail every time
I am taping the picture I love so well on the wall:
moonless black night beyond country-plaid curtains   85
everything illuminated out of empty space
I hang the black linen dress on my body
the hanging night, the drifting night, the moaning night
daughter of troubled sleep
This occurs to me   90
I hang up a mirror to catch stars, everything occurs to me out in the
night in my skull of empty space
I go outside in starry ice
I build up the house again in memory of empty space

This occurs to me about empty space   95
that it is nevered to be mentioned again
Fancy this
imagine this
painting the phenomenal world
there's talk of dressing the body with strange adornments   100
to remind you of a vow to empty space
there's talk of the discourse in your mind like a silkworm
I wish to venture into a not-chiseled place
I pour sand on the ground
Objects and vehicles emerge from the fog   105
the canyon is dangerous tonight
suddenly there are warning lights
The patrol is helpful in the manner of guiding
there is talk of slowing down
there is talk of a feminine deity   110
I bind her with a briar
I bind with the tooth of a tiger
I bind with my quartz crystal
I magnetize the worlds
I cover myself with jewels   115
I drink amrita
there is some new detail
there is a spangle on her shoe
there is a stud on her boot
the tires are studded for the difficult climb   120
I put my hands to my face
I am putting makeup on empty space
I wanted to scare you with the night that scared me
the drifting night, the moaning night
Someone was always intruding to make you forget empty space   125
you put it all on
you paint your nails
you put on scarves
all the time adorning empty space
Whatever-your-name-is I tell you "empty space"   130
with your fictions with dancing come around to it
with your funny way of singing come around to it
with your smiling come to it
with your enormous retinue & accumulation come around to it
with your extras come round to it   135
with your good fortune, with your lazy fortune come round to it
when you look most like a bird, that is the time to come around to it

when you are cheating, come to it
when you are in your anguished head
when you are not sensible   140
when you are insisting on the
praise from many tongues
It begins with the root of the tongue
it begins with the root of the heart
there is a spinal cord of wind   145
singing & moaning in empty space

[1984]

LARRY LEVIS   [1946–1996]

The Poem You Asked For

My poem would eat nothing.
I tried giving it water
but it said no,

worrying me.
Day after day,   5
I held it up to the light,

turning it over,
but it only pressed its lips
more tightly together.

It grew sullen, like a toad   10
through with being teased.
I offered it all my money,

my clothes, my car with a full tank.
But the poem stared at the floor.
Finally I cupped it in   15

my hands, and carried it gently
out into the soft air, into the
evening traffic, wondering how

to end things between us.
For now it had begun breathing,   20
putting on more and

more hard rings of flesh.
And the poem demanded the food,
it drank up all the water,

beat me and took my money,   25
tore the faded clothes
off my back,

said Shit,
and walked slowly away,
slicking its hair down.   30

Said it was going
over to your place.

[1972]

LINDA HOGAN   [b. 1947]

The History of Red

First
there was some other order of things
never spoken
but in dreams of darkest creation.

Then there was black earth,   5
lake, the face of light on water.
Then the thick forest all around
that light,
and then the human clay
whose blood we still carry   10
rose up in us
who remember caves with red bison
painted in their own blood,
after their kind.

A wildness   15
swam inside our mothers,
desire through closed eyes,
a new child
wearing the red, wet mask of birth,

delivered into this land   20
already wounded,
stolen and burned
beyond reckoning.

Red is this yielding land
turned inside out   25
by a country of hunters
with iron, flint and fire.
Red is the fear
that turns a knife back
against men, holds it at their throats,   30
and they cannot see the claw on the handle,
the animal hand
that haunts them
from some place inside their blood.

So that is hunting, birth,   35
and one kind of death.
Then there was medicine, the healing of wounds.
Red was the infinite fruit
of stolen bodies.
The doctors wanted to know   40
what invented disease
how wounds healed
from inside themselves
how life stands up in skin,
if not by magic.   45

They divined the red shadows of leeches
that swam in white bowls of water;
they believed stars
in the cup of sky,
They cut the wall of skin   50
to let
what was bad escape
but they were reading the story of fire
gone out
and that was science.   55

As for the animal hand on death's knife,
knives have as many sides
as the red father of war
who signs his name
in the blood of other men.   60

And red was the soldier
who crawled
through a ditch
of human blood in order to live.
It was the canal of his deliverance.   65
It is his son who lives near me.
Red is the thunder in our ears
when we meet.
Love, like creation,
is some other order of things.   70

Red is the share of fire
I have stolen
from root, hoof, fallen fruit.
And this was hunger.

Red is the human house   75
I come back to at night
swimming inside the cave of skin
that remembers bison.
In that round nation
of blood   80
we are all burning,
red, inseparable fires
the living have crawled
and climbed through
in order to live   85
so nothing will be left
for death at the end.

This life in the fire, I love it,
I want it,
this life.   90

[1993]

AI   [b. 1947]

Why Can't I Leave You?

You stand behind the old black mare,
dressed as always in that red shirt,
stained from sweat, the crying of the armpits,

that will not stop for anything,
stroking her rump, while the barley goes unplanted.   5
I pick up my suitcase and set it down,
as I try to leave you again.
I smooth the hair back from your forehead.
I think with your laziness and the drought too,
you'll be needing my help more than ever.   10
You take my hands, I nod
and go to the house to unpack,
having found another reason to stay.

I undress, then put on my white lace slip
for you to take off, because you like that   15
and when you come in, you pull down the straps
and I unbutton your shirt.
I know we can't give each other any more
or any less than what we have.
There is safety in that, so much   20
that I can never get past the packing,
the begging you to please, if I can't make you happy,
come close between my thighs
and let me laugh for you from my second mouth.

                                                                [1972]

YUSEF KOMUNYAKAA   [b. 1947]

Facing It

My black face fades,
hiding inside the black granite.
I said I wouldn't,
dammit: No tears.
I'm stone. I'm flesh.   5
My clouded reflection eyes me
like a bird of prey, the profile of night
slanted against morning. I turn
this way—the stone lets me go.
I turn that way—I'm inside   10
the Vietnam Veterans Memorial
again, depending on the light

to make a difference.
I go down the 58,022 names,
half-expecting to find   15
my own in letters like smoke.
I touch the name Andrew Johnson;
I see the booby trap's white flash.
Names shimmer on a woman's blouse
but when she walks away   20
the names stay on the wall.
Brushstrokes flash, a red bird's
wings cutting across my stare.
The sky. A plane in the sky.
A white vet's image floats   25
closer to me, then his pale eyes
look through mine. I'm a window.
He's lost his right arm
inside the stone. In the black mirror
a woman's trying to erase names: 30
No, she's brushing a boy's hair.

                                                            [1988]

JANE KENYON   [1947–1995]

From Room to Room

Here in this house, among photographs
of your ancestors, their hymnbooks and old
shoes . . .

       I move from room to room,
a little dazed, like the fly. I watch it   5
bump against each window.

I am clumsy here, thrusting
slabs of maple into the stove.
Out of my body for a while,
weightless in space. . . .   10

          Sometimes
the wind against the clapboard
sounds like a car driving up to the house.

My people are not here, my mother
and father, my brother. I talk   15
to the cats about weather.

"Blessed be the tie that binds . . ."
we sing in the church down the road.
And how does it go from there? The tie . . .

the tether, the hose carrying   20
oxygen to the astronaut,
turning, turning outside the hatch,
taking a look around.

[1978]

HEATHER McHUGH   [b. 1948]

What He Thought

for Fabbio Doplicher

We were supposed to do a job in Italy
and, full of our feeling for
ourselves (our sense of being
Poets from America) we went
from Rome to Fano, met   5
the mayor, mulled
a couple matters over (what's
cheap date, they asked us; what's
flat drink). Among Italian literati

we could recognize our counterparts: 10
the academic, the apologist,
the arrogant, the amorous,
the brazen and the glib—and there was one

administrator (the conservative), in suit
of regulation gray, who like a good tour guide   15
with measured pace and uninflected tone narrated
sights and histories the hired van hauled us past.
Of all, he was most politic and least poetic,
so it seemed. Our last few days in Rome
(when all but three of the New World Bards had flown)   20

I found a book of poems this
unprepossessing one had written: it was there
in the *pensione* room (a room he'd recommended)
where it must have been abandoned by
the German visitor (was there a bus of *them*?) 25
to whom he had inscribed and dated it a month before.
I couldn't read Italian, either, so I put the book
back into the wardrobe's dark. We last Americans

were due to leave tomorrow. For our parting evening then
our host chose something in a family restaurant, and there 30
we sat and chatted, sat and chewed,
till, sensible it was our last
big chance to be poetic, make
our mark, one of us asked
                        "What's poetry? 35
Is it the fruits and vegetables and
marketplace of Campo dei Fiori, or
the statue there?" Because I was

the glib one, I identified the answer
instantly, I didn't have to think—"The truth 40
is both, it's both," I blurted out. But that
was easy. That was easiest to say. What followed
taught me something about difficulty,
for our underestimated host spoke out,
all of a sudden, with a rising passion, and he said: 45

The statue represents Giordano Bruno,
brought to be burned in the public square
because of his offense against
authority, which is to say
the Church. His crime was his belief 50
the universe does not revolve around
the human being: God is no
fixed point or central government, but rather is
poured in waves through all things. All things
move. "If God is not the soul itself, He is 55
the soul of the soul of the world." Such was
his heresy. The day they brought him
forth to die, they feared he might
incite the crowd (the man was famous
for his eloquence). And so his captors 60
placed upon his face
an iron mask, in which

he could not speak. That's
how they burned him. That is how
he died: without a word, in front   65
of everyone.
        And poetry—
              (we'd all
put down our forks by now, to listen to
the man in gray; he went on   70
softly)—
        poetry is what

he thought, but did not say.

                       [1994]

LESLIE MARMON SILKO   [b. 1948]

Prayer to the Pacific

I traveled to the ocean
        distant
              from my southwest land of sandrock
              to the moving blue water
           Big as the myth of origin.   5

Pale
pale water in the yellow-white light of
              sun   floating west
                to China
              where ocean herself was born.   10
Clouds that blow across the sand are wet.

Squat in the wet sand and speak to the Ocean:
        I return to you   turquoise   the red coral you sent us,
            sister spirit of Earth.
Four round stones in my pocket   I carry back the ocean   15
            to suck and to taste.

Thirty thousand years ago
           Indians came riding across the ocean
           carried by giant sea turtles.

Waves were high that day   20
        great sea turtles waded   slowly out
            from the gray sundown sea.

Grandfather Turtle rolled in the sand   four times
                        and disappeared
                                swimming into the sun.   25

And so   from that time
            immemorial,
                    as the old people say,
rain clouds drift from the west
                    gift from the ocean.   30

Green leaves in the wind
Wet earth on my feet
            swallowing raindrops
                    clear from China.

                                                            [1981]

SEKOU SUNDIATA   [b. 1948]

Blink Your Eyes

Remembering Sterling A. Brown

I was on my way to see my woman
but the Law said I was on my way
thru a red light red light red light
and if you saw my woman
you could understand,   5
I was just being a man
It wasn't about no light
it was about my ride
and if you saw my ride
you could dig that too, you dig?   10
Sunroof stereo radio black leather
bucket seats sit low you know,
the body's cool, but the tires are worn.
Ride when the hard time come, ride
when they're gone, in other words   15
the light was green.

I could wake up in the morning
without a warning
and my world could change:
blink your eyes.   20

All depends, all depends on the skin,
all depends on the skin you're living in.

Up to the window comes the Law
with his hand on his gun
what's up? what's happening?   25
I said I guess
that's when I really broke the law.
He said *a routine, step out the car*
a routine, assume the position.
Put your hands up in the air   30
you know the routine, like you just don't care.
License and registration.
Deep was the night and the light
from the North Star on the car door, deja vu
we've been through this before,   35
why did you stop me?
Somebody had to stop you.
I watch the news, you always lose.
You're unreliable, that's undeniable.
This is serious, you could be dangerous.   40

I could wake up in the morning
without a warning
and my world could change:
blink your eyes.
All depends, all depends on the skin,   45
all depends on the skin you're living in.

New York City, they got laws
can't no bruthas drive outdoors,
in certain neighborhoods, on particular streets
near and around certain types of people.   50
They got laws.
All depends, all depends on the skin,
all depends on the skin you're living in.

[1995]

AGHA SHAHID ALI   [1949–2001]

I Dream It Is Afternoon
When I Return to Delhi

At Purana Qila I am alone, waiting
for the bus to Daryaganj. I see it coming,
but my hands are empty.
"Jump on, jump on," someone shouts,
"I've saved this change for you   5
for years. Look!"
A hand opens, full of silver rupees.
"Jump on, jump on." The voice doesn't stop.
There's no one I know. A policeman,
handcuffs silver in his hands,   10
asks for my ticket.

I jump off the running bus,
sweat pouring from my hair.
I run past the Doll Museum, past
headlines on the Times of India   15
building, PRISONERS BLINDED IN A BIHAR
JAIL, HARIJAN VILLAGES BURNED BY LANDLORDS.
Panting, I stop in Daryaganj,
outside Golcha Cinema.

Sunil is there, lighting   20
a cigarette, smiling. I say,
"It must be ten years, you haven't changed,
it was your voice on the bus!"
He says, "The film is about to begin,
I've bought an extra ticket for you,"   25
and we rush inside:

Anarkali is being led away,
her earrings lying on the marble floor.
Any moment she'll be buried alive.
"But this is the end," I turn   30
toward Sunil. He is nowhere.
The usher taps my shoulder, says
my ticket is ten years old.

Once again my hands are empty.
I am waiting, alone, at Purana Qila.   35

Bus after empty bus is not stopping.
Suddenly, beggar women with children
are everywhere, offering
me money, weeping for me.

[1987]

VICTOR HERNÁNDEZ CRUZ   [b. 1949]

Problems with Hurricanes

A campesino looked at the air
And told me:
With hurricanes it's not the wind
or the noise or the water.
I'll tell you he said: 5
it's the mangoes, avocados
Green plantains and bananas
flying into town like projectiles.

How would your family
feel if they had to tell   10
The generations that you
got killed by a flying
Banana.

Death by drowning has honor
If the wind picked you up   15
and slammed you
Against a mountain boulder
This would not carry shame
But
to suffer a mango smashing   20
Your skull
or a plantain hitting your
Temple at 70 miles per hour
is the ultimate disgrace.

The campesino takes off his hat—   25
As a sign of respect
towards the fury of the wind
And says:
Don't worry about the noise

Don't worry about the water   30
Don't worry about the wind—
If you are going out
beware of mangoes
And all such beautiful
sweet things.   35

                                                      [1991]

MARK HALLIDAY   [b. 1949]

Functional Poem

Is there any reason why a poem shouldn't
at least occasionally
come through for us in a concrete way and
get something done?

Because I need to get something across   5
to a particular individual
with whom I have no normal contact,
I mean I never see this guy, and yet
I've got something to say to him—
and me being a poet I naturally   10
have to use
the means at my disposal.

The individual to whom I refer
is a young man with blond hair,
I admit from a certain point of view   15
many people would consider him handsome although
he's what I call rather heavy-set i.e.
chubby. Well-dressed, the guy has money, I'm sure
he wears those yellow-white cotton pants
made for people like golfers and princes   20
who can take everything slow and cool—
not that he does. Because

the one time I saw this guy
on a hot inter-suburban street some years ago
he was driving his white Camaro   25
with his radio on terrifically loud with

some old Beach Boys song which I normally like
but it seemed a sacrilege for this rich guy to have
that old gentle lighthearted music in his Camaro —
the song was a hit when this character was about   30
five years old, for god's sake! —
but anyway he cuts right in front of me,
I'm driving my father's old VW,
he almost clips my fender, gives me this look,
like "You're over the hill, man, get off the road" —   35
I'm under 35 and this guy is telling me
I'm over the hill! So naturally
I give him a blast on the horn.
So then the bastard slows way way down.
So I pass him, except all of a sudden   40
he speeds up to keep even with me,
I'm stuck out in the left lane
and here comes a frigging truck or something!
So I hit the brakes and duck in behind him
in his beautiful creamy white Camaro   45
with the Beach Boys and a little cooler of
Miller High Life in the back seat, I'm sure.
Almost immediately he does the slow-down thing again —

and this time he lets me pass him.
But then about thirty seconds later   50
vrrrroooooommm! — he's passing me
but there's traffic coming toward us,
God, my heart seized up like a broken clutch —
but
he made it, the bastard,   55
I admit he had great acceleration,
and nerve, too, the guy had nerve —
he pulled away into the distance,
going even faster to show me that
the near-miss never scared him for a second.   60

Okay. Now, I've thought it over,
and I realize that what's wrong with this individual
is not that he's rich, or that he's young,
or that he's a little on the heavy side.
That stuff is his business, and the same goes   65
for the loud radio as far as I'm concerned and
the fast driving too, even, in most situations.
But what's wrong with the guy is

that he made me run the risk of
severe damage to life and limb or   70
possibly a fatality, i.e. I could have been killed.
And that is just not acceptable.
I'm saying, this person cannot be permitted
to do such a thing.

Now, I know all your theories, by the way,   75
about "Poetry makes nothing happen"
and art is not a tool or weapon et cetera.
But on the other hand it *is* a way of giving messages,
and if I'm being a little more honest about this
than most poets, then so be it;   80
and I'm just giving that blond individual
this message:

Don't go around interfering with somebody else's
right to live, you stupid jerk.
Why don't you consider some other life-style   85
less dangerous to others and yourself as well?
Why don't you read some poetry once in a while?
If this poem can do a job on you,
maybe others can, too. Why don't you
take some of your gas money and   90
subscribe to a few poetry magazines?
Think about it.

Readers, if you see the above individual,
or somebody like him, could you
please just pass along this message.   95

[1987]

RAY A. YOUNG BEAR   [b. 1950]

From the Spotted Night

In the blizzard
while chopping wood
the mystical whistler
beckons my attention.
Once there were longhouses   5
here. A village.

In the abrupt spring floods
swimmers retrieved our belief.
So their spirit remains.
From the spotted night   10
distant jets transform
into fireflies who float
towards me like incandescent
snowflakes.
The leather shirt   15
which is suspended
on a wire hanger
above the bed's headboard
is humanless; yet when one
stands outside the house,   20
the strenuous sounds
of dressers and boxes
being moved can be heard.
We believe someone wears
the shirt and rearranges   25
the heavy furniture,
although nothing
is actually changed.
Unlike the Plains Indian shirts
which repelled lead bullets,   30
ricocheting from them
in fiery sparks,
this shirt is the means;
this shirt *is* the bullet.

[1990]

CAROLYN FORCHÉ   [b. 1950]

The Colonel

What you have heard is true. I was in his house. His wife carried a tray of
coffee and sugar. His daughter filed her nails, his son went out for the
night. There were daily papers, pet dogs, a pistol on the cushion beside
him. The moon swung bare on its black cord over the house. On the television was a cop show. It was in English. Broken bottles were embedded
in the walls around the house to scoop the kneecaps from a man's legs or

cut his hands to lace. On the windows there were gratings like those in liquor stores. We had dinner, rack of lamb, good wine, a gold bell was on the table for calling the maid. The maid brought green mangoes, salt, a type of bread. I was asked how I enjoyed the country. There was a brief commercial in Spanish. His wife took everything away. There was some talk then of how difficult it had become to govern. The parrot said hello on the terrace. The colonel told it to shut up, and pushed himself from the table. My friend said to me with his eyes: say nothing. The colonel returned with a sack used to bring groceries home. He spilled many human ears on the table. They were like dried peach halves. There is no other way to say this. He took one of them in his hands, shook it in our faces, dropped it into a water glass. It came alive there. I am tired of fooling around he said. As for the rights of anyone, tell your people they can go fuck themselves. He swept the ears to the floor with his arm and held the last of his wine in the air. Something for your poetry, no? he said. Some of the ears on the floor caught this scrap of his voice. Some of the ears on the floor were pressed to the ground.

[1978]

ANNE CARSON   [b. 1950]

Sumptuous Destitution

"Sumptuous destitution"
Your opinion gives me a serious feeling: I would like to be what you deem me.
          (Emily Dickinson letter 319 to Thomas Higginson)

is a phrase
You see my position is benighted.   5
          (Emily Dickinson letter 268 to Thomas Higginson)

scholars use
She was much too enigmatical a being for me to solve in an hour's interview.   (Thomas Higginson letter 342a to Emily Dickinson)

of female   10
God made me [Sir] Master—I didn't be—myself.
          (Emily Dickinson letter 233 to Thomas Higginson)

silence.
Rushing among my small heart—and pushing aside the blood—
          (Emily Dickinson letter 248 to Thomas Higginson) 15

Save what you can, Emily.
And when I try to organize — my little Force explodes — and leaves me bare
and charred.   (Emily Dickinson letter 271 to Thomas Higginson)

Save every bit of thread.
Have you a little chest to put the Alive in?   20
                    (Emily Dickinson letter 233 to Thomas Higginson)

One of them may be
By Cock, said Ophelia.
                    (Emily Dickinson letter 268 to Thomas Higginson)

the way out of here.

                                                        [2000]

JOHN YAU   [b. 1950]

Chinese Villanelle

I have been with you, and I have thought of you
Once the air was dry and drenched with light
I was like a lute filling the room with description

We watched glum clouds reject their shape
We dawdled near a fountain, and listened   5
I have been with you, and I have thought of you

Like a river worthy of its gown
And like a mountain worthy of its insolence . . .
Why am I like a lute left with only description

How does one cut an axe handle with an axe   10
What shall I do to tell you all my thoughts
When I have been with you, and thought of you

A pelican sits on a dam, while a duck
Folds its wings again; the song does not melt
I remember you looking at me without description   15

Perhaps a king's business is never finished,
Though "perhaps" implies a different beginning
I have been with you, and I have thought of you
Now I am a lute filled with this wandering description

                                                        [1979]

JORIE GRAHAM   [b. 1950]

Reading Plato

This is the story
    of a beautiful
lie, what slips
    through my fingers,
your fingers. It's winter,   5
    it's far

in the lifespan
    of man.
Bareheaded, in a soiled
    shirt,   10
speechless, my friend
    is making

lures, his hobby. Flies
    so small
he works with tweezers and   15
    a magnifying glass.
They must be
    so believable

they're true—feelers,
    antennae,   20
quick and frantic
    as something
drowning. His heart
    beats wildly
in his hands. It is   25
    blinding
and who will forgive him
    in his tiny
garden? He makes them
    out of hair,   30

deer hair, because it's hollow
    and floats.
Past death, past sight,
    this is
his good idea, what drives   35
    the silly days

together. Better than memory. Better
    than love.
Then they are done, a hook
    under each pair   40
of wings, and it's Spring,
    and the men

wade out into the riverbed
    at dawn. Above,
the stars still connect-up   45
    their hungry animals.
Soon they'll be satisfied
    and go. Meanwhile

upriver, downriver, imagine, quick
    in the air,   50
in flesh, in a blue
    swarm of
flies, our knowledge of
    the graceful

deer skips easily across   55
    the surface.
Dismembered, remembered,
    it's finally
alive. Imagine
    the body   60

they were all once
    a part of,
these men along the lush
    green banks
trying to slip in   65
    and pass

for the natural world.

                    [1983]

JOY HARJO   [b. 1951]

She Had Some Horses

She had some horses.

She had horses who were bodies of sand.
She had horses who were maps drawn of blood.
She had horses who were skins of ocean water.
She had horses who were the blue air of sky.   5
She had horses who were fur and teeth.
She had horses who were clay and would break.
She had horses who were splintered red cliff.

She had some horses.

She had horses with long, pointed breasts.   10
She had horses with full, brown thighs.
She had horses who laughed too much.
She had horses who threw rocks at glass houses.
She had horses who licked razor blades.

She had some horses.   15

She had horses who danced in their mothers' arms.
She had horses who thought they were the sun and their
bodies shone and burned like stars.
She had horses who waltzed nightly on the moon.
She had horses who were much too shy, and kept quiet   20
in stalls of their own making.

She had some horses.

She had horses who liked Creek Stomp Dance songs.
She had horses who cried in their beer.
She had horses who spit at male queens who made   25
them afraid of themselves.
She had horses who said they weren't afraid.
She had horses who lied.
She had horses who told the truth, who were stripped
bare of their tongues.   30

She had some horses.

She had horses who called themselves, "horse."
She had horses who called themselves, "spirit," and kept
their voices secret and to themselves.
She had horses who had no names.   35
She had horses who had books of names.

She had some horses.

She had horses who whispered in the dark, who were afraid to speak.
She had horses who screamed out of fear of the silence, who
carried knives to protect themselves from ghosts.   40
She had horses who waited for destruction.
She had horses who waited for resurrection.

She had some horses.

She had horses who got down on their knees for any saviour.
She had horses who thought their high price had saved them.   45
She had horses who tried to save her, who climbed in her
bed at night and prayed as they raped her.

She had some horses.

She had some horses she loved.
She had some horses she hated.   50

These were the same horses.

                                                              [1983]

GARRETT KAORU HONGO   [b. 1951]

Yellow Light

One arm hooked around the frayed strap
of a tar-black, patent-leather purse,
the other cradling something for dinner:
fresh bunches of spinach from a J-Town *yaoya*,°   *vegetable stand or seller*
sides of split Spanish mackerel from Alviso's,   5
maybe a loaf of Langendorf;° she steps
off the hissing bus at Olympic and Fig,
begins the three-block climb up the hill,
passing gangs of schoolboys playing war,
Japs against Japs, Chicanas chalking sidewalks   10
with the holy double-yoked crosses of hopscotch,
and the Korean grocer's wife out for a stroll
around this neighborhood of Hawaiian apartments
just starting to steam with cooking
and the anger of young couples coming home   15

6. **Langendorf:** A well-known bakery in California.

from work, yelling at kids, flicking on
TV sets for the Wednesday Night Fights.

If it were May, hydrangeas and jacaranda
flowers in the streetside trees would be
blooming through the smog of late spring.   20
Wisteria in Masuda's front yard would be
shaking out the long tresses of its purple hair.
Maybe mosquitoes, moths, a few orange butterflies
settling on the lattice of monkey flowers
tangled in chain-link fences by the trash.   25

But this is October, and Los Angeles
seethes like a billboard under twilight.
From used-car lots and the movie houses uptown,
long silver sticks of light probe the sky.
From the Miracle Mile, whole freeways away,   30
a brilliant fluorescence breaks out
and makes war with the dim squares
of yellow kitchen light winking on
in all the side streets of the Barrio.

She climbs up the two flights of flagstone   35
stairs to 201-B, the spikes of her high heels
clicking like kitchen knives on a cutting board,
props the groceries against the door,
fishes through memo pads, a compact,
empty packs of chewing gum, and finds her keys.   40

The moon then, cruising from behind
a screen of eucalyptus across the street,
covers everything, everything in sight,
in a heavy light like yellow onions.

                                                              [1982]

DAVID MURA   [b. 1952]

Grandfather-in-Law

It's nothing really, and really, it could have been worse, and of course, he's
        now several years dead,
and his widow, well, if oftentimes she's somewhat distracted, overly
        cautious when we visit—

after all, Boston isn't New York—she seems, for some reason, enormously
    proud that there's now a writer in the family,
and periodically, sends me clippings about the poet laureate, Thoreau,
    Anne Sexton's daughter, Lowell, New England literary lore—
in which I fit, if I fit at all, simply because I write in English—as if color
    of skin didn't matter anymore,   5
Still, years ago, during my first visit to Boston, when we were all asleep,
he, who used to require that my wife memorize lines of Longfellow or
    Poe and recite them on the phone,
so that, every time he called, she ran outdoors and had to be coaxed
    back, sometimes with threats, to talk to Pops
(though she remembers too his sly imitations of Lincoln, ice cream at
    Brighams, burgers and fries, all the usual grandfatherly treats),
he, who for some reason was prejudiced against Albanians—where on
    earth did he find them I wondered—   10
who, in the thirties, would vanish to New York, catch a show, buy a suit,
    while up north,
the gas and water bills pounded the front door (his spendthrift ways
    startled me with my grandfather's resemblance),
who for over forty years came down each morning, "How's the old goat?"
    with a tie only his wife could knot circling his neck,
he slipped into my wife's room—we were unmarried at the time—and
    whispered so softly she thought
he almost believed she was really asleep, and was saying this like a wish
    or spell, some bohunk miscalculated Boston sense of duty: 15
"Don't make a mistake with your life, Susie. Don't make a mistake . . ."
Well. The thing that gets me now, despite the dangling rantings I've let
    go, is that, at least at that time,
he was right: There was, inside me, some pressing, raw unpeeled
    persistence, some libidinous desire for dominance
that, in the scribbled first drafts of my life, seemed to mark me as wastrel
    and rageful, bound to be unfaithful,
to destroy, in some powerful, nuclear need, fissioned both by childhood
    and racism, whatever came near—   20
And I can't help but feel, forgiving him now, that if she had listened, if
    she had been awake,
if this flourishing solace, this muscled-for-happiness, shared by us now,
    had never awakened,
he would have become for me a symbol of my rage and self-destruction,
    another raw, never healing wound,
and not this silenced grandfatherly presence, a crank and scoundrel, red-
    necked Yankee who created the delicate seed of my wife, my child.

[1989]

RITA DOVE   [b. 1952]

The Satisfaction Coal Company

1

What to do with a day.
Leaf through *Jet*. Watch T.V.
Freezing on the porch
but he goes anyhow, snow too high
for a walk, the ice treacherous.   5
Inside, the gas heater takes care of itself;
he doesn't even notice being warm.

Everyone says he looks great.
Across the street a drunk stands smiling
at something carved in a tree.   10
The new neighbor with the floating hips
scoots out to get the mail
and waves once, brightly,
storm door clipping her heel on the way in.

2

Twice a week he had taken the bus down Glendale hill   15
to the corner of Market. Slipped through
the alley by the canal and let himself in.
Started to sweep
with terrible care, like a woman
brushing shine into her hair,   20
same motion, same lullaby.
No curtains—the cop on the beat
stopped outside once in the hour
to swing his billy club and glare.

It was better on Saturdays   25
when the children came along:
he mopped while they emptied
ashtrays, clang of glass on metal
then a dry scutter. Next they counted
nailheads studding the leather cushions.   30
Thirty-four! they shouted,
that was the year and
they found it mighty amusing.

But during the week he noticed more—
lights when they gushed or dimmed   35

at the Portage Hotel, the 10:32
picking up speed past the B & O switchyard,
floorboards trembling and the explosive
kachook kachook kachook kachook
and the oiled rails ticking underneath.   40

3

They were poor then but everyone had been poor.
He hadn't minded the sweeping,
just the thought of it—like now
when people ask him what he's thinking
and he says *I'm listening.*   45

Those nights walking home alone,
the bucket of coal scraps banging his knee,
he'd hear a roaring furnace
with its dry, familiar heat. Now the nights
take care of themselves—as for the days,   50
there is the canary's sweet curdled song,
the wino smiling through his dribble.
Past the hill, past the gorge
choked with wild sumac in summer,
the corner has been upgraded.   55
Still, he'd like to go down there someday
to stand for a while, and get warm.

[1986]

NAOMI SHIHAB NYE   [b. 1952]

The Small Vases from Hebron°

Tip their mouths open to the sky.
Turquoise, amber,
the deep green with fluted handle,
pitcher the size of two thumbs,
tiny lip and graceful waist.   5

Hebron: An ancient city in the West Bank area of Israel, a sacred place for both
Muslims and Jews. It has been a focus of tension between Israelis and Palestin-
ians since the 1967 Arab-Israeli war.

Here we place the smallest flower
which could have lived invisibly
in loose soil beside the road,
sprig of succulent rosemary,
bowing mint.   10

They grow deeper in the center of the table.

Here we entrust the small life,
thread, fragment, breath.
And it bends. It waits all day.
As the bread cools and the children   15
open their gray copybooks
to shape the letter that looks like
a chimney rising out of a house.

And what do the headlines say?

Nothing of the smaller petal   20
perfectly arranged inside the larger petal
or the way tinted glass filters light.
Men and boys, praying when they died,
fall out of their skins.
The whole alphabet of living,   25
heads and tails of words,
sentences, the way they said,
"Ya'Allah!" when astonished,
or "ya'ani" for "I mean"—
a crushed glass under the feet   30
still shines.
But the child of Hebron sleeps
with the thud of her brothers falling
and the long sorrow of the color red.

                                            [1998]

ALICE FULTON   [b. 1952]

You Can't Rhumboogie in a Ball and Chain

for Janis Joplin°

You called the blues' loose black belly lover
and in Port Arthur they called you pig-face.
The way you chugged booze straight, without a glass,
your brass-assed language, slingbacks with jeweled heel,
proclaimed you no kin to their muzzled blood.   5
No Chiclet-toothed Baptist boyfriend for you.

Strung-out, street hustling showed men wouldn't buy you.
Once you clung to the legs of a lover,
let him drag you till your knees turned to blood,
mouth hardened to a thin scar on your face,   10
cracked under songs, screams, never left to heal.
Little Girl Blue, soul pressed against the glass.

That voice rasping like you'd guzzled fiberglass,
stronger than the four armed men behind you.
But a pale horse lured you, docile, to heel: 15
warm snow flanks pillowed you like a lover.
Men feared the black holes in your body and face,
knew what they put in would return as blood.

Craving fast food, cars, garish as fresh blood,
diners with flies and doughnuts under glass,   20
Formica bars and a surfer's gold face,
in nameless motels, after sign-off, you
let TV's blank bright stare play lover,
lay still, convinced its cobalt rays could heal.

Your songs that sound ground under some stud's heel,   25
swallowed and coughed up in a voice like blood:
translation unavailable, lover!
No prince could shoe you in unyielding glass,
stories of exploding pumpkins bored you
who flaunted tattooed breast and hungry face.   30

That night needing a sweet-legged sugar's face,
a hot, sky-eyed Southern comfort to heal

Janis Joplin: (1943–1970), Blues singer in the 1960s and 1970s. Born and raised
in Port Arthur, Texas, her life was blessed by an innate musical talent and cursed
by alcohol and drugs. She died of an overdose at age twenty-seven.

the hurt of senior proms for all but you,
plain Janis Lyn, self-hatred laced your blood.
You knew they worshiped drained works, emptied glass,   35
legend's last gangbang the wildest lover.

Like clerks we face your image in the glass,
suggest lovers, as accessories, heels.
"It's your shade, this blood dress," we say. "It's you."

[1983]

ALBERTO RÍOS [b. 1952]

Nani° *diminutive for "grandmother"*

Sitting at her table, she serves
the sopa de arroz to me
instinctively, and I watch her,
the absolute *mamá,* and eat words
I might have had to say more   5
out of embarrassment. To speak,
now-foreign words I used to speak,
too, dribble down her mouth as she serves
me albondigas. No more
than a third are easy to me.   10
By the stove she does something with words
and looks at me only with her
back. I am full. I tell her
I taste the mint, and watch her speak
smiles at the stove. All my words   15
make her smile. Nani never serves
herself, she only watches me
with her skin, her hair. I ask for more.

I watch the *mamá* warming more
tortillas for me. I watch her   20
fingers in the flame for me.
Near her mouth, I see a wrinkle speak
of a man whose body serves
the ants like she serves me, then more words
from more wrinkles about children, words   25
about this and that, flowing more
easily from these other mouths. Each serves
as a tremendous string around her,

holding her together. They speak
nani was this and that to me   30
and I wonder just how much of me
will die with her, what were the words
I could have been, was. Her insides speak
through a hundred wrinkles, now, more
than she can bear, steel around her,   35
shouting, then, What is this thing she serves?

She asks me if I want more.
I own no words to stop her.
Even before I speak, she serves.

[1982]

GARY SOTO   [b. 1952]

The Elements of San Joaquin

for César Chávez°

FIELD

The wind sprays pale dirt into my mouth
The small, almost invisible scars
On my hands.

The pores in my throat and elbows
Have taken in a seed of dirt of their own.   5

After a day in the grape fields near Rolinda
A fine silt, washed by sweat,
Has settled into the lines
On my wrists and palms.

Already I am becoming the valley,   10
A soil that sprouts nothing.
For any of us.

César Chávez: (1927–1993), Hispanic-American labor leader and activist known
for creating the United Farm Workers and for leading a nationwide boycott of
California table grapes in 1968 as part of an effort to achieve labor contracts for
field workers.

WIND

A dry wind over the valley
Peeled mountains, grain by grain,
To small slopes, loose dirt   15
Where red ants tunnel.
The wind strokes
The skulls and spines of cattle
To white dust, to nothing,

Covers the spiked tracks of beetles,   20
Of tumbleweed, of sparrows
That pecked the ground for insects.

Evenings, when I am in the yard weeding,
The wind picks up the breath of my armpits
Like dust, swirls it   25
Miles away

And drops it
On the ear of a rabid dog,
And I take on another life.

WIND

When you got up this morning the sun   30
Blazed an hour in the sky,

A lizard hid
Under the curled leaves of manzanita°
And winked its dark lids.

Later, the sky grayed,   35
And the cold wind you breathed
Was moving under your skin and already far
From the small hives of your lungs.

STARS

At dusk the first stars appear.
Not one eager finger points toward them.   40
A little later the stars spread with the night
And an orange moon rises
To lead them, like a shepherd, toward dawn.

33. manzanita: An evergreen shrub or small tree found in arid regions of the
western United States.

SUN

In June the sun is a bonnet of light
Coming up,   45
Little by little,
From behind a skyline of pine.

The pastures sway with fiddle-neck,
Tassels of foxtail.

At Piedra   50
A couple fish on the river's edge,
Their shadows deep against the water.
Above, in the stubbled slopes,
Cows climb down
As the heat rises   55
In a mist of blond locusts,
Returning to the valley.

RAIN

When autumn rains flatten sycamore leaves,
The tiny volcanos of dirt
Ants raised around their holes,   60
I should be out of work.

My silverware and stack of plates will go unused
Like the old, my two good slacks
Will smother under a growth of lint
And smell of the old dust   65
That rises
When the closet door opens or closes.

The skin of my belly will tighten like a belt
And there will be no reason for pockets.

HARVEST

East of the sun's slant, in the vineyard that never failed,   70
A wind crossed my face, moving the dust
And a portion of my voice a step closer to a new year.

The sky went black in the ninth hour of rolling trays,
And in the distance ropes of rain dropped to pull me
From the thick harvest that was not mine.   75

FOG

If you go to your window
You will notice a fog drifting in.

The sun is no stronger than a flashlight.
Not all the sweaters
Hung in closets all summer   80

Could soak up this mist. The fog:
A mouth nibbling everything to its origin,
Pomegranate trees, stolen bicycles,

The string of lights at a used-car lot,
A Pontiac with scorched valves.   85

In Fresno the fog is passing
The young thief prying a window screen,
Graying my hair that falls
And goes unfound, my fingerprints
Slowly growing a fur of dust—   90
One hundred years from now
There should be no reason to believe
I lived.

DAYBREAK

In this moment when the light starts up
In the east and rubs   95
The horizon until it catches fire,

We enter the fields to hoe,
Row after row, among the small flags of onion,
Waving off the dragonflies
That ladder the air.   100

And tears the onions raise
Do not begin in your eyes but in ours,
In the salt blown
From one blister into another;

They begin in knowing   105
You will never waken to bear
The hour timed to a heart beat,
The wind pressing us closer to the ground.

When the season ends,
And the onions are unplugged from their sleep,   110
We won't forget what you failed to see,
And nothing will heal
Under the rain's broken fingers.

[1977; rev. 1995]

JIMMY SANTIAGO BACA   [b. 1952]

Family Ties

Mountain barbecue.
They arrive, young cousins singly,
older aunts and uncles in twos and threes,
like trees. I play with a new generation
of children, my hands in streambed silt   5
of their lives, a scuba diver's hands, dusting
surface sand for buried treasure.
Freshly shaved and powdered faces
of uncles and aunts surround taco
and tamale tables. Mounted elk head on wall,   10
brass rearing horse cowboy clock
on fireplace mantle. Sons and daughters
converse round beer and whiskey table.
Tempers ignite on land grant issues.
Children scurry round my legs.   15
Old bow-legged men toss horseshoes on lawn,
other farmhands from Mexico sit on a bench,
broken lives repaired for this occasion.
I feel no love or family tie here. I rise
to go hiking, to find abandoned rock cabins   20
in the mountains. We come to a grass clearing,
my wife rolls her jeans up past ankles,
wades ice cold stream, and I barefooted,
carry a son in each arm and follow.
We cannot afford a place like this.   25
At the party again, I eat bean and chile
burrito, and after my third glass of rum,
we climb in the car and my wife drives
us home. My sons sleep in the back,
dream of the open clearing,   30
they are chasing each other with cattails
in the sunlit pasture, giggling,
as I stare out the window
at no trespassing signs white flashing past.

[1989]

JUDITH ORTIZ COFER   [b. 1952]

Cold as Heaven

Before there is a breeze again
before the cooling days of Lent, she may be gone.
My grandmother asks me to tell her
again about the snow.
We sit on her white bed   5
in this white room, while outside
the Caribbean sun winds up the world
like an old alarm clock. I tell her
about the enveloping blizzard I lived through
that made everything and everyone the same;   10
how we lost ourselves in drifts so tall
we fell through our own footprints;
how wrapped like mummies in layers of wool
that almost immobilized us, we could only
take hesitant steps like toddlers   15
toward food, warmth, shelter.
I talk winter real for her,
as she would once conjure for me to dream
at sweltering siesta time,
cool stone castles in lands far north.   20
Her eyes wander to the window,
to the teeming scene of children
pouring out of a yellow bus, then to the bottle
dripping minutes through a tube
into her veins. When her eyes return to me,   25
I can see she's waiting to hear more
about the purifying nature of ice,
how snow makes way for a body,
how you can make yourself an angel
by just lying down and waving your arms   30
as you do when you say
good-bye.

[1995]

ANITA ENDREZZE   [b. 1952]

The Girl Who Loved the Sky

Outside the second grade room,
the jacaranda tree blossomed
into purple lanterns, the papery petals
drifted, darkening the windows.
Inside, the room smelled like glue.   5
The desks were made of yellowed wood,
the tops littered with eraser rubbings,
rulers, and big fat pencils.
Colored chalk meant special days.
The walls were covered with precise   10
bright tulips and charts with shiny stars
by certain names. There, I learned
how to make butter by shaking a jar
until the pale cream clotted
into one sweet mass. There, I learned   15
that numbers were fractious beasts
with dens like dim zeros. And there,
I met a blind girl who thought the sky
tasted like cold metal when it rained
and whose eyes were always covered   20
with the bruised petals of her lids.

She loved the formless sky, defined
only by sounds, or the cool umbrellas
of clouds. On hot, still days
we listened to the sky falling   25
like chalk dust. We heard the noon
whistle of the pig-mash factory,
smelled the sourness of home-bound men.
I had no father; she had no eyes;
we were best friends. The other girls   30
drew shaky hop-scotch squares
on the dusty asphalt, talked about
pajama parties, weekend cook-outs,
and parents who bought sleek-finned cars.
Alone, we sat in the canvas swings,   35
our shoes digging into the sand, then pushing,
until we flew high over their heads,
our hands streaked with red rust
from the chains that kept us safe.

I was born blind, she said, an act of nature.   40
Sure, I thought, like birds born
without wings, trees without roots.
I didn't understand. The day she moved
I saw the world clearly; the sky
backed away from me like a departing father.   45
I sat under the jacaranda, catching
the petals in my palm, enclosing them
until my fist was another lantern
hiding a small and bitter flame.

[1988]

RAY GONZÁLEZ   [b. 1952]

Praise the Tortilla,
Praise the Menudo,
Praise the Chorizo

I praise the tortilla in honor of El Panzón,
who hit me in school every day and made me see
how the bruises on my arms looked like
the brown clouds on my mother's tortillas.
I praise the tortilla because I know   5
they can fly into our hands like
eager flesh of the one we love,
those soft yearnings we delight in biting
as we tear the tortilla and wipe the plate clean.

I praise the menudo as visionary food that it is,   10
the tripas y posole tight flashes of color
we see as the red caldo smears across our notebooks
like a vision we have not had in years,
our lives going down like the empty bowl
of menudo exploding in our stomachs   15
with the chili piquin of our poetic dreams.

I praise the chorizo and smear it
across my face and hands,
the dayglow brown of it painting me
with the desire to find out   20
what happened to la familia,
why the chorizo sizzled in the pan

and covered the house with a smell
of childhood we will never have again,
the chorizo burrito hot in our hands,   25
as we ran out to play and show the vatos
it's time to cut the chorizo,
tell it like it is before la manteca runs down
our chins and drips away.

[1992]

MARK DOTY   [b. 1953]

Tiara

Peter died in a paper tiara
cut from a book of princess paper dolls;
he loved royalty, sashes

and jewels. I don't know,
he said, when he woke in the hospice,   5
I was watching the Bette Davis film festival

on Channel 57 and then—
At the wake, the tension broke
when someone guessed

the casket closed because   10
he was *in there in a big wig
and heels,* and someone said,

*You know he's always late,
he probably isn't here yet—
he's still fixing his makeup.*   15

And someone said he asked for it.
Asked for it—
when all he did was go down

into the salt tide
of wanting as much as he wanted,   20
giving himself over so drunk

or stoned it almost didn't matter who,
though they were beautiful,
stampeding into him in the simple,

ravishing music of their hurry.   25
I think heaven is perfect stasis
poised over the realms of desire,

where dreaming and waking men lie
on the grass while wet horses
roam among them, huge fragments   30

of the music we die into
in the body's paradise.
Sometimes we wake not knowing

how we came to lie here,
or who has crowned us with these temporary,   35
precious stones. And given

the world's perfectly turned shoulders,
the deep hollows blued by longing,
given the irreplaceable silk

of horses rippling in orchards,   40
fruit thundering and chiming down,
given the ordinary marvels of form

and gravity, what could he do,
what could any of us ever do
but ask for it?   45

[1991]

RICHARD JONES   [b. 1953]

Cathedral

Songbirds live
in the old cathedral,
caged birds bought at the street market
and freed as a kind of offering.
Now doves and finches and parakeets   5
nest in the crooks of the nave's highest arches,
roosting on the impossibly high
sills of stained glass windows,
looking down into the valley of the altar
as if from cliffs.   10

Twice a day, you'll hear them singing:
at dawn
when the blue light
of angels' wings
and the yellow light of halos   15
flood into their nests to wake them;
and during mass
when the organ fills
the valley below with thunder.
These birds love thunder,   20
never having seen a drop of rain.
They love it when the people below stand up
and sing. They fly
in mad little loops
from window to window,   25
from the tops of arches
down toward the candles and tombs,
making the sign of the cross.

If you look up during mass
to the world's light falling   30
through the arms of saints,
you can see birds flying
through blue columns of incense
as if it were simple wood smoke
rising from a cabin's chimney   35
in a remote and hushed forest.

[1994]

JANE HIRSHFIELD   [b. 1953]

The Stone of Heaven

Here, where the rivers dredge up
the very stone of Heaven, we name its colors—
muttonfat jade, kingfisher jade, jade of appleskin green.

And here, in the glittering
hues of the Flemish Masters, we sample their wine;   5
rest in their windows' sun-warmth,
cross with pleasure their scrubbed tile floors.

Everywhere the details leap like fish — bright shards
of water out of water, facet-cut, swift-moving
on the myriad bones.   10

Any woodthrush shows it — he sings,
not to fill the world, but because he is filled.

But the world does not fill with us,
it spills and spills, whirs with owl-wings,
rises, sets, stuns us with planet-rings, stars.   15
A carnival tent, a fluttering of banners.

O baker of yeast-scented loaves,
sword dancer,
seamstress, weaver of shattering glass,
O whirler of winds, boat-swallower,   20
germinant seed,
O seasons that sing in our ears in the shape of O —
we name your colors muttonfat, kingfisher, jade,
we name your colors anthracite, orca, growth-tip of pine,
we name them arpeggio, pond,   25
we name them flickering helix within the cell, burning coal tunnel,
    blossom of salt,
we name them roof flashing copper, frost-scent at morning, smoke-singe
    of pearl,
from black-flowering to light-flowering we name them,
from barest conception, the almost not thought of, to heaviest matter,
    we name them,
from glacier-lit blue to the gold of iguana we name them,   30
and naming, begin to see,
and seeing, begin to assemble the plain stones of earth.

                                                                                    [1994]

LORNA DEE CERVANTES   [b. 1954]

Freeway 280

Las casitas° near the gray cannery,   *little houses*
nestled amid wild abrazos° of climbing roses   *bear hugs*
and man-high red geraniums
are gone now. The freeway conceals it
all beneath a raised scar.   5

But under the fake windsounds of the open lanes,
in the abandoned lots below, new grasses sprout,
wild mustard remembers, old gardens
come back stronger than they were,
trees have been left standing in their yards.   10
Albaricoqueros, cerezos, nogales° . . .   *apple, cherry, walnut trees*
Viejitas' come here with paper bags to gather greens.   *old women*
Espinaca, verdolagas, yerbabuena° . . .   *spinach, purslane, mint*

I scramble over the wire fence
that would have kept me out.   15
Once, I wanted out, wanted the rigid lanes
to take me to a place without sun,
without the smell of tomatoes burning
on swing shift in the greasy summer air.

Maybe it's here   20
en los campos extraños de esta ciudad°
where I'll find it, that part of me
mown under
like a corpse
or a loose seed.   25

                                                                  [1981]

21. en . . . ciudad: In the strange fields of this city.

                    THYLIAS MOSS   [b. 1954]

                         Tornados

Truth is, I envy them
not because they dance; I out jitterbug them
as I'm shuttled through and through legs
strong as looms, weaving time. They
do black more justice than I, frenzy   5
of conductor of philharmonic and electricity, hair
on end, result of the charge when horns and strings release
the pent up Beethoven and Mozart. Ions played

instead of notes. The movement
is not wrath, not hormone swarm because   10

I saw my first forming above the church a surrogate
steeple. The morning of my first baptism and
salvation already tangible, funnel for the spirit
coming into me without losing a drop, my black
guardian angel come to rescue me before all the words   15

get out, *I looked over Jordan and what did I see coming for*
to carry me home. Regardez,° it all comes back, even the first   *look*
grade French, when the tornado stirs up the past, bewitched spoon
lost in its own spin, like a roulette wheel that won't
be steered, like the world. They drove me underground,   20
tornado watches and warnings, atomic bomb drills. Adult
storms so I had to leave the room. Truth is

the tornado is a perfect nappy curl, tightly wound,
spinning wildly when I try to tamper with its nature, shunning
the hot comb and pressing oil even though if absolutely straight   25
I'd have the longest hair in the world. Bouffant tornadic
crown taking the royal path on a trip to town, stroll down
Tornado Alley where it intersects Memory Lane. Smoky spirit-
clouds, shadows searching for what cast them.

[1991]

LOUISE ERDRICH   [b. 1954]

A Love Medicine

Still it is raining lightly
in Wahpeton. The pickup trucks
sizzle beneath the blue neon
bug traps of the dairy bar.

Theresa goes out in green halter and chains   5
that glitter at her throat.
This dragonfly, my sister,
she belongs more than I
to this night of rising water.

The Red River swells to take the bridge.   10
She laughs and leaves her man in his Dodge.
He shoves off to search her out.
He wears a long rut in the fog.

And later, at the crest of the flood,
when the pilings are jarred from their sockets   15
and pitch into the current,
she steps against the fistwork of a man.
She goes down in wet grass
and his boot plants its grin
among the arches of her face.   20

Now she feels her way home in the dark.
The white-violet bulbs of the streetlamps
are seething with insects,
and the trees lean down aching and empty.
The river slaps at the dike works, insistent.   25

I find her curled up in the roots of a cottonwood.
I find her stretched out in the park, where all night
the animals are turning in their cages.
I find her in a burnt-over ditch, in a field
that is gagging on rain,   30
sheets of rain sweep up down
to the river held tight against the bridge.

We see that now the moon is leavened and the water,
as deep as it will go,
stops rising. Where we wait for the night to take us   35
the rain ceases. *Sister, there is nothing
I would not do.*

[1984]

CORNELIUS EADY   [b. 1954]

My Mother,
If She Had Won Free Dance Lessons

Would she have been a person
With a completely different outlook on life?
There are times when I visit
And find her settled on a chair
In our dilapidated house,   5
The neighborhood crazy lady
Doing what the neighborhood crazy lady is supposed to do,
Which is absolutely nothing

And I wonder as we talk our sympathetic talk,
Abandoned in easy dialogue,   10
I, the son of the crazy lady,
Who crosses easily into her point of view
As if yawning
Or taking off an overcoat.
Each time I visit   15
I walk back into our lives

And I wonder, like any child who wakes up one day to find themself
Abandoned in a world larger than their
   Bad dreams,
I wonder as I see my mother sitting there,   20
Landed to the right-hand window in the living room,
Pausing from time to time in the endless loop of our dialogue
To peek for rascals through the
Venetian blinds,

I wonder a small thought.   25
I walk back into our lives.
Given the opportunity,
How would she have danced?
Would it have been as easily

As we talk to each other now,   30
The crazy lady
And the crazy lady's son,
As if we were old friends from opposite coasts
Picking up the thread of a long conversation,

Or two ballroom dancers   35
Who only know
One step?

What would have changed
If the phone had rung like a suitor,
If the invitation had arrived in the mail   40
Like Jesus, extending a hand?

[1986]

MARILYN CHIN   [b. 1955]

Turtle Soup

for Ben Huang

You go home one evening tired from work,
and your mother boils you turtle soup.
Twelve hours hunched over the hearth
(who knows what else is in that cauldron).

You say, "Ma, you've poached the symbol of long life;   5
that turtle lived four thousand years, swam
the Wei, up the Yellow, over the Yangtze.
Witnessed the Bronze Age, the High Tang,
grazed on splendid sericulture."
(So, she boils the life out of him.)   10

"All our ancestors have been fools.
Remember Uncle Wu who rode ten thousand miles
to kill a famous Manchu and ended up
with his head on a pole? Eat, child,
its liver will make you strong."   15

"Sometimes you're the life, sometimes the sacrifice."
Her sobbing is inconsolable.
So, you spread that gentle napkin
over your lap in decorous Pasadena.

Baby, some high priestess has got it wrong.   20
The golden decal on the green underbelly
says "Made in Hong Kong."

Is there nothing left but the shell
and humanity's strange inscriptions,
the songs, the rites, the oracles?   25

[1987]

CATHY SONG   [b. 1955]

Girl Powdering Her Neck

From a Ukiyo-e Print by Utamaro

The light is the inside
sheen of an oyster shell,
sponged with talc and vapor,
moisture from a bath.

A pair of slippers   5
are placed outside
the rice-paper doors.
She kneels at a low table
in the room,
her legs folded beneath her   10
as she sits on a buckwheat pillow.

Her hair is black
with hints of red,
the color of seaweed
spread over rocks.   15

Morning begins the ritual
wheel of the body,
the application of translucent skins.
She practices pleasure:
the pressure of three fingertips   20
applying powder.
Fingerprints of pollen
some other hand will trace.

The peach-dyed kimono
patterned with maple leaves   25
drifting across the silk,
falls from right to left
in a diagonal, revealing
the nape of her neck
and the curve of a shoulder   30
like the slope of a hill
set deep in snow in a country
of huge white solemn birds.
Her face appears in the mirror,

Kitagawa Utamaro (1753–1806), *Girl Powdering Her Neck*
(Musée Guimet, Paris).

a reflection in a winter pond,   35
rising to meet itself.

She dips a corner of her sleeve
like a brush into water
to wipe the mirror;
she is about to paint herself.   40
The eyes narrow
in a moment of self-scrutiny.
The mouth parts
as if desiring to disturb
the placid plum face;   45
break the symmetry of silence.
But the berry-stained lips,
stenciled into the mask of beauty,
do not speak.

Two chrysanthemums   50
touch in the middle of the lake
and drift apart.

                                                              [1983]

KIMIKO HAHN   [b. 1955]

When You Leave

This sadness could only be a color
if we call it *momoiro,* Japanese

for *peach-color,* as in the first story
Mother told us: It is the color of the hero's skin

when the barren woman discovered him   5
inside a peach floating down the river.

And of the banner and gloves she sewed
when he left her to battle the horsemen, then found himself

torn, like fruit off a tree. Even when he met a monkey
dog and bird he could not release   10

the color he saw when he closed his eyes.
    In his boat
the lap of the waves against the hold

was too intimate as he leaned back to sleep.
  He wanted   15
to leave all thoughts of peach behind him—

the fruit that brought him to her
and she, the one who opened the color forever.

[1989]

JIM DANIELS   [b. 1956]

Short-order Cook

An average joe comes in
and orders thirty cheeseburgers and thirty fries.

I wait for him to pay before I start cooking.
He pays.
He ain't no average joe.   5

The grill is just big enough for ten rows of three.
I slap the burgers down
throw two buckets of fries in the deep frier
and they pop pop spit spit . . .
psss . . .   10
The counter girls laugh.
I concentrate.
It is the crucial point—
they are ready for the cheese:
my fingers shake as I tear off slices   15
toss them on the burgers/fries done/dump/
refill buckets/burgers ready/flip into buns/
beat that melting cheese/wrap burgers in plastic/
into paper bags/fries done/fill thirty bags/
bring them to the counter/wipe sweat on sleeve   20
and smile at the counter girls.
I puff my chest out and bellow:
"Thirty cheeseburgers, thirty fries!"
They look at me funny.
I grab a handful of ice, toss it in my mouth   25
do a little dance and walk back to the grill.
Pressure, responsibility, success,
thirty cheeseburgers, thirty fries.

[1985]

LI-YOUNG LEE   [b. 1957]

Eating Alone

I've pulled the last of the year's young onions.
The garden is bare now. The ground is cold,
brown and old. What is left of the day flames
in the maples at the corner of my
eye. I turn, a cardinal vanishes.   5
By the cellar door, I wash the onions,
then drink from the icy metal spigot.

Once, years back, I walked beside my father
among the windfall pears. I can't recall
our words. We may have strolled in silence. But   10
I still see him bend that way—left hand braced
on knee, creaky—to lift and hold to my
eye a rotten pear. In it, a hornet
spun crazily, glazed in slow, glistening juice.

It was my father I saw this morning   15
waving to me from the trees. I almost
called to him, until I came close enough
to see the shovel, leaning where I had
left it, in the flickering, deep green shade.

White rice steaming, almost done. Sweet green peas   20
fried in onions. Shrimp braised in sesame
oil and garlic. And my own loneliness.
What more could I, a young man, want.

[1986]

MARTÍN ESPADA   [b. 1957]

The Saint Vincent de Paul
Food Pantry Stomp

Madison, Wisconsin, 1980

Waiting for the carton of food
given with Christian suspicion
even to agency-certified charity cases
like me,

thin and brittle   5
as uncooked linguini,
anticipating the factory-damaged cans
of tomato soup, beets, three-bean salad
in a welfare cornucopia,
I spotted a squashed dollar bill   10
on the floor, and with
a Saint Vincent de Paul food pantry stomp
pinned it under my sneaker,
tied my laces meticulously,
and stuffed the bill in my sock   15
like a smuggler of diamonds,
all beneath the plaster statue wingspan
of Saint Vinnie,
who was unaware
of the dance   20
named in his honor
by a maraca shaker
in the salsa band
of the unemployed.

[1990]

WANG PING   [b. 1957]

Syntax

She walks to a table
She walk to table

She is walking to a table
She walk to table now

What difference does it make   5
What difference it make

In Nature, no completeness
No sentence really complete thought

Language, like woman,
Look best when free, undressed.   10

[1999]

TOM ANDREWS   [1961–2001]

The Hemophiliac's Motorcycle

For the sin against the holy ghost is ingratitude.
—Christopher Smart, Jubilate Agno°

May the Lord Jesus Christ bless the hemophiliac's motorcycle, the smell
  of knobby tires,
Bel-Ray oil mixed with gasoline, new brake and clutch cables and
  handlebar grips,
the whole bike smothered in WD40 (to prevent rust, and to make the
  bike shine),
may He divine that the complex smell that simplified my life was
  performing the work of the spirit,
a window into the net of gems, linkages below and behind the given
  material world,   5
my little corner of the world's danger and sweet risk, a hemophiliac
  dicing on motocross tracks
in Pennsylvania and Ohio and West Virginia each Sunday from April
  through November,
the raceway names to my mind then a perfect sensual music, Hidden
  Hills, Rocky Fork, Mt. Morris, Salt Creek,
and the tracks themselves part of that music, the double jumps and off-
  camber turns, whoop-de-doos and fifth-gear downhills,
and me with my jersey proclaiming my awkward faith—"Powered By
  Christ," it said above a silk-screened picture of a rider in a radical
  cross-up,   10
the bike flying sideways off a jump like a ramp, the rider leaning his
  whole body into a left-hand corner—
may He find His name glorified in such places and smells,
and in the people, Mike Bias, Charles Godby, Tracy Woods, David and
  Tommy Hill, Bill Schultz°—
their names and faces snowing down to me now as I look upward to the
  past—
friends who taught me to look at the world luminously in front of my eyes,   15

Epigraph: In 1756 Christopher Smart (1722–1771) was seized by an urge to pray
publicly, sometimes forcing passerby to kneel with him. He was placed in an institution, where he began pouring out innovative poetry, including *Jubilate Agno*
(Rejoice in the Lamb). It is, in part, a liturgy of worship, joining the material and
spiritual universe in prayers of praise and thanksgiving. The most famous section
is on his cat Jeoffry (see p. 43).
13. Mike Bias . . . Bill Schultz: Motocross racers.

to find for myself the right rhythm of wildness and precision, when to
    hold back and when to let go,
each of them with a style, a thumbprint, a way of tilting the bike this
    way or that out of a berm shot, or braking heavily into a corner,
may He hear a listening to the sure song of His will in those years,
for they flooded me with gratitude that His informing breath was
    breathed into me,
gratitude that His silence was the silence of all things, His presence
    palpable everywhere in His absence,   20
gratitude that the sun flashed on the Kanawha River, making it shimmer
    and wink,
gratitude that the river twisted like a wrist in its socket of bottomland,
    its water part of our speech
as my brother and I drifted in inner tubes fishing the Great White Carp,
gratitude that plump squirrels tight-walked telephone lines and trellises
    of honeysuckle vines
and swallows dove and banked through the limbs of sycamore trees,
    word-perfect and sun-stunned   25
in the middle of the afternoon, my infusion of factor VIII° sucked in and
    my brother's dialysis sucked in and out—
both of us bewildered by the body's deep swells and currents and eerie
    backwaters,
our eyes widening at the white bursts on the mountain ash, at
    earthworms inching into oil-rainbowed roads—
gratitude that the oak tops on the high hills beyond the lawns fingered
    the denim sky
as cicadas drilled a shrill voice into the roadside sumac and
    peppergrass,   30
gratitude that after a rain catbirds crowded the damp air, bees spiraling
    from one exploding blossom to another,
gratitude that at night the star clusters were like nun buoys moored to
    a second sky, where God made room for us all,
may He adore each moment alive in the whirring world,
as now sitting up in this hospital bed brings a bright gladness for the
    human body, membrane of web and dew
I want to hymn and abide by, splendor of tissue, splendor of cartilage
    and bone,   35
splendor of the taillike spine's desire to stretch as it fills with blood
after a mundane backward plunge on an iced sidewalk in Ann Arbor,
splendor of fibrinogen and cryoprecipitate, loosening the blood pooled
    in the stiffened joints

---

26. **factor VIII:** An enzyme essential to blood clotting.

so I can sit up oh sit up in radiance, like speech after eight weeks of
    silence,
and listen for Him in the blood-rush and clairvoyance of the healing
    body,   40
in the sweet impersonal luck that keeps me now
from bleeding into the kidney or liver, or further into the spine,
listen for Him in the sound of my wife and my father weeping and
    rejoicing,
listen as my mother kneels down on the tiled floor like Christopher
    Smart
praying with strangers on a cobbled London street, kneels here in broad
    daylight   45
singing a "glorious hosanna from the den"
as nurses and orderlies and patients rolling their IV stands behind them
    like luggage
stall and stare into the room and smile finally and shuffle off, having
    heard God's great goodness lifted up
on my mother's tongue, each face transformed for a moment by ridicule
or sympathy before disappearing into the shunt-light of the hallway,   50
listen for Him in the snap and jerk of my roommate's curtain as he
    draws it open
to look and look at my singing mother and her silent choir
and to wink at me with an understanding that passeth peace, this kind,
    skeletal man
suffering from end-stage heart disease who loves science fiction and
    okra,
who on my first night here read aloud his grandson's bar mitzvah speech
    to me,   55
". . . In my haftorah portion, the Lord takes Ezekiel to a valley full of
    bones,
the Lord commands him to prophesy over the bones so they will become
    people. . . ,"
and solemnly recited the entire text of the candlelighting ceremony,
"I would like to light the first candle in memory of Grandma Ruth, for
    whom I was named,
I would like Grandma Dot and Grandpa Dan to come up and light the
    second candle,   60
I would like Aunt Mary Ann and my Albuquerque cousins Alanna and
    Susanna to come up and light the third candle. . . ,"
his voice rising steadily through the vinegary smell and brutal hush in
    the room,
may the Lord hear our listening, His word like matchlight cupped to a
    cigarette

the instant before the intake of breath, like the smoke clouds pooled in
    the lit tobacco
before flooding the lungs and bloodstream, filtering into pith and
    marrow,   65
may He see Himself again in the hemophiliac's motorcycle
on a certain Sunday in 1975 — Hidden Hills Raceway, Gallipolis, Ohio,
a first moto holeshot and wire-to-wire win, a miraculously benign
    sideswipe early on in the second moto
bending the handlebars and front brake lever before the possessed
    rocketing up through the pack
to finish third after passing Brian Kloser on his tricked-out Suzuki
    RM125   70
midair over the grandstand double jump —
may His absence arrive like that again here in this hygienic room,
not with the rush of a peaked power band and big air over the jumps
but with the strange intuitive calm of that race, a stillness somehow
    poised
in the body even as it pounded and blasted and held its line across the
    washboard track,   75
may His silence plague us like that again,
may He bless our listening and our homely tongues.

                                                                          [1994]

VIRGIL SUÁREZ   [b. 1962]

The Ways of Guilt

Guilt is magical.
— from "Adultery," a poem by James Dickey

My father calls a day
too late, merely to remind
me that once again
I've forgotten my mother's

birthday, never mind his,   5
which is a month earlier,
and which I have also
forgotten. He lowers

his voice so that he can
tell me that he will call   10

my mother and tell her
that I have just called

to wish her a happy
birthday—never mind
that I'm a day too late.   15
My mother, after he puts

her on, manages to say
that it's all right, all right
for a son to forget a parent's
birthday, but a mother   20

or father (I'm a father
of two)—and she stops
at "father" to suck
in her breath—should never

forget a son or daughter's   25
birthday, that would certainly
be unpardonable, like a tiger
eating her cubs. After we

hang up, I think of all those
moments, painfully awkward   30
and embarrassing when my
parents, left without any other

alternative, reverted to what always
works: guilt. As I hang up
my three-year-old daughter   35
Alexandria walks into the kitchen

for a glass of cold water. She
looks up at me & must sense
something in the way I look
for she asks, "Daddy, are you   40

happy?" This is something
she's learned at school,
from hearing her teacher say
bad behavior doesn't make

her happy. This is also the   45
same child who's asked
in the past where laughter
goes. I look at her & smile

just to reassure her that yes,
I am happy, for the moment,   50
anyway. Perhaps happiest
to know that when the moment

comes in her own life, I too
will know what buttons to push.
What strings   55
to pull.

[1997]

TIMOTHY LIU   [b. 1965]

Thoreau

My father and I have no place to go.
His wife will not let us in the house—
afraid of catching AIDS. She thinks
sleeping with men is more than a sin,
my father says, as we sit on the curb   5
in front of someone else's house.
Sixty-four years have made my father
impotent. Silver roots, faded black
dye mottling his hair make him look
almost comical, as if his shame   10
belonged to me. Last night we read
Thoreau in a steak house down the road
and wept: *If a man does not keep pace*
with his companions, let him travel
to the music that he hears, however   15
measured or far away. The orchards
are gone, his village near Shanghai
bombed by the Japanese, the groves
I have known in Almaden—apricot,
walnut, peach and plum—hacked down.   20

[1995]

SHERMAN ALEXIE   [b. 1966]

Postcards to Columbus

Beginning at the front door of the White House, travel west
for 500 years, pass through small towns and house fires, ignore
hitchhikers and stranded motorists, until you find yourself
back at the beginning of this journey, this history and country

folded over itself like a Mobius strip. Christopher Columbus   5
where have you been? Lost between Laramie and San Francisco
or in the reservation HUD house, building a better mousetrap?
Seymour saw you shooting free throws behind the Tribal School

in a thunderstorm. Didn't you know lightning strikes the earth
800 times a second? But, Columbus, how could you ever imagine   10
how often our lives change? *Electricity is lightning pretending
to be permanent* and when the Indian child pushes the paper clip

into the electrical outlet, it's applied science, insane economics
of supply and demand, the completion of a 20th century circuit.
Christopher Columbus, you are the most successful real estate agent   15
who ever lived, sold acres and acres of myth, a house built on stilts

above the river salmon travel by genetic memory. Beneath the burden
of 15,000 years my tribe celebrated this country's 200th birthday
by refusing to speak English and we'll honor the 500th anniversary
of your invasion, Columbus, by driving blindfolded cross-country   20

naming the first tree we destroy *America*. We'll make the first guardrail
we crash through our national symbol. Our flag will be a white sheet
stained with blood and piss. Columbus, can you hear me over white noise
of your television set? Can you hear ghosts of drums approaching?

[1993]

ALLISON JOSEPH   [b. 1967]

On Being Told I Don't Speak
Like a Black Person

Emphasize the "h," you hignorant ass,
was what my mother was told
when colonial-minded teachers

slapped her open palm with a ruler
in that Jamaican schoolroom.   5
Trained in England, they tried
to force their pupils to speak
like Eliza Doolittle after
her transformation, fancying themselves
British as Henry Higgins,   10
despite dark, sun-ripened skin.
Mother never lost her accent,
though, the music of her voice
charming everyone, an infectious lilt
I can imitate, not duplicate.   15
No one in the States told her
to eliminate the accent,
my high school friends adoring
the way her voice would lift
when she called me to the phone,   20
A-ll-i-son, it's friend Cathy.
Why don't you sound like her?,
they'd ask. I didn't sound
like anyone or anything,
no grating New Yorker nasality,   25
no fastidious British mannerisms
like the ones my father affected
when he wanted to sell someone
something. And I didn't sound
like a Black American,   30
college acquaintances observed,
sure they knew what a black person
was supposed to sound like.
Was I supposed to sound lazy,
dropping syllables here, there,   35
not finishing words but
slurring the final letter so that
each sentence joined the next,
sliding past the listener?
Were certain words off limits,   40
too erudite, too scholarly
for someone with a natural tan?
I asked what they meant,
and they stuttered, blushed,
said you know, Black English,   45
applying what they'd learned

from that semester's text.
Does everyone in your family
speak alike?, I'd question,
and they'd say don't take this the   50
wrong way, nothing personal.

Now I realize there's nothing
more personal than speech,
that I don't have to defend
how I speak, how any person,   55
black, white, chooses to speak.
Let us speak. Let us talk
with the sounds of our mothers
and fathers still reverberating
in our minds, wherever our mothers   60
or fathers come from:
Arkansas, Belize, Alabama,
Brazil, Aruba, Arizona.
Let us simply speak
to one another,   65
listen and prize the inflections,
differences, never assuming
how any person will sound
until her mouth opens,
until his mouth opens,   70
greetings familiar
in any language.

[1999]

Biographical Notes on the Authors
[Arranged Alphabetically]

This section offers brief biographical sketches of the 200 known authors of the poems included in this book. For fuller biographical information, the most convenient print sources are the *Dictionary of Literary Biography* (Detroit: Gale, 1978–), currently at 254 volumes; and *Contemporary Authors,* also published by Gale (original series, 195 volumes; new revised series, currently 103 volumes). Biographical information for many authors can also be found on the Internet. The Academy of American Poets Web site (http://www.poets.org/poets/index.cfm) is particularly valuable and convenient; we are indebted to it for many of the entries. The "Modern American Poetry" Web site (http://www.english.uiuc.edu/maps/poets.htm) also is excellent and very convenient. The Bedford/St. Martin's LitLinks site (http://www.bedfordstmartins.com/litlinks) is another useful resource. Sites for many individual authors — personal home pages for some contemporary poets and sites maintained by scholars or fans of writers old and new — are available as well. To emphasize how poets work with and are influenced by each other, when the names of poets represented in this anthology appear within a biographical entry, they are in small caps as a reminder that those biographical notes will shed further light on the author at hand.

Ai (b. 1947), who has described herself as one-half Japanese, one-eighth Choctaw, one-fourth Black, and one-sixteenth Irish, was born Florence Anthony in Albany, Texas, and grew up in Tucson, Arizona. She legally changed her name to "Ai," which means "love" in Japanese. She received a B.A. in Japanese from the University of Arizona and an M.F.A. from the University of California at Irvine. She is the author of half a dozen books of poetry, among them *Vice* (1999), which won the National Book Award for poetry. She has taught at Wayne State University, George Mason University, and the University of Kentucky, and she currently teaches at Oklahoma State University and lives in Stillwater, Oklahoma.

Sherman Alexie (b. 1966), of Spokane/Coeur d'Alene Indian descent, was born on the Spokane Indian Reservation in Wellpinit, Washington. He earned his B.A. from Washington State University in Pullman. He has published eight books of poetry and several novels and collections of short fiction, including *The Lone Ranger and Tonto Fistfight in Heaven* (1993). He wrote the script for the film *Smoke Signals* on the basis of one of his short stories. "Postcards to Columbus" reflects Alexie's concern about the devaluation of his native culture.

Agha Shahid Ali (1949–2001) was born in New Delhi and grew up Muslim in Kashmir. He was educated at the University of Kashmir, Srinagar, and at the University of Delhi. He earned a Ph.D. from Pennsylvania State University in 1984 and an M.F.A. from the University of Arizona in 1985. He was a poet (author of eight books of poetry), critic (author of *T. S. Eliot as Editor*, 1986), translator (*The Rebel's Silhouette: Selected Poems* by Faiz Ahmed Faiz, 1992), and editor (*Ravishing Disunities: Real Ghazals in English*, 2000). He held teaching positions at the University of Delhi and at several colleges and universities in the United States. "I Dream It Is Afternoon When I Return to Delhi" shows Ali's use of Western formal cultural principles in work that focuses on his own cultural background.

Tom Andrews (1961–2001) was born and grew up in West Virginia. He graduated from Hope College and earned his M.F.A. at the University of Virginia. He published three books of poems and a memoir, *Codeine Diary* (1998), about his coming to terms with his hemophilia and his determined refusal to let it circumscribe his life. He edited collections of essays on WILLIAM STAFFORD and CHARLES WRIGHT. "The Hemophiliac's Motorcycle" is written as a single sentence and displays the same spirit of celebration one finds in CHRISTOPHER SMART's *Jubilate Agno*.

Matthew Arnold (1822–1888) was born in the small English village of Laleham and raised at Rugby School, where his father was headmaster. He attended Oxford University and, in 1857, was elected professor of poetry at Oxford, a position he held for ten years, writing mostly literary criticism. He also worked for thirty-five years as an inspector of schools and made two lecture tours of the United States.

John Ashbery (b. 1927) grew up on a farm near Rochester, New York. He attended Harvard University and later Columbia University. He studied in France for two years and then stayed

on, writing art criticism. Returning to New York, he taught, edited *Art News*, and wrote for *Newsweek*. He is the author of twenty books of poetry, including *Some Trees* (1956), which was selected by W. H. AUDEN for the Yale Younger Poets Series, and *Self-Portrait in a Convex Mirror* (1975), which received the Pulitzer Prize for poetry, the National Book Critics Circle Award, and the National Book Award. He has also published literary criticism, a book of art criticism, a collection of plays, and a novel. "One Coat of Paint" is typical of the way Ashbery combines varied syntactical devices and leads a sentence away from what its opening would usually predict.

Margaret Atwood (b. 1939) was born in Ottawa and raised in Ontario and Quebec. She studied at the University of Toronto, published her first book shortly afterward, and then earned an M.A. at Harvard University. She is the author of at least fifteen books of poetry, ten novels, five collections of short fiction, four collections of nonfiction, and several books for children and is the editor of an anthology of Canadian writers. Much of her work, like the poem in this anthology, reflects her feminist concerns. She has served as a writer-in-residence and a lecturer at many colleges and universities. She lives in Toronto.

W. [ystan] H. [ugh] Auden (1907–1973) was born in York, England. He went to private school and then to Oxford University, where he began to write poetry. He supported himself by teaching and publishing and wrote books based on his travels to Iceland, Spain, and China. He also wrote (with Chester Kallman) several librettos, including the one for Igor Stravinsky's *The Rake's Progress*

(1951). He lived in the United States from 1939 until his death and became a U.S. citizen in 1946. His work combines lively intelligence, quick wit, careful craftsmanship, and social concern.

Jimmy Santiago Baca (b. 1952) was born in Sante Fe, New Mexico, of Chicano and Apache heritage. Abandoned by his parents at the age of two, he lived with one of his grandparents for several years before being placed in an orphanage. He lived on the streets as a youth and was imprisoned for six years for drug possession. In prison, he taught himself to read and write and began to compose poetry. A fellow inmate convinced him to submit some of his poems for publication. He has since published seven books of poetry, a memoir, a collection of stories and essays, a play, and a screenplay. He lives outside Albuquerque in a one-hundred-year-old adobe house.

Jim Barnes (b. 1933), born in Oklahoma of Choctaw and Welsh heritage, worked for ten years as a lumberjack. He studied at Southeastern Oklahoma State University and received his Ph.D. from the University of Arkansas. Author of several books of poetry, he often uses formalist techniques to comment on the difficulties faced by Native Americans. Currently professor of comparative literature at Northeast Missouri State University, he is the founder and editor of the *Chariton Review*.

Aphra Behn (1640–1689) was born in East Kent of middle-class parents and in her early twenties traveled to Suriname, on the northern coast of South America. When she returned to England, she married a London merchant who died, probably of the plague, the following year. In financial difficulty, Behn worked as a spy in Antwerp for King Charles II but was not paid, so she turned to writing. She first wrote plays, as well as verse, and then turned to the emerging genre of prose fiction, in which she is best known for *Oroonoko*, which is set in Suriname.

John Berryman (1914–1972) was born John Smith in McAlester, Oklahoma; he took the name of his stepfather after his father's suicide. He attended a private school in Connecticut, Columbia College, and Clare College, Cambridge. He taught at Wayne State University, Harvard University, Princeton University, and the University of Minnesota. His early work was traditional, highly crafted, and admired, but only later, when he was in his forties, did his poetry emerge as boldly original and innovative. *77 Dream Songs*, published in 1964 and awarded a Pulitzer Prize, unveiled the alter egos "Henry" and "Mr. Bones" in a sequence of sonnet-like poems whose unusual diction, difficult syntax, leaps in language and tone, and mixture of lyricism and comedy reached depths of the human spirit and psyche. He added to the sequence in the following years until they totaled nearly four hundred in *The Dream Songs* (1969). Berryman suffered throughout his life from mental and emotional difficulties and commited suicide by jumping off a bridge in Minneapolis.

Elizabeth Bishop (1911–1979), born in Worcester, Massachusetts, was raised in Nova Scotia by her grandparents after her father died and her mother was committed to an asylum. She attended Vassar College, intending to study medicine, but was encouraged by MARIANNE

MOORE to be a poet. From 1935 to 1937 she traveled in France, Spain, northern Africa, Ireland, and Italy and then settled in Key West, Florida, for four years, after which she lived in Rio de Janeiro for almost twenty years. She wrote slowly and carefully and produced a small body of poetry (totaling only around one hundred poems), technically sophisticated, formally varied, witty, and thoughtful, revealing in precise, true-to-life images her impressions of the physical world. She served as Consultant in Poetry at the Library of Congress from 1949 to 1950.[1]

William Blake (1757–1827) was born and lived in London. His only formal schooling was in art—he studied for a year at the Royal Academy and was apprenticed to an engraver. He worked as a professional engraver, doing commissions and illustrations, assisted by his wife, Catherine Boucher. Blake started writing poetry at the age of eleven and later engraved and hand-printed his own poems, in very small batches, with his own hand-colored illustrations. His early work showed a strong social conscience, and his later work turned increasingly mythic and prophetic.

Robert Bly (b. 1926) was born in Madison, Minnesota, and served in the navy during World War II. He studied at St. Olaf College for a year before going to Harvard University. He lived in New York for a few years, then earned

an M.A. from the University of Iowa Writers' Workshop. He received a Fulbright grant in 1956 to travel to Norway and began to translate Norwegian poetry into English. In 1966 he founded (with David Ray) American Writers Against the Vietnam War. He has published more than thirty books of poetry, many books of translations, and a number of nonfiction books and has edited numerous collections of poetry. A best-selling author, (his controversial 1990 best-seller *Iron John* was a key book in the "men's movement") he is also a challenging critic of contemporary consumerist culture. "Driving to Town Late to Mail a Letter" is an example of his ability to discover a moment of epiphany in the most common of situations. He now lives on a farm near the small town of Moose Lake, Minnesota.

Louise Bogan (1897–1970) was born in Maine and educated in Boston. For thirty-eight years she was the poetry editor at the *New Yorker*. She was reclusive and disliked talking about herself, and for that reason details are scarce regarding her private life. The majority of her poetry was written in the earlier half of her life and published in the *New Republic*, the *Nation*, *Poetry*, *Scribner's*, *Atlantic Monthly*, and in several volumes of collected verse. Her poetry is notable for its strict adherence to lyrical forms while maintaining a high emotional pitch. "Women," like much of her verse, explores the perpetual disparity of heart and mind.

---

1. The first appointment of a Consultant in Poetry at the Library of Congress was made in 1937. The title was changed to Poet Laureate Consultant in Poetry in 1986. Appointments are made for one year, beginning in September, and sometimes have been renewed for a second year.

Eavan Boland (b. 1944) was born in Dublin and educated there and in London and New York. She has taught at Trinity College and University College, Dublin; Bowdoin College; and the University of Iowa. She currently is a professor of English at Stanford University. She is the author of eight volumes of poetry and a collection of essays, coeditor of *The Making of a Poem: A Norton Anthology of Poetic Forms* (2000), and a regular reviewer for the *Irish Times*.

Anne Bradstreet (c. 1612–1672), born in Northampton, England, was educated by tutors, reading chiefly religious writings and the Bible. In 1628 she married Simon Bradstreet, a brilliant young Puritan educated at Cambridge. They were among the earliest settlers of the Massachusetts Bay Colony, in 1630, and her father and husband were leading figures in its governance. She wrote regularly in both prose and verse throughout her busy and difficult years in Massachusetts.

Emily Brontë (1818–1848) was the fifth of six children, three of whom (Emily, Charlotte, and Anne) became famous novelists. She was brought up, like her siblings, by her aunt at Haworth in Yorkshire, where her father was a clergyman. Emily was educated at home and spent the rest of her life there, near the wild Yorkshire moors she loved. Charlotte sent some of the sisters' poetry to be published, under pseudonyms, in 1846, but the venture was not successful and the Brontës then turned to writing novels. Emily is best known for the novel *Wuthering Heights*.

Gwendolyn Brooks (1917–2000), born in Topeka, Kansas, was raised in Chicago and wrote her first poems at age seven. She began studying poetry at the Southside Community Art Center. Her second collection of poems, *Annie Allen* (1949), earned the first Pulitzer Prize given to an African American poet. She served as Consultant in Poetry at the Library of Congress from 1985 to 1986 and worked in community programs and poetry workshops in Chicago to encourage young African American writers.

Sterling A. Brown (1901–1989) was born in Washington, D.C., and educated at Dunbar High School, Williams College, and Harvard University. He taught for more than fifty years at Howard University. Like many other black poets of the period, he expresses his concerns about race in America. His first book of poems, *Southern Road* (1932), was well received by critics, and Brown became part of the artistic tradition of the Harlem Renaissance. Brown was deeply interested in African American music and dialect. He became one of the great innovators in developing poetry related to jazz. His work is known for its frank, unsentimental portraits of black people and their experiences and its successful incorporation of African American folklore and contemporary idiom.

Elizabeth Barrett Browning (1806–1861) was born in Durham, England, and studied with her brother's tutor. Her first book of poetry was published when she was thirteen, and she soon became the most famous female poet to that point in English history. A riding accident at the age of sixteen left her a semi-invalid in the house of her possessive father, who had forbidden any of his eleven children to marry. She and ROBERT BROWNING were forced to elope (she was thirty-nine at the time); they lived in Florence, Italy, where she died fifteen years later. Her best-known book of poems was *Sonnets from the Portuguese*, a sequence of forty-four sonnets recording the growth of her love for Robert.

Robert Browning (1812–1889) was the son of a bank clerk in Camberwell, then a suburb of London. As an aspiring poet in 1844, he admired ELIZABETH BARRETT's poetry and began a correspondence with her that led to one of the world's most famous romances. Their courtship lasted until 1846 when they were secretly wed and ran off to Italy, where they lived until Elizabeth's death in 1861. The years in Florence were among the happiest for both of them. To her he dedicated *Men and Women*, which contains his best poetry. Although she was the more popular poet during her lifetime, his reputation grew upon his return to London after her death, assisted somewhat by public sympathy for him. The late 1860s were the peak of his career: he and TENNYSON were mentioned together as the foremost poets of the age.

Charles Bukowski (1920–1994), born in Andernach, Germany, came to the United States at age three and grew up in poverty in Los Angeles, drifted extensively, and for much of his life made his home in San Pedro, working for many years in the U.S. Postal Service. He was familiar with the people of the streets, skid row residents, hustlers, and a transient lifestyle. He began writing in childhood, and published his first story at age twenty-four and his first poetry when he was thirty-five. He

published many books of poetry, in addition to novels and short stories reminiscent of Ernest Hemingway. He is very popular in Europe. His style, which exhibits a strong sense of immediacy and a refusal to embrace standard formal structures, was influenced by the Beat movement.

Robert Burns (1759–1796) was born in Ayrshire in southwestern Scotland, the son of a poor farming family. His formal education lasted only to about his ninth year, when he was needed to work on the farm, but he read widely and voraciously whenever he could find time. His first book of poems, published in 1785, sold out within a month. Despite living in poverty, he poured out a flood of his finest poems in the early 1790s. He is regarded as Scotland's national bard for his ability to depict with loving accuracy the life of his fellow rural Scots. His use of dialect brought a stimulating, much-needed freshness and raciness into English poetry, but his greatness extends beyond the limits of dialect: his poems are written about Scots, but, in tune with the rising humanitarianism of his day, they apply to a multitude of universal problems.

Thomas Campion (1567–1620) was born in London and educated at Cambridge University. After studying law at Gray's Inn and medicine at the University of Caen, he set up a medical practice in London. His first book was a collection of poems in Latin, *Thomae Campiani Poemata* (1595), and his love of quantitative versification (see **quantitative verse** in the glossary) carried over to his English poems. He published a book of prosody, *Observations* *in the Art of English Poesy*, in 1602, defending quantitative verse against the accentual, rhymed verse more characteristic of English poetry. He was a composer as well as a poet and one of the great writers of song in English. In 1601, he contributed twenty-one songs and a brief treatise on song to Philip Rosseter's *Book of Ayeres* and went on to publish four books of airs himself, the last in 1617. He also wrote a number of masques for performance at King James's court. He died in London, probably of the plague.

Hayden Carruth (b. 1921) was born in Waterbury, Connecticut, and educated at the University of North Carolina at Chapel Hill and the University of Chicago. For many years he lived in northern Vermont. He now lives in upstate New York, where until recently he taught in the graduate creative writing program at Syracuse University. He has been editor of *Poetry*, poetry editor of *Harper's*, and, for twenty years, an advisory editor of the *Hudson Review*. Noted for the breadth of his linguistic and formal resources, influenced by jazz and the blues, Carruth has published twenty-nine books, chiefly poetry but also a novel, four books of criticism, and two anthologies. Many of his best-known poems are about the people and places of northern Vermont, as well as rural poverty and hardship, and reflect his political radicalism and sense of cultural responsibility.

Anne Carson (b. 1950) was born to a banker's family and raised in various Ontario towns. A scholar trained in the classics (Ph.D., University of Toronto), Carson has developed an independent voice as a poet and an essayist. Her work challenges preconceived notions of poetry, fusing classical topics with a unique and thoroughly modern style and sensibility. She has taught at a number of colleges and universities, following a pattern of teaching one semester in Canada and at least one semester in the United States.

Lorna Dee Cervantes (b. 1954) was born in San Francisco and grew up in San Jose. There she studied at San Jose City College and San Jose State University. She has been a member of the Chicana Theatre Group, has worked at the Centro Cultural de la Gente, and founded Mango Publications, a small press that prints Chicano and diverse books as well as a literary journal. She is coeditor of *Red Dirt*, a cross-cultural poetry journal. Cervantes, who considers herself "a Chicana writer, a feminist writer, a political writer," lives in Colorado and is a professor at the University of Colorado at Boulder.

Marilyn Chin (b. 1955) is a first-generation Chinese American, born in Hong Kong and raised in Portland, Oregon. In addition to publishing several books of poetry, she has coedited *Dissident Song: A Contemporary Asian American Anthology* (1991) and co-translated *The Selected Poems of Ai Qing* (1985). An activist who sees herself as pitted against the dominant culture in which she lives, she writes poetry that reflects the difficulty of bridging two cultures and conveys a sense of exile and loss. She teaches at San Diego State University.

Lucille Clifton (b. 1936) was born in Depew, New York, and studied at Howard University. In addition to many books of poetry, she has published a memoir and more than sixteen books for children. She has taught at several colleges and worked in the Office of Education in Washington, D.C. She has served as poet laureate for the State of Maryland and is currently Distinguished Professor of Humanities at St. Mary's College of Maryland. Her poems typically reflect her ethnic pride, womanist principles, and race and gender consciousness.

Judith Ortiz Cofer (b. 1952) was born in Puerto Rico and raised in New Jersey. A writer of poetry, prose, and fiction, she often combines genres in the same collection. Her poetry and prose reflect her rich cultural and linguistic background. She currently lives in Georgia, where she is a professor at the University of Georgia.

Samuel Taylor Coleridge (1772–1834) was born in Devonshire and sent to school in London after his father's death. He went to Jesus College, Cambridge, in 1791, and dropped out twice without a degree. In 1798 Coleridge and WILLIAM WORDSWORTH published *Lyrical Ballads*, which initiated the Romantic movement in English poetry and established both of their reputations. After 1802 Coleridge became addicted to opium, used as a treatment for physical discomfort and seizures. He and his wife were separated, his friendship with Wordsworth broke up, and his poetic output stopped. From 1816 to his death he lived under constant medical supervision, but still published a journal and wrote several plays, pieces of criticism, and philosophical and religious treatises.

Billy Collins (b. 1941), born and raised in New York City, is the author of several collections of poems. Perhaps no poet since ROBERT FROST has managed to combine high critical acclaim with such broad popular appeal. The typical Collins poem opens on a clear and hospitable note but soon takes an unexpected turn; poems that begin in irony may end in a moment of lyric surprise. Collins sees his poetry as "a form of travel writing" and considers humor "a door into the serious." Collins is Distinguished Professor of Literature at Lehman College of the City University of New York and a writer-in-residence at Sarah Lawrence College. He was appointed Poet Laureate Consultant in Poetry at the Library of Congress from 2001 to 2002.

Jayne Cortez (b. 1936) was born in Arizona, grew up in the Watts section of Los Angeles, and now lives in New York City. A poet and performance artist, she has published several collections of poetry and made a number of recordings, often performing her poetry with the jazz group the Firespitters. Her poems have been translated into twenty-eight languages. In 1964 she founded the Watts Repertory Company, and in 1972 she formed her own publishing company, Bola Press.

Hart Crane (1899–1932), born in Garrettsville, Ohio, began writing verse in his early teenage years. Though he never attended college, he read widely on his own. An admirer of T. S. ELIOT, Crane combined the influences of European literature and traditional versification with a particularly American sensibility derived from WALT WHITMAN.

His major work, the book-length poem *The Bridge* (1930), expresses in ecstatic terms a vision of the historical and spiritual significance of America. Like Eliot, Crane used the landscape of the modern, industrialized city to create a powerful new symbolic literature. He committed suicide in 1932, at the age of thirty-three, by jumping from the deck of a steamship sailing back to New York from Mexico.

Stephen Crane (1871–1900), born in Newark, New Jersey, was the fourteenth and youngest child of a Methodist minister. He started to write stories at the age of eight and at sixteen was writing feature articles for the *New York Tribune*. He attended Lafayette College and Syracuse University and then returned to New York where he lived in poverty as a freelance writer and journalist. His experience in the Bowery slums supplied detail for his first, self-published novel, *Maggie: A Girl of the Streets* (1893), a pioneer work of the naturalistic movement. His most famous novel, *The Red Badge of Courage*, a realistic depiction of the Civil War from the point of view of an ordinary soldier, was published in 1895 and was a resounding success. His achievements as a novelist won him assignments as a special newspaper correspondent and enabled him to travel widely, reporting on the Spanish-American and Graeco-Turkish wars. In addition to several volumes of essays and short stories, he published two collections of poems, *The Black Riders* (1895) and *War Is Kind* (1899). He settled briefly in England and died from tuberculosis in Badenweiler, Germany, a few months before his twenty-ninth birthday.

Robert Creeley (b. 1926), born in Arlington, Massachusetts, attended Harvard University, then lived in France and Spain before joining the faculty of Black Mountain College (an experimental arts college in North Carolina) in 1954, where he edited the *Black Mountain Review*. His influence helped to define an emerging countertradition to the literary establishment. He has published more than sixty books of poetry in the United States and abroad. Since 1989 he has been Samuel P. Capen Professor of Poetry and Humanities at the State University of New York, Buffalo. "Time" illustrates his technique of fracturing lines to convey tension, anxiety, and fragmentation of the psyche.

Victor Hernández Cruz (b. 1949) was born in Aguas Buenas, Puerto Rico, and moved to New York City with his family at the age of five. His first book of poetry was published when he was seventeen. A year later, he moved to California's Bay Area and published his second book. In 1971 Cruz visited Puerto Rico and reconnected with his ancestral heritage; eighteen years later, he returned to Puerto Rico to live. He now divides his time between Puerto Rico and New York. Much of his work explores the relation between the English language and his native Spanish, playing with grammatical and syntactical conventions within both languages to create his own bilingual idiom.

Countee Cullen (1903–1946) was born either in Louisville, Kentucky, Baltimore, Maryland, or (as he himself claimed) New York City. He was adopted by the Reverend Frederick A. Cullen and his wife and grew up, as he put it, "in the conservative atmosphere of a Methodist parsonage." He studied at New York University and Harvard University. A forerunner of the Harlem Renaissance movement, he was in the 1920s the most popular black literary figure in America. From the 1930s until his death, he wrote less and worked as a junior high school French teacher. For many years after his death, his reputation was eclipsed by that of other Harlem Renaissance writers, particularly LANGSTON HUGHES and Zora Neale Hurston; recently, however, there has been a resurgence of interest in his life and work.

e. e. cummings (1894–1962) was born in Cambridge, Massachusetts, where his father was a Unitarian minister and a sociology lecturer at Harvard University. He graduated from Harvard and then served as an ambulance driver during World War I. *The Enormous Room* (1922) is an account of his confinement in a French prison camp during the war. After the war, he lived in rural Connecticut and Greenwich Village, with frequent visits to Paris. In his work, Cummings experimented radically with form, punctuation, spelling, and syntax, abandoning traditional techniques and structures to create a new, highly idiosyncratic means of poetic expression. At the time of his death in 1962, he was the second most widely read poet in the United States, after ROBERT FROST.

Jim Daniels (b. 1956) was born in Detroit, where he, his brothers, his father, and his grandfather all have worked in the auto industry. He graduated with a B.A. from Alma College in Michigan and earned his M.F.A. from Bowling Green University. He presently lives in Pittsburgh, where he teaches at Carnegie Mellon University. Daniels's poems often reflect and honor the lives of the working class.

Toi Derricotte (b. 1941) was born and raised in Detroit, where she earned a B.A. in special education from Wayne State University. She is the author of several collections of poetry as well as a memoir, *The Black Notebooks* (1997). With poet CORNELIUS EADY, she co-founded Cave Canem, which offers workshops and retreats for African American poets. Among many honors she has received is the Distinguished Pioneering of the Arts Award from the United Black Artists. Derricotte teaches creative writing at the University of Pittsburgh.

Emily Dickinson (1830–1886) was born in Amherst, Massachusetts, and lived there her entire life, rarely leaving. She briefly attended a women's seminary but became homesick and left before a year was out. Dickinson never married and became reclusive later in life, forgoing even the village routines and revelries she enjoyed. She published very few of the more than 1,700 poems she wrote; most were written for herself or for inclusion in her many letters. Not until 1955 was there a complete edition of her poems attempting to present them as originally written.

John Donne (1572–1631) was born in London to a prosperous Catholic family (through his mother he was related to Sir Thomas More and the playwright John Heywood). Donne studied at Oxford University for several years but did not take a degree. He fought with Sir Walter Raleigh in two naval strikes against Spain. In 1601 Donne's promising political career was permanently derailed by his precipitous marriage to Anne More without her father's consent. He was briefly imprisoned, lost a very promising position with Sir Thomas Egerton, and spent years seeking further political employment before finally being convinced by King James in 1615 to become a priest of the Church of England. His life was described by Isaac Walton later in the century as being divided into two parts. In Phase I he was "Jack Donne" of Lincoln's Inn: when young, Donne employed a sophisticated urban wit that created in his earlier poetry a sort of jaded tone. "The Flea" presumably appeared during this stage of his life and illustrates its characteristics well (a typical **metaphysical poem**—see the glossary). In Phase II he was John Donne, dean of St. Paul's: after Donne took holy orders in 1615, his poetry became markedly less amorous and more religious in tone. His *Holy Sonnets* (of which "Batter my heart, three-personed God" is one) are as dense and complex as his earlier work, with his talent now directed toward exploration of his relationship with God.

H. D. [Hilda Doolittle] (1886–1961) was born in Bethlehem, Pennsylvania. She went to private schools in Philadelphia and then dropped out of Bryn Mawr after a year because of ill health. She moved to England, where an old friend (and fiancé for a time), EZRA POUND, encouraged her to write and sent some of her poetry to a journal. H. D. became a leader of Pound's Imagist group but eventually moved away from it. From 1933 to 1934 she visited

Freud as a patient and later wrote *Tribute to Freud* (1956). Besides poetry, she wrote novels and translated Greek.

Mark Doty (b. 1953) is the author of six collections of poetry and two memoirs—*Heaven's Coast* (1996), about the loss of his partner, Wally Roberts, and *Firebird* (1999), a gay coming-of-age story, a chronicle of a gradual process of finding in art a place of personal belonging. He has taught at Brandeis University, Sarah Lawrence College, Vermont College, and the University of Iowa Writers' Workshop. He now lives in Provincetown, Massachusetts, and Houston, Texas, where he teaches at the University of Houston.

Rita Dove (b. 1952) was born in Akron, Ohio; her father was the first research chemist to break the race barrier in the tire industry. She graduated from Miami University in Oxford, Ohio, with a degree in English; after a year at Tübingen University in Germany on a Fulbright fellowship, she joined the University of Iowa Writers' Workshop, where she earned her M.F.A. in 1977. She has taught at Tuskegee Institute and Arizona State University and now is on the faculty of the University of Virginia. She was appointed Poet Laureate Consultant in Poetry at the Library of Congress in 1993, making her the youngest person—and the first African American—to receive this highest official honor in American letters. She was awarded the Pulitzer Prize in 1987 for *Thomas and Beulah*, a book-length sequence loosely based on the lives of her grandparents. "The Satisfaction Coal Company" is from that book ("he" is Thomas; "they" are Thomas and Beulah); it reflects Dove's concern for those living workaday lives and her celebration of their worth and dignity.

Michael Drayton (1563–1631) was born a year before Shakespeare and in the same county, Warwickshire, England. He wrote sonnets, pastorals, odes, verse epistles, satires, and historical epics. His masterpiece is a topographical work on England titled *Poly-Olbion*, a poem celebrating all the counties of England and Wales. He was an influential writer of religious poetry as well. "Since there's no help, come let us kiss and part" is the sixty-first in a sequence of sonnets addressed to "Idea," the embodiment of the Platonic idea of virtue and beauty.

Paul Laurence Dunbar (1872–1906) was the first African American to gain national eminence as a poet. Born and raised in Dayton, Ohio, he was the son of ex-slaves. He was an outstanding student. The only African American in his class, he was both class president and class poet. Although he lived to be only thirty-three years old, Dunbar was prolific, writing short stories, novels, librettos, plays, songs, and essays as well as the poetry for which he became well known. He was popular with both black and white readers of his day. His style encompasses two distinct voices — the standard English of the classical poet and the evocative dialect of the turn-of-the-century black community in America.

Robert Duncan (1919–1988) was born in Oakland, California, and raised by adoptive parents who were devout theosophists and instilled in him a lifelong interest in occult spirituality. He entered the University of California at Berkeley in 1936 and moved into leftist politics and a bohemian lifestyle. He was drafted in 1941 but was discharged after declaring his homosexuality. His 1944 essay "The Homosexual in Society" compared the situation faced by homosexuals in modern society with that of blacks and Jews. Influenced by a variety of poets, Duncan credited a long correspondence with DENISE LEVERTOV with helping him find a new poetics — a magical, mystical blend of the experimental with the traditional. His first book, *Heavenly City, Earthly City*, was published in 1947, the same year he met Charles Olson, whose literary theories helped shape Duncan's "grand collage" concept of verse. He returned to San Francisco in 1948, becoming part of the San Francisco Renaissance and cultivating the role of a guru, discoursing on literature, spiritualism, and sexual diversity. He became affiliated with Olson's Black Mountain movement and taught at Black Mountain College in 1956. His reputation as a poet was established by three major collections: *The Opening of the Field* (1960), *Roots and Branches* (1964), and *Bending the Bow* (1968). He was awarded the Harriet Monroe Memorial Prize in 1961, a Guggenheim Fellowship in 1963, the Levinson Prize in 1964, and the National Poetry Award in 1985.

Cornelius Eady (b. 1954) was born and raised in Rochester, New York, and attended Monroe Community College and Empire State College. He began writing as a teenager. His poems are his biography, their subjects ranging from blues musicians to the witnessing of his father's death. He has published six volumes of poetry. With poet TOI

DERRICOTTE, he co-founded Cave Canem, which offers workshops and retreats for African American poets, and with composer Diedre Murray he has collaborated on two highly acclaimed music-dramas. Formerly the director of the Poetry Center at the State University of New York, Stony Brook, he is currently Distinguished Writer-in-Residence at the City College of New York.

T.[homas]   S.[tearns]   Eliot (1888–1965) was born and raised in St. Louis. He went to prep school in Massachusetts and then to Harvard University, where he earned an M.A. in philosophy in 1910 and started his doctoral dissertation. He studied at the Sorbonne, Paris, and then at Marburg, Germany, in 1914. The war forced him to Oxford, where he married and abandoned philosophy for poetry. After teaching and working in a bank, he became an editor at Faber and Faber and editor of the journal *Criterion* and was the dominant force in English poetry for several decades. He became a British citizen and a member of the Church of England in 1927. He won the Nobel Prize in literature in 1948. He also wrote plays, essays, and a series of poems on cats that became the basis of a musical by Andrew Lloyd Weber. The poems included in this anthology show Eliot's use of collage techniques to embody the fragmentation he saw in culture and individual psyches in his day.

Elizabeth I (1533–1603) was queen of England from 1558 to 1603. In addition to being well educated and a skillful politician and ruler, she wrote extensively, mostly speeches and translations but also a few original poems in the forms and manner typical of her time. Though the attribution of "When I was fair and young" has been questioned, it is credited to her in the most recent collection of Queen Elizabeth I's works.

Anita Endrezze (b. 1952) was born in Long Beach, California, of Yaqui and European ancestry, and earned her M.A. from Eastern Washington University. She is a poet, writer, and painter (in watercolor and acrylics) who also works in fiber and creates handmade books. She is a member of Atlatl, a Native American arts service organization. In addition to her poetry, she has published a children's novel, *The Mountain and the Guardian Spirit*, in Danish as well as other novels, short stories, and nonfiction. Currently, she lives in Everett, Washington, where she is a storyteller, teacher, and writer.

Louise Erdrich (b. 1954) was born in Minnesota to a French Ojibwe mother and a German-born father. She grew up near the Turtle Mountain Reservation in North Dakota and is a member of the Turtle Mountain Band of Chippewa. Her grandfather was tribal chief of the reservation. She was among the first women admitted to Dartmouth College, where she began writing; she also studied at Johns Hopkins University. Erdrich is best known for her novels and nonfiction. "Love Medicine" is also the title of her first novel (1984).

Martín Espada (b. 1957) was born in Brooklyn, New York, and has an eclectic résumé: radio journalist in Nicaragua, welfare rights paralegal, advocate for mental patients, night desk clerk in a transient hotel, attendant in a primate nursery, groundskeeper at a minor league ballpark, bindery worker in a printing plant, bouncer in a bar, and practicing lawyer in Chelsea, Massachusetts. Author of five books of poetry, he is regarded as one of the leading poets of Puerto Rican heritage in the United States. He presently teaches at the University of Massachusetts, Amherst.

Anne Finch, Countess of Winchilsea [Anne Kingsmill] (1661–1720) was born into an aristocratic family and went to the court of Charles II at age twenty-three as a maid of honor (attendant) to the duchess of York. She married one of the Gentlemen of the Bedchamber, but they were both forcibly retired when James II was deposed. After two years, her husband inherited a title and an estate, where they lived in the Kentish countryside. From the safety of a private country house, she bravely published a volume of her poetry, despite the mockery that she received as an aristocratic woman writer. The poem included in this anthology is the introduction to that volume, a vigorous protest against the neglect and subordination of women.

Carolyn Forché (b. 1950) was born in Detroit, attended Michigan State University, and earned an M.F.A. from Bowling Green State University. She achieved immediate success as a writer, winning the Yale Younger Poets Prize in 1976. Her work underwent a remarkable shift following a year spent on a Guggenheim fellowship in El Salvador, where she worked with human rights activist Archbishop Oscar Humberto Romero and with Amnesty International. The shock of witnessing countless atrocities in Central America led her to begin writing what she calls "poetry of witness." The volume *The Country Between Us* (1981) stirred immediate controversy because of its overtly political topics and themes. "The Colonel," a prose poem in which the speaker conveys a horrific story with chilling flatness, is probably the most disturbing and memorable poem in the book. Over the years her quest to understand the individual's struggle with social upheaval and political turmoil has taken her from El Salvador to the occupied West Bank, Lebanon, and South Africa. She is currently a faculty member at George Mason University in Virginia.

Philip Freneau (1752–1832), widely regarded as the father of American literature, came from a wealthy New York family. At Princeton University, he was a roommate of James Madison. He was an activist, a public writer, the "poet of the Revolution," but also a private romantic poet who spent two years in the West Indies writing of the beauties of nature and learning navigation, after which he took to sea as a ship's captain. Some of his best poems, including "The Indian Burying Ground" and the beautiful lyric "The Wild Honey Suckle" (which established him as an important American precursor of the Romantics), were written in stolen moments during the hectic 1780s. In 1801 he retired to a farm, worked on his poems, and wrote essays attacking the greed and selfishness of corrupt politicians.

Robert Frost (1874–1963) was born in San Francisco and lived there until he was eleven. When his father died, the family moved to Massachusetts, where Robert did well in school, especially in the classics but dropped out of both Dartmouth College and Harvard University. He went unrecognized as a poet until 1913, when he was first published in England, where he had moved with his wife and four children. Upon returning to the United States, he quickly achieved success with more publications and became the most celebrated poet in mid-twentieth-century America. He held a teaching position at Amherst College and received many honorary degrees as well as an invitation to recite a poem at John F. Kennedy's inauguration. Although his work is principally associated with the life and landscape of New England, and although he was a poet of traditional verse forms and meters, he is also a quintessentially modern poet in his adherence to language as it is actually spoken, in the psychological complexity of his portraits, and in the degree to which his work is infused with layers of ambiguity and irony.

Alice Fulton (b. 1952) was born and grew up in Troy, New York. Winner of many fellowships and awards, she is the author of five books of poetry and a collection of essays. She has taught at the University of California, Los Angeles, Ohio State University, and the University of North Carolina, Wilmington and for eighteen years at the University of Michigan. She was a member of the American delegation at the 1988 Chinese-American Writers' Conference, held in Beijing, Xian, Leshan, Wuhan, and Shanghai. Fulton currently teaches at the Cornell University. "You Can't Rhumboogie in a Ball and Chain" is a **sestina** (see the glossary). The poem's form with its repetition is partic-

ularly interesting in light of the obsessive nature of its content.

Richard Garcia (b. 1941) was born in San Francisco, a first-generation American (his mother was from Mexico, his father from Puerto Rico). While still in high school, he had a poem published by City Lights in a Beat anthology. After publishing his first collection in 1972, however, he did not write poetry again for twelve years, until an unsolicited letter of encouragement from Octavio Paz inspired him to resume. Since then, his work has appeared widely in literary magazines such as the *Kenyon Review, Parnassus,* and the *Gettysburg Review,* as well as two later books, *The Flying Garcias* (1993) and *Rancho Notorious* (2001). He is also the author of a bilingual children's book, *My Aunt Otilia's Spirits* (1987). Garcia has lived in Colorado, Mexico, and Israel, and now makes his home in Los Angeles, where he is poet-in-residence at Childrens Hospital.

Jack Gilbert (b. 1925) was born in Pittsburgh and educated there and in San Francisco. He toured fifteen countries in 1975 as a lecturer on American literature for the U.S. State Department. He has lived for extended periods in New York, San Francisco, Japan, and the Greek islands. His book *Views of Jeopardy* was the 1962 winner of the Yale Younger Poets Series. Both it and *Monolithos* (1982) were nominated for the Pulitzer Prize. His work is characterized by a sparse, concrete, yet powerfully affecting style that the critic David St. John called the "stoniest and most aesthetic Romanticism in American poetry." In his poetry Gilbert makes extensive use of myth, fascinated by the contemporaneity of ancient ideas and themes.

Allen Ginsberg (1926–1997) was born in Newark, New Jersey, and graduated from Columbia University, after several suspensions, in 1948. Several years later, Ginsberg left for San Francisco to join other poets of the Beat movement. His poem "Howl," the most famous poem of the movement, was published in 1956 by Lawrence Ferlinghetti's City Lights Books; the publicity of the ensuing censorship trial brought the Beats to national attention. Ginsberg was co-founder with ANNE WALDMAN of the Jack Kerouac School of Disembodied Poetics at the Naropa Institute in Boulder, Colorado. In his later years he became a distinguished professor at Brooklyn College.

Louise Glück (b. 1943) was born in New York City and educated at Sarah Lawrence College and Columbia University. She has published numerous collections of poetry, including *The Triumph of Achilles* (1985), which received the National Book Critics Circle Award and the Poetry Society of America's Melville Kane Award; *Ararat* (1990), which received the Rebekah Johnson Bobbitt National Prize for Poetry; and *The Wild Iris* (1992), which received the Pulitzer Prize and the Poetry Society of America's William Carlos Williams Award. She has also published *Proofs and Theories: Essays on Poetry* (1994). Glück teaches at Williams College and lives in Cambridge, Massachusetts.

Ray Gonzalez (b. 1952) received his M.F.A. in creative writing from Southwest Texas State University. He has published five books of poetry, including *The Heat of Arrivals* (which won the 1997 Josephine Miles Book Award) and *Cabato Sentora* (1999). He is also the author of *Memory Fever: A Journey Beyond El Paso del Norte* (1993), a book of essays dealing with growing up in the Southwest, and editor of twelve anthologies. He served as poetry editor for *The Bloomsbury Review* for eighteen years. In 1989 he was awarded the Colorado Governor's Award for Excellence in the Arts. He has taught at the University of Illinois, Chicago, and now teaches at the University of Minnesota.

George Gordon, Lord Byron (1788–1824) was one of the great Romantic poets, although he is best known for his lighthearted and humorous verse, such as *Don Juan*. He was born in London and raised in Scotland; he studied at Harrow and at Trinity College, Cambridge. He inherited the title of sixth baron Byron (with estate) at age ten. The last few years of his life were spent in Italy, and he died in Greece after joining the Greek forces in their war for independence.

Jorie Graham (b. 1950) was born in New York City. She attended New York University as an undergraduate and received an M.F.A. from the University of Iowa Writers' Workshop. She is the author of eight collections of poetry, including *The Dream of the Unified Field: Selected Poems 1974–1994*, which won the 1996 Pulitzer Prize for poetry. She has also edited two anthologies, *Earth Took of Earth: 100 Great Poems of the English Language* (1996) and *The Best American Poetry 1990*. She has taught at the University of Iowa and is currently the Boylston Professor of

Rhetoric and Oratory at Harvard University. Her use of formal constraints with daring innovations, illustrated in "Reading Plato," has influenced many contemporary poets.

Thomas Gray (1716–1771) was born in London and educated at Eton and at Cambridge University, where he studied literature and history. In November 1741 his father died, and Gray moved with his mother and aunt to the village of Stoke Poges in Buckinghamshire, where he wrote his first important English poems, the "Ode on the Spring," "Ode on a Distant Prospect of Eton College," and "Hymn to Adversity," and began his masterpiece, "Elegy Written in a Country Churchyard," called the most famous and diversified of all graveyard poems. These poems solidified his reputation as one of the most important poets of the eighteenth century. In 1757 he was named poet laureate but refused the position. In 1762 he applied for the Regius Professorship of Modern History at Cambridge but was rejected; however, he was given the position in 1768, when the successful candidate was killed. A painfully shy and private person, he never delivered any lectures as a professor.

Marilyn Hacker (b. 1942) was born in New York City. She is the author of nine books of poetry, including *Presentation Piece* (1974), which was the Lamont Poetry Selection of the Academy of American Poets and a National Book Award winner, and *Selected Poems, 1965–1990* (1994), which received the Poets' Prize. She was editor of the *Kenyon Review* from 1990 to 1994 and has received numerous honors and awards.

She lives in New York City and Paris. Often labeled a neo–formalist, Hacker often handles traditional forms in fresh ways, as "Villanelle" illustrates.

Kimiko Hahn (b. 1955) was born in Mt. Kisco, New York, to two artists; her mother is from Hawaii and her father is from Wisconsin. Hahn majored in English and East Asian studies at the University of Iowa and received an M.A. in Japanese literature at Columbia University. She is the author of numerous books of poems, including *The Unbearable Heart* (1996), which received an American Book Award. In 1995 she wrote ten portraits of women for a two-hour HBO special titled *Ain't Nuthin' but a She-Thing*. She has taught at Parsons School of Design, the Poetry Project at St. Mark's Church, and Yale University. She lives in New York and is an associate professor in the English Department at Queens College/CUNY.

Mark Halliday (b. 1949) earned his Ph.D. in English from Brandeis University. He has taught at Wellesley College, the University of Pennsylvania, Western Michigan University, Indiana University, and, since 1996, at Ohio University. He has published three books of poetry—*Little Star* (1987), which received a National Poetry Series Award; *Tasker Street* (1992), which won the Juniper Prize; and *Selfwolf* (1999)—as well as two works of criticism. He often combines humor with serious implications. "Functional Poem" is a good example of conveying irony through an off-handed tone.

Thomas Hardy (1840–1928) was born in a cottage in Higher Bockhampton,

Dorset, near the regional market town of Dorchester in southwestern England. Apprenticed at age sixteen to an architect, he spent most of the next twenty years restoring old churches. He had always had an interest in literature and started writing novels in his thirties, publishing more than a dozen. In 1896 Hardy gave up prose and turned to poetry, writing until his death at age eighty-eight. He had a consistently bleak, even pessimistic, outlook on life. Many of his works stress the dark effects of "hap" (happenstance, coincidence) in the world, which is a central motif in "The Convergence of the Twain."

Joy Harjo (b. 1951) was born in Tulsa, Oklahoma. Her mother was of Cherokee-French descent and her father was Creek. She moved to the Southwest and began writing poetry in her early twenties. She then earned her B.A. at the University of New Mexico and her M.F.A. from the University of Iowa Writers' Workshop. Harjo has published several volumes of poetry, including *In Mad Love and War* (1990), which received an American Book Award and the Delmore Schwartz Memorial Award. She also performs her poetry and plays saxophone with her band, Poetic Justice. She is professor of English at the University of New Mexico, Albuquerque. Of "She Had Some Horses" Harjo has said, "This is the poem I'm asked most about and the one I have the least to say about. I don't know where it came from."

Michael S. Harper (b. 1938) was born in Brooklyn and grew up surrounded by jazz. When his family moved to Los Angeles, he worked at all kinds of jobs,

from the post office to professional football. He studied at the City College of Los Angeles, California State University, Los Angeles, and the University of Iowa Writers' Workshop. He has written ten more than ten books of poetry, including *Dear John, Dear Coltrane* (1970), which was nominated for the National Book Award, and edited or co-edited several collections of African American poetry. He is University Professor and professor of English at Brown University, where he has taught since 1970. He lives in Barrington, Rhode Island.

Robert Hass (b. 1941) was born in San Francisco. His books of poetry include *Field Guide* (1973), which was selected by STANLEY KUNITZ for the Yale Younger Poets Series. He has also translated with Czeslaw Milosz several volumes of Milosz's poetry, including *Facing the River* (1995) and *Treatise on Poetry* (2001). He is the author or editor of several other collections of essays and translations, including *The Essential Haiku: Versions of Basho, Buson, and Issa* (1994) and *Twentieth Century Pleasures: Prose on Poetry* (1984). He served as Poet Laureate Consultant in Poetry at the Library of Congress from 1995 to 1997. He lives in California and teaches at the University of California, Berkeley. "Late Spring" shows Hass's quiet, penetrating way of looking at and responding to the outside world and its effects on the inner world of the observer.

Robert Hayden (1913–1980) was raised in a poor neighborhood in Detroit and had an emotionally tumultuous childhood. Because of impaired vision, he was unable to participate in sports and spent his time reading instead. He graduated from high school in 1932 and attended Detroit City College (later Wayne State University). His first book of poems, *Heart-Shape in the Dust*, was published in 1940. After working for newspapers and on other projects, he studied under W. H. AUDEN in the graduate creative writing program at the University of Michigan. He taught at Fisk University and at the University of Michigan. His poetry gained international recognition in the 1960s, and he was awarded the grand prize for poetry at the First World Festival of Negro Arts in Dakar, Senegal, in 1966 for his book *Ballad of Remembrance*. In 1976 he became the first black American to be appointed as Consultant in Poetry at the Library of Congress.

Samuel Hazo (b. 1928), of Lebanese and Syrian heritage, is a highly influential Arab American writer of verse, educator, and advocate on behalf of poetry. He is the author of numerous collections of poetry, fiction, and essays. He is founder, director, and president of the International Poetry Forum in Pittsburgh and McAnulty Distinguished Professor of English Emeritus at Duquesne University. He is the recipient of the 1986 Hazlett Memorial Award for Excellence in the Arts. In 1993 he was chosen to be the first state poet of the Commonwealth of Pennsylvania, a position he still holds.

Seamus Heany (b. 1939) grew up on a small farm near Castledawson, County Derry, Northern Ireland. He was educated at St. Columb's College, a Catholic boarding school situated in the city of Derry, and then at Queen's University, Belfast. As a young English teacher in Belfast in the early 1960s, he joined a poetry workshop and began writing verse. Subsequently he became a major force in contemporary Irish literature. The author of many volumes of poetry and essays as well as at least one play, he is well known at present for his best-selling verse translation of *Beowulf* (2000). He held the chair of professor of poetry at Oxford University from 1989 to 1994. Heaney has been a resident of Dublin since 1976, but since 1981 he has spent part of each year teaching at Harvard University. He was awarded the Nobel Prize in literature in 1995.

Lyn Hejinian (b. 1941), poet, essayist, and translator, was born in the San Francisco Bay area and lives in Berkeley. She was educated at Harvard University and has traveled and lectured extensively in Russia and Europe. Author or coauthor of fourteen books of poetry, she is one of the leading **L-A-N-G-U-A-G-E Poets** (see the glossary). She has also published autobiographical writing and, more recently, translations from Russian of the works of Arkadii Dragomoschenko. From 1976 to 1984, Hejinian was editor of Tuumba Press, and since 1981 she has been the co-editor of *Poetics Journal*. She is also the co-director of Atelos, a literary project commissioning and publishing cross-genre works by poets. "A Mask of Anger" shows her attention to the potential language has for shaping consciousness.

George Herbert (1593–1633) was the fifth son in an ancient and wealthy Welsh family. He studied at Cambridge, graduating with honors, and was elected public orator of the university.

He served in Parliament for two years but fell out of political favor and become rector of Bemerton near Salisbury. Herbert was a model Anglican priest and an inspiring preacher. All of his poetry, religious in nature, was published posthumously in 1633. "Easter-wings" is among the earliest of concrete poems (see the glossary), and "The Pulley" is a fine example of metaphysical wit (see the glossary).

Mary (Sidney) Herbert, Countess of Pembroke (1561–1621) was an important literary patron and writer of the Elizabethan period. In addition to editorial work and translations, she wrote a number of original poems. She also contributed 107 poetic renderings of psalms to a series of 150 begun by her brother Sir Philip Sidney, each written in a different stanzaic and metrical pattern. "Psalm 100 *Jubilate Deo*" is from that volume.

Robert Herrick (1591–1674), the son of a well-to-do London goldsmith, was apprenticed to his uncle (also a goldsmith), studied at Cambridge University, then lived for nine years in London, where he hobnobbed with a group of poets that included BEN JONSON. Under familial pressure to do something more worthwhile, Herrick became an Anglican priest. He was given the parish of Dean Prior, Devonshire—a rural place that at first he hated—and there he quietly wrote poems about imagined mistresses and pagan rites (as in his well-known "Corinna's Going A-Maying") and deft but devout religious poems. When he returned to London in 1648, having been ejected from his pulpit by the Puritan revolution, he published his poetry in a volume with two titles, *Hesperides* for the

secular poems, *Noble Numbers* for those with sacred subjects. Probably his most famous poem is "To the Virgins, to Make Much of Time," a short lyric on the traditional **carpe diem** theme (see the glossary).

Conrad Hilberry (b. 1928) grew up in Michigan. He earned his B.A. at Oberlin College and his M.A. and Ph.D. at the University of Wisconsin and taught at Kalamazoo College until his recent retirement. Hilberry has published several collections of poetry and has been poetry editor of *Passages North* and of the anthology *Poems from the Third Coast* (1976). Hillberry has been praised for his mastery of tone, through which he achieves subtleties of implication in his work, as is evidenced in "Player Piano."

Geoffrey Hill (b. 1932) is a major presence in contemporary British poetry. Born in Bromsgrove, Worcestershire, he attended the local grammar school there before going on to study English language and literature at Keble College, Oxford. He taught at Leeds University from 1954 until 1980, when he moved to Emmanuel College, Cambridge. In 1988 he became University Professor and a professor of literature and religion at Boston University.

Jane Hirshfield (b. 1953) is the author of five books of poetry, editor and co-translator of two anthologies of poetry by women, and author of a collection of essays, *Nine Gates: Entering the Mind of Poetry* (1997). A graduate of Princeton University, she studied Soto Zen from 1974 to 1982, including three years of monastic practice, the influence of which is apparent in her work. "For me, poetry, like Zen practice, is a path toward deeper and more life. There are ways to wake up into the actual texture of one's own existence, to widen it, to deepen and broaden it, and poetry is one of the things that does that." She teaches at Bennington College and lives in the San Francisco Bay area.

Linda Hogan (b. 1947), a poet, novelist, essayist, playwright, and activist widely considered to be one of the most influential and provocative Native American figures in the contemporary American literary landscape, was born in Denver. Because her father, who was from the Chickasaw Nation, was in the army and was transferred frequently during Hogan's childhood, she lived in various locations while she was growing up, but considers Oklahoma to be her true home. In her late twenties, while working with orthopedically handicapped children, she began writing during her lunch hours, although she had no previous experience as a writer and little experience reading literature. She pursued her writing by commuting to the University of Colorado, Colorado Springs, for her undergraduate degree and earning an M.A. in English and creative writing at the University of Colorado, Boulder, in 1978. She has published more than a dozen books—poetry, novels, and nonfiction—and received numerous awards for her work. She teaches creative writing at the University of Colorado.

Garrett Kaoru Hongo (b. 1951) was born in Volcano, Hawaii, grew up on Oahu and in Los Angeles, and did graduate work in Japanese language and literature at the University of Michigan. Hongo has published several books of poetry, including *The River of Heaven*

(1988), which was the Lamont Poetry Selection of the Academy of American Poets and a finalist for the Pulitzer Prize. He has also written *Volcano: A Memoir of Hawai'i* (1995) and edited collections of Asian American verse. He currently teaches at the University of Oregon, Eugene, where he directed the creative writing program from 1989 to 1993. His work often uses rich textures and sensuous detail to comment on conditions endured by Japanese Americans during World War II and thereafter.

Gerard Manley Hopkins (1844–1889) was born in London, the eldest of eight children. His father was a ship insurer who also wrote a book of poetry. Hopkins studied at Balliol College, Oxford, and, after converting to Catholicism, taught in a school in Birmingham. In 1868 he became a Jesuit and burned all of his early poetry, considering it "secular" and worthless. He then worked as a priest and teacher in working-class London, Glasgow, and Merseyside, and later as professor of classics at University College, Dublin. Hopkins went on to write many poems on spiritual themes, but he published little during his lifetime; his poems were not known until they were published by his friend Robert Bridges in 1918. They convey a spiritual sensuality, celebrating the wonder of nature both in their language and in their rhythms (which he called "sprung rhythm"; see the glossary under **accentual meter**).

A. E. Housman (1859–1936) was born in Fockbury, Worcestershire. A promising student at Oxford University, he failed his final exams (because of emotional turmoil possibly caused by his suppressed homosexual love for a fellow student) and spent the next ten years feverishly studying and writing scholarly articles while working as a clerk at the patent office. Housman was rewarded with the chair of Latin at University College, London, and later at Cambridge University. His poetry, like his scholarship, was meticulous, impersonal in tone, and limited in output: two slender volumes—*A Shropshire Lad* (1896) and *Last Poems* (1922)—during his lifetime, and a small book titled *More Poems* (1936) after his death. His poems often take up the theme of doomed youths acting out their brief lives in the context of the human histories implicit in agricultural communities and activities, especially the English countryside and traditions he loved.

Susan Howe (b. 1937), born in Boston to Irish American parents, studied painting at the School of the Museum of Fine Arts, Boston. Her painting moved toward collage and then toward performance art, which eventually led her to poetry. She has been an actor and a stage manager at Dublin's Gate Theatre. She is the author of several books of poems, including *Pierce-Arrow* (1999), and two volumes of criticism: *My Emily Dickinson* (1985), and *The Birth-Mark: Unsettling the Wilderness in American Literary History* (1993), which was named an International Book of the Year by the *Times Literary Supplement*. Since 1989 she has been a professor of English at the State University of New York, Buffalo. She lives in Guilford, Connecticut.

Langston Hughes (1902–1967) was born in Joplin, Missouri, and grew up in Lincoln, Illinois, and Cleveland, Ohio. During his high-school years he began writing poetry. He attended Columbia University for a year, then held odd jobs as an assistant cook, a launderer, and a busboy and traveled to Africa and Europe working as a seaman. In 1924 he moved to Harlem. Hughes's first book of poetry, *The Weary Blues*, was published in 1926. He finished his college education at Lincoln University in Pennsylvania three years later. He wrote novels, short stories, plays, songs, children's books, essays, and memoirs as well as poetry, and is also known for his engagement with the world of jazz and the influence it had on his writing. His life and work were enormously important in shaping the artistic contributions of the Harlem Renaissance of the 1920s.

Randall Jarrell (1914–1965) was born in Nashville, Tennessee, and earned his B.A. and M.A. at Vanderbilt University. From 1937 to 1939 he taught at Kenyon College, where he met JOHN CROWE RANSOM and ROBERT LOWELL, and afterward he taught at the University of Texas. He served in the air force during World War II. Jarrell's reputation as a poet was established in 1945 with the publication of his second book, *Little Friend, Little Friend*, which documents the intense fears and moral struggles of young soldiers. Other volumes followed, all characterized by great technical skill, empathy with others, and deep sensitivity. Following the war, Jarrell began teaching at the University of North Carolina, Greensboro, and remained there, except for occasional absences to teach elsewhere, until his death. Besides poetry, he wrote a satirical novel, several children's books, numerous poetry reviews—collected in *Poetry and the Age* (1953)—and a translation of Goethe's *Faust*.

Robinson Jeffers (1887–1962) was born in Pittsburgh, where his father was a professor of Old Testament literature and biblical history at Western Theology Seminary. He began to learn Greek from his father at the age of five, and his early lessons were followed by travel in Europe, which included schooling in Zurich, Leipzig, and Geneva. He moved with his family to southern California in 1903. After graduating from Occidental College in 1906 and pursuing graduate studies in medicine and forestry, Jeffers decided to concentrate on poetry. In 1914 he settled in Carmel, California, and built a stone cottage and a forty-foot stone tower on land overlooking Carmel Bay and facing Point Lobos, where he lived the rest of his life (Tor House and Hawk Tower are open to the public — see www.torhouse.org). Much of Jeffers's verse celebrates the awesome beauty of the Carmel–Big Sur region, often contrasting the intense, rugged beauty of the landscape with the degraded and introverted condition of modern man.

Richard Jones (b. 1953) was born in London, where his father was serving in the U.S. Air Force, and studied at the University of Virginia. Jones is the author of several books of poems, including *The Blessing: New and Selected Poems*, which received the Midland Authors Award for Poetry for 2000. His most recent "publication," *Body and Soul*, is on compact disc and discusses the art of poetry. He has also published two critical anthologies and has been the editor of the literary journal *Poetry East* since 1979. He has taught at Piedmont College and the University of Virginia and presently is professor of English and director of the creative

writing program at DePaul University in Chicago.

Ben Jonson (1572–1637), born in London, was the stepson of a bricklayer (his father died before he was born). He attended Westminster School and then joined the army. Jonson later worked as an actor and as the author of comedies such as *Everyman in His Humor* (in which SHAKESPEARE acted the lead), *Volpone*, and *The Alchemist*. He wrote clear, elegant, "classical" poetry that contrasted with the intricate, subtle, "metaphysical" poetry of his contemporaries JOHN DONNE and GEORGE HERBERT. He was named poet laureate and was the idol of a generation of English writers, who dubbed themselves the Sons of Ben.

Allison Joseph (b. 1967) was born in London to Caribbean parents and grew up in Toronto and the Bronx. She earned her B.A. from Kenyon College and her M.F.A. from Indiana University. She is the author of three collections of poetry: *What Keeps Us Here* (winner of Ampersand Press's 1992 Women Poets Series Competition and the John C. Zacharis First Book Award), *Soul Train* (1997), and *In Every Seam* (1997). Her poems are often attuned to the experiences of women and minorities. She formerly taught at the University of Arkansas and currently is an associate professor at Southern Illinois University, Carbondale, where she is editor of the *Crab Orchard Review*.

John Keats (1795–1821) was born in London. His father, a worker at a livery stable who married his employer's daughter and inherited the business, was killed by a fall from a horse when

Keats was eight. When his mother died of tuberculosis six years later, Keats and his siblings were entrusted to the care of a guardian, a practical-minded man who took Keats out of school at fifteen and apprenticed him to a doctor. As soon as he qualified for medical practice, in 1815, he abandoned medicine for poetry, which he had begun writing two years earlier. In 1818, the year he contracted tuberculosis, he also fell madly in love with a pretty, vivacious young woman named Fanny Brawne, whom he could not marry because of his poverty, illness, and devotion to poetry. In the midst of such stress and emotional turmoil, his masterpieces poured out between January and September 1819: the great odes, a number of sonnets, and several longer lyric poems. In February 1820, his health failed rapidly; he went to Italy in the autumn, in hopes that the warmer climate would improve his health, and died there on February 23, 1821. His poems are rich with sensuous, lyrical beauty and emotional resonance, reflecting his delight in life as well as his awareness of life's brevity and difficulty.

Jane Kenyon (1947–1995) was born in Ann Arbor, Michigan, and grew up in the Midwest. She earned her B.A. and M.A. from the University of Michigan. During her lifetime Kenyon published four books of poetry and also translated the work of Anna Akhmatova. Two additional volumes have been published posthumously. A few months before her death in April 1995 from leukemia, she was named poet laureate of New Hampshire.

Galway Kinnell (b. 1927) was born in Providence, Rhode Island, and attended Princeton University and the University of Rochester. He served in the U.S. Navy and then visited Paris on a Fulbright fellowship. Returning to the United States, he worked for the Congress on Racial Equality and then traveled widely in the Middle East and Europe. He has taught in France, Australia, and Iran as well as at numerous colleges and universities in the United States. He has published many books of poetry, including *Selected Poems* (1980), for which he received both the Pulitzer Prize and the National Book Award. He has also published translations of works by Yves Bonnefoy, Yvanne Goll, François Villon, and Rainer Maria Rilke. He divides his time between Vermont and New York City, where he is the Erich Maria Remarque Professor of Creative Writing at New York University.

Etheridge Knight (1933–1991) was born in Corinth, Mississippi. He dropped out of school at age sixteen and served in the U.S. Army in Korea from 1947 to 1951, returning with a shrapnel wound that caused him to fall deeper into a drug addiction that had begun during his service. In 1960 he was arrested for robbery and sentenced to eight years in an Indiana state prison. During this time he began writing poetry. His first book, *Poems from Prison* (1968), was published one year before his release. The book was a success, and Knight joined other poets in what came to be called the Black Arts Movement, the aesthetic and spiritual sister of the Black Power concept. He went on to write several more books of poetry and to receive many prestigious honors and awards. In 1990 he earned a B.A. in American poetry and criminal justice from Martin Center University in Indianapolis.

Kenneth Koch (1925–2002) was born in Cincinnati and, after service in World War II, received his B.A. from Harvard University and his Ph.D. from Columbia University. As a young poet, Koch was known for his association with the New York school of poetry, a cosmopolitan movement influenced by the Beats, French surrealism and European avant-gardism in general. In addition to many books of poetry, including *One Train* and *On the Great Atlantic Rainway: Selected Poems, 1950–1988* (both 1994), which together won the Bollingen Prize in 1995, and *New Addresses* (2000), a finalist for the National Book Award, he wrote plays, a novel, a libretto, criticism, and several influential books on teaching creative writing to children, including *Wishes, Lies, and Dreams* (1970) and *Rose, Where Did You Get That Red?* (1973). He lived in New York City, where he was professor of English at Columbia University.

Yusef Komunyakaa (b. 1947) was born and grew up in Bogalusa, Louisiana. He earned degrees at the University of Colorado, Colorado State University, and the University of California, Irvine. His numerous books of poems include *Neon Vernacular: New and Selected Poems, 1977–1989* (1994), for which he received the Pulitzer Prize and the Kingsley Tufts Poetry Award, and *Thieves of Paradise* (1998), which was a finalist for the National Book Critics Circle Award. Other publications include *Blues Notes: Essays, Interviews & Commentaries* (2000), *The Jazz Poetry Anthology* (coedited with J. A. Sascha Feinstein, 1991), and *The Insomnia of Fire* by Nguyen Quang Thieu (co-translated with Martha Collins, 1995). He is a professor in the Council of Humanities and the creative writing program at Princeton University. He lives in New York City.

Maxine Kumin (b. 1925) was born in Philadelphia and received her B.A. and M.A. at Radcliffe College. She has published several books of poetry, including *Up Country: Poems of New England* (1972), for which she received the Pulitzer Prize. She is also the author of a memoir, *Inside the Halo and Beyond: The Anatomy of a Recovery* (2000); four novels; a collection of short stories; more than twenty children's books; and four books of essays. She has taught at the University of Massachusetts, Columbia University, Brandeis University, and Princeton University. She has served as Consultant in Poetry to the Library of Congress and as poet laureate of New Hampshire where she lives.

Stanley Kunitz (b. 1905) was born in Worcester, Massachusetts, and earned his B.A. and M.A. at Harvard University. His first two books of poetry attracted little attention, but after service in World War II he continued to write and achieved great success and recognition. Among his many books of poetry are *Selected Poems, 1928–1958*, which won the Pulitzer Prize for 1959, and *Passing Through: The Later Poems, New and Selected* (1995), which won the National Book Award. In addition to publishing several translations, he edited the Yale Series of Younger Poets from 1969 to 1977 and is editor of *The Essential Blake* (1987) and *Poems of John Keats* (1964—his work has been called a contemporary extension of the vision of JOHN KEATS). In 2000 he was named Poet Laureate Consultant in Poetry at the Library of Congress. He taught for many years in the graduate writing program at Columbia University. He lives in New York City and Provincetown, Massachusetts.

Philip Larkin (1922–1985) was born into a working-class family in Coventry, England. He received a scholarship to attend Oxford University. With his second volume of poetry, *The Less Deceived* (1955), Larkin became the preeminent poet of his generation and a leading voice of what came to be called "The Movement," a group of young English writers who rejected the prevailing fashion for neo-Romantic writing exemplified by W. B. YEATS and DYLAN THOMAS. Like THOMAS HARDY, a major influence on his work, Larkin focused on intense personal emotion but strictly avoided sentimentality or self-pity. In addition to writing poetry, Larkin was a highly respected jazz critic. He worked as a librarian in the provincial city of Hull, where he died in 1985.

Li-Young Lee (b. 1957) was born in Jakarta, Indonesia, to Chinese parents. His father, who had been personal physician to Mao Tse-tung, relocated his family to Indonesia, where he helped found Gamaliel University. In 1959 the Lee family fled the country to escape anti-Chinese sentiment, and they settled in the United States in 1964. Lee studied at the University of Pittsburgh, the University of Arizona, and the Brockport campus of the State University of New York. He has taught at several universities, including Northwestern University and the University of Iowa. In addition to several books of poetry, he has published a prose memoir, *The Winged Seed* (1995). In his

poems one often senses a profound sense of exile, the influence of his father's presence, and a rich spiritual sensuality.

Denise Levertov (1923–1997) was born in Ilford, Essex. Her mother was Welsh and her father was a Russian Jew who became an Anglican priest. She was educated at home and claimed to have decided to become a writer at the age of five. Her first book, *The Double Image* (1946), brought her recognition as one of a group of poets dubbed the "New Romantics"—her poems often blend the sense of an objective observer with the sensibility of a spiritual searcher. She moved to the United States after marrying the American writer Mitchell Goodman. There she turned to free-verse poetry, and with her first American book, *Here and Now* (1956), she became an important voice in the American avant-garde. In the 1960s, she became involved in the movement protesting the Vietnam war. Levertov went on to publish more than twenty collections of poetry, four books of prose, and three volumes of poetry in translation. From 1982 to 1993, she taught at Stanford University. She spent the last decade of her life in Seattle.

Philip Levine (b. 1928) was born in Detroit and received his degrees from Wayne State University and the University of Iowa. He is the author of many books of poetry, including *The Simple Truth* (1994), which won the Pulitzer Prize. He has also published a collection of essays, edited *The Essential Keats* (1987), and coedited and translated two books of poetry, by Spanish poet Gloria Fuertes and Mexican poet Jamie Sabines. He lives in New York City and Fresno, California, and teaches at New York University.

Larry Levis (1946–1996) grew up on a farm near Fresno, California. He earned his B.A. from Fresno State College (now California State University), an M.A. from Syracuse University, and a Ph.D. from the University of Iowa. He published six collections of poetry—several of them receiving major awards—and a collection of short fiction. He taught at the University of Missouri, the University of Utah, and Virginia Commonwealth University. Levis died of a heart attack at the age of forty-nine. PHILIP LEVINE wrote that he had years earlier recognized Levis as "the most gifted and determined young poet I have ever had the good fortune to have in one of my classes."

Timothy Liu (b. 1965) was born in San Jose, California, to parents who had immigrated from the Chinese mainland. He studied at Brigham Young University, the University of Houston, and the University of Massachusetts, Amherst. He is the author of several books of poetry (including *Vox Angelica*, which won the 1992 Norma Farber First Book Award from the Poetry Society of America) and the editor of *Word of Mouth: An Anthology of Gay American Poetry* (2000). He is an assistant professor at William Paterson University and lives in Hoboken, New Jersey.

Audre Lorde (1934–1992) was born in New York City to West Indian parents. She grew up in Manhattan and attended Roman Catholic schools. While she was still in high school, her first poem appeared in *Seventeen* magazine. She earned her B.A. from Hunter College in New York City and her M.A. in library science from Columbia University. In 1968 she left her job as head librarian at the University of New York to become a lecturer and creative writer. She accepted a poet-in-residence position at Tougaloo College in Mississippi, where she discovered a love of teaching, published her first volume of poetry, *The First Cities* (1968), and met her long-term partner, Frances Clayton. Many other volumes of poetry followed, several winning major awards. She also published four volumes of prose, among them *The Cancer Journals* (1980), which chronicled her struggles with cancer, and *A Burst of Light* (1988), which won a National Book Award. In the 1980s, Lorde and writer Barbara Smith founded Kitchen Table: Women of Color Press. She was also a founding member of Sisters in Support of Sisters in South Africa, an organization that worked to raise awareness about women under apartheid. She was the poet laureate of New York from 1991 to 1992.

Richard Lovelace (1618–1657) was born into a prominent family in Kent, England, and went to Oxford, where his dashing appearance and wit made him a social and literary favorite. He fought in the English civil war on the Royalist side and was imprisoned and exiled. Later he fought in France against the Spanish and was again imprisoned on his return to England. After his release he spent ten years in poverty and isolation before his death. He was a leader of the "Cavalier poets," followers of King Charles I who were soldiers and courtiers but also wrote well-crafted, light-hearted lyric poetry.

"To Lucasta, Going to the Wars" is an excellent example of the type.

Robert Lowell (1917–1978) was born in Boston into a prominent New England family. He attended Harvard University and then Kenyon College, where he studied under JOHN CROWE RANSOM. At Louisiana State University he studied with Robert Penn Warren and Cleanth Brooks as well as Allen Tate. He was always politically active—a conscientious objector during World War II and a Vietnam protestor—and suffered from manic depression. Lowell's reputation was established early: his second book, *Lord Weary's Castle*, was awarded the Pulitzer Prize for poetry in 1947. In the mid-1950s he began to write more directly from personal experience and loosened his adherence to traditional meter and form. The result was a watershed collection of the "confessional" school, *Life Studies* (1959), which changed the landscape of modern poetry, much as T. S. ELIOT's *The Waste Land* had done three decades earlier. He died suddenly from a heart attack at age sixty.

Christopher Marlowe (1564–1593) was born in Canterbury the same year as WILLIAM SHAKESPEARE. The son of a shoemaker, he needed the help of scholarships to attend King's School, Canterbury, and Corpus Christi College, Cambridge. He was involved in secret political missions for the government. He was one of the most brilliant writers of his generation in narrative poetry, lyric poetry, and drama (his best-known play is *Doctor Faustus*). He died after being stabbed in a bar fight, reportedly over his bill, at the age of twenty-nine. "The Passionate Shep-

herd to His Love" is among the most famous of Elizabethan songs.

Andrew Marvell (1621–1678) was born in Hull, Yorkshire, and educated at Trinity College, Cambridge. After traveling in Europe, he worked as a tutor and in a government office (as assistant to JOHN MILTON) and later became a member of Parliament for Hull. Marvell was known in his lifetime as a writer of rough satires in verse and prose. His "serious" poetry, like "To His Coy Mistress," was not published until after his death. It is a famous exploration of the **carpe diem** theme (see the glossary).

Heather McHugh (b. 1948) was born to Canadian parents in San Diego and grew up in Virginia. She is a graduate of Radcliffe College and the University of Denver. McHugh has published numerous books of poetry, a book of prose, and four books of translations. She teaches as a core faculty member in the M.F.A. Program for Writers at Warren Wilson College and as Milliman Writer-in-Residence at the University of Washington, Seattle. She has been a visiting professor at the University of Iowa Writers' Workshop and has held chairs at the University of California, Berkeley, the University of Alabama, and the University of Cincinnati.

Claude McKay (1890–1948), the son of poor farm workers, was born in Sunny Ville, Jamaica. He was educated by his older brother, who possessed a library of English novels, poetry, and scientific texts. At age twenty, McKay published a book of verse called *Songs of Jamaica*, recording his impressions of black life in Jamaica in dialect. In 1912, he traveled to the United States to attend Tuskegee Institute. He soon left to study agriculture at Kansas State University. In 1914 he moved to Harlem and became an influential member of the Harlem Renaissance. After committing himself to Communism and traveling to Moscow in 1922, he lived for some time in Europe and Morocco, writing fiction. McKay later repudiated Communism, converted to Roman Catholicism, and returned to the United States. He published several books of poetry as well as an autobiography, *A Long Way from Home* (1937). He wrote a number of sonnets protesting the injustices of black life in the United States, "America" among them. They are of interest for the way they use the most Anglo of forms to contain and intensify what the poem's language is saying.

James Merrill (1926–1995) was born in New York City, son of Charles Merrill, co-founder of Merrill Lynch. At the age of eight, he was already writing poems, and at age sixteen, while he was in prep school, his father had a book of them privately printed under the title *Jim's Book*. He received his B.A. from Amherst College after service in World War II interrupted his education. He taught for a year at Bard College and spent two and a half years traveling in Europe. In 1955 he moved to the small coastal town of Stonington, Connecticut, with his companion David Jackson. He published a memoir and two novels in addition to more than two dozen books of poetry, for which he won numerous prestigious awards, including the Pulitzer Prize for *Divine Comedies* (1976), which was composed with the help of a Ouija board. Merrill

is recognized as one of the most complex and erudite of modern poets.

W. S. Merwin (b. 1927) was born in New York City and lived in New Jersey and Pennsylvania during his pre-college years. He studied creative writing and foreign languages at Princeton University and became a translator, living mostly in England and France until 1968, when he returned to the United States. He is the author of many books of poetry, including *A Mask for Janus* (1952), which was selected by W. H. Auden for the Yale Series of Younger Poets, and *Carrier of Ladders* (1970), which received the Pulitzer Prize. He has also published nearly twenty books of translation, including Dante's *Purgatorio* (2000); numerous plays; and four books of prose, including *The Lost Upland* (1992), his memoir of life in the south of France. He lives in Hawaii and is active in environmental movements.

Edna St. Vincent Millay (1892–1950) was born in Rockland, Maine, and was encouraged to write from an early age by her mother. In 1912, at her mother's urging, Millay entered her poem "Renascence" into a contest; she won fourth place, publication in *The Lyric Year*, and a scholarship to Vassar. She spent the Roaring Twenties in Greenwich Village acting, writing plays and prize-winning poetry, and living a bohemian lifestyle. In 1923 her book *The Harp Weaver* was awarded the Pulitzer Prize. Millay continued to write and take an active part in political affairs for several decades thereafter, despite a diminished literary reputation.

John Milton (1608–1674), son of a well-off London businessman, was educated at St. Paul's School and at home with private tutors. After graduating with an M.A. from Christ's College, Cambridge, he spent the next six years reading at home. Milton had written verse since his university days, but he broke off to write prose tracts in favor of Oliver Cromwell, in whose government he later headed a department. The strain of long hours of reading and writing for the revolutionary cause aggravated a genetic weakness and resulted in his total blindness around 1651. He wrote his most famous works, *Paradise Lost* (1667), *Paradise Regained* (1671), and *Samson Agonistes* (1671), by dictating them to his daughter and other amanuenses.

Marianne Moore (1887–1972) was born near St. Louis and grew up in Carlisle, Pennsylvania. After studying at Bryn Mawr College and Carlisle Commercial College, she taught at a government Indian school in Carlisle. She moved to Brooklyn, where she became an assistant at the New York Public Library. She loved baseball and spent a good deal of time watching her beloved Brooklyn Dodgers. She began to write **Imagist poetry** (see the glossary) and to contribute to the *Dial,* a prestigious literary magazine. She served as acting editor of the *Dial,* from 1925 to 1929 and later was editor for four years. Moore was widely recognized for her work, receiving among other honors the Bollingen Prize, the National Book Award, and the Pulitzer Prize.

Robert Morgan (b. 1944) is a native of the North Carolina mountains. He was raised on land settled by his Welsh ancestors. He is an accomplished poet,

novelist, and short story writer. His four historical novels, two collections of short fiction, and nine volumes of poetry reveal an indelible sense of place for those familiar with or strangers to the Blue Ridge Mountains and address themes that matter to all people in all places: birth and death, love and loss, joy and sorrow, the necessity for remembrance, and the inevitability of forgetting. He was educated at the University of North Carolina, Chapel Hill, and earned an M.F.A. from the University of North Carolina, Greensboro. In 1971 Morgan began teaching at Cornell University, where, since 1992, he has been the Kappa Alpha Professor of English.

Thylias Moss (b. 1954) was born in Cleveland, Ohio. She attended Syracuse University and received her B.A. from Oberlin College and M.F.A. from the University of New Hampshire. She is the author of numerous books of poetry; a memoir, *Tale of a Sky-Blue Dress* (1998); two children's books; and two plays, *Talking to Myself* (1984) and *The Dolls in the Basement* (1984). She lives in Ann Arbor, where she is a professor of English at the University of Michigan.

David Mura (b. 1952), a third-generation Japanese American, was born in Great Lakes, Illinois, and graduated from Grinnell College in Iowa; he did graduate work at the University of Minnesota and Vermont College. Mura is a poet, creative nonfiction writer, critic, playwright, and performance artist. He is the author of numerous books of poetry, including *After We Lost Our Way* (1989), which was selected by GERALD STERN as a National Poetry

Series winner, and two memoirs, *Turning Japanese: Memoirs of a Sansei* (1991), which was a New York Times Notable Book of the Year, and *Where the Body Meets Memory: An Odyssey of Race, Sexuality & Identity* (1996). Mura is the artistic director of the Asian-American Renaissance, an arts organization in Minnesota.

John Frederick Nims (1913–1999) was born in Muskegon, Michigan, and studied at DePaul University, the University of Notre Dame, and the University of Chicago, where he received his Ph.D. in 1945. By that time, he had already distinguished himself as a poet and critic. He went on to teach at Harvard University, the University of Florence, the University of Toronto, the Bread Loaf School of English, Williams College, and the University of Missouri, among others. He was editor of *Poetry* magazine from 1978 to 1984. He was the author of many books of poetry and many translations, as well as several critical works and a widely used textbook, *Western Wind: An Introduction to Poetry* (1983).

Naomi Shihab Nye (b. 1952), born in St. Louis of a Palestinian father and an American mother, grew up in both the United States and Jerusalem. She received her B.A. from Trinity University in San Antonio, Texas, where she still resides with her family. The author of many books of poems, she has also written short stories and books for children and has edited anthologies, several of which focus on the lives of children and represent work from around the world. She is also a singer-songwriter and on several occasions has traveled to the Middle East and Asia for the U.S. Information Agency, promoting international goodwill through the arts. Nye's work often attests to a universal sense of exile, from place, home, love, and one's self and the way the human spirit confronts them.

Frank (Francis Russell) O'Hara (1926–1966) was born in Baltimore and grew up in Massachusetts. He studied piano at the New England Conservatory in Boston from 1941 to 1944 and served in the South Pacific and Japan during World War II. He majored in English at Harvard, then received his M.A. in English at the University of Michigan in 1951. He moved to New York, where he worked at the Museum of Modern Art and began writing poetry seriously as well as composing essays and reviews on painting and sculpture. His first volume of poems, *A City in Winter*—thirteen poems together with two drawings by the artist Larry Rivers—was published in 1952. Other collaborations with artists followed. His first major collection of poetry was *Meditations in an Emergency* (1957). His poetry is often casual, relaxed in diction, and full of specific detail, seeking to convey the immediacy of life. He described his work as "I do this I do that" poetry because his poems often read like entries in a diary, as in the opening lines of "The Day Lady Died." He was killed at forty when he was struck by a sand buggy while vacationing on Fire Island, New York.

Sharon Olds (b. 1942) was born in San Francisco and educated at Stanford and Columbia Universities. She has written eight books of poetry and received numerous important prizes and awards. In the words of Elizabeth Frank, "she and her work are about nothing less than the joy of making—of making love, making babies, making poems, making sense of love, memory, death, the feel—the actual bodily texture, of life." Named New York State Poet in 1998, Olds teaches poetry workshops at New York University's graduate creative writing program, along with workshops at Goldwater Hospital in New York, a public facility for physically disabled persons.

Mary Oliver (b. 1935) was born in Cleveland and educated at Ohio State University and Vassar College. She is the author of ten volumes of poetry, including *American Primitive* (1983), for which she won the Pulitzer Prize, and three books of prose. She holds the Catharine Osgood Foster Chair for Distinguished Teaching at Bennington College and lives in Provincetown, Massachusetts, and Bennington, Vermont. Oliver is one of the most respected of poets concerned for the natural world.

George Oppen (1908–1984) was born in New Rochelle, New York, the son of George August Oppenheimer, a diamond merchant, and Elsie Rothfeld. He described his schooling as "minimal." In 1927 he married Mary Colby. The couple rejected the comfortable world of Oppen's parents and chose a life of independence. He was a leading figure among the "Objectivists," a group of poets who shared the conviction that the poet must be faithful to the world of facts ("The Forms of Love" is an example of the philosophy of Objectivism). His first book of poems, *Discrete Series*, was published in 1934 by the

Objectivist Press, after which he stopped writing poetry for nearly twenty-five years in favor of political activism, even living as an exile in Mexico during the McCarthy era. After returning to poetry, he received the 1969 Pulitzer Prize for poetry for *Of Being Numerous* (1968).

Simon J. Ortiz (b. 1941) was born and raised in the Acoma Pueblo Community in Albuquerque, New Mexico. He received his early education from the Bureau of Indian Affairs school on the Acoma reservation, later attending the University of New Mexico and completing his M.F.A. at the University of Iowa, where he was a part of the International Writing Program. Unlike most Native American contemporary writers, Ortiz is a full-blooded Native American, and his first language was Keresan. By learning English, he found a way to communicate with those outside his immediate culture. His poetry explores the significance of individual origins and journeys, which he sees as forming a vital link in the continuity of life. His many writing accomplishments include poems, short stories, essays, and children's books. Ortiz has taught Native American literature and creative writing at San Diego State University, Navajo Community College, Marin College, the Institute for the Arts of the American Indian, and the University of New Mexico. He is currently a faculty member at the University of Toronto.

Wilfred Owen (1893–1918) was born in Oswestry, Shropshire, and went to school at Birkenhead Institute and Shrewsbury Technical School. He studied at London University but was forced to withdraw for financial reasons. After that he went to Dunsden, Oxfordshire, as a vicar's assistant. At Dunsden, Owen grew disaffected with the church and left to teach in France. He enlisted in 1915 and six months later was hospitalized in Edinburgh, where he met Siegfried Sassoon, whose war poems had just been published. Owen was sent back to the front and was killed one week before the armistice. He is the most widely recognized of the "war poets," a group of World War I writers who brought the realism of war into poetry.

Linda Pastan (b. 1932) was born in New York City, graduated from Radcliffe College, and earned an M.A. from Brandeis University. She has published many books of poetry and received numerous awards for them, including a Dylan Thomas Award. Her deeply emotional poetry often has grief at its center. Her work is referred to as "spare, plain-spoken" poetry, a kind of plainsong. Pastan served as poet laureate of Maryland from 1991 to 1994. She presently lives in Potomac, Maryland.

writes not only poetry but also short stories, novels, essays, and nonfiction, and she has served as an anthology editor and translator. Her work often reveals how living in two different languages can create very different experiences of the world.

Robert Pinsky (b. 1940) was born in Long Branch, New Jersey. He is the author of six books of poetry, including *The Figured Wheel: New and Collected Poems, 1966–1996* (1996), which won the 1997 Lenore Marshall Poetry Prize and was a Pulitzer Prize nominee. He has also published four books of criticism, two books of translation, and a computer novel, *Mindwheel*. In 1999 he co-edited with Maggie Dietz *Americans' Favorite Poems: The Favorite Poem Project Anthology*. He is currently poetry editor of the weekly Internet magazine *Slate*. He teaches in the graduate writing program at Boston University, and in 1997 he was named Poet Laureate Consultant in Poetry at the Library of Congress. He lives in Newton Corner, Massachusetts.

Marge Piercy (b. 1936) was born in working-class Detroit and studied at the University of Michigan and Northwestern University. She has published fourteen books of poetry, fifteen novels, and a collection of essays on poetry, *Parti-Colored Blocks for a Quilt* (1982). Much of her work deals with subtle and blatant forms of oppression of women.

Wang Ping (b. 1957) received her B.A. from Beijing University and came to the United States in 1985. She earned a Ph.D. at New York University. Ping

Sylvia Plath (1932–1963) grew up in a middle-class family in Boston and showed early promise as a writer, having stories and poems published in magazines such as *Seventeen* while she was in high school. As a student at Smith College, she was selected for an internship at *Mademoiselle* magazine and spent a month working in New York in the summer of 1953. Upon her return home, she suffered a serious breakdown and attempted suicide, was institutionalized, and then returned to Smith College for her senior year in 1954. She received a Fulbright fellowship to study at Cambridge University in England, where she met the poet Ted Hughes. They were married in 1956. They lived in the United States as well as England, and Plath studied under ROBERT LOWELL at Boston University. Their marriage broke up in 1962, and from her letters and poems it appears that she was approaching another breakdown. On February 11, 1963, she committed suicide. Four books of poetry appeared during her lifetime, and her *Selected Poems* was published in 1985. The powerful, psychologically intense poetry for which she is best known (including "Daddy") was written after 1960, influenced by the "confessional" style of LOWELL (see **confessional poetry** in the glossary).

Edgar Allan Poe (1809–1849) was born in Boston. His parents were touring actors; both died before he was three years old, and he was taken into the home of John Allan, a prosperous merchant in Richmond, Virginia, and baptized Edgar Allan Poe. His childhood was uneventful, although he studied in England for five years (1815–1820). In 1826 he entered the University of Virginia but, because of gambling debts, stayed for only a year. He began to write and published a book of poems in 1827. He joined the army and gained an appointment to West Point, but was dismissed after six months for disobeying orders. He turned to fiction writing and journalism to support himself. He began publishing stories and was appointed editor of the *Southern Literary Messenger* in Richmond, but his job was terminated after two years because of his drinking. He achieved success as an artist and editor in New York City (1837), then in Philadelphia (1838–1844), and again in New York (1844–1849), but

failed to satisfy his employers and to secure a livelihood, and thus lived in or close to poverty his entire life. He is famous for his horror tales and is credited with inventing the detective story, as well as for writing poetry with a prominent use of **rhythms**, **alliteration**, and **assonance** (see the glossary) that gives it a strongly musical quality.

Alexander Pope (1688–1744) was born in London to a successful textile merchant and spent his childhood in the country, stunted by tuberculosis of the spine (his height never exceeded four and a half feet). Pope was also limited by his Catholicism, which prevented him from going to university, voting, or holding public office. He instead turned to writing and gained considerable fame for his satire *The Rape of the Lock* and his translations of Homer. Fame also brought ridicule and vehement attacks from critics holding different political views, and Pope struck back with nasty satires on his detractors. Later in his career, he wrote a good deal of ethical and philosophical verse.

Ezra Pound (1885–1972) was born in Idaho but grew up outside Philadelphia; he attended the University of Pennsylvania for two years and graduated from Hamilton College. He taught for two years at Wabash College, then left for Europe, living for the next few years in London, where he edited *Little Review* and founded several literary movements—including the Imagists and the Vorticists. After moving to Italy, he began his major work, the *Cantos*, and became involved in fascist politics. During World War II he did radio broadcasts from Italy in support of

Mussolini, for which he was indicted for treason in the United States. Judged mentally unfit for trial, he remained in an asylum in Washington, D.C., until 1958, when the charges were dropped. Pound spent his last years in Italy. He is generally considered the poet most responsible for defining and promoting a modernist aesthetic in poetry.

writers who sought to preserve a traditional aesthetic ideal that was firmly rooted in classical values and forms. As a critic, he promulgated the highly influential New Criticism, which focused attention on texts as self-sufficient entities, to be analyzed through rigorous methodologies intended to reveal their depth, subtleties, and intricacies of technique and theme.

Dudley Randall (1914–2002) was born in Washington, D.C., and lived most of his life in Detroit. His first published poem appeared in the *Detroit Free Press* when he was thirteen. He worked for Ford Motor Company and then for the U.S. Postal Service and served in the South Pacific during World War II. He graduated from Wayne State University in 1949 and then from the library school at the University of Michigan. In 1965 Randall established the Broadside Press, one of the most important publishers of modern black poetry. "Ballad of Birmingham," written in response to the 1963 bombing of a church in which four girls were killed, has been set to music and recorded. It became an anthem for many in the civil rights movement.

John Crowe Ransom (1888–1974) was born in Pulaski, Tennessee, the son of a preacher. He studied at Vanderbilt University and then at Christ Church College, Oxford, on a Rhodes scholarship. After service in World War I, he taught first at Vanderbilt and later at Kenyon College, where he edited the *Kenyon Review*. He published three volumes of highly acclaimed poetry, but after 1927 principally devoted himself to critical writing. He was a guiding member of the Fugitives, a group of

Henry Reed (1914–1986) was born in Birmingham, Warwickshire, and was educated at the University of Birmingham, where his circle of friends included W. H. AUDEN and Louis MacNiece. His service in the British army during World War II provided the basis for his famous *Lessons of the War* (three related poems, of which "Naming of Parts" is the first). In addition to his one early volume of poetry, he is well known in Britain for his many radio plays; he also published translations and a book on the novel.

Adrienne Rich (b. 1929) was born in Baltimore, the elder daughter of a forceful Jewish intellectual who encouraged and critiqued her writing. While she was at Radcliffe College in 1951, W. H. AUDEN selected her book *A Change of World* for the Yale Younger Poets Award. She became involved in radical politics, especially in the opposition to the Vietnam War, and taught inner-city minority youth. She had felt a tension as she modeled her early poetry on that of male writers, and in the 1970s Rich became a feminist, freeing herself from her old models and becoming an influential figure in contemporary American literature. She is the author of nearly twenty volumes of poetry and several books of nonfiction prose. In 1999 Rich received the Lifetime Achievement Award from the Lannan Foundation. Since 1984 she has lived in California.

Alberto Ríos (b. 1952) was born to a Guatemalan father and an English mother in Nogales, Arizona, on the Mexican border. He earned a B.A. in English and one in psychology and an M.F.A. at the University of Arizona. In addition to seven books of poetry, he has published two collections of short stories. His work often fuses realism, surrealism, and magical realism, as exemplified by "Nani." Since 1994 he has been Regents Professor of English at Arizona State University, where he has taught since 1982. He lives in Chandler, Arizona.

Edwin Arlington Robinson (1869–1935) was born in Head Tide, Maine, and grew up in the equally provincial Maine town of Gardiner, the setting for much of his poetry. He was forced to leave Harvard University after two years because of his family's financial difficulties. He published his first two books of poetry in 1896 and 1897 ("Richard Cory" appeared in the latter). For the next quarter-century Robinson chose to live in poverty and write his poetry, relying on temporary jobs and charity from friends. President Theodore Roosevelt, at the urging of his son Kermit, used his influence to get Robinson a sinecure job in the New York Custom House in 1905, giving him time to write. He published numerous books of mediocre poetry in the next decade. The tide turned for him with *The Man Against the Sky* (1916); the numerous volumes that followed received high praise and sold well. He

was awarded three Pulitzer Prizes: for *Collected Poems* in 1921, *The Man Who Died Twice* in 1924, and *Tristram* in 1927. Robinson was the first major American poet of the twentieth century, unique in that he devoted his life to poetry and willingly paid the price in poverty and obscurity.

Theodore Roethke (1908–1963) was the son of a commercial greenhouse operator in Saginaw, Michigan. As a child, he spent much time in the greenhouse, and the impressions of nature he formed there later influenced the subjects and imagery of his verse. Roethke graduated from the University of Michigan and studied at Harvard University. Although he published only eight books of poetry, they were held in high regard by critics, some of whom considered him among the best poets of his generation. *The Waking* was awarded the Pulitzer Prize in 1954; *Words for the Wind* (1958) received the Bollingen Prize and the National Book Award. He taught at many colleges and universities and gained a reputation as an exceptional teacher of poetry writing, although his career was interrupted several times by serious mental breakdowns.

Christina Rossetti (1830–1894), born in London into a literary family (her brother Dante Gabriel Rossetti was one of the Pre-Raphaelite group), began writing poetry at an early age. Ill health saved her from a career as a governess; instead she nursed her ailing father and worked at the St. Mary Magdalen Home for Fallen Women. Rossetti had a strong Anglican religiosity that led her to give up theater and opera and turn down two offers of marriage. She wrote six collections of poetry, as well as short stories, nursery rhymes, and religious essays.

Sonia Sanchez (b. 1934) was born Wilsonia Driver in Birmingham, Alabama. In 1943 she moved to Harlem with her sister to live with their father and his third wife. She earned a B.A. in political science from Hunter College in 1955 and studied poetry writing with LOUISE BOGAN at New York University. In the 1960s she became actively involved in the social movements of the times, and she has continued to be a voice for social change. She has published more than a dozen books of poetry, many plays, and several books for children, and she has edited two anthologies of literature. She began teaching in the San Francisco area in 1965 and was a pioneer in developing black studies courses at what is now San Francisco State University, from 1968 to 1969. She was the first Presidential Fellow at Temple University, where she began teaching in 1977, and held the Laura Carnell Chair in English there until her retirement in 1999. She lives in Philadelphia.

Anne Sexton (1928–1974) was born in Newton, Massachusetts, and dropped out of Garland Junior College to get married. After suffering nervous breakdowns following the births of her two children, she was encouraged to enroll in writing programs. Studying under ROBERT LOWELL at Boston University, she was a fellow student with SYLVIA PLATH. Like the work of other "confessional" poets, Sexton's poetry includes an intimate view of her life and emotions. She made the experience of being a woman a central issue in her poetry, bringing into it such subjects

as menstruation, abortion, and drug addiction. She published at least a dozen books of poetry—*Live or Die* was awarded the Pulitzer Prize for poetry in 1966—as well as four children's books co-authored with MAXINE KUMIN. Sexton's emotional problems continued, along with a growing addiction to alcohol and sedatives, and she committed suicide in 1974.

William Shakespeare (1564–1616) was born in Stratford-upon-Avon, England, where his father was a glovemaker and bailiff, and he presumably went to grammar school there. He married Anne Hathaway in 1582, and sometime before 1592 he left for London to work as a playwright and actor. Shakespeare joined the Lord Chamberlain's Men (later the King's Men), an acting company for which he wrote thirty-five plays, before retiring to Stratford around 1612. In addition to being a skillful dramatist, he was perhaps the finest lyric poet of his day, as exemplified by songs scattered through his plays, two early nondramatic poems (*Venus and Adonis* and *The Rape of Lucrece*), and the sonnet sequence expected of all noteworthy writers in the Elizabethan age. Shakespeare's sonnets were probably written in the 1590s, although they were not published until 1609.

Percy Bysshe Shelley (1792–1822) was born into a wealthy aristocratic family in Sussex County, England. He was educated at Eton and then went on to Oxford University, but was expelled after six months for writing a defense of atheism, the first price he would pay for his nonconformity and radical (for his time) commitment to social justice. The following year he eloped with

Harriet Westbrook, daughter of a tavern keeper, despite his belief that marriage was a tyrannical and degrading social institution (she was sixteen, he eighteen). He became a disciple of the radical social philosopher William Godwin, fell in love with Godwin's daughter, Mary Wollstonecroft Godwin (the author, later, of *Frankenstein*), and went to live with her in France. Two years later, after Harriet committed suicide, they married and moved to Italy, where they shifted about restlessly and Shelley was generally short on money and in poor health. In such trying circumstances he wrote his greatest works. He died at age thirty, when the boat he was in was overturned by a sudden storm.

Sir Philip Sidney (1554–1586) was born into an important aristocratic family in Elizabethan England. He attended Shrewsbury School and Oxford University, although he left without a degree and completed his education through extended travel on the Continent. He was the epitome of the well-rounded courtier idealized in his era, excelling as a soldier, writer, literary patron, and diplomat. He was the author of an important work of prose fiction *(Arcadia)*, a landmark essay in literary criticism *(The Defense of Poesy)*, and an important sonnet cycle (*Astrophil and Stella*, which includes "Loving in truth, and fain in verse my love to show"). His poetry has been labeled "news from the heart."

Leslie Marmon Silko (b. 1948) was born in Albuquerque of mixed Pueblo, Mexican, and white ancestry and grew up on the Laguna Pueblo Reservation in New Mexico. She earned her B.A.

(with honors) from the University of New Mexico. In a long and productive writing career (she was already writing stories in elementary school), she has published poetry, novels, short stories, essays, letters, and film scripts. She taught creative writing first at the University of New Mexico and later at the University of Arizona. She has been named a Living Cultural Treasure by the New Mexico Humanities Council and has received the Native Writers' Circle of the Americas Lifetime Achievement Award. Her work is a graphic telling of the life of native peoples, maintaining its rich spiritual heritage while exposing the terrible consequences of European domination. Silko lives today on a ranch in the mountains a few miles northwest of Tucson, Arizona.

Charles Simic (b. 1938) was born in Belgrade, Yugoslavia. In 1953 he, his mother, and his brother joined his father in Chicago, where he lived until 1958. His first poems were published when he was twenty-one. In 1961 he was drafted into the U.S. Army, and in 1966 he earned his B.A. from New York University. His first book of poems, *What the Grass Says*, was published in 1967. Since then he has published more than sixty books of poetry, translations, and essays, including *The World Doesn't End: Prose Poems* (1990), for which he received the Pulitzer Prize for poetry. Since 1973 he has lived in New Hampshire, where he is a professor of English at the University of New Hampshire.

Edith Sitwell (1887–1964) was born into an aristocratic and literary family in late Victorian England. She both shocked and amused people by her writing, eccentric behavior, and dramatic Elizabethan dress. Influenced by Baudelaire and the symbolists, T. S. ELIOT's poetry, Stravinsky's music, and abstract art, Sitwell introduced verbal and rhythmic innovations that contrasted sharply with then-current verse.

Christopher Smart (1722–1771) was born in Shipbourne, Kent. He attended the Durham School and was later educated at Pembroke College, Cambridge, where he won prizes for his poetry. After college, Smart lived in London, editing and writing copy for periodicals and composing songs for the popular theater. In 1752 he published his first collection, *Poems on Several Occasions*. In the 1750s Smart developed a form of religious mania that compelled him to continuous prayer. From 1756 on, he was confined, with one brief intermission, until 1763 in St. Luke's Hospital and then in Mr. Potter's Madhouse in Bethnal Green. During his confinement, he wrote what many see as his most original and lasting works—*A Song to David* and *Jubilate Agno*, with its well-known homage to his cat, Jeoffry. Smart ranks as one of the most respected and influential religious poets in English literature.

Gary Snyder (b. 1930) was born in San Francisco and grew up in Oregon and Washington. He studied anthropology at Reed College and Oriental languages at the University of California, Berkeley, where he became associated with the Beat movement; however, his poetry often deals with nature rather than the urban interests more typical of Beat poetry. He has published sixteen books of poetry and prose, including *Turtle Island* (1974), which won the Pulitzer Prize for poetry. Snyder is active in the environmental movement and spent a number of years in Japan devoting extensive study to Zen Buddhism. He teaches at the University of California, Davis.

Cathy Song (b. 1955) was born in Hawaii and lived in the small town of Wahiawa on Oahu. She left Hawaii for the East Coast, studying at Wellesley College and then at Boston University. Her first book, *Picture Bride*, was chosen by Richard Hugo for the Yale Series of Younger Poets in 1982. Since then she has published three other books of poetry. She lives in Honolulu and teaches at the University of Hawaii at Manoa.

Gary Soto (b. 1952) grew up in Fresno, California. He earned his B.A. from California State University, Fresno, and M.F.A. from the University of California, Irvine. He worked his way through college at jobs such as picking grapes and chopping beets. Much of his poetry comes out of and reflects his working background, that of migrant workers and tenant farmers in the fields of southern California, and provides glimpses into the lives of families in the barrio. Soto's language comes from earthy, gritty, raw everyday American speech. His first book, *The Elements of San Joaquin*, won the 1976 United States Award from the International Poetry Forum. He has published ten collections of poetry, two novels, four essay collections, and numerous young adult and children's books and has edited three anthologies. He lives in Berkeley, California.

Edmund Spenser (1552–1599), a contemporary of WILLIAM SHAKESPEARE, was the greatest English nondramatic poet of his time. Best known for his romantic and national epic *The Faerie Queene*, Spenser wrote poems of a number of other types as well and was important as an innovator in metrics and forms (as in his development of the special form of sonnet that bears his name—see **Spenserian Sonnet** in the glossary). "One day I wrote her name upon the strand" is number 75 in *Amoretti*, a sequence of sonnets about a courtship addressed to a woman named Elizabeth, probably Elizabeth Boyle, who became his second wife.

William Stafford (1914–1995) was born in Hutchinson, Kansas, and studied at the University of Kansas and then at the University of Iowa Writers' Workshop. In between, he was a conscientious objector during World War II and worked in labor camps. In 1948 Stafford moved to Oregon, where he taught at Lewis and Clark College until he retired in 1980. His first major collection of poems, *Traveling through the Dark*, was published when Stafford was forty-eight. It won the National Book Award in 1963. He went on to publish more than sixty-five volumes of poetry and prose and came to be known as a very influential teacher of poetry. From 1970 to 1971 he was Consultant in Poetry at the Library of Congress.

Gertrude Stein (1874–1946) was born in Allegheny, Pennsylvania. After attending Radcliffe College, Harvard University, and Johns Hopkins Medical School, she moved to France in 1903 and became a central figure in the Parisian art world. An advocate of the avant-garde, her salon became a gathering place for the "new moderns." What Henri Matisse and Pablo Picasso achieved in the visual arts, Stein attempted in her writing. Her first published book, *Three Lives* (1909), the stories of three working-class women, has been called a minor masterpiece. A number of other books followed, including *The Autobiography of Alice B. Toklas* (1933), actually Stein's own autobiography.

Gerald Stern (b. 1925) was born in Pittsburgh and studied at the University of Pittsburgh and Columbia University. Stern came late to poetry: he was forty-six when he published his first book. Since then he has published more than ten collections of poems. Stern has often been compared to WALT WHITMAN and JOHN KEATS for his exploration of the self and the sometimes ecstatic exuberance of his verse. He taught at Columbia University, New York University, Sarah Lawrence College, the University of Pittsburgh, and the University of Iowa Writers' Workshop, among others, until his retirement in 1995. He now lives in Easton, Pennsylvania, and New York City.

Wallace Stevens (1879–1955) was born in Reading, Pennsylvania, and attended Harvard University for three years. He tried journalism and then attended New York University Law School, after which he worked as a legal consultant. He spent most of his life working as an executive for the Hartford Accident and Indemnity Company, spending his evenings writing some of the most imaginative and influential poetry of his time. Although now considered one of the major American poets of the century, he did not receive widespread recognition until the publication of his *Collected Poems* just a year before his death.

Virgil Suárez (b. 1962) was born in Havana, Cuba. Eight years later he left with his parents for Spain, where they lived until they came to the United States in 1974. He is the author of several collections of poetry, several novels, and a volume of short stories and the editor of several best-selling anthologies. His work often reflects the impact of the diaspora on the everyday life of Cuban and other exiles. He is professor of creative writing at Florida State University.

Sekou Sundiata (b. 1948) was born and raised in Harlem. His work is deeply influenced by the music, poetry, and oral traditions of African American culture. A self-proclaimed radical in the 1970s, for the past several decades he has used poetry to comment on the life and times of our culture. His work, which encompasses print, performance, music, and theater, has received praise for its fusion of soul, jazz, and hiphop grooves with political insight, humor, and rhythmic speech. He regularly records and performs on tour with artists such as Craig Harris and Vernon Reid.

Jonathan Swift (1667–1745) was born in Ireland of English parents and educated at Kilkenny College and Trinity College, Dublin. He worked in England for a decade as a private secretary and for four years as a political writer, but spent the rest of his life in Ireland, as dean of St. Patrick's Cathedral in Dublin. Although he is best known for his satires in prose (such as *Gulliver's Travels* and "A Modest Proposal"), Swift's original ambition was to be a poet, and he wrote occasional verse throughout his life.

James Tate (b. 1943), a native of Kansas City, Missouri, studied at the University of Missouri and Kansas State College during his undergraduate years. He then earned his M.F.A. at the University of Iowa Writers' Workshop in 1967, the same year his first poetry collection, *The Lost Pilot*, was published (it was selected by Dudley Fitts for the Yale Series of Younger Poets). He is the author of numerous books of poetry, including *Selected Poems* (1991), which won the Pulitzer Prize and the William Carlos Williams Award. Tate's poems often include highly unusual juxtapositions of imagery, tone, and context, as is evident in "The Wheelchair Butterfly." Tate has taught at the University of Iowa, the University of California, Berkeley, and Columbia University and now teaches at the University of Massachusetts, Amherst.

Edward Taylor (c.1642–1729) was born in England and emigrated to the colonies, where he became a clergyman in Westfield, a frontier village in what is now Massachusetts. Taylor regarded his poems as sacramental acts of private devotion and asked that they never be published. When he died, his manuscripts were placed in the Yale University library, and two centuries passed before his work was discovered.

The selection of his poems published in 1939 established him as a writer of genuine power, perhaps unsurpassed in America until William Cullen Bryant appeared a century and a half later.

Alfred, Lord Tennyson (1809–1892) was born in Somersby, Lincolnshire, and grew up there in the tense atmosphere of his unhappy father's rectory. He went to Trinity College, Cambridge, but was forced to leave because of family and financial problems, so he returned home to study and practice the craft of poetry. His early volumes, published in 1830 and 1832, received bad reviews, but his *In Memoriam* (1850), an elegy on his close friend Arthur Hallam, who died of a brain seizure, won acclaim. He was unquestionably the most popular poet of his time (the "poet of the people") and arguably the greatest of the Victorian poets. He succeeded WILLIAM WORDSWORTH as poet laureate, a position he held from 1850 until his death.

Dylan Thomas (1914–1953) was born in Swansea, Wales, and after grammar school became a journalist. He worked as a writer for the rest of his life. His first book of poetry, *Eighteen Poems*, appeared in 1934 and was followed by *Twenty-five Poems* (1936), *Deaths and Entrances* (1946), and *Collected Poems* (1952). His poems are often rich in textured rhythms and images. He also wrote prose, chiefly short stories collectively appearing as *Portrait of the Artist as a Young Dog* (1940), and a number of film scripts and radio plays. His most famous work, *Under Milk Wood*, written as a play for voices, was first performed in New York on May 14, 1953. Thomas's radio broadcasts and

his lecture tours and poetry readings in the United States brought him fame and popularity. Alcoholism contributed to his early death in 1953.

Jean Toomer (1894–1967) was born in Washington, D.C., of mixed French, Dutch, Welsh, Negro, German, Jewish, and Indian blood (according to him). Although he passed for white during certain periods of his life, he was raised in a predominantly black community and attended black high schools. He began college at the University of Wisconsin but transferred to the College of the City of New York. He spent several years publishing poems and stories in small magazines. In 1921 he took a teaching job in Georgia and remained there four months; the experience inspired *Cane* (1923), a book of prose poetry describing the Georgian people and landscape that became a central work of the Harlem Renaissance. He later experimented in communal living and both studied and tried to promulgate the ideas of Quakerism and the Russian mystic George Gurdjieff. From 1950 on he published very little, writing mostly for himself.

Quincy Troupe (b. 1943) was born in New York City and grew up in East St. Louis, Illinois. He earned degrees from Grambling College and Los Angeles City College. He is a poet, biographer, journalist, editor, and teacher. In addition to poetry, he has written *Miles: The Autobiography* (1989), which received an American Book Award; *James Baldwin: The Legacy* (1989); and *Miles and Me: A Memoir of Miles Davis* (2000). He also edited *Giant Talk: An Anthology of Third World Writing* (1975) and is a founding editor of *Confrontation: A*

Journal of Third World Literature and American Rag. He taught creative writing for the Watts Writers' Movement from 1966 to 1968 and served as director of the Malcolm X Center in Los Angeles during the summers of 1969 and 1970. He is professor of creative writing and American literature at the University of California, San Diego.

Jean Valentine (b. 1934) was born in Chicago and raised in New York and Boston. She is a graduate of Radcliffe College. Her first book, *Dream Barker,* was selected for a Yale Younger Poets Award in 1965. Since then she has published eight books of poetry. She teaches at Sarah Lawrence College and New York University and lives in New York City.

Ellen Bryant Voigt (b. 1943) was born in Danville, Virginia, and studied at Converse College, the University of South Carolina, and the University of Iowa, where she earned an M.F.A. in music and literature. She is a pianist as well as a writer; her highly tuned musical ear is evident in the rich textures of sound in her poetry. She is the author of six collections of poetry and *The Flexible Lyric* (1999), a collection of craft essays. She has taught at Goddard College, where she founded the writing program, at M.I.T., and now teaches at Warren Wilson College in North Carolina, where she is the founding director of the writing program. She lives in Marshfield, Vermont, and is currently the Vermont State Poet.

Derek Walcott (b. 1930), born on the eastern Caribbean island of St. Lucia, moves between the African heritage of his family and the English cultural heritage of his reading and education. Both of his parents were educators who immersed themselves in the arts. His early training was in painting, which like his poetry was influenced by his Methodist religious training. He attended St. Mary's College and the University of the West Indies in Jamaica. His first book, *Twenty-Five Poems* (1948), appeared when he was eighteen, and he has published prolifically since then: nearly twenty books of poetry, more than twenty-five plays, and a book of nonfiction. His work, which explores both the isolation of the artist and regional identity, is known for blending Caribbean, English, and African traditions. He was awarded the Nobel Prize for literature in 1992, the academy citing him for "a poetic oeuvre of great luminosity, sustained by a historical vision, the outcome of a multicultural achievement." He teaches creative writing at Boston University every fall and lives the rest of the year in St. Lucia.

Anne Waldman (b. 1945) was born in Millville, New Jersey, and grew up in Greenwich Village. She is associated with the bohemian poetics of the Lower East Side in New York and with "Beat poetics." She attended Bennington College, co-founded the literary magazine *Angel Hair,* and for ten years directed the St. Mark's Church Poetry Project in New York City. She became a Buddhist, guided by the Tibetan Chogyam Trungpa Rinpoche, who would also become ALLEN GINSBERG's guru. She and Ginsberg worked together to create the Jack Kerouac School of Disembodied Poetics, at Trungpa's Naropa Institute in Boulder, Colorado. Both an author and a performance artist, she has published more than forty books and gives exuberant, highly physical readings of her own work. She now lives in Boulder and New York City.

Edmund Waller (1606–1687) was born into a wealthy English family and attended Eton College and Cambridge University. He was elected to Parliament and married a rich woman who died soon after. He was later exiled for involvement in a Royalist plot. Waller's poems, first published while he was in exile, enjoyed great popularity; he pioneered the smooth, balanced, antithetical **pentameter couplets** that became the staple of English poetry in the late seventeenth century and most of the eighteenth. After the restoration of the monarchy in 1660, he again joined Parliament, where he remained for many years.

James Welch (b. 1940) was born in Browning, Montana. His father was a member of the Blackfoot tribe, his mother of the Gros Ventre tribe. He attended schools on the Blackfoot and Fort Belknap reservations and took a degree from the University of Montana, where he studied under Richard Hugo. Welch has published many books of poetry, fiction, and nonfiction. His hard, spare poems often evoke the bleakest side of contemporary Native American life. He received a Lifetime Achievement Award for literature from the Native Writers' Circle in 1997. He makes his home on a farm outside Missoula, Montana.

Walt Whitman (1819–1892) was born in rural Long Island, the son of a farmer and carpenter. He attended grammar school in Brooklyn and took his first job as a printer's devil for the *Long Island Patriot*. Attending the opera, dabbling in politics, participating in street life, and gaining experience as student, printer, reporter, writer, carpenter, farmer, seashore observer, and teacher provided the bedrock for his future poetic vision of an ideal society based on the realization of self. Although Whitman liked to portray himself as uncultured, he read widely in the King James Bible, SHAKESPEARE, Homer, Dante, Aeschylus, and Sophocles. He worked for many years in the newspaper business and began writing poetry only in 1847. In 1855, at his own expense, Whitman published the first edition of *Leaves of Grass*, a thin volume of twelve long untitled poems. Written in a highly original and innovative **free verse**, influenced significantly by music, with a wide-ranging subject matter, the work seemed strange to most of the poet's contemporaries—but they did recognize its value: Ralph Waldo Emerson wrote to him shortly after Whitman sent him a copy, "I greet you at the beginning of a great career." He spent much of the remainder of his life revising and expanding this book. *Leaves of Grass* today is considered a masterpiece of world literature, marking the beginning of modern American poetry, and Whitman is widely regarded as America's national poet.

Richard Wilbur (b. 1921) was born in New York City and grew up in rural New Jersey. He attended Amherst College and began writing poetry during World War II while fighting in Italy and France. Afterward, he studied at Harvard University and then taught there and at Wellesley College, Wesleyan University, and Smith College. He has published many books of poetry, including *Things of This World* (1956), for which he received the Pulitzer Prize for poetry and the National Book Award, and *New and Collected Poems* (1988), which also won a Pulitzer Prize. He has always been respected as a master of formal constraints, comparing them to the genie in the bottle: the restraints stimulate the imagination to achieve results unlikely to be reached without them. He has also published numerous translations of French plays, two books for children, a collection of prose pieces, and editions of WILLIAM SHAKESPEARE and EDGAR ALLAN POE. In 1987 he was appointed Poet Laureate Consultant in Poetry at the Library of Congress. He now lives in Cummington, Massachusetts.

Nancy Willard (b. 1936) was raised in Ann Arbor, Michigan, and educated at the University of Michigan and Stanford University. She is a noted writer of books for children. *A Visit to William Blake's Inn: Poems for Innocent and Experienced Travelers* (1981) was the first book of poetry to win the prestigious Newbery Medal, which recognizes the most distinguished American children's book published the previous year. She is an excellent poet, essayist, and novelist. Her work in all genres frequently leads to experiencing the common in a most uncommon way. She teaches at Vassar College and lives in Poughkeepsie, New York.

William Carlos Williams (1883–1963) was born in Rutherford, New Jersey; his father was an English emigrant and his mother was of mixed Basque descent from Puerto Rico. He decided to be both a writer and a doctor while in high school in New York City. He graduated from the medical school at the University of Pennsylvania, where he was a friend of EZRA POUND and HILDA DOOLITTLE. After an internship in New York, writing poems between seeing patients, Williams practiced general medicine in Rutherford (he was ALLEN GINSBERG's pediatrician). His first book of poems was published in 1909, and he subsequently published poems, novels, short stories, plays, criticism, and essays. Initially one of the principal poets of the **Imagist** movement (see the glossary), Williams sought later to invent an entirely fresh—and distinctly American—poetic whose subject matter was centered on the everyday circumstances of life and the lives of common people. Williams, like Wallace Stevens, became one of the major poets of the twentieth century and exerted great influence upon poets of his own and later generations.

Nellie Wong (b. 1940) was born and raised in Oakland, California's Chinatown during the 1940s. Since she began writing in the 1970s, she has spoken out against the oppression of all people, in particular, workers, women, minorities, and immigrants, and has worked steadily with community-based and international organizations to achieve racial justice. She is known as both a poet and a feminist human rights activist. She is the author of three poetry volumes and the co-editor of an anthology of political essays, *Voices of Color* (1999). She has taught creative writing at several colleges in the Bay area. Until her retirement, she worked as senior analyst in the Office of Affirmative Action/Equal Opportunity at the University of San Francisco. She lives in San Francisco and continues to speak at conferences nationwide on issues of race, gender, class, literature, labor, and community organizing.

William Wordsworth (1770–1850) was born and raised in the Lake District of England. Both his parents died by the time he was thirteen. He studied at Cambridge, toured Europe on foot, and lived in France for a year during the first part of the French Revolution. He returned to England, leaving behind a lover, Annette Vallon, and their daughter, Caroline, from whom he was soon cut off by war between England and France. He met SAMUEL TAYLOR COLERIDGE, and in 1798 they published *Lyrical Ballads*, the first great work of the English Romantic movement. He changed poetry forever by his decision to use common language in his poetry instead of heightened **poetic diction** (see the glossary). In 1799 he and his sister Dorothy moved to Grasmere, in the Lake District, where he married Mary Hutchinson, a childhood friend. His greatest works were produced between 1797 and 1808. He continued to write for the next forty years but never regained the heights of his early verse. In 1843 he was named poet laureate, a position he held until his death in 1850.

Charles Wright (b. 1935) was born in Pickwick Dam, Tennessee, and grew up in Tennessee and North Carolina. He studied at Davidson College, served a four-year stint in Italy as a captain in the U.S. Army Intelligence Corps, and then continued his education at the University of Iowa Writers' Workshop and at the University of Rome on a Fulbright fellowship. He has published many books of poetry—including *Black Zodiac*, which won the Pulitzer Prize

for poetry in 1997—two volumes of criticism, and a translation of Eugenio Montale's poetry. Wright's poems have been labeled impressionistic, combining images from the natural world, Catholicism, and the rural South. He taught at the University of California, Irvine, for almost twenty years and now is Souder Family Professor of English at the University of Virginia.

James Wright (1927–1980) grew up in Martin's Ferry, Ohio. He attended Kenyon College, where his study under JOHN CROWE RANSOM sent his early poetry in a formalist direction. After spending a year in Austria on a Fulbright fellowship, he returned to the United States and earned an M.A. and a Ph.D. at the University of Washington, studying under THEODORE ROETHKE and STANLEY KUNITZ. He went on to teach at the University of Minnesota, Macalester College, and Hunter College. His working-class background and the poverty that he saw during the Depression stirred a sympathy for the poor and "outsiders" of various sorts that shaped the tone and content of his poetry. He published numerous books of poetry; his *Collected Poems* received the Pulitzer Prize in 1972.

Lady Mary Wroth (c.1587–c.1651), niece of SIR PHILIP SIDNEY and MARY SIDNEY HERBERT, was one of the best and most prolific women writers of the English Renaissance and an important literary patron. Her husband's early death left her deeply in debt. She wrote *Pamphilia to Amphilanthus*, the only known English sonnet sequence on love themes by a woman; seventy-four poems that appeared in *Urania* (the first full-length work of prose fiction by a woman); and several other pieces. BEN JONSON said that reading her sonnets had made him "a better lover and a much better poet."

Sir Thomas Wyatt (1503–1542) was born in Kent and educated at St. John's College, Cambridge. He spent most of his life as a courtier and diplomat, serving King Henry VIII as ambassador to Spain and as a member of several missions to Italy and France. These travels introduced Wyatt to Italian writers of the High Renaissance, whose work he translated, thus introducing the sonnet form into English. He was arrested twice and charged with treason, sent to the Tower of London, and acquitted in 1541. Aristocratic poets at the time rarely published their poems themselves: works circulated in manuscript and in published collections ("miscellanies") gathered by printers. The most important of these is a volume published by Richard Tottel in 1557 titled *Songs and Sonnets* but more commonly known as *Tottel's Miscellany*, which includes ninety-seven of Wyatt's sonnets and delightful lyrics.

John Yau (b. 1950) was born in Lynn, Massachusetts, a year after his parents emigrated from China. He received a B.A. from Bard College and an M.F.A. from Brooklyn College, where he studied with JOHN ASHBERY. He has published several books of poetry and two books of criticism, edited an anthology of fiction, organized a retrospective of Ed Moses's paintings and drawings, and written a long essay on ROBERT CREELEY's poetry and poetics. Yau lives in Manhattan and teaches at the Maryland Institute College of Art.

William Butler Yeats (1865–1939) was born in Sandymount, Dublin, to an Anglo-Irish family. On leaving high school in 1883 he decided to be an artist, like his father, and attended art school, but soon gave it up to concentrate on poetry. His first poems were published in 1885 in the *Dublin University Review*. Religious by temperament but unable to accept orthodox Christianity, Yeats throughout his life explored esoteric philosophies in search of a tradition that would substitute for a lost religion. He became a member of the Theosophical Society and the Order of the Golden Dawn, two groups interested in Eastern occultism, and later developed a private system of symbols and mystical ideas. Through the influence of Lady Gregory, a writer and promoter of literature, he became interested in Irish nationalist art, helping to found the Irish National Theatre and the famous Abbey Theatre. He was actively involved in Irish politics, especially after the Easter Rising of 1916. He continued to write and to revise earlier poems, leaving behind, at his death, a body of verse that, in its variety and power, placed him among the greatest twentieth-century poets of the English language. He was awarded the Nobel Prize for Literature in 1923.

Al Young (b. 1939) was born at Ocean Springs, Mississippi, and lived for a decade in the South, then moved to Detroit. He attended the University of Michigan and the University of California, Berkeley. Young has been a professional guitarist and singer, a disk jockey, a medical photographer, and a warehouseman and has written six books of poetry, five novels, several memoirs, essays, and film scripts. He has edited a number of books, including *Yardbird Lives!* (1978) and *African American Literature: A Brief Introduction and Anthology* (1995). In the 1970s and 1980s, Young co-founded the journals *Yardbird Reader* and *Quilt* with poet-novelist Ishmael Reed. He lives in Palo Alto, California.

David Young (b. 1936) was born in Davenport, Iowa. He earned a B.A. from Carleton College and an M.A. and a Ph.D. from Yale University. He is the author of nine books of poetry and several volumes of translations and has published five volumes of criticism and prose, among them studies of WILLIAM SHAKESPEARE and WILLIAM BUTLER YEATS and *Seasoning: A Poet's Year, with Seasonal Recipes* (1999). He has edited several anthologies, including *Models of the Universe: An Anthology of the Prose Poem* (1995, with Stuart Friebert), and is coeditor of the literary magazine *Field,* of the *Field* Translation Series, and of the *Field* Contemporary Poetry Series. He lives in Oberlin, Ohio, where he is Longman Professor of English and Creative Writing at Oberlin College.

Ray A. Young Bear (b. 1950) was born and raised in the Mesquakie Tribal Settlement near Tama, Iowa. His poetry has been influenced by his maternal grandmother, Ada Kapayou Old Bear, and his wife, Stella L. Young Bear. He attended Claremont College in California as well as Grinnell College, the University of Iowa, Iowa State University, and Northern Iowa University. He has been a visiting faculty member at Eastern Washington University and the University of Iowa. Young Bear and his wife co-founded the Woodland Song and Dance Troupe

of Arts Midwest in 1983. Young Bear's group has performed traditional Mesquakie music in the United States and the Netherlands. A writer of poetry, fiction, and nonfiction, he has contributed to contemporary Native American poetry and the study of it for nearly three decades.

Paul Zimmer (b. 1934) was born in Canton, Ohio, and educated at Kent State University. He is the author of more than a dozen poetry collections, including *The Great Bird of Love*, which was selected for the National Poetry Series in 1998. He has become well known for his many poems in the voice of the persona "Zimmer," a kind of Buster Keaton everyman. Zimmer has directed the university presses at the University of Georgia, the University of Iowa, and the University of Pittsburgh and was instrumental in the foundation of an influential poetry series at each.

Louis Zukofsky (1904–1978) was the son of immigrant Russian Jews and grew up on the Lower East Side of Manhattan. His "Poem Beginning 'The'" brought him to the attention of EZRA POUND, at whose behest he was invited to edit a special issue of *Poetry* magazine, for which he coined the term "Objectivist" poetry. He became a leading member of the Objectivist group, together with WILLIAM CARLOS WILLIAMS, Charles Reznikoff, GEORGE OPPEN, and Carl Rakosi. Widely considered an important forerunner of contemporary avant-garde writing, he was an accomplished writer of fiction, a ceaseless experimenter in poetry and theory, and one of the most influential poets and critics of his era.

Glossary of Poetic Terms

This selective glossary is intended to help readers who seek a better understanding of poetic terms and techniques. It often provides examples and explanations in addition to definitions, and it can be used as a reference, as needed, or it can be read straight through. Becoming more aware of the tools and techniques poets work with can help one experience a poem more richly and fully. We have drawn numerous illustrations from John Frederick Nims's "Love Poem" (p. 173), because it provides particularly clear and memorable examples of many figures of speech.

For a more complete, book-length guide to literary terminology, see Ross Murfin and Supryia Ray, *The Bedford Glossary of Critical and Literary Terms* (2nd ed., 2003); M. H. Abrams, *A Glossary of Literary Terms* (7th ed., 1999); or William Harmon and C. Hugh Holman, *A Handbook to Literature* (8th ed., 2000), all excellent resources on which we have drawn frequently. The most authoritative work is the massive *New Princeton Encyclopedia of Poetry and Poetics,* ed. Alex Preminger and T. V. Brogan (3rd ed., 1993). Several glossaries of literary terms are available on the Internet.

Accent   The stress, or greater emphasis, given to some syllables of words relative to that received by adjacent syllables.

Accentual meter   A metrical system in which the number of accented, or stressed, syllables per line is regular (all lines having the same number, or the corresponding lines of different stanzas having the same number), while the number of unstressed syllables in lines varies randomly. Accentual meter with two accented syllables in each half-line, linked by a system of alliteration, was the principle of Old English poetry (up to the eleventh century), and some modern poets — e.g., W. H. Auden — have sought to revive it. Gerard Manley Hopkins developed a unique variety of accentual verse he called *sprung rhythm* (see pp. 117–19).

Accentual-syllabic verse   Verse whose meter takes into account both the number of syllables per line and the pattern of accented and unaccented syllables. The great majority of metrical poems in English are accentual-syllabic. Cf. **quantitative verse.**

Alexandrine   A poetic line with six iambic feet (iambic hexameter).

Allegory   A form or manner, usually narrative, in which objects, persons, and actions make coherent sense on a literal level but also are equated in a sustained and obvious way with (usually) abstract meanings that lie outside the story. A classic example in prose is John Bunyan's *The Pilgrim's Progress;* in narrative poetry, Edmund Spenser's *The Faerie Queene.* Edward Taylor's "Housewifery" (p. 27), though not narrative, is allegorical in approach.

Alliteration   The repetition of identical consonant sounds in the stressed syllables of words relatively near to each other (in the same line or adjacent lines, usually). Alliteration is most common at the beginnings of words or syllables ("as the grass was green") but can involve consonants within words and syllables as well ("green and carefree, famous among the barns"). Alliteration applies to sounds, not spelling: "And honoured among foxes and pheasants" (examples from Dylan Thomas, "Fern Hill," p. 176). Cf. **consonance**.

Allusion   A figure of speech that echoes or makes brief reference to a literary or artistic work or a historical figure, event, or object; for example, the references to Lazarus and Hamlet in "The Love Song of J. Alfred Prufrock" (p. 147). It is usually a way of placing one's poem within, or alongside, a whole other context that is evoked in a very economical fashion. See also **intertextuality**.

Ambiguity   In expository prose, an undesirable doubtfulness or uncertainty of meaning or intention, resulting from imprecision in use of words or construction of sentences. In poetry, the desirable condition of admitting more than one possible meaning, resulting from the capacity of language to function on levels other than the literal. Related terms sometimes employed are "ambivalence" and "polysemy."

Anapest   A metrical foot consisting of three syllables, with two unaccented syllables followed by an accented one (˘˘´). In "anapestic meter," anapests are the predominant foot in a line or poem. The following line from William Cowper's "The Poplar Field" is in anapestic meter: "And thĕ whis|pĕrĭng soúnd|ŏf thĕ cóol| cŏlŏnnáde."

Anaphora   Repetition of the same word or words at the beginning of two or more lines, clauses, or sentences. For examples, see the portion of Christopher Smart's *Jubilate Agno* included in the anthology (p. 43); Walt Whitman employs it extensively in "Song of Myself" (p. 92) and "When Lilacs Last in the Dooryard Bloom'd" (p. 104).

Anticlimax   An arrangement of details such that one of lesser importance appears after one or ones of greater importance, where an even greater one is expected; for example, "Not louder shrieks by dames to heaven are cast, / When husbands die, or lapdogs breathe their last" (Alexander Pope, "The Rape of the Lock," p. 29).

Antithesis   A figure of speech in which contrasting words, sentences, or ideas are expressed in balanced, parallel grammatical structures; for example, "She had some horses she loved. / She had some horses she hated" (Joy Harjo, "She Had Some Horses," p. 291) illustrates antithesis.

Apostrophe   A figure of speech in which an absent person, an abstract quality, or a nonhuman entity is addressed as though present. It is a particular type of personification. See, as examples, Ben Jonson, "On My First Son" (p. 13) and John Keats, "Ode on a Grecian Urn" (p. 80).

Approximate rhyme   See **slant rhyme**.

Archetype   An image, symbol, character type, or plot line that occurs frequently enough in literature, religion, myths, folktales, and fairy tales to be recognizable as an element of universal experience and thus to evoke a deep emotional response. In "Spring and Fall" (p. 119) Gerard Manley Hopkins develops the archetypes in his title, those of spring (archetype for birth and youth) and fall (archetype for old age and the approach of death).

Assonance   The repetition of identical or similar vowel sounds in words relatively near to each other (usually within a line or in adjacent lines) whose consonant sounds differ. It can be initial ("*a*pple . . . *a*nd h*a*ppy *a*s") or, more commonly, internal ("gr*ee*n and car*e*fr*ee*," "T*i*me h*e*ld m*e* gr*ee*n and d*y*ing") (examples from Dylan Thomas, "Fern Hill," p. 176).

Aubade   A dawn song, ordinarily expressing the regret of two lovers that day has come to separate them.

Ballad   A poem that tells a story and was meant to be recited or sung; originally a folk art, transmitted orally from person to person and generation to generation. Many of the popular ballads were not written down and published until the eighteenth century, though their origins may have been centuries earlier. See "Lord Randal" and "Sir Patrick Spens" (pp. 1 and 2) as examples of popular Scottish ballads.

Ballad stanza   A quatrain in iambic meter rhyming *abcb* with (usually) four feet in the first and third lines, three in the second and fourth. See, for example, Robert Burns, "A Red, Red Rose" (p. 49).

Blank verse   Lines of unrhymed iambic pentameter. It is the most widely used verse form of poetry in English because it is the closest to the natural rhythms of English speech. Shakespeare's plays as well as Milton's *Paradise Lost* and *Paradise Regained*, Wordsworth's *Prelude*, and countless other long poems were composed in blank verse because it is well suited to narrative, dialogue, and reflection. For two poems based on blank verse but using it freely, see Robert Frost's "After Apple-Picking" and "Birches" (pp. 131, 133).

Cacophony   A harsh or unpleasant combination of sounds. An example can be found in Alexander Pope's, "An Essay on Criticism," lines 368–69: "But when loud surges lash the sounding shore, / The hoarse, rough verse should like the torrent roar." Cf. **euphony**.

Caesura   A pause or break within a line of verse, usually signaled by a mark of punctuation.

Carpe diem   "Seize the day," a Latin phrase from an ode by Horace. It is the label for a theme common in literature, especially sixteenth- and seventeenth-century English love poetry, that life is short and fleeting and that therefore we must make the most of present pleasures. See Robert Herrick, "To the Virgins, to Make Much of Time" (p. 14) and Andrew Marvell, "To His Coy Mistress" (p. 24).

Chaucerian stanza   A seven-line iambic stanza rhyming *ababbcc*, sometimes having an alexandrine (hexameter) closing line. See, for example, Sir Thomas Wyatt, "They flee from me" (p. 3).

Closed form   Any structural pattern or repetition of meter, rhyme, or stanza. Cf. **open form**.

Compression   The dropping of a syllable to make a line fit the meter, sometimes marked with an apostrophe (e.g., John Keats, "The Eve of St. Agnes" [p. 68], line 16: "praying in dumb orat'ries"). One common device is elision, the dropping of a vowel at the beginning or end of a word (e.g., John Donne, "A Valediction: Forbidding Mourning" [p. 11], lines 7 and 28: "'Twere profanation of our joys" and "To move, but doth, if th' other do").

Conceit   A figure of speech that establishes a striking or far-fetched analogy between seemingly very dissimilar things, either the exaggerated, unrealistic comparisons of love poems (such as those used in Shakespeare's Sonnet 18 [p. 8] and parodied in Sonnet 130 [p. 10]) or the complex analogies of metaphysical wit (as in John Donne's "The Flea," p. 12).

Concrete poem   A poem shaped in the form of the object the poem describes or discusses. See, for example, George Herbert's "Easter-wings" (p. 15).

Confessional poetry   Poetry about personal, private issues that usually speaks directly, without the use of a persona. See, for example, Robert Lowell, "Skunk Hour" (p. 182) and Sylvia Plath, "Daddy" (p. 222).

Connotation   The shared or communal range of emotional implications and associations a word may carry in addition to its dictionary definitions. Cf. **denotation**.

Consonance   The repetition of consonant sounds in words whose vowels are different. In perfect examples, all the consonants are alike—*live, love; chitter, chatter; reader, rider;* but words in which all the consonants following the main vowels are identical also are considered consonance—*dive, love; swatter, chitter; sound, bond; gate* and *mat, set, pit.*

Convention   A rule, method, practice, or characteristic established by usage; a customary feature.

Couplet   Two consecutive lines of poetry with the same end rhyme. English (Shakespearean) sonnets end with a couplet (see pp. 8–10); for an entire poem in tetrameter couplets, see Andrew Marvell, "To His Coy Mistress" (p. 24). See also **heroic couplets**.

Dactyl   A metrical foot consisting of three syllables, an accented one followed by two unaccented ones (ˊˇˇ). In "dactylic meter," dactyls are the predominant foot of a line or poem. The following lines from Thomas Hardy's "The Voice" are in dactylic meter: "Wóman mŭch|mĭssed, hŏw yŏu|cáll tŏ m̌e,|cáll tŏ m̌e, / Sáyiňg tĥat|nów yŏu aře|nót aš yŏu|wére."

Denotation   The basic meaning of a word; its dictionary definition.

Diction   Choice of words; the kind of words, phrases, and figurative language used to make up a work of literature. See also **poetic diction**.

Dimeter   A line of verse consisting of two metrical feet.

Double rhyme   A rhyme in which the accented, rhyming syllable is followed by one or more identical, unstressed syllables: *thrilling* and *killing, marry* and *tarry.* Formerly known as "feminine rhyme."

Dramatic irony   A situation in which a reader or audience knows more than the speakers or characters, either about the outcome of events or the discrepancy between a meaning intended by a speaker or character and that recognized by the reader or audience.

Dramatic monologue   A poem with only one speaker, overheard in a dramatic moment (usually addressing another character or characters who do not speak), whose words reveal what is going on in the scene and expose significant depths of the speaker's temperament, attitudes, and values. See Robert Browning, "My Last Duchess" (p. 89) and T. S. Eliot, "The Love Song of J. Alfred Prufrock" (p. 147).

Elegy   In Greek and Roman literature, a serious, meditative poem written in "elegiac meter" (alternating hexameter and pentameter lines); since the 1600s, a sustained and formal poem lamenting the death of a particular person, usually ending with a consolation, or setting forth meditations on death or another solemn theme. See Thomas Gray's "Elegy Written in a Country Churchyard" (p. 39), John Milton's pastoral elegy "Lycidas" (p. 17), and Walt Whitman's "When Lilacs Last in the Dooryard Bloom'd" (p. 104). The adjective "elegiac" is also used to describe a general tone of sadness or a worldview that emphasizes suffering and loss. It is most often applied to Anglo-Saxon poems like *Beowulf* or *The Seafarer,* but can also be used for modern poems as, for example, A. E. Housman's poems in *A Shropshire Lad.*

Elision   See **compression**.

End rhyme   Rhyme at the ends of lines in a poem.

End-stopped line   A line in which both the grammatical structure and the thought reach completion at the end. Cf. **run-on line**.

English sonnet   A sonnet consisting of three quatrains (four-line units, typically rhyming *abab cdcd efef*) and a couplet (two rhyming lines). Usually the subject is introduced in the first quatrain, expanded in the second, and expanded still further in the third; the couplet adds a logical, pithy conclusion or gives a surprising twist. Also called the Shakespearean sonnet (see examples on pp. 8–10). Cf. **Spenserian sonnet**.

Enjambment   See **run-on line**.

Epic   A long narrative poem that celebrates the achievements of great heroes and heroines, often determining the fate of a tribe or nation, in formal language and an elevated style. Examples include Homer's *Iliad* and *Odyssey,* Virgil's *Aeneid,* and John Milton's *Paradise Lost.*

Epigram   Originally an inscription, especially an epitaph; in modern usage a short poem, usually polished and witty with a surprising twist at the end. (Its other dictionary definition, "any terse, witty, pointed statement," generally does not apply in poetry.)

Epigraph   In literature, a quotation at the beginning of a poem or on the title page or the beginning of a chapter in a book. See the epigraph from Dante at the beginning of T. S. Eliot, "The Love Song of J. Alfred Prufrock" (p. 147).

Epiphany   An appearance or manifestation, especially of a divine being; in literature, since James Joyce adapted the term to secular use in 1944, a sudden sense of radiance and revelation one may feel while perceiving a commonplace object; a moment or event in which the essential nature of a person, a situation, or an object is suddenly perceived. The term is more common in narrative than in lyric poetry. William Wordsworth, in "Ode: Intimations of Immortality" (p. 55), writes about epiphanies, although the poem itself does not depict them; Robert Bly depicts one in "Driving to Town Late to Mail a Letter" (p. 201).

Euphony   Language that strikes the ear as smooth, musical, and agreeable. An example can be found in Alexander Pope's, "An Essay on Criticism," lines 366–67: "Soft is the strain when Zephyr gently blows, / And the smooth stream in smoother numbers flows." Cf. **cacophony**.

Exact rhyme   Rhyme in which all sounds following the vowel sound are the same: *spite* and *night, art* and *heart, ache* and *fake, card* and *barred.*

Exaggeration   See **hyperbole**.

Extension   Pronunciation that adds a syllable for the sake of the meter. See, for example, the ninth line of John Donne's sonnet "Batter my heart, three-personed God" (p. 13): "and would be lovèd fain."

Falling meter   Meter using a foot (usually a trochee or a dactyl) in which the first syllable is accented, followed by unaccented syllables that give a sense of stepping down. Cf. **rising meter**.

Feminine rhyme   See **double rhyme**.

Figure of speech and **figurative language**   Uses of language that depart from standard or literal usage in order to achieve a special effect or meaning.

Fixed form   Poetry written in definite, repeating patterns of line, rhyme scheme, or stanza.

Foot   The basic unit in metrical verse, comprised of (usually) one stressed and one or more unstressed syllables. See also **anapest, dactyl, iamb, spondee,** and **trochee**.

Form   (1) Genre or literary type (e.g., the lyric form); (2) patterns of meter, lines, and rhymes (stanzaic form); (3) the organization of the parts of a literary work in relation to its total effect (e.g., "The form [structure] of this poem is very effective").

Free verse   See **open form**.

Genre   A recurring type of literature; a literary form as defined by rules or conventions followed in it (e.g., tragedy, comedy, epic, lyric, pastoral, novel, short story, essay).

Haiku   A lyric form, originating in Japan, of seventeen syllables in three lines, the first and third having five syllables and the second seven, presenting an image of a natural object or scene that expresses a distinct emotion or spiritual insight. Gary Snyder incorporates haiku into "Hitch Haiku" (p. 217).

Half rhyme   See **slant rhyme**.

Heptameter   A poetic line with seven metrical feet.

Heroic couplets   Couplets in iambic pentameter with a full stop, usually, at the end. See Alexander Pope, "The Rape of the Lock" (p. 00). Also called "closed couplets."

Hexameter   A poetic line with six metrical feet. See also **alexandrine**.

Hyperbole   Exaggeration; a figure of speech in which something is stated more strongly than is logically warranted. Hyperbole is often used to make a point emphatically, as when Hamlet protests that he loved Ophelia much more than her brother did: "Forty thousand brothers / Could not with all their quantity of love / Make up my sum" (5.1.272–74). See also Robert Burns, "A Red, Red Rose" (p. 49).

Iamb   A metrical foot consisting of two syllables, an unaccented one followed by an accented one (˘ ´). In iambic meter (the most widely used of English metrical forms), iambs are the predominant foot in a line or poem. The following line from Thomas Gray's "Elegy Written in a Country Churchyard" (p. 39) is in iambic meter: "Thĕ cúr | fĕw tólls | thĕ knéll | ŏf párt | ĭng dáy."

Image   (1) A word or group of words that refers to a sensory experience or to an object that can be known by one or more of the senses. "Imagery" signifies all such language in a poem or other literary work collectively and can include any of the senses; see, for example, the first stanza of John Keats's "The Eve of St. Agnes" (p. 68). See also **synesthesia**. (2) A metaphor or other comparison. "Imagery" in this sense refers to the characteristic that several images in a poem have in common, for example, the military imagery in the octave of Donne's sonnet "Batter my heart, three-personed God" and the erotic imagery at the end (p. 13).

Imagist poetry   Poetry that relies on sharp, concrete images, written in a highly concentrated style that is suggestive rather than discursive. See, for example, H. D.'s "Garden" (p. 143).

Implied metaphor   Metaphor in which the *to be* verb is omitted and one aspect of the comparison is implied, rather than stated directly. "A car thief is a dirty dog" is direct metaphor; "some dirty dog stole my car" contains an implied metaphor. Examples are "whose hands *shipwreck* vases," "A *wrench* in clocks and the solar system," "In *traffic* of wit expertly manoeuvre" in John Frederick Nims, "Love Poem" (p. 173).

Internal rhyme   Rhyme that occurs between words within a line, between words within lines near each other, or between a word within a line and one at the end of the same or a nearby line. Edgar Allan Poe's "Annabel Lee" (p. 84) offers many examples: "chilling / And killing," "Can ever dissever," "And the stars never rise but I see the bright eyes."

Intertextuality   The implied presence of previous texts within a literary work or as its context. Devices used to achieve this include allusion and choice of genre. An intertextual approach assumes that interpretation is incomplete until the relation of the new work to its predecessors—response, opposition, development—has been considered.

Irony   A feeling, tone, mood, or attitude arising from the awareness that what is (reality) is opposite from, and usually worse than, what seems (appearance). What a person *says* may be ironic (see **verbal irony**), or a discrepancy between what a character knows or means and what a reader or audience knows can be ironic (see **dramatic irony**), or, without centering on one person, a general situation can be seen as ironic (**situational irony**). Irony should not be confused with mere coincidence. See also **Socratic irony**.

Italian sonnet   A sonnet composed of an octave (an eight-line unit), rhyming *abbaabba*, and a sestet (a six-line unit), often rhyming *cdecde* or *cdcdcd*, although variations are frequent. The octave usually develops an idea, question, or problem; then the poem pauses, or "turns," and the sestet completes the idea, answers the question, or resolves the difficulty. Sometimes called a Petrarchan sonnet. See Gerard Manley Hopkins, "God's Grandeur" (p. 117).

Juxtaposition   Placement of things side by side or close together for comparison or contrast or to create something new from the union, without necessarily making them grammatically parallel. See Alexander Pope, "The Rape of the Lock" (p. 29), 1. 72: "Dost sometimes counsel take—and sometimes tea."

Language poetry   Poetry evincing skepticism about the ability of written language to record, represent, communicate, or express anything other than its own linguistic apparatus. See Lyn Hejinian, "A Mask of Anger" (p. 256).

Line   A sequence of words printed as a separate entity on a page; the basic structural unit in poetry (except prose poems).

Literal   In accordance with the primary or strict meaning of a word or words; not figurative or metaphorical.

Litotes   See **understatement**.

Lyric   Originally, a poem sung to the accompaniment of a lyre; now a short poem expressing the personal emotion and ideas of a single speaker.

Masculine rhyme   See **single rhyme**.

Metaphor   A figure of speech in which two things usually thought to be dissimilar are treated as if they were alike and have characteristics in common. "Whose *palms are bulls* in china" (John Frederick Nims, "Love Poem," p. 173). See also **implied metaphor**.

Metaphysical poetry   The work of a number of seventeenth-century poets that was characterized by philosophical subtlety and intellectual rigor; subtle, often outrageous logic; imitation of actual speech, sometimes resulting in "rough" meter and style; and far-fetched analogies. John Donne, "A Valediction: Forbidding Mourning" and "The Flea" (pp. 11 and 12) exemplify the type. See also **conceit**.

Meter   A steady beat, or measured pulse, created by a repeating pattern of accents, syllables, or both.

Metonymy   A figure of speech in which the name of one thing is substituted for that of something closely associated with it, as in commonly used phrases such as "The *White House* announced today..." (the name of the building is substituted for the president or the staff members who issued the announcement), "He's got *a Constable* on his wall," "The *trains* are on strike," or "*Wall Street* is in a panic." In the last line of John Frederick Nims's "Love Poem" (p. 173 "All the toys of the world would break," *toys* is substituted for "things that give happiness" (as toys do to a child). See also **synecdoche**.

Mock epic   A literary form that imitates the grand style and conventions of the epic genre, such as the opening statement of a theme, an address to the muse, long formal speeches, and epic similes, but applies them to a subject unworthy of such exalted treatment. In "The Rape of the Lock" (p. 29) Alexander Pope uses the form for comic effect and at the same time treats seriously the great epic themes concerning human destiny and mortality. Also called "mock heroic." See also **epic**.

Monometer   A poetic line with one metrical foot.

Narrative   A story in prose or verse; an account of events involving characters and a sequence of events, told by a storyteller (narrator).

Near rhyme   See **slant rhyme**.

Octameter   A poetic line with eight metrical feet.

Octave   The first eight lines of an Italian sonnet.

Ode   A long lyric poem, serious (often intellectual) in tone, elevated and dignified in style, dealing with a single theme. The ode is generally more complicated in form than other lyric poems. Some odes retain a formal division into strophe, antistrophe, and epode, which reflects the ode's origins in the chorus of Greek tragedy. See William Wordsworth, "Ode: Intimations of Immortality" (p. 55), Percy Bysshe Shelley, "Ode to the West Wind" (p. 65), and John Keats, "Ode on a Grecian Urn" (p. 80).

Onomatopoeia   The use of words whose sounds supposedly resemble the sounds they denote (such as *thump, rattle, growl, hiss*), or a group of words whose sounds help to convey what is being described; for example, Emily Dickinson's "I heard a Fly *buzz*—when I died" (p. 114).

Open form   A form free of any predetermined metrical and stanzaic patterns. Cf. **closed form**.

Ottava rima   An eight-line stanza in iambic pentameter rhyming *abababcc*. See William Butler Yeats, "Among School Children" (p. 125).

Overstatement   See **hyperbole**.

Oxymoron   A figure of speech combining in one phrase (usually adjective-noun) two seemingly contradictory elements, such as "loving hate" or "feather of lead, bright smoke, cold fire, sick health" (Shakespeare, *Romeo and Juliet* 1.1.176–80). Oxymoron is a type of **paradox**.

Pantoum A poem composed of quatrains rhyming *abab* in which the second and fourth lines of each stanza serve as the first and third lines of the next, this process continuing through the last stanza (it repeats the first and third lines of the first stanza in reverse order, so the poem ends with the same line with which it began). See Nellie Wong, "Grandmother's Song" (p. 246).

Paradox A figure of speech in which a statement initially seeming self-contradictory or absurd turns out, seen in another light, to make good sense. The closing lines of John Donne's sonnet "Batter my heart, three-personed God" (p. 13) are paradoxical: "for I, / Except you enthrall me, never shall be free, / Nor ever chaste, except you ravish me." See also **oxymoron**.

Parallelism (1) A verbal arrangement in which elements of equal weight within phrases, sentences, or paragraphs are expressed in a similar grammatical order and structure. It can appear within a line or pair of lines ("And he was always quietly arrayed, / And he was always human when he talked"—Edwin Arlington Robinson, "Richard Cory" [p. 129]) or, more noticeably, as a series of parallel items, as in Langston Hughes's "Harlem" (p. 161). (2) A principle of poetic structure in which consecutive lines in open form are related by a line's repeating, expanding on, or contrasting with the idea of the line or lines before it, as in the poems of Walt Whitman (pp. 92–111).

Parody Now, a humorous or satirical imitation of a serious piece of literature or writing. In the sixteenth and seventeenth centuries, poets such as George Herbert practiced "sacred parody" by adapting secular lyrics to devotional themes.

Partial rhyme See **slant rhyme**.

Pastoral A poem (also called an "eclogue," a "bucolic," or an "idyll") that expresses a city poet's nostalgic image of the simple, peaceful life of shepherds and other country folk in an idealized natural setting. Christopher Marlowe's "The Passionate Shepherd to His Love" (p. 7) uses some pastoral conventions, as do certain elegies (including John Milton's "Lycidas," p. 17).

Pause See **caesura**.

Pentameter A poetic line with five metrical feet.

Persona Literally, the mask through which actors spoke in Greek plays. In some critical approaches of recent decades, the "character" projected by the author, the "I" of a narrative poem or novel, or the speaker whose voice is heard in a lyric poem. In this view, the poem is an artificial construct distanced from the poet's autobiographical self. Cf. **voice**.

Personification A figure of speech in which something nonhuman is treated as if it had human characteristics or performed human actions. Sometimes it involves abstractions, as in Thomas Gray's phrase "Fair Science frowned" ("Elegy Written in a Country Churchyard," p. 42); science cannot literally frown. In other cases concrete things are given human characteristics, as in the phrase "Wearing white for Eastertide" from A. E. Housman's "Loveliest of trees, the cherry now" (p. 120). Cherry trees do not actually wear clothes—they are being given, briefly, a human attribute. Difficulty can arise when personification is redefined (incorrectly) as treating something nonhuman in terms of anything alive rather than specifically human: "the mouth of time" in Nancy Willard's "Questions My Son Asked Me, Answers I Never Gave Him" (p. 236) is metaphor, not personification, since animals as well as humans have mouths. See also **apostrophe**.

Petrarchan sonnet   See **Italian sonnet**.

Poem   A term whose meaning exceeds all attempts at definition. Here is a slightly modified version of an attempt at definition by William Harmon and C. Hugh Holman in *A Handbook to Literature* (1996): A poem is a literary composition, written or oral, typically characterized by imagination, emotion, sense impressions, and concrete language that invites attention to its own physical features, such as sound or appearance on the page.

Poetic diction   In general, specialized language used in or considered appropriate to poetry. In the late seventeenth and the eighteenth centuries, a refined use of language that excluded "common" speech from poetry as indecorous—and substituted elevated circumlocutions, archaic synonyms, or such forms as *ope* and *e'er*.

Prose poem   A poem printed as prose, with lines wrapping at the right margin rather than being divided through predetermined line breaks. See Carolyn Forché, "The Colonel" (p. 286).

Prosody   The principles of versification, especially of meter, rhythm, rhyme, and stanza forms.

Pun   A play on words based on similarity in sound between two words having very different meanings. Also called "paronomasia." See the puns on "heart" and "kindly" in Sir Thomas Wyatt's "They flee from me" (p. 3).

Quantitative verse   Verse whose meter is based on the length of syllables (phonetic length being a distinguishing feature of ancient Greek and Latin, whereas English is an accentual language). Classical poetry exhibits a great variety of meters, and some English poets in the late 1500s attempted to fashion English verse on this principle. In *Evangeline* Henry Wadsworth Longfellow used dactylic hexameter in imitation of Virgil's *Aeneid*, but defined it by accent, not quantity. Cf. **accentual-syllabic verse**.

Quatrain   A stanza of four lines or other four-line unit within a larger form, such as a sonnet.

Refrain   One or more identical or deliberately similar lines repeated throughout a poem, such as the final line of a stanza or as a block of lines between stanzas or sections.

Rhyme   The repetition of the accented vowel sound of a word and all succeeding consonant sounds. See also **exact rhyme**; **slant rhyme**.

Rhyme royal   An alternative term for **Chaucerian stanza**, because it was used by King James I of Scotland in his poem *The Kingis Quair* ("The King's Book"), written about 1424.

Rhyme scheme   The pattern of end rhymes in a poem or stanza; the recurring sequence is usually described by assigning a letter to each word-sound, the same word-sounds having the same letter (e.g., a quatrain might be *abcb*).

Rhythm   The patterned "movement" of language created by the choice of words and their arrangement, usually described through such metaphors as fast or slow, smooth or halting, graceful or rough, deliberate or frenzied, syncopated or disjointed. Rhythm in poetry is affected, in addition to meter, by such factors, as line length, line endings, pauses (or lack of them) within lines, spaces within, at the beginning or end of, or between lines, word choice, and combinations of sounds.

Rising meter   A foot (usually an iamb or an anapest) in which the final, accented syllable is preceded by one or two unaccented syllables, thus giving a sense of stepping up. Cf. **falling meter**.

Run-on line   A line whose sense and grammatical structure continue to the next. In the following lines by William Stafford ("Traveling through the Dark," p. 176), the first line is run-on, the second end-stopped: "Traveling through the dark I found a deer / dead on the edge of the Wilson River road." Also called "enjambment." Cf. **end-stopped line**.

Sarcasm   A harsh and cutting form of verbal irony, often involving apparent praise that is obviously not meant: "Oh, no, these are fine. I *prefer* my eggs thoroughly charred."

Satire   A work, or manner within a work, that combines a critical attitude with humor and wit with the intent of improving humanity or human institutions. Alexander Pope's "The Rape of the Lock" (p. 29), for example, satirizes the values and attitudes of members of the wealthy, indolent upper classes of his day.

Scansion   The division of metrical verse into feet in order to determine and label its meter. Scanning a poem involves marking its stressed syllables with an accent mark [´] and its unstressed syllables with a curved line [˘], using a vertical line to indicate the way it divides into feet, and then describing (or labeling) the type of foot used most often and the line length—that is, the number of feet in each line. See also **foot** and **line**.

Sestet   The last six lines of an Italian sonnet.

Sestina   A lyric poem consisting of six six-line stanzas and a three-line concluding stanza (or "envoy"). The six end-words of the first stanza must be used as the end-words of the other five stanzas, in a specified pattern (the first line ends with the end-word from the last line of the previous stanza, the second line with that of the first line of the previous stanza, the third line with that of the previous fifth line, the fourth line with that of the previous second line, the fifth line with that of the previous fourth line, the sixth line with that of the previous third line). The three lines of the envoy must use the end-words of lines five, three, and one from the first stanza, in that order, and must include the other three end-words within the lines. See Alice Fulton, "You Can't Rhumboogie in a Ball and Chain" (p. 298).

Shakespearean sonnet   See **English sonnet**.

Shaped poem   See **concrete poem**.

Simile   Expression of a direct similarity, using such words as *like, as,* or *than,* between two things usually regarded as dissimilar, as in "Shrinking from far *headlights pale as a dime*" (John Frederick Nims, "Love Poem," p. 173). It is important to distinguish *simile* from *comparison,* in which the two things joined by "like" or "as" are *not* dissimilar.

Single rhyme   A rhyme in which the stressed, rhyming syllable is the final syllable: *west* and *vest, away* and *today.* Formerly called "masculine rhyme."

Situational irony   The mood evoked when an action intended to have a certain effect turns out to have a different and more sinister effect. See Thomas Hardy, "The Convergence of the Twain" (p. 116).

Slant rhyme   Consonance at the ends of lines; for example, *Room* and *Storm, firm* and *Room,* and *be* and *Fly* in Emily Dickinson's "I heard a Fly buzz—when I died" (p. 114). It can also be internal, if repeated enough to form a discernible pattern.

Socratic irony   A pose of self-deprecation, or of belittling oneself, in order to tease the reader into deeper insight.

Sonnet   A fourteen-line poem usually written in iambic pentameter; originally lyrical love poems, sonnets came to be used also for meditations on religious themes, death, and nature, and are now open to all subjects. Some variations in form have been tried: Sir Philip Sidney's "Loving in truth, and fain in verse my love to show" (p. 5) is in hexameters; George Meredith wrote sixteen-line sonnets; John Milton's "On the New Forcers of Conscience under the Long Parliament" is a "caudate" (tailed) sonnet with a six-line coda appended; and Gerard Manley Hopkins designed "Pied Beauty" (p. 119) as a "curtal" (abbreviated) sonnet (six lines in place of the octave, then four lines, and a half-line ending in place of the sestet). See **English sonnet** and **Italian sonnet.**

Sonnet sequence   A group of sonnets so arranged as to imply a narrative progression in the speaker's experience or attitudes; used especially in the sixteenth century. Also called "sonnet cycle."

Spenserian sonnet   A variation of the English sonnet that employs the structure of three quatrains plus a couplet but joins the quatrains by linking rhymes: *abab bcbc cdcd ee.* For examples, see pp. 5 and 6.

Spenserian stanza   A stanza of nine iambic lines, the first eight pentameter and the ninth hexameter, rhyming *ababbcbcc* (see John Keats, "The Eve of St. Agnes," p. 68).

Spondee   A metrical foot made up of two stressed syllables (´´), with no unstressed syllables. Spondees could not, of course, be the predominant foot in a poem; they are usually substituted for iambic or trochaic feet as a way of increasing emphasis, as in this line from John Donne's "Batter my heart, three-personed God," (p. 13): "As yet | but knock, | breathe, shine, | and seek | to mend."

Sprung rhythm   See **accentual meter.**

Stanza   A grouping of poetic lines into a section, either according to form—each section having the same number of lines and the same prosody (see Percy Bysshe Shelley's "Ode to the West Wind," p. 65)—or according to thought, creating irregular units comparable to paragraphs in prose (as in William Wordsworth's "Ode: Intimations of Immortality," p. 55).

Stress   See **accent.**

Structure   (1) The planned framework—the general plan or outline—of a literary work; (2) narrower patterns within the overall framework. Cf. **form.**

Substitution   The use of a different kind of foot in place of the one normally demanded by the predominant meter of a poem, as a way of adding variety, emphasizing the dominant foot by variation from it, speeding up or slowing down the pace, or signaling a switch in meaning.

Surrealism   An artistic movement that attempted to portray or interpret the workings of the unconscious mind, especially as realized in dreams, by an irrational, noncontextual choice and arrangement of images or objects. Now more often used to refer to anything defying the normal sense of reality.

Syllabic verse   A metrical pattern in which all lines in the poem have the same number of syllables (as in Sylvia Plath's "Metaphors," p. 221) or all first lines of stanzas have the same number, all second lines the same, and so on (see Dylan Thomas's "Fern Hill," p. 176)—while the stressed syllables are random in number and placement.

Symbol   Something that is itself and also stands for something else; a literary symbol is a prominent or repeated image or action that is present in the poem (or story or play) and can be seen, touched, smelled, heard, tasted, or experienced imaginatively but also conveys a cluster of abstract meanings beyond itself. Most critics agree that the tiger in William Blake's "The Tyger" (p. 47) and the wrecked vessel in Adrienne Rich's "Diving into the Wreck" (p. 214), for example, carry symbolic meaning.

Synecdoche   A special kind of metonymy in which a part of a thing is substituted for the whole of which it is a part, as in the commonly used phrases "give me a hand," "lend me your ears," or "many mouths to feed." See, for example, "whose *hands* shipwreck vases" and "For should your *hands* drop white and empty" (John Frederick Nims, "Love Poem," p. 173).

Synesthesia   Description of one kind of sense experience in relation to another, such as attribution of color to sounds ("blue notes") and vice versa ("a loud tie") or of taste to sounds ("sweet music"). See, for example, "With Blue—uncertain stumbling Buzz—" (Emily Dickinson, "I heard a Fly buzz—when I died," p. 114).

Tercet   A stanza of three lines, each usually ending with the same rhyme; but see **terza rima**. Cf. **triplet**.

Terza rima   A poetic form consisting of three-line stanzas (tercets) with interlinked rhymes, *aba bcb cdc ded efe*, etc., made famous by Dante's use of it in *The Divine Comedy*. Terza rima is used in Percy Bysshe Shelley's "Ode to the West Wind" (p. 65).

Tetrameter   A poetic line with four metrical feet. Robert Frost's line "The woods are lovely, dark, and deep" ("Stopping by Woods on a Snowy Evening," p. 135) is an example of iambic tetrameter.

Text   Traditionally, a piece of writing. In recent reader response criticism, "text" has come to mean the words with which the reader interacts; in this view, a poem is not an object, not a shape on the page or a spoken performance, but what is completed in the reader's mind.

Theme   The central idea embodied or explored in a literary work, for some idea-based approaches to literature; the general concept, explicit or implied, that the work incorporates and makes persuasive to the reader.

Title   The name attached to a work of literature. For poetry, a title in some cases is an integral part of a poem and needs to be considered in interpreting it; see, for example, George Herbert's "The Pulley" (p. 15). In other cases the name has been added as a means of identifying the poem and is not integral to interpretation. Sometimes the poem is untitled and the first line is used as a convenient way of referring to it, but should not be thought of as a title and does not follow the capitalization rules for titles.

Tone   The attitude, or "stance," toward the subject and toward the reader or audience implied in a literary work; the "tone of voice" it seems to project (serious or playful; exaggerated or understated; formal or informal; ironic or straightforward; or a complex mixture of more than one of these).

Transferred epithet   A figure of speech in which a modifier that ought, strictly, to apply to one word is transferred to another word that it does not strictly fit. In "The drunk clambering on his undulant floor" (John Frederick Nims, "Love Poem," p. 173), the drunk's perception, not the floor, is undulating.

Trimeter   A poetic line with three metrical feet.

Triplet   A group of three consecutive lines with the same rhyme, often used for variation in a long sequence of couplets. Cf. **tercet**.

Trochee   A metrical foot consisting of two syllables, an accented one followed by an unaccented one (˘). In trochaic meter, trochees are the predominant foot in a line or poem. The following lines from William Blake's introduction to *Songs of Innocence* are in trochaic meter (each line lacking the final unaccented syllable): "Piping │down the│valleys│wild, / Piping│Songs of│pleasant│glee, / On a│cloud I│ saw a│child, / And he│laughing│said to│me."

Understatement   A figure of speech expressing something in an unexpectedly restrained way. Paradoxically, to de-emphasize through understatement can be a way of emphasizing, of making people react with "there must be more to it than that." When Mercutio in *Romeo and Juliet*, after being stabbed by Tybalt, calls his wound "a scratch, a scratch" (3.1.92), he is understating, for the wound is serious—he calls for a doctor in the next line, and he dies a few minutes later.

Verbal irony   A figure of speech in which what is said is nearly the opposite of what is meant (such as saying "Lovely day out" when the weather actually is miserable). See Stephen Crane's "Do not weep, maiden, for war is kind" (p. 130).

Villanelle   A nineteen-line lyric poem divided into five tercets and a final four-line stanza, rhyming *aba aba aba aba aba abaa*. Line 1 is repeated to form lines 6, 12, and 18; line 3 is repeated to form lines 9, 15, and 19. See Elizabeth Bishop, "One Art" (p. 172), and Dylan Thomas, "Do not go gentle into that good night" (p. 178).

Voice   The supposed authorial presence in poems that do not obviously employ persona as a distancing device.

Michael S. Harper. "Nightmare Begins Responsibility" from *Images of Kin: New and Selected Poems* by Michael S. Harper. Copyright © 1977 by Michael S. Harper. Used with permission of the author and the University of Illinois Press.

Robert Hass. "Late Spring" from *Human Wishes* by Robert Hass. Copyright © 1989 by Robert Hass. Reprinted by permission of HarperCollins Publishers, Inc.

Robert Hayden. "Those Winter Sundays," copyright © 1966 by Robert Hayden, from *Angle of Ascent: New and Selected Poems* by Robert Hayden. Used by permission of Liveright Publishing Corporation.

Samuel Hazo. "For Fawzi in Jerusalem" from *Blood Rights* (University of Pittsburgh Press, 1968). Copyright © 1968 by Samuel Hazo. Reprinted by permission of the author.

Seamus Heaney. "Digging" from *Poems 1965–1975* by Seamus Heaney. Copyright © 1980 by Seamus Heaney. Reprinted by permission of Farrar, Straus and Giroux, LLC, and Faber and Faber Ltd.

Lyn Hejinian. "A Mask of Anger." Copyright © by Lyn Hejinian. Reprinted by permission of the author and Burning Deck Press, 71 Elmgrove Avenue, Providence, RI 02906.

Conrad Hilberry. "Player Piano" from *Player Piano: Poems* by Conrad Hilberry. Copyright © 1999 by Conrad Hilberry. Reprinted by permission of Louisiana State University Press.

Geoffrey Hill. "In Memory of Jane Fraser" from *Collected Poems* by Geoffrey Hill. Copyright © 1985 by Geoffrey Hill. Reprinted by permission of Oxford University Press.

Jane Hirshfield. "The Stone of Heaven" from *The October Palace* by Jane Hirshfield. HarperPerennial, 1994. Copyright © 1994 by Jane Hirshfield. Reprinted by permission of HarperCollins Publishers, Inc.

Linda Hogan. "The History of Red" from *The Book of Medicines* by Linda Hogan. Copyright © 1993 by Linda Hogan. Reprinted by permission of Coffee House Press.

Garrett Kaoru Hongo. "Yellow Light" from *Yellow Light*. Copyright © 1982 by Garrett Kaoru Hongo. Wesleyan University Press.

Susan Howe. From "Speeches at the Barriers," from *The Europe of Trusts: Selected Poems* (Los Angeles: Sun & Moon Press, 1990), pp. 101–102. Copyright © 1990 by Susan Howe. Reprinted by permission of the publisher.

Langston Hughes. "Harlem" and "The Negro Speaks of Rivers" from *The Collected Poems of Langston Hughes* by Langston Hughes. Copyright © 1994 by the Estate of Langston Hughes. Used by permission of Alfred A. Knopf, a division of Random House, Inc.

Randall Jarrell. "The Woman at the Washington Zoo" from *The Complete Poems* by Randall Jarrell. Copyright © 1969 and copyright renewed © 1997 by Mary von S. Jarrell. Reprinted by permission of Farrar, Straus and Giroux, LLC.

Robinson Jeffers. "Hurt Hawks" from *The Selected Poetry of Robinson Jeffers* by Robinson Jeffers. Copyright © 1928 and renewed 1956 by Robinson Jeffers. Reprinted by permission of Random House, Inc.

Richard Jones. "Cathedral" from *The Blessing: New and Selected Poems.* Copyright © 2000 by Richard Jones. Reprinted by permission of Copper Canyon Press.

Allison Joseph. "On Being Told I Don't Speak Like a Black Person," first published in *Many Mountains Moving* and reprinted in *Outsiders* (ed. Laure-Anne Bosselaar, Milkweed Editions, 1999), appears by permission of the author.

Jane Kenyon. "From Room to Room" from *From Room to Room.* Copyright © 1978 by Jane Kenyon. Reprinted with the permission of Alice James Books.

Galway Kinnell. "The Bear" from *Body Rags* by Galway Kinnell. Copyright © 1965, 1966, 1967 by Galway Kinnell. Reprinted by permission of Houghton Mifflin Company. All rights reserved.

Etheridge Knight. "Hard Rock Returns to Prison from the Hospital for the Criminal Insane" from *The Essential Etheridge Knight* by Etheridge Knight. Copyright © 1986 by Etheridge Knight. Reprinted by permission of the University of Pittsburgh Press.

Kenneth Koch. "The History of Jazz." Copyright © 1962 by Kenneth Koch. Reprinted by permission of the author's estate.

Yusef Komunyakaa. "Facing It" from *Neon Vernacular*, copyright © 1993 by Yusef Komunyakaa. Wesleyan University Press.

Maxine Kumin. "The Excrement Poem" from *Our Ground Time Here Will Be Brief: New and Selected Poems.* Copyright © 1982 by Maxine Kumin. Also from *Selected Poems 1960–1990* by Maxine Kumin. Reprinted by permission of W. W. Norton & Company. Used by permission of W. W. Norton & Company, Inc.

Stanley Kunitz. "Father and Son" from *The Poems of Stanley Kunitz 1928–1978.* Copyright © 1979 by Stanley Kunitz. Used by permission of W. W. Norton & Company, Inc.

Philip Larkin. "High Windows" from *Collected Poems* by Philip Larkin. Copyright © 1988, 1989 by the Estate of Philip Larkin. Reprinted by permission of Farrar, Straus and Giroux, LLC. Also from *High Windows.* Copyright © 1974 by Philip Larkin. Reprinted by permission of Faber and Faber Ltd.

Li-Young Lee. "Eating Alone" from *Rose.* Copyright © 1986 by Li-Young Lee. Reprinted with the permission of BOA Editions, Ltd.

Denise Levertov. "February Evening in New York" from *Collected Earlier Poems 1940–1960.* Copyright © 1960, 1979 by Denise Levertov. Reprinted by permission of New Directions Publishing Corp.

Philip Levine. "What Work Is" from *What Work Is* by Philip Levine. Copyright © 1992 by Philip Levine. Used by permission of Alfred A. Knopf, a division of Random House, Inc.

Larry Levis. "The Poem You Asked For" from *Wrecking Crew* by Larry Levis. Copyright © 1972 by Larry Levis. Reprinted by permission of University of Pittsburgh Press.

Timothy Liu. "Thoreau" from *Burnt Offerings*. Copyright © 1995 by Timothy Liu. Reprinted by permission of Copper Canyon Press.

Audre Lorde. "Coal" from *Undersong: Chosen Poems, Old and New* by Audre Lorde. Copyright © 1992, 1976, 1970, 1968 by Audre Lorde. Used by permission of W. W. Norton & Company, Inc.

Robert Lowell. "Skunk Hour" from *Selected Poems* by Robert Lowell. Copyright © 1976 by Robert Lowell. Reprinted by permission of Farrar, Straus and Giroux, Inc.

Heather McHugh. "What He Thought" from *Hinge & Sign: Poems , 1968–1993*. Copyright © 1994 by Heather McHugh. Wesleyan University Press.

James Merrill. "The Pier: Under Pisces" from *Collected Poems* by James Merrill, J. D. McClatchy and Stephen Yenser, editors. Copyright © 2001 by the Literary Estate of James Merrill at Washington University. Used by permission of Alfred A. Knopf, a division of Random House, Inc.

W. S. Merwin. "Yesterday" from *Opening the Hand* by W. S. Merwin. Copyright © 1983 by W. S. Merwin. Reprinted by permission of the author.

Robert Morgan. "Mountain Bride" from *Groundwork* (1979). Reprinted by permission of Gnomon Press.

Thylias Moss. "Tornados" from *Rainbow Remnants in Rock Bottom Ghetto Sky* by Thylias Moss. Copyright © 1991 by Thylias Moss. Used by permission of W. W. Norton & Company, Inc.

David Mura. "Grandfather-in-Law" from *After We Lost Our Way* (E. P. Dutton). Copyright © 1989 by David Mura. Reprinted by permission of the author.

John Frederick Nims, "Love Poem" from *Selected Poems*. Copyright © 1982 by the University of Chicago. Reprinted by permission of the University of Chicago Press.

Naomi Shihab Nye. "The Small Vases from Hebron" from *Fuel*. Copyright © 1998 by Naomi Shihab Nye. Reprinted with the permission of BOA Editions, Ltd.

Frank O'Hara. "The Day Lady Died." Copyright © 1964 by Frank O'Hara. Reprinted by permission of City Lights Books.

Sharon Olds. "I Go Back to May 1937" from *The Gold Cell* by Sharon Olds. Copyright © 1987 by Sharon Olds. Used by permission of Alfred A. Knopf, a division of Random House, Inc.

Mary Oliver. "August" from *American Primitive* by Mary Oliver. Copyright © 1994 by Mary Oliver. Reprinted by permission of Little, Brown and Company.

George Oppen. "The Forms of Love" from *Collected Poems* by George Oppen. Copyright © 1975 by George Oppen. Reprinted by permission of New Directions Publishing Corp.

Simon J. Ortiz. "Speaking." Previously published in *Woven Stone*, University of Arkansas Press, 1992. Copyright © 1992. Reprinted by permission of the author.

Linda Pastan. "An Early Afterlife" from *Carnival Evening — New and Selected Poems: 1968–1998* by Linda Pastan. Copyright © 1998 by Linda Pastan. Used by permission of W. W. Norton & Company, Inc.

Marge Piercy. "Barbie Doll" from *Circles on the Water* by Marge Piercy. Copyright © 1982 by Marge Piercy. Used by permission of Alfred A. Knopf, a division of Random House, Inc.

Wang Ping. "Syntax" from *New Generation: Poems from China Today*, ed. Wang Ping et al. (Brooklyn, NY: Hanging Loose Press, 1999). Copyright © 1999. Reprinted by permission.

Robert Pinsky. "Shirt" from *The Figured Wheel: New and Collected Poems, 1966–1996* by Robert Pinsky. Copyright © 1996 by Robert Pinsky. Reprinted by permission of Farrar, Straus and Giroux, LLC.

Sylvia Plath. "Metaphors" from *Crossing the Water* by Sylvia Plath. Copyright © 1960 by Ted Hughes. Copyright renewed. "Daddy" from *Ariel* by Sylvia Plath. Copyright © 1963 by Ted Hughes. Copyright renewed. Reprinted by permission of HarperCollins Publishers, Inc., and Faber and Faber Ltd.

Dudley Randall. "Ballad of Birmingham" from *Cities Burning*. Copyright © 1968 by Dudley Randall. Reprinted by permission of Broadside Press.

John Crowe Ransom. "Bells for John Whiteside's Daughter" from *Selected Poems*, Third Edition, revised and enlarged, by John Crowe Ransom. Copyright © 1924, 1927 by Alfred A. Knopf, Inc., and renewed 1952, 1955 by John Crowe Ransom. Used by permission of Alfred A. Knopf, a division of Random House, Inc.

Henry Reed. "Lessons of War" (1. Naming of Parts) from *Henry Reed: Collected Poems*, ed. Jon Stallworthy. Copyright © 1991 by the Executor of Henry Reed's Estate. Reprinted by permission of Oxford University Press.

Adrienne Rich. "Diving into the Wreck" from *The Fact of a Doorframe: Poems Selected and New, 1950–1984* by Adrienne Rich. By permission of the author and W. W. Norton & Company. Inc. Copyright © 1984 by Adrienne Rich. Copyright © 1975, 1978 by W. W. Norton & Company, Inc. Copyright © 1981 by Adrienne Rich.

Alberto Ríos. "Nani" from *Whispering to Fool the Wind* by Alberto Ríos. Copyright © 1982 by Alberto Ríos. Reprinted by permission of the author.

Theodore Roethke. "My Papa's Waltz," copyright 1942 by Hearst Magazines, Inc. From *The Collected Poems of Theodore Roethke* by Theodore Roethke. Used by permission of Doubleday, a division of Random House, Inc.

Sonia Sanchez. "An Anthem" from *Under a Soprano Sky* by Sonia Sanchez (Africa World Press, 1987). Copyright © 1987 by Sonia Sanchez. Reprinted by permission.

Anne Sexton. "Cinderella" from *Transformations*. Copyright © 1971 by Anne Sexton. Reprinted by permission of Houghton Mifflin Company. All rights reserved.

Leslie Marmon Silko. "Prayer to the Pacific." Copyright © 1981 by Leslie Marmon Silko. Reprinted from *Storyteller* by Leslie Marmon Silko, published by Seaver Books, New York, New York. By permission of the publisher.

Charles Simic. "Begotten of the Spleen" from *Charles Simic: Selected Early Poems*. Copyright © 1999 by Charles Simic. Reprinted by permission of George Braziller, Inc.

Edith Sitwell. "Lullaby" from *The Collected Poems of Edith Sitwell* by Edith Sitwell (Sinclair-Stevenson). Copyright © 1968 by Edith Sitwell. Reprinted by permission of David Higham Associates.

Gary Snyder. "Hitch Haiku" from *The Back Country*. Copyright © 1968 by Gary Snyder. Reprinted by permission of New Directions Publishing Corp.

Cathy Song. "Girl Powdering Her Neck" from *Picture Bride*. Copyright © 1983 by Yale University Press. Reprinted by permission of Yale University Press.

Gary Soto. "The Elements of San Joaquin" from *New and Selected Poems* by Gary Soto. Copyright © 1995, published by Chronicle Books, LLC, San Francisco.

William Stafford. "Traveling through the Dark," copyright © 1962, 1998 by the Estate of William Stafford. Reprinted from *The Way It Is: New & Selected Poems* with the permission of Graywolf Press, Saint Paul, Minnesota.

Gerald Stern. "Cow Worship" from *This Time: New and Selected Poems* by Gerald Stern. Copyright © 1998 by Gerald Stern. Used by permission of W. W. Norton & Company, Inc.

Wallace Stevens. "Disillusionment of Ten O'Clock," "Sunday Morning," and "The Emperor of Ice-Cream," from *The Collected Poems of Wallace Stevens* by Wallace Stevens. Copyright © 1954 by Wallace Stevens and renewed 1982 by Holly Stevens. Used by permission of Alfred A. Knopf, a division of Random House, Inc.

Virgil Suárez. "The Ways of Guilt" is reprinted with permission from the publishers of *Spared Angola* (Houston: Arte Público Press—University of Houston, 1997).

Sekou Sundiata. "Blink Your Eyes." Copyright © 1995 by Sekou Sundiata. Reprinted by permission.

James Tate. "The Wheelchair Butterfly" from *Selected Poems*. Copyright © 1991 by James Tate. Reprinted by permission of the author.

Dylan Thomas, "Do not go gentle into that good night" and "Fern Hill" from *The Poems of Dylan Thomas*. Copyright © 1945 by The Trustees for the Copyrights of Dylan Thomas. Reprinted by permission of New Directions Publishing Corp.

Jean Toomer. "Reapers" from *Cane* by Jean Toomer. Copyright 1923 by Boni & Liveright, renewed 1951 by Jean Toomer. Used by permission of Liveright Publishing Corporation.

Quincy Troupe. "Snake-Back Solo 2" from *Avalanche* (Minneapolis: Coffee House Press, 1996). Copyright © 1996 by Quincy Troupe. Used by permission of the author.

Jean Valentine. "December 21st" from *The Messenger* by Jean Valentine. Copyright © 1979 by Jean Valentine. Reprinted by permission of Farrar, Straus and Giroux, Inc.

Ellen Bryant Voigt. "Woman Who Weeps" from *Two Trees* by Ellen Bryant Voigt. Copyright © 1992 by Ellen Bryant Voigt. Used by permission of W. W. Norton & Company, Inc.

Derek Walcott. "Sea Grapes" from *Collected Poems 1948–1984* by Derek Walcott. Copyright © 1986 by Derek Walcott. Reprinted by permission of Farrar, Straus and Giroux, Inc.

Anne Waldman. "Makeup on Empty Space" from *Helping the Dreamer: New and Selected Poems, 1966–1988*. Copyright © 1989 by Anne Waldman. Reprinted by permission of Coffee House Press.

James Welch. "Christmas Comes to Moccasin Flat" from *Riding the Earthboy 40* by James Welch. Harper & Row. Copyright © 1971 by James Welch. Reprinted by permission of James Welch. All rights reserved.

Richard Wilbur. "Love Calls Us to the Things of This World" from *Things of This World*. Copyright © 1956 and renewed 1984 by Richard Wilbur. Reprinted by permission of Harcourt, Inc.

Nancy Willard. "Questions My Son Asked Me, Answers I Never Gave Him" from *Household Tales of Moon and Water*. Copyright © 1982 by Nancy Willard. Reprinted by permission of Harcourt, Inc.

William Carlos Williams. "Spring and All," "The Red Wheelbarrow," and "This Is Just to Say" from *Collected Poems: 1909–1939, Volume I*. Copyright © 1938 by New Directions Publishing Corp. Reprinted by permission of New Directions Publishing Corp.

Nellie Wong. "Grandmother's Song" from *Dreams in Harrison Railroad Park* by Nellie Wong. Copyright © 1977 by Nellie Wong. Reprinted by permission of Kelsey Street Press.

Charles Wright. "March Journal" from *The World of the Ten Thousand Things: Poems, 1980–1990* by Charles Wright. Copyright © 1990 by Charles Wright. Reprinted by permission of Farrar, Straus and Giroux, Inc.

James Wright. "A Blessing" from *The Branch Will Not Break* by James Wright. Copyright © 1961 by James Wright. Wesleyan University Press.

John Yau. "Chinese Villanelle." Copyright © 1989 by John Yau. Reprinted from *Radiant Silhouette: New and Selected Work 1974–1988* with the permission of the author.

William Butler Yeats. "The Second Coming," copyright © 1924 by Macmillan Publishing Company, renewed 1952 by Bertha Georgie Yeats. "Among School Children," "Leda and the Swan," and "Sailing to Byzantium," copyright © 1928 by Macmillan Publishing Company; copyright renewed 1956 by Bertha Georgie Yeats. Reprinted with the permission of Scribner, an imprint of Simon & Schuster Adult Publishing Group, from *The Collected Poems of W. B. Yeats, Volume 1: The Poems, Revised*, edited by Richard J. Finneran.

Al Young. "A Dance for Ma Rainey." Copyright © 1969 and 1992 by Al Young. Reprinted with the permission of the author.

David Young. "The Portable Earth-Lamp" from *The Planet on the Desk: Selected and New Poems 1960–1990*. Copyright © 1991 by David Young. Wesleyan University Press.

Ray A. Young Bear. "From the Spotted Night" from *The Invisible Musician,* copyright © 1990 by Ray A. Young Bear. Reprinted by permission of Holy Cow! Press.

Paul Zimmer. "Zimmer Imagines Heaven" from *Family Reunion: Selected and New Poems* by Paul Zimmer. Copyright © 1983 by Paul Zimmer. Reprinted by permission of the University of Pittsburgh Press.

Louis Zukofsky. Excerpt from "A" 15. From *"A,"* pp. 359–375. Copyright © 1978 by Celia Zukofsky and Louis Zukofsky. By permission of The Johns Hopkins University Press.

Index of Authors, Titles, and First Lines